SOFTWARE DEVELOPMENT: A RIGOROUS APPROACH

Prentice-Hall International
Series in Computer Science

C. A. R. Hoare, Series Editor

Published

Future Titles

SOFTWARE DEVELOPMENT: A RIGOROUS APPROACH

CLIFF B. JONES

IBM ESRI
La Hulpe, Belgium

Prentice/Hall International

ENGLEWOOD CLIFFS, N.J. LONDON NEW DELHI SINGAPORE
SYDNEY TOKYO TORONTO WELLINGTON

Library of Congress Cataloguing in Publication Data

JONES, CLIFFORD B 1944–
    Software development.

    Bibliography: p.
    Includes index.
    1. Electronic digital computers – Programming.
I. Title
QA76.6.J66   001.6'42   79-14806
ISBN 0-13-821884-6

British Library Cataloguing in Publication Data

JONES, CLIFFORD
    Software development.
    1. Programming (Electronic computers)
    I. Title
    001.6'425   QA76.6
    ISBN 0-13-821884-6

© 1980 by PRENTICE-HALL INTERNATIONAL, INC., LONDON

ISBN 0-13-821884-6

PRENTICE-HALL INTERNATIONAL, INC., *London*
PRENTICE-HALL OF AUSTRALIA PTY. LTD., *Sydney*
PRENTICE-HALL OF CANADA, LTD., *Toronto*
PRENTICE-HALL OF INDIA PRIVATE LIMITED, *New Dehli*
PRENTICE-HALL OF JAPAN, INC., *Tokyo*
PRENTICE-HALL OF SOUTHEAST ASIA PTE., LTD., *Singapore*
PRENTICE-HALL INC., *Englewood Cliffs, New Jersey*
WHITEHALL BOOKS LIMITED, *Wellington, New Zealand*

10   9   8   7   6   5   4   3   2   1

Printed in the United States of America

CONTENTS

LIST OF ILLUSTRATIONS

TABLE OF SYMBOLS

Arithmetic and Logical Operators

+ *plus*, - *minus*, * *multiply*, / *integer division*, ** *exponentiation*
$\wedge$ *and*, $\vee$ *or*, $\Rightarrow$ *implies*, $\Leftrightarrow$ *equivalence*, $\sim$ *not*
A *for all*, **E** *there exists*, **E!** *there exists exactly one*
ι *the unique object*
(**A**$x\epsilon X$)(...) *bounded quantification*

Set Notation

$\{\,\}$ *set brackets*
$\{x \mid p(x)\}$ *set of elements such that*
$x \epsilon X$ *is a member*
$\cup$ *union*, $\cap$ *intersection*, - *difference*, **union** *distributed union*
$\subseteq$ *subset*, $\subset$ *proper subset*
card *cardinality*
$Bool = \{\text{TRUE,FALSE}\}$
$Nat = \{1,2,...\}$
$Nat0 = \{0,1,2,...\}$
$Int = \{...,-2,-1,0,1,2,...\}$

List Notation

$<\,>$ *list brackets*
hd *head*, **tl** *tail*, **len** *length*, (i) *indexing*,
$\mid\mid$ *concatenation*, **elems** *collect to a set*, **conc** *distributed concatenation*

Mapping Notation

[ ] *mapping brackets*
dom *domain*, **rng** *range*, (i) *application*, † *overwrite*, $\mid$ *restrict*

PREFACE

Without the ability to record its results, neither a science nor even a civilization could make progress. This book teaches a method for recording specifications and designs of computer systems.

Two major problems exist with the production of computer programs (i.e. software). Firstly the created programs are frequently not satisfactory to the people who have to use them and secondly their production is too costly. Newspaper stories of the effects of computer errors are myriad. Programmers are only too aware of the human contribution to these errors. The problem of the productivity of the development of computer systems is also linked to errors. Errors which are made in the specification or early design stages are frequently uncovered late in the development cycle and result in enormous correction costs. Even this does not express the full dissatisfaction with computer programs. There is another major problem in that the systems created are often unnecessarily difficult to use.

The computer industry faces a crisis which has been created by its success. More and more powerful systems are demanded as industry puts greater reliance on computers. In order to be able to produce such systems, new development methods must be employed.

This book is intended for a course which will bring the results of computer science into software development practice. The pre-requisites are simple. Some programming experience is necessary. Furthermore, the reader is assumed to have made errors in his programs and to be dissatisfied with this state of affairs. The programs presented in this book are written in the PL/I language. But, for the majority of the examples, the language constructs which are used are common to nearly all languages. No previous exposure to formal methods is assumed. The book is self-contained in that all required notation is taught.

The ideas covered in this book can be considered under the headings of specification and design. The techniques for recording specifications in a precise and concise way have enabled the author and his colleagues to analyze many existing computing concepts and systems. Not only has this proved to be a powerful way of understanding such systems, but it has also facilitated their documentation. However, the ultimate advantage of such a specification tool is for the design of new systems. If used in this way, systems will be created whose architecture makes them much more usable.

For design purposes, a method is taught which permits the coherent documentation of a design. A record of why each stage of design is believed to be correct is an integral part of the documentation. For this reason the design documentation can be reviewed easily and the danger of errors remaining undetected is almost eliminated.

Webster's Dictionary defines *rigorous* as "scrupulously accurate, precise." The approach taken here is rigorous: it is intended to be precise without being completely formal. Thus the aim is to show ways in which the confidence placed in newly developed software can be drastically increased. Just as in other engineering disciplines, in order to work reliably, one must first learn a formal basis. The final rigorous method is not, however, very mathematical. The crucial point is that, having learnt the theory, one can safely reason at a rigorous level. What one writes will fit into a framework and because of this the developer, or others, will know how to complete the formal details if necessary.

The book is divided into three parts. The first part is devoted to programs which manipulate numbers. Key techniques are introduced based on this simple data type. Pre- and post-conditions provide precise specifications of a program. The development of the control structure of a program can be put on a firm footing by showing how one can prove that the specification is met.

The second part of the book concentrates on data structures. Here, the advantages of documenting programs by using abstract data types are shown to be precision, conciseness, and manipulability. This material shows the applicability of the computer science results to data processing applications. The refinement of such data types onto those available in programming languages is also covered.

The techniques presented in the first two parts of the book are collected in the third part into a coherent development method. A number of examples of the application of this method are given.

Many exercises are included as well as a glossary and appendices which are to be used as reference material both during and after studying the text.

The material has been developed in an industrial environment where it has been taught many times. One pattern in which it has been used is in two or three week intensive courses. In industry courses, the sections marked with * are normally omitted. If all of the remaining material is taught, the students should be able to document both specifications and design in a precise notation. Another possibility is to concentrate on specification methods: in this case chapters 5, 6, 11, and the refinement sections of chapters 12, 14 should also be omitted.

A number of sections have been included (marked *) which make the material suitable for an M.Sc. course. For such an audience, references are provided to related literature.

It is a pleasure to be able to acknowledge the help that I have received with the creation of this book. The current text has evolved over two years in the courses which I taught at the IBM European Systems Research Institute—the students there have provided much useful criticism. In particular Soren Brandt and Andre Fischer checked the whole text.

The method of production of this book deserves fuller description elsewhere. I should, however, like to express my gratitude to Derek Andrews, Neal Eisenberg, and Charles Goldfarb without whom it would have been impossible for me to employ the new technology which was used to typeset this book.

My cooperation with Prentice-Hall International has been a pleasure from beginning to end—I should like to thank Derek Coleman, Ron Decent, Henry Hirschberg and Tony Hoare for their help and encouragement.

A debt of another kind is that to the sources of the ideas. Much of the work presented in this book has been developed in conjunction with my colleagues and friends at the IBM Laboratory Vienna. A continued source of inspiration and criticism has been the meetings of IFIP Working Group 2.3.

Examples and exercises have been taken from the works of P.Henderson, G.Hay, B.Jousset, D.Parnas and P.D.Wright. Permission to use the cartoon in chapter 1 was granted by the A.L.I. Press Agency, Brussels.

Chapter 1

INTRODUCTION

Structure of the Book

The body of the book is divided into three parts. Within each part there are several chapters. Each chapter is broken down into a number of sections and sub-sections. An overview of the organization is given in fig. 1.

The purpose of part A (chapters 2-6) is to bring the reader to the point where he can prove programs correct. Since this idea is probably unfamiliar, it is shown for numerical programs where there are no additional problems of unfamiliar notation. Thus, apart from the notation of logic which is being taught, only the familiar algebra (of numbers) is used.

Part B (chapters 7-16) moves away from numerical algorithmic problems into techniques which can be shown to apply to data manipulating problems. This part of the book discusses how abstract data types can be used in writing specifications and in the development of programs.

These first two parts of the book present the basic techniques; both parts cover specification and then proof; both parts begin formally and then develop a less formal (but rigorous) style of proof when enough practice has been gained to make this safe. Part C (chapters 17-22) fits the various techniques into an overall systematic approach to program design and applies the method to a number of problems.

The book is basically self-contained in that all required notation is taught. Readers who are totally unfamiliar with logic notation would benefit from studying chapters 1-3 and 14-15 of Lipschutz(64). (This is the form of reference used throughout the book: the number in brackets following the first author's name refers to the year of publication. A detailed bibliography is given at the end of the book). Four of the chapters (13, 15, 16, and 18) and a number of sections are marked, in the table of contents, with an asterisk: these present additional material

1

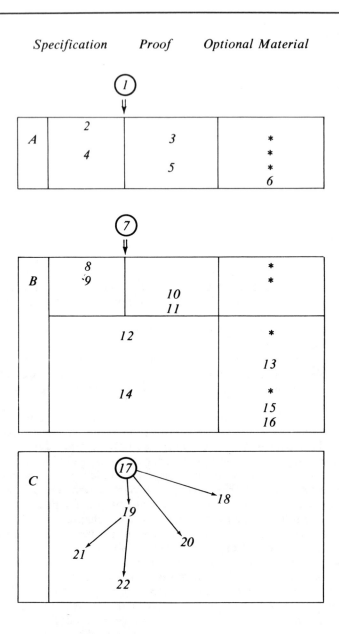

Figure 1   Organization

and are not necessary for a comprehension of the main text. Because it is mainly intended for university use, the optional material is presented in a more condensed form.

The programming language PL/I has been used because it is likely to be familiar to practising programmers. The full language is far from ideal for program proofs. It is, however, in the spirit of the approach of this book to try to use a large language in a constrained way and then to consider the features of the language as required. Here, a subset of PL/I is used which is simple enough for the reader to have no difficulty in translating into, say, Pascal.

At the back of the book there is a glossary of technical terms for reference (terms in this glossary are marked on first reference thus—*predicate*). Similarly, appendices are given which include reference material of use during, and after, reading the book (e.g. appendix C provides access to a number of definitions which are developed as examples or exercises). Many exercises are provided since practice with unfamiliar notation is the only way to gain confidence. Answers are provided for those exercises which check the reader's comprehension of the notation. Most chapters contain a section of summary exercises—these vary in difficulty but are generally more complex than those in the body of the chapters.

Background

The overall requirement for a more effective way of developing software systems is taken for granted here. From the viewpoint of those who wish to see computers assist in solving their problems, there are two major problems: software development is both highly error-prone and is disproportionately costly. The principal bottleneck (both financially and in terms of time) in implementing computer systems is now the production of the software.

The above shortcomings are of concern in all computer applications. As regards freedom from errors, most people would agree that the requirements on, for example, missile early warning, patient monitoring or nuclear power station control systems should be as stringent as possible. Leaving aside such emotive examples one moves into an area where the penalty for failure is easier to translate into financial terms. Much of modern business life relies on computers. If the payroll program fails, it is no longer practical to think in terms of manual backup. In some industries, the cost of the failure could be a strike and attendant loss of production. When assessing the cost of a program failure, such items must be considered as well as expenses related to lost files or security breaches.

Programmers do not usually work in a vacuum. Whoever is paying the salaries of programmers today has cause for complaint at the cost of creating programs.

Having identified that a problem exists, the next step towards its solution is the location of some plausible cause. In the case of software development, the cause is not hard to find. The scale of the applications which are tackled by software developers has grown far more rapidly than the available tools. Twenty years ago the limitations of the machine (memory size etc.) imposed a limit on the size of programs. The increase in machine power and size has been prodigious. But there is a growth which is more significant than the number of lines of code in programs. This is the complexity of interaction with other systems. Perhaps the most dramatic way an experienced programmer can appreciate this is by considering his bookshelf over the years. For the early machines a principles of operation document was perhaps one centimeter thick and was almost all that was needed. Today, with access methods, operating systems, database systems etc., one meter of manuals is almost certainly a minimum. This gives some measure of the complexity of the programs with which today's systems must interact.

Although there have been some minor changes in the development approach (these are reviewed in the next section), these changes are insignificant compared with those of the problem domain. Programmers could be likened to children who, having mastered the construction of small bridges with Lego bricks, are then entrusted with the construction of a full-scale suspension bridge without learning any new methods—not surprisingly their systems often fall down.

★   ★   ★

Before going into more detail on methods, some terminology for the phases of the process of producing software are given. The following terms are used:

> requirements
> specification
> design
> module development and testing
> system test
> maintenance

The phase of analyzing the **requirements** for a system is a rather informal one. An understanding of the general application area must be gained and a list of desirable features should be built up for a system. This book does not venture into this area at all. An attempt to bring some order into this process is described in Langefors(73). The specifications described in this book can easily be related to the information flow diagrams used by Langefors.

It is the role of a **specification** to record precisely what the function of a system is. It is derived from the requirements and could not be created without them. The specification should avoid going into details of implementation because the external appearance of the system should be more stable (e.g. across time and multiple implementations) than the design. Furthermore, the user of a system should be shielded from implementation details, although he will obviously want to read the specification.

Design and **module development** are both treated as problem decomposition steps: they have in common the production of solutions and differ only in that the former create further problem specifications while the latter develop code.

Specification and design are the main areas of concern in this book. The intent is to explain a method which will virtually eliminate errors in these phases. It is the need to rework development based on faulty design decisions which reduces productivity. This book makes an indirect contribution to testing and maintenance although they are not specifically discussed below.

Theory versus Practice

Accepting that the twin problems of errors and production costs extend to most program development environments does not imply that the same solutions will be universally applicable. There are areas of computer applications where it is possible to have pre-packaged solutions or program generators. The hope that such approaches could be generalized to cover all computer problems bears a resemblance to the search for a philosopher's stone—in this case it would transmute non-procedural descriptions into golden programs.

The aim of this book is to show methods which will aid the development of versatile programs which are novel enough to require some inventiveness in their design.

In order to put the rigorous approach in context, this sub-section reviews the general influence that theoretical ideas have already had on software development practice. One aid to tracing this influence is a categorization of programming problems. A first-level split can be made between algorithmic and data manipulating programs. Problems in the algorithmic category can usually be specified briefly but their specification gives no guide to the solution. Many data processing problems require almost no calculation in their solution. Their difficulty comes from locating and manipulating large quantities of data. Of course, the division is not neatly defined and, if a second-level split is made of algorithmic problems, part of the reason becomes apparent. Algorithmic problems which deal with numbers have been widely studied and a rich body of documented knowledge exists. Non-numeric problems (e.g. sorting) have been studied to varying degrees; parsing is one area which has perhaps been overstudied. Non-numerical algorithmic problems and data processing problems obviously overlap.

* * *

Looking first at theory, one can distinguish scientific and stylistic results. The truth of the scientific results has been established—only their usefulness can be questioned; with the stylistic observations their usefulness is often more apparent than their universality.

Stylistic results are reviewed first. The idea of *top-down* development was perhaps best explained in Dijkstra(69). The general idea of solving complex problems by decomposing them into smaller problems is, of course, very much older. It must also be understood that the proposal requires the creation of hierarchically structured documentation for a system. This is an important point. Whenever steps in a development method are proposed in this book, they are not meant as a straitjacket for thinking. Obviously one often needs to experiment and backtrack (see Naur(72)). But, both as a check and to provide readable documentation of a system, it should be possible to create design documents which link together hierarchically. The documentation of a project is also essential to make progress visible and to reduce unnecessary repetition of work.

Another issue of style, which was also raised by E.W.Dijkstra, is the question of the dangers involved in programs which use (or overuse) *GOTO* statements (see Dijkstra(68), Knuth(74)). Both of these concerns with style would appear to be applicable to all classes of programming problems.

Continuing the review of theoretical work, attention is now turned to the results which are making computing into a scientific subject.

Perhaps the most important single result is the ability to prove programs correct. It is fairly obvious that programs can theoretically be proved correct: specifications can be formalized (as is shown in this book); programs themselves are written in formal languages; therefore, the assertion that a program fulfils a specification is a mathematical statement. As in school mathematics, if such an assertion is true it must be possible to prove it. The reader may remember Pythagoras' theorem about the squares on the sides of right-angled triangles: this was justified by a proof rather than by measuring a few triangles. The question then is whether program proofs can be made practical. Starting with the *inductive assertion method* (Floyd(67), Naur(66)), and continuing with Hoare(69), Wirth(71) and Dijkstra(76), styles have evolved which have made program proofs easier to construct. There is also the work on *symbolic execution* (see Burstall(74)) which is the basis of some automatic program verifiers. The evolution of development styles based on proof methods is discussed below. It is unfortunate that most of the early applications of proof techniques were in the area of algorithmic problems since this has tended to cloud the argument of their real scope of applicability.

Other work in software development has concentrated on providing formal definitions of systems and, as a special case, programming languages (for a review see Lucas(78)). Such definitions have been applied to problems in both the algorithmic and the data processing class.

These theoretical results link together and support each other's messages; proofs can only be given with respect to formal specifications; so-called *abstract data types* are essential for limiting detail in specifications and proofs; programs in which *GOTO* statements are used carelessly are virtually impossible to reason about; etc.

★   ★   ★

What is happening in practice? What methods are being used by people whose salaries depend on the programs they write? The vast majority of such programmers are, of course, working on data processing problems.

Considering firstly the area of system specification, there are already some large scale applications of formal definition techniques: an international standards committee produced ECMA(76); an American government department has required that all potential vendors provide formal definitions of the *Ada* language; some computer manufacturers are making use of such techniques for controlling large projects (e.g. Berthaud(78)). Use is growing where the need is greatest—on really complex projects.

In the design area, a number of different headings must be considered. The general idea of a top-down approach is now widely accepted. Decomposition implies that intermediate stages be documented and the form of documentation should be considered. Few formal design descriptions, as shown in theoretical papers, have been used in practice. Rather, techniques like HIPO charts (see Stay(76)) and pseudo-code (see IBM(b)) are being used in attempts to structure the use of well-chosen natural language to document design. Because the language itself is not formal, there are no fixed criteria for evaluation and the quality of such documentation is, at best, variable and difficult to measure.

The next heading to be considered could be called "tactics": given a problem, one can ask for advice on finding good designs. This is a pragmatic problem and there has been little theoretical work. Myers(75) has provided some useful ways of assessing the independence of modules. Jackson(75) proposes very usable design rules based on the data structures a program is to manipulate. This is a technique which is, therefore, applicable to the more data-oriented forms of problem.

Another facet of design to consider is verification. Here the influence of the theoretical work on practice is, so far, almost non-existent. Not only have formal proofs not been used, but also—much more disappointingly—there would appear to be no acceptance of the idea that a designer has a responsibility to record some reason for believing his work to be correct. A specification is given him (WHAT his program should do); he eventually produces a proposed solution (HOW his specification will be met) but the reason (WHY) he believed this to be correct is lost forever. Rather, in practice, the idea of *walk-throughs* or *inspections* have gradually become accepted (see Fagan(76)).

The usefulness of testing is well summarized by the quote from E.W.Dijkstra:

> Program testing can be used to show the presence of bugs, never to show their absence.

In a sense, even this comment is kind to testing. The problem is magnified by the fact that any errors located as late as testing will be difficult, and therefore expensive, to remove if they were made early in the design. Experience (see T.C.Jones(77)) shows that indeed many errors located in completed programs do come from early in design. It is, of course, for this reason that some form of review during design can be a much more effective way of eliminating errors. The only question to be resolved is what should go on at such a review. It is proposed in chapter 17 that such a review is the ideal forum for the designer to present an argument (WHY) for correctness.

In the area of code development the idea of **structured code** has, after much unconstructive debate, become fairly widely adopted in practice.

In practice, most software undergoes some testing and it is clear that testing does have a role to play even in a more rigorous development environment. A good review of this role is given in Gerhart(77).

The concern with human aspects of program development has received some attention. Weinberg(71) is still, perhaps, the best review of this area. The organizational structure called **chief programmer team** is considered valuable in many environments (see Baker(72)).

★   ★   ★

Before discussing which ideas should now be transferred from theory to practice, it is worthwhile reviewing the effectiveness of the transfer of two of the concepts mentioned above. Both top-down development and structured code are applicable to the whole range of programming problems. The former, when not taught too dogmatically, has been widely accepted; the latter has frequently suffered from the way it was taught, but even so has met with disproportionate resistance. Why? There is a key difference. Top-down design is a constructive proposal, avoid *GOTO* is a negative one. One can argue that what is required for a new method to be really useful is that it offers a constructive discipline rather than a (simple) test of created programs. One can also deduce some rules for the teaching of methods—but rather than list these, the author will try to follow them.

It was pointed out in the preceding section that today's situation is not acceptable. The reluctance of the software industry to provide guarantees for software systems is a clear indication of the lack of confidence in the methods being used. What then is the gap between theory and practice? More importantly, which ideas would appear to be ripe for application?

This book shows how precise specifications for programs can be written for data-processing problems. To achieve this, formal definition methods are explained and then shown to provide a basis for precise, though not fully formal, specifications. A similar approach is taken with correctness arguments. For these to be sound (or **rigorous**) the writer needs to understand what would comprise a formal proof—having learnt this foundation it will rarely be necessary to apply it in practice. To support correctness arguments, the specification techniques are applied to the documentation of sub-components during development. The ideas which this book aims to bring into practical use are marked with an asterisk in fig. 2. The rest of the figure summarizes the points made in this section.

Central to showing the applicability of these methods to programs

	Theory	Practice	Transfer
Specification	formal	natural language	*
Development	top-down	top-down	good
- Documentation	formal	--- pseudo-code HIPO	*
- Tactics	---	Myers Jackson	
- Verification	proofs argument	--- --- reviews testing	*
Coding	structured	structured	poor
Human Aspects	---	Weinberg Chief Programmer Team	

Figure 2   Theory versus Practice

which manipulate data, is the use of **abstract data types**. There is no magic remedy for software ills. The author believes software development to be difficult and therefore doubts the possibility of such remedies. But what is being offered is a constructive discipline, one which gives support throughout the development process.

Merits of a Rigorous Approach

An approach more rigorous than that currently being taken, is required. The objective of this book might be stated as providing ways of increasing confidence in the software systems we develop. In order to achieve both fewer remaining errors and higher productivity it is necessary to reduce the probability of making errors—in particular, design errors.

Three main arguments are given for showing that an understanding

of formal methods is important. Firstly, they are the foundation of the
subject. Most areas of knowledge go through an informal phase before an
underlying theory is developed. Computing is unique in the number of
practitioners it absorbed before its theory was available. One aim of this
book is to show how ideas (or hints) can be adopted from the formal
work to ensure a sounder, more rigorous, way of working. This is the
second reason for understanding more formal methods. The third
argument is more contentious. It is the author's belief that, for difficult
computing problems, future methods must become more formal.

To illustrate these three arguments the area of specifications is
considered. The necessity of precise specifications comes from the
following facts:

- they are the basis of development
- they provide the communication between the user and the
  developer
- they often serve as a standards document across implementations.

But one can be more precise about *precision*. A specification should be
unambiguous, non-contradictory, and complete. In order to possess all of
these qualities, certain properties can be deduced about the languages in
which specifications are written. This topic is taken up in more detail in
chapter 2, for now only the conclusion that the specification language
must be formal is considered. What is a formal language? All
programming languages (e.g. ALGOL, PL/I) are formal. The
distinction is whether the class of meaningful statements can be
characterized and a meaning given to each member of that class. The
important point is that this property does not hold for the languages of
everyday discourse (e.g. English)—for an interesting, and humorous,
review see Hill(72). This book shows how problems like *bill of materials*
can be specified in a few lines if the right sort of specification language is
employed.

There are, however, some objections to the use of special purpose
specification languages. One of the roles of a specification is communication. Users who are outside the computing area are less likely to learn a
specification language than the developers. This is not, however, an
argument for abandoning specification languages. Because a specification is also to be the basis of development, the members of the computer
area must obtain a higher level of formality. If they use specification
languages, the systems they design will anyway be better structured.
Furthermore, from a precise specification, one can derive a well-
structured document in English. An ill-structured English description is,
on the other hand, no basis for the development of a computer system.

A second objection to the use of special specification languages is the
effort required to learn them, even for computer professionals. Two
points should be made. Consider the cartoon in fig. 3. The man with the
hammer is not seeking any complex properties of number theory; he does
not even want to know what power of *10* is involved; he wants a

Are you sure there isn't a simpler means of writing
'The Pharaoh had 10,000 soldiers?'

Figure 3   Cartoon

shorthand. The same is true of the use of notation in this book. When sets are introduced, it is to cover a few items of notation which make it possible to write some specifications naturally and concisely. The second point about notation can be made by considering two simple arithmetic calculations such as:

*a) CXXVIII * IV*
b) MMMMXCVI / CCLVI

These computations are, at best, very cumbersome in the wrong notation. A good notation (like Arabic numerals) makes them trivial and opens the way to much more complex calculations. A.N.Whitehead (see Whitehead(59)) wrote:

> By relieving the brain of all unnecessary work, a good notation sets it free to concentrate on more advanced problems, and in effect increases the mental power of the race.

The use of apposite notation will make it possible to manipulate specifications; manipulate to prove properties of the system; manipulate to show the implementation correct.

One advantage of learning formal specification methods is that they provide a basis. On this basis, this book shows how rigorous specifications, which have a formal structure but some informal functions, can be created.

Hints for everyday work on specifications are:

- precise specifications are possible, even for large systems
- the structure of a specification is crucial
- using abstract data types leads to far clearer understanding
- there is a separate class of languages (distinct from natural or programming languages) appropriate for specifications.

It is easy to show how formal methods will influence the future. Examples of the use of formal specification have already been given. There is nothing to prevent writing formal specifications (see Hansal(76), Nilsson(76)) for database systems. As reliance on complex computer systems increases so must the precision with which they are controlled.

Specific Approach of this Book

In 1970, full of ideas on formal definition and proof, the author returned from Vienna to manage a group of programmers in the U.K. The brave announcement that such methods would now be used was met with scepticism and a challenge to prove an existing program correct. The chosen test consisted of several hundred lines of PL/I, had been written by a good programmer and had worked operationally for some time. There was too great a quantity of detailed information and the attempt at the proof was a failure. Instead, an alternative test was agreed: the author was to develop a new program from the original specification. This was done using a form of the methods of this book. Progress was monitored carefully by the group to ensure no testing was performed. The author's program ran first time. More importantly a subsequent comparison with the original program uncovered several errors in the latter. (A development of this program is given in chapter 18.)

Stories like this abound and are the cause of the shift from program proofs to systematic development methods—see Hoare(71), Wirth(71) and Jones(72). One could add to Dijkstra's pungent aphorism on testing:

Program proofs can show the absence of bugs, not avoid their insertion.

Moving from proofs to the application of correctness arguments in development is also the key to higher productivity; early elimination of errors avoids the very time-consuming rework involved in their late location. The development process is, at last, provided with positive criteria for successful completion of a design stage.

The approach in this book, then, is based on a development process, the eventual result of which can be fitted into a hierarchical (top-down) design documentation. Clearly, each stage has to be documented. This documentation contains:

- specification of the problem

- proposed solution. Written in terms of
- units about which assumptions are recorded
- a correctness argument

The assumptions at one stage of development, if not fulfilled by available software, become the specifications for the next stage of development.

All of this documentation is rigorous, in the sense that it has a formal structure but uses informal comments in a controlled way. For example, correctness arguments may consist of one or two definitions and the claim that these fit with the checklist of results for the relevant type of development stage. If, for some reason, it is necessary to be more formal, the formal structure makes this a simple task. Fig. 4 presents an overview of the method.

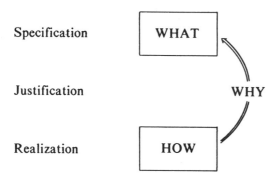

Figure 4   The Rigorous Method

Let us try and clarify the distinction between *rigorous* and *formal*. A completely formal proof of correctness could be checked by a suitable program. This, of course, would provide a great deal of confidence in correctness. However, there is also a cost. Such a proof must be at an incredible level of detail. In mathematics textbooks the normal way of presenting proofs is to document enough steps to convince the reader. This has two advantages. In nearly all cases it achieves this objective; if it fails to do so, it has still shown how the overall task can be decomposed. The doubtful reader can then try to fill in the details of the step which he finds unconvincing. There are, of course, occasional errors in mathematics books but, because of the use of rigorous arguments, their frequency is minute compared with the occurrence of errors in programs. There is a range of possibilities from no correctness argument, via rigorous argument, to formal proofs. There tends to be a diminishing return with excessive use of formal proofs. A great many errors can be located by outlining a rigorous argument; fewer errors and far greater cost will result from formalizing such proofs. But the reason rigorous arguments are so efficacious is that the writer is able to formalize them. Thus the reader of this book first learns how to produce formal proofs so that he can reason safely at a rigorous level. The use of rigorous correctness arguments uncovered many errors in the development of the examples in this book; it is not claimed that all programs are error-free but there are certainly far fewer errors than there would otherwise have been.

The aim then is for designers to record their reasons for believing their work to be correct. This will help them be correct and provide subsequent reviewers with a way of checking for correctness. It must be understood that recording the correctness argument is the responsibility of the developer. It is not workable to separate the tasks.

Summary

Two reasons cited in Linden(72) for the growth of interest in work on program correctness are:

> 1) The inability to design and implement software systems which can be guaranteed correct is severely restricting computer applications in many important areas.
> 2) Debugging and maintaining large computer programs is now well recognized as one of the most serious and costly problems facing the computer industry.

The aim of this book is to present a collection of techniques which can be merged into a rigorous method for developing computer software.

For further discussion of topics in this chapter, the reader is referred to Linden(72) and Jones(77a). When considering the predictions of delay in adoption of methods it is important to remember that the former paper was published in 1972. A more up-to-date review is given in Gerhart(78).

The notation used in this book is part of a meta-language used for specifying systems and languages. A formal definition of the meta-language is given in Jones(78).

Summary Exercises

Exercise 1.1:   Considering the categorization of programs:

Algorithmic
   Numeric
   Non-numeric
Data Manipulation

Identify problems from your experience which fit each category.

Exercise 1.2: Name an area of commercial data processing where algorithms are well documented.

Exercise 1.3: Discuss why testing is inadequate as a way of ensuring program correctness and include some calculations on the number of test-cases required for various purposes (e.g. to execute all paths in a program).

Exercise 1.4: Discuss why program proof ideas are of most significance in the context of a development method.

Exercise 1.5: Discuss why the separation of the tasks of designing, and arguing the correctness of a design, is bad.

Part A

PROGRAMS WHICH MANIPULATE NUMBERS

The major portion of the specification language used in this book consists of notation taken from established areas of mathematics. A simple analogy may help to motivate the adoption of formal notation. The reader will recall the following kind of problem:

> John has three red toys and James has more green toys than the total number owned by John and Jack together. Jack has ... . How many toys are owned by each boy?

The way to handle such problems is to reduce them to symbols and then manipulate algebraic expressions. One feature of such problems is that a certain amount of irrelevant information is usually included. In the analogous situation with specifications, there is normally plenty of irrelevant information; unfortunately, one cannot rely on all of the essential information being present. It is to be expected that specifications will also be more tractable in a mathematical notation.

This part of the book shows that the use of logic notation makes an enormous step towards comprehensible and manipulable specifications. The next part of the book carries the process further and brings in notations like that of set theory. One advantage of such formal specifications is that it will be easy to identify any incompleteness in a specification.

S.D.R.A.—C

Functions will be considered before examining programs. Functions are an established part of mathematics and thus it is only necessary to present standard notation. The concept of assignment is central to programming languages and brings with it a notion of program variables denoting different values at different points in time; the methods of handling functions have to be extended to cope with this notion of time.

With both functions and programs the order is firstly to show how specifications are written and then to address the problem of correctness proofs.

The specifications presented both for functions (chapter 2) and for programs (chapter 4) consist of *type information* and *pre-post-conditions*. The functions or programs which fulfil the specifications are referred to as *realizations*. The language for expressing realizations (i.e. the programming language in the case of programs) is, itself, a formal language in the sense that it has a fixed meaning. It is therefore possible to prove that realizations fulfil their specifications in a way which is akin to proofs of theorems in mathematics. In chapter 3, techniques such as reasoning by cases and induction are introduced. Chapter 5 introduces lists of rules for reasoning about programming constructs; it shows how proofs can be used in a top-down *decomposition* process leading from specification to program.

This part of the book is concerned exclusively with programs which manipulate numbers, so that the new concepts of precise specification and proof are presented to the reader in a familiar domain. The reader whose normal programming work involves data manipulation rather than arithmetic is asked to show patience (and await part B): the overall structure of the specifications shown here is a part of the rigorous method.

The reader may feel that this first part of the book is similar to practicing scales on a musical instrument. Simple examples are chosen so that the specifications can be grasped quickly. One example is much like the next—but there is a steady progression. The reader will gain confidence in writing proofs and will gradually find that he can safely make larger steps. This is particularly important with the lists of properties given for reasoning about programming constructs. As the student becomes familiar with the rules he will find that they can be used as mental checklists.

The material of chapters 2 and 3 will be familiar to university students who can confine themselves to a review of the notation.

Following the major four chapters, chapter 6 discusses a number of further topics including how a general solution for a problem can be documented and thus provide the basis for a number of programs.

Chapter 2

SPECIFYING FUNCTIONS

If one wishes to have something constructed, it is necessary to provide a description of its required properties. The term *specification* can be used for such a description. The greater the degree of complexity of the required properties, the higher the degree of precision necessary in the specification. Thus a familiar object like a child's wooden building block can be specified by a few dimensions, while the properties required of a modern aeroplane can only be specified by employing methods from many scientific disciplines.

When the discussion is focussed on computer systems, it is only necessary to acknowledge the complexity of the systems which are to be created in order to realize that precise specifications are of tantamount importance in this area. Furthermore, for large computer systems, it is to be expected that the appropriate means of writing specifications will rely on other scientific disciplines. This chapter shows how the notation of logic can be employed to increase the precision of specifications. This notation is especially important because it can be used to link together expressions written in other notations.

A specification can be viewed as a contract between, on the one hand, those who wish to use the object being described and, on the other hand, those who are to build the object. For the user, this contract states the properties on which he is relying. The developer has a different view of the same document: for him it states the behavior of the object he must build. Both of these views lead, however, to the conclusion that the specification should describe only the external view of a system (WHAT it does) and omit the description of the realization (HOW it works). The user is not concerned with how the system is to be constructed and should certainly not have to disentangle the description of its function from that of its design. The work of the system developer is precisely to create the design. Any attempt to pre-empt the design decisions in the specification is likely to be premature. Large tasks are tackled more easily in pieces and the separation of the descriptions of what a system is to do and how it is to do it is obviously an advantageous one.

To illustrate this split, two examples are considered. The first example is taken, not from computing, but from the everyday world.

Consider the features of a motor car which are of importance to its user. Clearly certain space requirements for the passengers and luggage are of interest; some measure of the performance is also of concern; there are people whose interest extends to size of the engine. But nobody who is purely a user should be concerned with the sizes of screws used in the carburettor or the tensile strengths of the materials. To describe what a user wants from a car is a lengthy task, but it is converted into one of gargantuan proportions if this description includes engineering details.

The task of sorting can be used as a simple computing example of the advantages of separating specification and realization. Essentially the specification for sorting needs to state (i) the required ordering relation between the output items and (ii) that these be a permutation of the input items. This external view is exactly what the user has to know. He is not interested in the particular algorithm to be used. The developer must choose that algorithm which fits the constraints best. Of course, performance will be a key consideration. The main point is that a short precise specification of the task to be performed can be written and that this, without any trace of the design, should comprise the specification.

A specification can be viewed as a contract and it is interesting to consider how these are written. A lawyer will claim to use natural language, but any layman who has to read a contract might be excused for disagreeing—in fact a very controlled and limited language is used to try to achieve precision. If the contract is for the construction of a house, an architect will record his part of the specification in a formal, pictorial, notation—the reader is invited to think what a description of a house would look like if only natural language were used.

Returning now to requirements for a specification, fig. 5 divides them into technical and usability considerations. The necessity of the technical requirements should be clear: precision avoids ambiguity, consistency avoids contradictions etc.

Technical
    Precise
    Consistent
    Complete

Usability
    Comprehensible
    Well-structured
    Concise
    Extendable

Figure 5   Requirements for Specifications

Given a set of requirements for specifications it is possible to discuss how they can be realized. The first three (technical) requirements necessitate that a formal language be used to write specifications. The use of the adjective *formal* is intended to distinguish those languages which have precise semantics. That is, every statement in the language has one exact meaning. The languages used in normal discourse have been dubbed **natural languages** by the computer community. It is well known that ambiguous sentences can be constructed, in languages like English, French or German. The reader should be familiar with at least one formal language. Any programming language is formal in the sense used here. Thus every program has a fixed meaning; ultimately this meaning is given by the compiler for the language. The first conclusion drawn for specifications, then, is that they must be written in a formal language.

Programming languages have been given as examples of formal languages, but it is not the intention to propose their use as specification languages. One reason for this is the desire to give implicit specifications (i.e. state what result is required) while the idea of a programming language is to show algorithms. In part B it is also shown that the data types of programming languages are too restrictive for use as specification languages.

Rather than develop a specification language from scratch the plan is to take as much as possible from established branches of mathematics. There are many advantages to be gained by this. Firstly, any familiarity with mathematical notation will reduce the amount of new notation to be learned. Secondly, and perhaps more importantly, the consistency of the notations is assured by the soundness of the disciplines underlying them. The main reason for adopting formal notation is that it will serve as a shorthand: in this chapter the symbols of logic are used as abbreviations for ideas which one would otherwise have to express in rather verbose sentences.

Specifications are first presented formally and in detail. Once the ability to handle the formal treatment of small examples has been mastered, it will be possible to rely on ideas which are familiar and which do not therefore have to be formally defined. Taking again the example of sorting, the concepts of ordered lists and of permutations might be accepted as understood by people familiar with sorting. Here these concepts are defined formally in order to gain practice in the use of the formalism. In an everyday environment, one could use such understood concepts without providing formal definitions. The essential point is that the use of a formal notation has forced a structure on the definition. At some level, parts of the definition may be given in natural language. However, such informal specifications can subsequently be replaced by formal ones if necessary. The structure of the definition will not be disrupted. In fact, precisely this structure provides the skeleton which can be fleshed out where required.

Having drawn some conclusions about them, it is time to look at some specifications.

Functions

A function can be defined by a rule which maps arguments into results. Thus:

$f1(x,y) \triangleq x * x + y - 1$

defines a function for which:

$f1(2,3) = 6$

(Arithmetic operators will be written as in PL/I, see the table of symbols.)

     To be more precise, an explicit function definition has a left-hand side and a right-hand side separated by the definition symbol ($\triangleq$). The left-hand side consists of the name of the function followed, in parenthesis, by a list of names for the *parameters*. The right-hand side is an expression built up from the parameter names, constants (e.g. *1*) and known operators (e.g. *, +, -) or functions. The parameters are only dummy variables (their actual identifiers are irrelevant) which show what computation is to be made with the actual *argument* values. Thus, fig. 6 shows the same function in a pictorial way.

      Figure 6   **Parameter Substitution**

     The right-hand expression defines, then, a computation, providing values are available for each of the parameters. Such values are called *arguments*. A function defines a value for a list of arguments. This value is determined by substituting, in an obvious way, the arguments for the names of the parameters throughout the right-hand side of the definition. This process can also be viewed in terms of fig. 6. Thus:

$f1(1,2)$
$= 1 * 1 + 2 - 1$
$= 2$

     The process of finding a function value for particular arguments is known as *applying* the function to the arguments. As well as applying functions to numbers, it is necessary to substitute arguments of other sorts. For example:

$f1(x_0,y_0) = x_0 * x_0 + y_0 - 1$
$f1(a+7,b*c) = (a+7) * (a+7) + (b*c) - 1$

     Very few functions yield results for all argument values. The function *f1* above, for example, uses arithmetic operators in its definition and is therefore only defined for numerical arguments. One way of restricting the arguments to which a function can be applied is by providing a type clause. A *type clause* contains the function name and a list of the names of sets from which arguments can be chosen. It is also useful to record the set of values of potential results of the function so this is appended, after an →, to the function type. Thus, for some arbitrary function f which takes n arguments from sets named $D1$ to Dn and yields results from the set R, the type definition is:

$f: D1\ D2 \dots Dn\ \rightarrow R$

The set of possible arguments defined by such a type clause is called its defined **domain** and the set of possible results its **range**. These terms are not used with precise formal meaning for functions since it is necessary to constrain the domain in other ways. Before going into this, the type clause for $f1$ can be shown. Assuming *Nat* to be the name of the set of natural numbers (e.g. *1, 2, ...*), it might be:

$f1: Nat\ Nat \rightarrow Nat$

Notice that other possibilities exist: the domain, and hence the range, could be extended to include negative and/or fractional values. In recording a particular type clause, all that is being claimed is that if arguments from the stated domain are chosen, the function, if it yields a result at all, will yield a result in the stated range.

Why the caveat of "if it yields a result"? While for simple functions, like $f1$, it is possible to simply name sets over which they will be defined, the ability of more complex functions to yield a result may depend on relationships holding between the values of arguments. This topic, however, comes closer to implicit specifications to which attention must now be turned.

Implicit Specifications

The explicit definition of a function is analogous to a program. This chapter is concerned with specifications and it is necessary to step back from the realization level to provide a definition of what a function should compute. In order to do this some logic notation is used. Such symbols as are used are also expressed in words since the logic notation itself is not introduced until the next section.

The essence of an *implicit specification* is to state the relationship required between arguments and results without having to write an explicit rule for computing the latter from the former. Consider, for example, the case of finding the square root of a number. To oversimplify for a moment, the required function can be specified by stating that the square of the result it yields for a given argument should be the same value as that argument. This specification gives no clue as to how to find square roots, it is simply a check which can be applied to establish whether an answer is acceptable. The specification, therefore, defines a class of possible functions. To be more realistic, it is necessary to consider what class of values is to be considered as the domain of the function, and, assuming these are not all perfect squares, to introduce the notion of a tolerance. Suppose it is required to state that a function *sqrt* should yield the square root of x_0 to within tolerance t_0. A specification would have to state that the absolute value of the difference between the square of the result and x_0 must be less than the tolerance. Using *r* as a name for the result:

$r = sqrt(x_0, t_0)$

then:

$abs(r**2 - x_0) \leq t_0$

This specification is, so far, incomplete in that the valid values for x_0 and t_0 have not been defined. *Real* will be used as the name of the set of all real numbers. A first restriction on arguments can, then, be provided by writing a type clause for the function *sqrt* such as:

sqrt: Real Real → Real

But this is still not enough. If *sqrt* is to yield a real number as result, it can only find the square root of non-negative numbers. Similarly, if the tolerance is to be used as above, it also must be non-negative. So any arguments x_0, t_0 must satisfy:

$x_0 \geq 0 \land t_0 \geq 0$

($\land$ being read as ***and***).

    Three pieces of information have been provided for the specification: a type clause; a pre-condition specifying assumptions on the input; a post-condition specifying the required relation between input and output values. A ***predicate*** is a function whose range is the two Boolean values **TRUE** and **FALSE**. The set containing exactly these two values is named *Bool*. The pre- and post-conditions are both predicates.

    The three pieces of specification information about a function can be collected into a standard form as shown in fig. 7. The pre-condition is a predicate of the arguments of the function and the post-condition a predicate of the arguments and the result. Although the names of the parameters of the predicates can be chosen freely, the use of suggestive names like *r* for the result will aid readability.

---

f: D1 D2 ... Dn → R
pre-f(d1,d2,...,dn) ≜ ...
post-f(d1,d2,...,dn,r) ≜ ...

where:

pre-f: D1 D2 ... Dn → Bool
post-f: D1 D2 ... Dn R → Bool

    Figure 7   **Implicit Function Specification**

A number of typographical conventions are used consistently

throughout this book as an aid to comprehension. The names of functions or predicates are written using lower-case letters, hyphens and digits; the first character is always a lower-case letter. Another convention dictates the naming of pre- and post-conditions. Their names are always constructed by using the appropriate prefix to the name of the function which is being specified. For the specific example of *sqrt* this gives:

sqrt: Real Real → Real
pre-sqrt(x,t) ≜ *x≥0 ∧ t≥0*
post-sqrt(x,t,r) ≜ *abs(r**2 - x) ≤ t*

Notice that the definition of the predicate *post-sqrt* uses the parame er name *r* for the result of the function. The meaning of this three-part specification is that, for any arguments which are defined to be valid, an acceptable *sqrt* function must yield results which (together with the inputs) give the value **TRUE** when the post-condition is applied to them. In formulae:

$x_0 \epsilon Real \wedge t_0 \epsilon Real \wedge pre\text{-}sqrt(x_0,t_0) \Rightarrow post\text{-}sqrt(x_0,t_0,sqrt(x_0,t_0))$

(the symbol ⇒, being read as ***implies***). Thus a *sqrt* function which computed:

sqrt(82,1) = 9

would satisfy the specification for these particular values.

Limitation to a function *f* of one argument makes it possible to emphasize graphically what the relation between the argument values should be: see fig. 8.

---

f: D → R
pre-f(d) ≜ ...
post-f(d,r) ≜ ...

$(\epsilon D \wedge pre\text{-}f(\quad) \Rightarrow post\text{-}f(\quad,f(\quad)))$

Figure 8   Meaning of Implicit Function Specification

Given a specification in the standard, three-part, format, it is clear what conditions must be fulfilled in order to satisfy the specification. Notice that the specification requires that some result is produced for every valid input. What is being specified is a function; a function yields a single result for given arguments; but the specification defines a class of acceptable functions which would each yield different results. Thus:

sqrt(82,1) = 9.1
sqrt(81,0) = -9

are both acceptable.

One obvious point about the specification of *sqrt* is that it is far shorter than an algorithm which would perform the calculation (e.g. successive approximation). This is possible because a convenient inverse operation exists; *square* is assumed to be available though *sqrt* is not. It is also important to remember the other property of such a specification: it is the specified properties which interest the user of the function. For many purposes one would wish to exclude negative results and perhaps one would want to allow negative arguments, and decide whether imaginary values or error messages should be the result. The point is that these issues should be discussed in terms of specification and the user need never know, still less read, the selected algorithm.

★   ★   ★

The trivial task of subtraction of integers is another which can easily be specified by an inverse operation. That is, subtraction can be defined, even if not available as a basic operation, in terms of addition. Using *Int* as the name of a set containing all integers (i.e. ...,-1,0,1,...), the specification of a subtraction function can be given as:

sub: Int Int → Int
pre-sub(x,y) ≜ **TRUE**
post-sub(x,y,r) ≜ $x = y + r$

The pre-condition will be **TRUE** for any values, this provides no limitation: *sub* must work for any integers. The school child learns the concept of subtraction $(x - y)$ by looking for the number which must be added to y to obtain x: this is exactly the form of the implicit specification.

Another example from school can be derived from the problem of subtraction. The first numbers one learns are the natural numbers and care is taken to avoid negative numbers. Remembering that the set named *Nat* contains only the integers *1* and above, a subtraction function which only yields positive results can be specified by:

subp: Nat Nat → Nat
pre-subp(x,y) ≜ $x > y$
post-subp(x,y,r) ≜ $x = y + r$

The interest is in the pre-condition. In order to guarantee that an answer exists, it is necessary to have a condition between the two values. This could not easily be specified by means of the type clause.

The next step is to look in more detail at the notation used to build up the predicates of the implicit function definitions.

Propositional Operators

When writing explicit arithmetic function definitions, the use of constants and operators is familiar. Thus:

2 + 3 * 6

is an arithmetic expression denoting the value *20*. Logical expressions also contain constants and operators but these are of the appropriate type. Only two logical constants exist, they are written:

TRUE, FALSE

These two values are called *Boolean* values after the English mathematician, George Boole, who wrote "The Laws of Thought" in 1854. Similarly, five Boolean or *propositional* operators are introduced. Components of logical expressions may also be *propositions* which are either true or false. For example:

0 ≤ 2

is a proposition whose value is **TRUE**. Whereas: *This book is printed on green paper* is a proposition whose value is **FALSE**. The use of the symbols for the Boolean values within the text tends to be rather ugly and can easily be avoided. Rather than *proposition whose value is* **FALSE**, expressions like *false proposition* are used below.

The propositional operators can be inserted between propositions to build up larger propositions. This is analogous to the way arithmetic expressions are constructed. The symbols chosen and their names are shown in the first two columns of fig. 9 (the priority column is explained below).

Operator	Name	Priority
~	not	highest
∧	and	-
∨	or	-
⇒	implies	-
⇔	equivalence	lowest

Figure 9   Propositional Operators and Their Priority

Arithmetic operators, such as +, apply to values taken from infinite sets. Thus it is not possible to define their meaning by a table of all possible combinations of operands. In comparison, the definition of the propositional connectives is trivial because it is straightforward to provide a tabular definition. Thus:

a	b	a ∧ b
TRUE	TRUE	TRUE
TRUE	FALSE	FALSE
FALSE	TRUE	FALSE
FALSE	FALSE	FALSE

Here, *a* and *b* can be replaced by Boolean valucs, propositions or larger logical expressions. Thus knowing that:

$0<2 , 2≤7$

are both true, the table shows that:

$0<2 ∧ 2≤7$

is also true. The above **truth-table** corresponds to the intuitive reading of **and**. The tables for the other operators can be constructed in a similar way.

Exercise 2.1:   Provide truth table definitions for:
a) *or*—remember the interpretation is either one, or the other, or both
b) *equivalence*—corresponding to equality
c) *not*—an operator with only one operand

The truth-table for the remaining operator (**implies**) is:

a	b	a ⟹ b
TRUE	TRUE	TRUE
TRUE	FALSE	FALSE
FALSE	TRUE	TRUE
FALSE	FALSE	TRUE

Once again, this corresponds to one's intuitive understanding providing the operator is used sensibly. Thus, reading $p⟹q$ as **if p then q**, it is obvious that:

$a=2 ⟹ a**2 = 4$

The lines of the truth table can be checked by considering possible values for *a*:

> first line, *a* as *2*
> third line, *a* as *-2*
> fourth line, *a* as *3*

This only leaves the second line which fits with the fact that:

$a=2 ⟹ a**2 = 7$

is considered to be false. Only if propositions are constructed where the operands have no logical connection can confusing propositions be constructed. Thus:

this book is printed on green paper $\Rightarrow$ *7>3*

is true according to the table but is also useless. Implication should present no difficulties within this book since it is only used where the operands have some connection. One way of avoiding the need for *implies* is to note that:

$a \Rightarrow b$, $\sim a \vee b$

have the same truth-table and are thus equivalent. This can easily be checked by using the basic truth-tables to construct:

a	b	$\sim a$	$\sim a \vee b$	$a \Rightarrow b$
TRUE	TRUE	FALSE	TRUE	TRUE
TRUE	FALSE	FALSE	FALSE	FALSE
FALSE	TRUE	TRUE	TRUE	TRUE
FALSE	FALSE	TRUE	TRUE	TRUE

This technique of constructing truth-tables to check that expressions have the same meaning allows one to check equivalences which will be of use later when logical expressions have to be manipulated. For this reason they are collected together in appendix C.

Exercise 2.2:   Many pairs of expressions have, like those shown above, the same truth-tables. These are used below in constructing chains of deductions. The reader should convince himself that the following pairs of expressions are equivalent. Any means may be used (e.g. writing truth-tables, using earlier results to prove later ones).

a) $a \wedge b$, $b \wedge a$
b) $a \wedge$ **TRUE** , a
c) $a \vee b$, $b \vee a$
d) **FALSE** $\vee b$, b

The next two rules are referred to as ***associative rules***:

e) $(a \wedge b) \wedge c$, $a \wedge (b \wedge c)$
f) $(a \vee b) \vee c$, $a \vee (b \vee c)$

distributive rules:

g) $a \wedge (b \vee c)$, $(a \wedge b) \vee (a \wedge c)$
h) $a \vee (b \wedge c)$, $(a \vee b) \wedge (a \vee c)$

de Morgan's laws:

i) $\sim (a \vee b)$, $\sim a \wedge \sim b$
j) $\sim (a \wedge b)$, $\sim a \vee \sim b$

double negation:

k)   ~(~a) , a

implication:

l)   ~(a⟹b) , a ∧ ~b

equivalence:

m)   a ⟺ b , (a ⟹ b) ∧ (b ⟹ a)

Exercise 2.3: Some logical expressions are true whatever values are chosen for their constituents: such expressions are called *tautologies*. Check (e.g. by constructing truth-tables) that the following expressions are tautologies:

a)   a ∨ ~a
b)   **FALSE** ⟹ a
c)   a ⟹ **TRUE**
d)   a ⟹ (b ⟹ a)
e)   a ⟹ (b ⟹ a∧b)
f)   a∧b ⟹ a
g)   b ⟹ (a ∨ b)
h)   (**TRUE** ⟹ a) ⟹ a
i)   (a ⟹ c) ⟹ (a∧b ⟹ c)
j)   (a ⟹ b) ⟹ ((a ⟹ ~b) ⟹ ~a)

In arithmetic expressions, one can reduce the number of parentheses required by establishing *priorities* for the operators. Thus:

$$x + y * z = x + (y * z)$$

because multiplication has a higher priority than the addition operator. Similarly, in building logical expressions some economy of parentheses can be gained by using the priorities shown in fig. 9. These are not used extensively but for example:

$$p1 \wedge p2 \vee p3 \wedge p4 \Rightarrow p5$$

is written rather than:

$$((p1 \wedge p2) \vee (p3 \wedge p4)) \Rightarrow p5$$

The high priority of the unary operator, *not*, has already been used in the exercises above. Furthermore, obvious abbreviations like:

$$0 \leq i \leq 7 \quad for \quad 0 \leq i \wedge i \leq 7$$

are used.

The usefulness of the propositions that can be built would be severely limited if only constants and operators were permitted. Explicit definitions can be written for functions which have Boolean values. Any function whose range is *Bool* is said to be a predicate. Using parameters and their substitution by arguments, as with functions, one can give an explicit definition of a predicate as:

$p1(x) \triangleq 0 < x \land x \leq 7$

and then note that:

$p1(1) \Leftrightarrow$ **TRUE**
$p1(8) \Leftrightarrow$ **FALSE**

Those values for which the predicate yields **TRUE** are said to *satisfy* the predicate. Thus *1, 7* satisfy *p1*, while *0, 8* do not satisfy *p1*. Thus propositions can be built up from predicates. This has, in fact, already been done in the preceding section, where:

$pre\text{-}sqrt(x_0, t_0) \Rightarrow post\text{-}sqrt(x_0, t_0, sqrt(x_0, t_0))$

was used.

Given this firmer understanding of basic (propositional) logic notation, it can now be used to write some useful predicates.

Assume a function (**mod**) is available which finds the modulus of *x* when divided by *y*:

x **mod** *y*

such that, for example:

7 **mod** *2 = 1*
81 **mod** *9 = 0*

This function can be used to define a predicate:

is-divisor: Int Int → Bool

which yields **TRUE** if and only if its second argument exactly divides the first:

$is\text{-}divisor(x,y) \triangleq (x \textbf{ mod } y) = 0$

It is a useful convention to use *is-* as a prefix for predicate names. Apart from pre- and post-conditions, this convention will be followed below.

Exercise 2.4: Define a predicate:

is-common-divisor: Int Int Int → Bool

which yields **TRUE** if and only if the third argument is a divisor of both of the first two arguments, e.g.

is-common-divisor(81,108,9) $\Leftrightarrow$ **TRUE**

(Hint: throughout this book, use earlier results to simplify tasks.)

Exercise 2.5: Define predicates which test whether their argument is an odd or even integer:

is-odd: Int → Bool
is-even: Int → Bool

Exercise 2.6: Provide an implicit specification (type clause, pre- and post-condition) of a function which, for a given real number x_0 and a given integer n_0, will find the n_0th root of x_0. Assume that there is no tolerance problem with the resulting real number and specify the function using its inverse.

Exercise 2.7: Specify a function which, for given real numbers x_0 and y_0 will find the result of dividing x_0 by y_0. Do not use a division symbol in the specification.

Exercise 2.8: A function for performing integer division which delivers two results (the quotient and remainder) might be specified:

idiv: Int Int → Int Int
pre-idiv(a,b) $\triangleq$ *a≥0* $\land$ *b>0*
post-idiv(a,b,q,r) $\triangleq$ ...

provide a definition of the predicate to replace the ellipsis points.

A number of examples of obtaining short specifications by employing inverse operations have been given. Other techniques will be presented in later chapters. The idea of using axioms is now introduced. The factorial function is presumed to be known. Factorial can be defined by two simple statements about natural numbers:

0! = 1
(n+1)! = (n+1) * n!

Since these statements are taken as basic and are not themselves questioned, they are called **axioms**. This can be used to specify a function:

fact: Int → Int
pre-fact(n) $\triangleq$ *n* $\geq$ *0*
post-fact(n,fn) $\triangleq$ *fn = n!*

The sequence of **Fibonacci numbers** is formed by adding two adjacent numbers of the sequence to compute the next. The sequence can be defined by the axioms:

fib(0) = 0
fib(1) = 1
fib(n+2) = fib(n) + fib(n+1)

and a function for producing the *nth* Fibonacci number specified by:

nfib: Int → Int
pre-nfib(n) $\triangleq$ *n* $\geq$ *0*
post-nfib(n,f) $\triangleq$ *f = fib(n)*

Such convenient axiomatic definitions are rarely available—the techniques of the later sections have a larger part to play in specifying programs.

It should be realized that for values outside (i.e. which do not satisfy) the pre-condition the function is not constrained in any way.

Quantifiers

It has been pointed out that the logic notation is essentially to be used as a way of recording concepts in a succinct and manipulable form. There are two other forms of expressions which must be modelled in logic notation, namely: *for all possible values such-and-such holds* or *there exists some value for which such-and-such holds*. The *quantifiers* provide natural models of these two forms.

Given the material in the preceding section, it is possible to construct such expressions as:

is-even(2) $\wedge$ is-even(4) $\wedge$ is-even(6) $\wedge$ is-even(8)

But it is not yet possible to state that for all possible natural numbers the result of multiplying them by *2* will yield an even number. As with propositional operators, the quantified formulae can be easily read. The symbol for the *universal quantifier* is **A**; reading this symbol as *for all*, and ϵ as *is a member of*, the above statement can be written:

*(**A**nϵNat)(is-even(n+n))*

A quantified expression is built up from a quantifier symbol (**A** in this case), a *bound variable*, a *constraint*, and a body which normally contains the bound variable one or more times. As with parameters, the bound variable is a place holder and could be replaced by a graphic notation as in fig. 10.

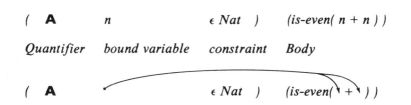

(**A**	*n*	*ϵ Nat)*	*(is-even(n + n))*
Quantifier	*bound variable*	*constraint*	*Body*

(**A**   *ϵ Nat)*   *(is-even(\ +\ ))*

Figure 10   Bounded Quantified Expression

Many treatments of logic do not use the constraint part of a quantified expression so, to be precise, the expressions used here should be called *bounded quantified expressions*. The constraint part of quantified expressions can be very significant. Some very plausible looking expressions like:

*(**A**n)(2*n>n)*

are not true (consider *-1*), unless care is taken to make clear the range of values which *n* is allowed to assume. Using *Nat* for the set of natural numbers: *1, 2, 3 ...* , it is true that:

*(**A**nϵNat)(2*n>n)*

This standard form for quantified expressions includes a constraint. The constraint is only omitted where the range of values under discussion is obvious from the context.

A useful key to understanding the universal quantifier is to think of it in terms of an abbreviation for a logical expression built up with **and** operators (such an expression is called a **conjunction**). Using:

$\{i{:}j\}$

as a way of denoting the set containing all integers between, and including, i and j, the expression:

$(\mathbf{A}n\epsilon\{2{:}4\})(p(n))$

is equivalent to:

$p(2) \wedge p(3) \wedge p(4)$

Such expansion is, of course, only possible when the range specifies a finite set of values for the bound variable. Thus:

$(\mathbf{A}n\epsilon Nat)(is\text{-}even(2^*n))$

would expand to an infinite expression:

$is\text{-}even(2) \wedge is\text{-}even(4) \wedge is\text{-}even(6) \wedge \ldots$

For this reason, quantifiers can be thought of as providing an abbreviation for expressions which one could not otherwise write.

Analogous to a conjunction, a logical expression whose main operator(s) are **or** is called a **disjunction**. Is there an analogous concept of quantified expressions corresponding to disjunctions such as:

$p(7) \vee p(8) \vee p(9) \qquad ?$

The answer is yes, this corresponds to an English expression like *there exists some value for which such-and-such holds*. Using the *existential quantifier* (**E**) the above expression can be written:

$(\mathbf{E}x\epsilon\{7{:}9\})(p(x))$

Here again, the constraint can allow an infinite set of values for the bound variable. For example:

$(\mathbf{E}x\epsilon Nat)(x \bmod 721 = 38)$

Notice that the quantified statement asserts the existence of one *or more* values. This meaning follows from considering an existentially quantified expression as an abbreviation for a disjunction.

With the use of quantifiers, the expressions now being constructed are part of the so-called *predicate calculus*. Quantifiers are used in some definitions and general statements. For example:

$(\mathbf{A}d\epsilon D)(pre\text{-}f(d) \Rightarrow post\text{-}f(d,f(d)))$

There is little need to manipulate quantifiers. Simple translations of the quantifiers will serve to clarify the subsequent manipulations. Two equivalences used are:

$(\mathbf{A}x\epsilon X)(p(x)) \Leftrightarrow \sim(\mathbf{E}x\epsilon X)(\sim p(x))$
$\sim(\mathbf{A}x\epsilon X)(p(x)) \Leftrightarrow (\mathbf{E}x\epsilon X)(\sim p(x))$

The use of the expansions of quantified expressions (to disjunctions and conjunctions) and the rules given in exercise 2.2 should make these equivalences obvious. Consider for example:

$(\mathbf{A}x\epsilon X)(p(x))$

the expansion of this into an (infinite) conjunction gives:

$p(x_1) \wedge p(x_2) \wedge \ldots$

Using the rule that double negation does not change an expression, the above formula is equivalent to:

$\sim(\sim(p(x_1) \wedge p(x_2) \wedge \ldots))$

To this one can apply another of the equivalences—de Morgan's law:

$\sim(\sim p(x_1) \vee \sim p(x_2) \vee \ldots)$

But considering the expansion of an existentially quantified expression to a disjunction, this can be seen to be equivalent to:

$\sim(\mathbf{E}x\epsilon X)(\sim p(x))$

The meaning of a constraint involving the empty set (written { }) is, by convention, true for the universal quantifier:

$(\mathbf{A}x\epsilon\{\ \})(p(x))$

and false for the existential quantifier:

$\sim(\mathbf{E}x\epsilon\{\ \})(p(x))$

If a proof of some property, say $p(x)$, is constructed without making any assumptions about x, then one can conclude:

$(\mathbf{A}x)(p(x))$

Similarly, if some particular object x_0 has been shown to give $p(x_0)$, then a valid conclusion is:

$(\mathbf{E}x)(p(x))$

Rather than write strings of the same quantifier and restriction, the expression:

$(\mathbf{E}x\epsilon Int)(\mathbf{E}y\epsilon Int)(is\text{-}common\text{-}divisor(x,y,z) \Rightarrow z=1)$

for example, will be abbreviated to:

$(\mathbf{E}x,y\epsilon Int)(is\text{-}common\text{-}divisor(x,y,z) \Rightarrow z=1)$

It is now time to return, equipped with the quantifier notation, to the topic of implicitly specifying functions (see fig. 7). Suppose it is required to specify a function which yields the **greatest common divisor** (**highest common factor**) of two natural numbers. Then:

gcd: Nat Nat → Nat
pre-gcd(x,y) ≜ **TRUE**
post-gcd(x,y,d) ≜
    is-common-divisor(x,y,d) ∧
    ~*(**E**e∈Nat)(e>d ∧ is-common-divisor(x,y,e))*

follows exactly the form of words one would use to explain the concept of greatest common divisor.

The *gcd* function is said to be *total* because it requires no extra input assumptions. This situation recurs often below and, since the pre-condition can be interpreted as defining extra freedom, it will be omitted for total functions. Thus a function for which no pre-condition is recorded must deliver a suitable result for all values in its domain.

Exercise 2.9:   Check which of the following expressions is true:

a)   *(**A**x)(x = x)*
b)   *(**E**x)(x ≠ x)*
c)   *(**E**x∈Nat)((7 **mod** x) > x)*
d)   *(**A**x∈Nat)(**E**y∈Nat)(is-divisor(x,y))*
e)   *(**E**y∈Nat)(**A**x∈Nat)(is-divisor(x,y))*
f)   *(**E**x,y∈Int)(is-common-divisor(x,y,z) ⇒ z=1)*
g)   *(**A**x∈Nat)(~is-prime(4*x))*
h)   *(**A**x∈Nat)(~is-prime(2*x))*

Exercise 2.10:   Express, using quantifiers, the facts that:
a) there is not a largest integer,
b) there is no integer beyond which no prime number can be found.

Exercise 2.11:   Define a function (giving the standard three parts) which delivers the *smallest common multiple* of two natural numbers as its result. For example:

scm(81,18) = 162

Exercise 2.12:   Modulus (**mod**) is introduced, and used above. It is written as though it were an infix operator. This can now, with the aid of quantifiers, be defined. Present a definition of a *mod* function (without, of course, using **mod**) which accepts two natural numbers as arguments. Since the result may be zero:

Nat0 = {0,1,2, ... }

is required.

Exercise 2.13:   Use quantifiers to complete the definition of:

is-prime(x) ≜ ...

for natural numbers.

Summary

This chapter has introduced the first collection of notation taken from mathematics as an aid to precise and concise specifications. A standard format (type clause, pre- and post-condition) has been introduced for implicitly specifying what a function should do. The type clause and pre-condition define the domain of the function—this is analogous to the input of a program. The type clause also specifies the type of the results of a function—this is analogous to the output of a program. The process part of the specification is defined implicitly in the post-condition.

Pre- and post-conditions are predicates. The necessary notation of logic (Boolean values, propositional operators and quantifiers) has been introduced and illustrated on small numerical specifications. An important distinction has been made between the external view of a function, given by its specification, and the internal view given by the explicit function definition. Other terms for this dichotomy are the extensional (external) and intentional view of functions.

Summary Exercises

Exercise 2.14: Comment on some other disciplines which have found it necessary to develop their own notation.

Exercise 2.15: In order to show the usefulness of the logic notation, rewrite in English the specifications of exercises 2.12 and 2.13 then ask somebody to review this for ambiguity and completeness.

Chapter 3

PROOFS ABOUT FUNCTIONS

Chapter 2 shows how specifications for functions can be written. Minor extensions are shown in the next chapter which covers the specification of programs. Thus, a valuable goal, that of precise specifications, is already within reach for numerical programs. Such specifications are, of course, valuable for communication and control. However, an even larger reward is attainable: correctness proofs can be based on precise specifications.

The correctness of a function can only be discussed with respect to a specification. Given a formal implicit specification and an explicit definition for a function, a proof can be constructed that the latter does, indeed, satisfy the former. For example, given the specification:

max: Int Int → Int
post-max(x,y,r) ≜ *r≥x* ∧ *r≥y* ∧ *(r=x* ∨ *r=y)*

and a realization:

max(x,y) ≜ **if** *x≥y* **then** *x* **else** *y*

it is proved that:

*(**A**x,y∊Int)(pre-max(x,y)* ⟹ *post-max(x,y,max(x,y)))*

Such proofs can be made so formal that they can be checked by a computer program. The first proofs are presented in considerable detail, but the ultimate aim is for a reasonable level of rigor. Thinking back to simple algebra, the reader will know that an expansion of:

(a+b)**2

can be achieved by steps like:

(a+b)*(a+b)
a*a + a*b + b*a + b*b
a**2 + 2*a*b + b**2

The reader could do the above expansion in one step, and practice with manipulating logical expressions will permit him to present more complex logical proofs at a rigorous (less formal) level. Rigorous, rather than machine-checked, proofs are what this book is trying to teach. This

chapter, then, shows how to prove that explicit definitions of functions
match the corresponding implicit specifications. In doing this for
functions, many of the key concepts which are required for program
proofs are introduced. Furthermore, these proofs about numerical
programs present, in a familiar framework, methods which are applicable
to more interesting data structures.

Unconditional Functions

This chapter, as a whole, is concerned with proving that explicit function
definitions satisfy the conditions given in their implicit specifications.
The first form of explicit definition, about which proofs are presented, is
the *unconditional* definition. That is, the definition consists of a simple
expression in terms of the parameters and operators. Such unconditional
functions are not very powerful (and, thus, the specifications and
programs look very similar) but they will provide a vehicle for the
presentation of the overall proof structure.

The simplest function is a *constant* function. Most pocket calcula-
tors are equipped with a way of generating the constant *pi*. Whatever
number is in the display, depression of the *pi* button replaces it with an
approximation to the value of *pi*. Thinking in terms of functions, this
suggests a function which, for any argument, delivers the value of π.
Thus an implicit specification reads:

$pi: Real \rightarrow Real$
$post\text{-}pi(x,r) \triangleq r = \pi$

Notice that the right-hand side of the definition of the predicate *post-pi*
does not need to refer to the name of the input parameter. There is no
difficulty in devising an appropriate function:

$pi(x) \triangleq \pi$

Referring back to fig. 8, which provides the meaning of the specification,
it is then required to show that (using a bounded quantifier):

$(\mathbf{A}x_0 \epsilon Real)(pre\text{-}pi(x_0) \Rightarrow post\text{-}pi(x_0,pi(x_0)))$

To show that this is true, the whole expression is reduced in steps to the
value **TRUE**. The first step is to notice that the bounded quantifier
limits the possible values for x_0: the limitation is not normally important
on unconditional functions though it is with conditional and recursive
functions. One must therefore prove (without restriction):

$pre\text{-}pi(x_0) \Rightarrow post\text{-}pi(x_0,pi(x_0))$

Substituting in the definition of *pre-pi* (remember that, for total
functions, the omitted predicate is **TRUE**):

$\mathbf{TRUE} \Rightarrow post\text{-}pi(x_0,pi(x_0))$

and using *post-pi* gives:

TRUE $\Rightarrow$ $pi(x_0)$ = π

Substituting again, this time with the definition of the function *pi* gives:

TRUE $\Rightarrow$ π = π

Since the right-hand side of this implication is true, the truth table for *implies* can be used to establish that the whole expression reduces to **TRUE**.

Just as in school algebra, the initial statement (the required theorem) has been transformed into what was required (the expression **TRUE**) in a series of simple steps. Each of these steps can be independently justified. The first phase consists of substituting definitions of predicates and functions; secondly, one can use other knowledge (in this case, only the meaning of *implies*) to simplify the expression. This structure of statement/substitution/simplification is the backbone of all the proofs in this chapter. It is illustrated graphically as in fig. 11. Notice that the order of the substitutions is unimportant since each is changing an expression to an equivalent one.

★　★　★

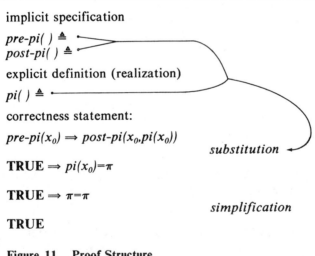

implicit specification

$pre\text{-}pi(\ )\ \triangleq$

$post\text{-}pi(\ )\ \triangleq$

explicit definition (realization)

$pi(\ )\ \triangleq$

correctness statement:

$pre\text{-}pi(x_0) \Rightarrow post\text{-}pi(x_0,pi(x_0))$

substitution

TRUE $\Rightarrow$ $pi(x_0)=\pi$

TRUE $\Rightarrow$ $\pi=\pi$

simplification

TRUE

Figure 11   Proof Structure

The above proof has been presented by the process of analysis by which it was found. This is typical of the way one works with proofs. Equally typical, is for many textbooks to present a synthetic form of the proof which builds up from the known facts to the required theorem. This does, in fact, make the proof easier to read. To illustrate this the above proof can be rewritten as follows. Given:

pre-pi(x) $\triangleq$ **TRUE**
post-pi(x,r) $\triangleq r = \pi$
pi(x) $\triangleq \pi$

Use *post-pi* to see:

post-pi(x_0,π)

therefore:

post-pi(x_0,pi(x_0))

thus by the meaning of ***implies***:

pre-pi(x_0) $\Rightarrow$ *post-pi(x_0,pi(x_0))*

Since this statement is general in x_0, one can conclude that:

$(\mathbf{A}x_0\epsilon Real)$*(pre-pi($x_0$)* $\Rightarrow$ *post-pi(x_0,pi(x_0)))*

This reordering of the steps may make reading easier but the concern in this book is with the creation of rigorous proofs and thus most of what follows uses the earlier analytic style.

★   ★   ★

Following the constant function, one can consider the ***identity*** function. That is, a function which yields as its result exactly the value of its argument. The implicit specification is as follows:

identity: Real $\longrightarrow$ *Real*
post-identity(x,r) $\triangleq r = x$

The obvious realization of this function is:

identity(x) $\triangleq x$

The statement to be proved is:

$(\mathbf{A}x_0\epsilon Real)$*(pre-identity($x_0$)* $\Rightarrow$ *post-identity(x_0,identity(x_0)))*

Proceeding as before, the bound will not be required and substituting for both the pre- and post-conditions gives:

TRUE $\Rightarrow$ *identity(x_0)* $= x_0$

When an implication arises with a left-hand side which is **TRUE**, it is clear that the right-hand side also has to be shown to be true in order to reduce the whole statement to **TRUE** (cf. rule (h) in exercise 2.3). It is therefore the practice below to drop the **TRUE** $\Rightarrow$ in order to reduce the length of formulae. Thus, the formula reduces to:

identity(x_0) $= x_0$

and using the explicit definition of *identity* gives:

$x_0 = x_0$

which is obviously true.

★   ★   ★

In the proofs given so far, the pre-condition has not played a part. Consider the following specification:

f: Int Int → Int
pre-f(x,y) ≜ *x = 2*
post-f(x,y,r) ≜ *r = 2*y*

This rather odd double function can be realized by:

f(x,y) ≜ *x*y*

which can be shown to satisfy:

pre-f(x,y) ⟹ *post-f(x,y,f(x,y))*

by substitution gives:

x=2 ⟹ *f(x,y) = 2*y*
x=2 ⟹ *x*y = 2*y*

which is obviously true.

If one tries to prove an incorrect function correct the proof will fail. For example, the above function is not correct if the pre-condition is ignored. The statement to be proved reduces to:

x * y = 2 * y

This is not, in general, true. When the attempt to reduce the correctness statement to true fails, one is forced to look for the mistake in the program.

Exercise 3.1:   Given the specification:

double: Int → Int
post-double(x,r) ≜ *r = 2*x*

and the function:

double(x) ≜ *x + x*

Prove the function satisfies the specification. (Obvious properties of arithmetic, such as *x+y=y+x*, should be used as required.)

Exercise 3.2:   The following can be taken as the specification for a function which **converts temperatures** from the Fahrenheit to Centigrade scales:

conv: Real → Real
post-conv(f,c) ≜ *c * 9/5 + 32 = f*

prove that:

conv(f) ≜ *(f-32) * 5/9*

satisfies the specification.

Exercise 3.3: Given the specification which changes *3* to *7* or *7* to *3*:

choose: Int $\longrightarrow$ *Int*
pre-choose(x) $\triangleq$ *x=3* $\lor$ *x=7*
post-choose(x,r) $\triangleq$ *x=3* $\land$ *r=7* $\lor$ *x=7* $\land$ *r=3*

show that:

choose(x) $\triangleq$ *10-x*

is correct.

Conditional Functions

It is time to introduce some more interesting ways of constructing function definitions. The unconditional functions of the preceding section can be thought of as the analogues of straight-line programs; branching programs can also be linked with a form of function description. That form is **conditional functions** and this section is concerned with proofs about these. The basic means of expressing conditional functions is the **conditional expression**. Readers who are familiar with *IF THEN ELSE* statements should have little difficulty in understanding these **if then else** expressions. An expression of the form:

if *b* **then** *c1* **else** *c2*

has a value which depends on the value of the sub-expression *b*: if this evaluates to **TRUE**, the value of the whole expression is the value of the sub-expression *c1*; if the sub-expression *b* has a value **FALSE**, then the value of the whole expression is the value of the sub-expression *c2*. Thus:

(if *x=1* **then** *1* **else** *2)* + **(if** *x≠1* **then** *1* **else** *2)*

is a rather cumbersome expression for the value *3*. Of more use is the definition of a function *max* which yields the maximum value of its two arguments:

max(x,y) $\triangleq$ **if** *x≥y* **then** *x* **else** *y*

Thus:

max(7,10) = 10 , max(8,3) = 8

How is this to be proved correct? Its correctness can only be discussed in terms of a specification; this can be given as:

max: Int Int $\longrightarrow$ *Int*
post-max(x,y,r) $\triangleq$ *r≥x* $\land$ *r≥y* $\land$ *(r=x* $\lor$ *r=y)*

The proof begins as in the last section and the initial statement is:

*(**A**x,y∈Int)(pre-max(x,y)* $\Rightarrow$ *post-max(x,y,max(x,y)))*

The argument must then be general for any integers, but here the restriction is important since the use of comparison may otherwise be invalid. So, for all integers, it must be shown:

pre-max(x,y) ⟹ *post-max(x,y,max(x,y))*

This gives:

TRUE ⟹ *post-max(x,y,max(x,y))*

At this point the definition of *post-max* could be used, but since the *r* term occurs four times it is preferable to consider the corresponding argument first. Thus using the definition of *max*, gives:

post-max(x,y, **if** *x≥y* **then** *x* **else** *y)*

How is one to proceed? Substitution into the definition of *post-max* would now create a really unwieldy expression. In such a situation, it is necessary to reason by cases. This will be the key to proofs about conditional expressions. In order to handle multiple cases the proof is divided by making temporary assumptions which make it possible to handle the cases one at a time. The two cases, *x≥y* and ∼*(x≥y)* are considered. The first assumption made is:

x ≥ y

Under this assumption, what has to be proved simplifies to:

post-max(x,y,x)

The definition of *post-max* can now be used to give:

x≥x ∧ *x≥y* ∧ *(x=x* ∨ *x=y)*

which simplifies to:

TRUE ∧ *x≥y* ∧ *(***TRUE** ∨ *x=y)*

and thus (using rules of exercise 2.2) to:

x ≥ y

which is exactly the temporary assumption. This leaves nothing to prove in this case. Of course, only one case has been considered so far. The alternative assumption is:

∼*(x≥y)*

or:

x < y

The formula which is to be proved now simplifies to:

post-max(x,y,y)

which becomes:

y≥x ∧ *y≥y* ∧ *(y=x* ∨ *y=y)*

which simplifies to:

$y \geq x$

This again follows from the temporary assumption.

(The assumption is unnecessarily strong. This results from the explicit definition being over-constrained in that:

$max(6,6)$

could yield either its first or its second argument as result; the choice to use the first value, embodied in the conditional expression, is arbitrary. Clearly, using the second would not change the result, but the effect of the asymmetry has reappeared in the proof. The reader who wishes to pursue this point is directed to the work on "Guarded Commands" in Dijkstra(75).)

Two cases have been considered. Since they are direct converses, no other possibility remains and the result (the correctness of *max*) has been proved for all cases.

The proofs are now becoming less automatic. Some choice has to be exercised as to the order in which substitution and case distinctions should be made. It is recommended to make case distinctions as soon as conditional expressions appear after substitution. Proliferating the conditional expression by substituting it further is likely to generate unnecessarily long expressions.

★   ★   ★

The reduction of an integer to one of three values indicating the sign of the original number can be used as a further example. (This is the *SIGN* built-in function of PL/I.) The implicit specification is as follows:

sign: Int → Int
$post\text{-}sign(x,r) \triangleq$
    $(x<0 \land r=-1) \lor$
    $(x=0 \land r=0) \lor$
    $(x>0 \land r=+1)$

Conditional expressions can be nested to provide the following realization:

$sign(x) \triangleq$
    if $x<0$ **then** *-1*
    else if $x=0$ **then** *0*
    else *+1*

To prove this correct it is necessary to show:

$post\text{-}sign(x_0, sign(x_0))$

(Notice that *pre-sign* is now being dropped as soon as it is noticed that its definition is **TRUE**.) Again, the most expedient substitution would appear to be for *sign*. This gives:

$post\text{-}sign(x_0,$ **if** $x_0<0$ **then** *-1* **else if** $x_0=0$ **then** *0* **else** *+1)*

Following the earlier structure, the proof proceeds by considering three cases. Firstly consider:

$x_0 < 0$

The formula to be proved reduces to:

post-sign$(x_0,-1)$

which using the definition of *post-sign* gives:

$(x_0{<}0 \wedge -1{=}{-}1) \vee (x_0{=}0 \wedge -1{=}0) \vee (x_0{>}0 \wedge -1{=}{+}1)$

or:

$(x_0{<}0) \vee$ **FALSE** $\vee$ **FALSE**
$x_0 < 0$

which follows from the temporary assumption and thus concludes this case. For the second case take the assumption:

$x_0 = 0$

Now the reduction of the conditional expression is made in two stages:

if $x_0{<}0$ **then** -1 **else if** $x_0{=}0$ **then** 0 **else** +1
    = **if** $x_0{=}0$ **then** 0 **else** +1
    = 0

Thus the formula to be proved reduces to:

post-sign$(x_0,0)$

which gives:

$(x_0{<}0 \wedge 0{=}{-}1) \vee (x_0{=}0 \wedge 0{=}0) \vee (x_0{>}0 \wedge 0{=}{+}1)$

This time it is the middle term of the disjunction which follows from the temporary assumption.

    Two cases have been considered ($x_0{<}0$ and $x_0{=}0$) but to cover all possible integers a third case must also be examined:

$x_0 > 0$

Here, the formula to be proved reduces to:

post-sign$(x_0, +1)$

and use of the definition of *post-sign* again gives an expression which follows from the assumption.

    All cases have now been considered and the proof of *sign* is complete.

Exercise 3.4:   Finding the *absolute value* of an integer can be specified as follows:

abs: Int $\longrightarrow$ *Nat0*
post-abs(x,r) $\triangleq r{\geq}0 \wedge (x{=}r \vee x{=}{-}r)$

Prove that the following conditional function satisfies the specification:

abs(x) $\triangleq$ **if** $x{<}0$ **then** -x **else** +x

Faced with the problem of finding an appropriate *abs* function a student suggested:

$abs2(x) \triangleq max(x,-x)$

Proving this correct provides the opportunity to use results which have gone before. It is required (with the new definition) to prove:

$post\text{-}abs(x_0,abs2(x_0))$

or:

$post\text{-}abs(x_0,max(x_0,-x_0))$

Now this is a use of *max* and, although it would be possible to substitute its definition, the proper interface is that described by the implicit specification given above. To record what follows from that specification a temporary name r is used: `

$r = max(x_0,-x_0)$

The post-condition of *max* gives:

$r{\geq}x_0 \land r{\geq}{-}x_0 \land (r{=}x_0 \lor r{=}{-}x_0)$

Noticing that:

$r{\geq}x_0 \land r{\geq}{-}x_0 \Rightarrow r{\geq}0$

it follows that:

$post\text{-}abs(x_0,r)$

By using functions which had been defined before, a proof about conditional functions had been avoided. Although this rather diverted the exercise it was a most valuable diversion. For one thing, using the specification of *max* rather than its realization was a correct decision. Although such simple functions as are being used here have trivial realizations, it must be remembered that for complex programs the specification is far easier to manipulate than the realization. A second respect in which the diversion was rewarding is that it points the way ahead to a development process where one begins with specifications of complex tasks and solves these in terms of simpler tasks. These simpler tasks become the subject of further development. The development process itself is covered later in this book, but some indication of how current techniques can readily be applied is given by the following exercise.

Exercise 3.5: Suppose a total multiplication routine is required for integers. (If the reader is disturbed by the unreality of a machine which does not provide such a basic instruction, he can assume the task is to microcode this instruction.) Thus the specification is:

$mult\text{: } Int \; Int \longrightarrow Int$
$post\text{-}mult(x,y,r) \triangleq r = x{*}y$

Some form of loop control variable must be found whose value can be used to limit the iteration. This is easier to achieve in a limited routine which assumes that one of its inputs is positive. Thus:

$multp: Int\ Int \rightarrow Int$
$pre\text{-}multp(x,y) \triangleq x \geq 0$
$post\text{-}multp(x,y,r) \triangleq r = x*y$

It is now possible to realize *mult* using *multp* as follows:

$mult(x,y) \triangleq$ **if** $x \geq 0$ **then** $multp(x,y)$ **else** $-multp(-x,y)$

Remembering:

$pre\text{-}multp(x_0,y_0) \Rightarrow post\text{-}multp(x_0,y_0,multp(x_0,y_0))$

prove the realization correct.

A further observation should be made about the structure of specifications. The specification of *mult*, for example, is functional in the sense that it defines exactly one answer. Furthermore, a multiplication symbol is used in the post-condition. This symbol is assumed to be understood; it is intended, however, that it should not be used in the realization. It would then be possible to replace *post-mult* by saying that the intended function should be equivalent to:

$mult(x,y) \triangleq x*y$

In other words, the post-condition could be expressed by writing an expression using operators which are not available in the realization. However, it must be remembered that this form is only applicable where one answer is fixed for given arguments (contrast with *sqrt* above). Furthermore, it is explained later that such shortening of post-conditions is unwise in the case of program specifications.

Recursive Functions

It is mentioned in the last two sections how the forms of function definitions shown can be viewed as analogues of program structures. But with straight-line and branching programs, the computations which can be generated are very short. The way of describing computations which can be much longer than the programs which evoke them is to use some form of repetitive concept (e.g. *DO* in PL/I, *for* in ALGOL 60). An analogous concept for functions exists in **recursion**. So far, function definitions have been stated in terms of previously defined functions (plus operators, parameters and constants). The only difference that distinguishes recursive functions is that the function being defined can also be used in the definition. This, of course, introduces a circularity which must be used with care. To provide a good example of the use of recursion, some notation is employed which is formally described in part B. For the time being, verbal descriptions of such formulae are included.

The problem to be considered is that of finding the largest number among a collection of numbers. The collection will be organized in a data structure called a **binary tree**. A binary tree consists of either an atomic data element (in this case a number) or is a node which consists of two parts, each of which is itself a binary tree. This description is expressed by the following (abstract syntax) formulae:

Bin-tree = Int | Node
Node:: LEFT:Bin-tree   RIGHT:Bin-tree

The precise meaning of these formulae is not important for now. Fig. 12 illustrates an instance of a binary tree (the nodes have been given names for subsequent use.)

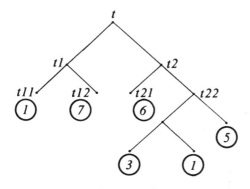

Figure 12   A Binary Tree

Representations, for example on arrays, are not difficult to invent. The function to be written here, however, is presented as though binary tree was a data type in its own right. The required function, *maxt*, is defined by a conditional expression. If the tree to be analyzed is an integer, then this integer is itself the maximum value of the (atomic) tree. If, on the other hand, the tree is a node containing two sub-trees, then the maximum value is the larger of the two numbers which are the maximum values contained in the two sub-trees. Finding the maximum of two numbers can be done by using the function *max* from the preceding section. How are the maximum values of the two sub-trees to be found? The answer is to use the function *maxt* which is being defined. Using *LEFT* and *RIGHT* as selectors which yield the sub-trees of a tree this can be written:

maxt(t) ≜
    if *t∈Int* **then** *t*
    else *max(maxt(LEFT(t)),maxt(RIGHT(t)))*

   The circularity or self-referencing which is used above requires some justification. Firstly, unconstrained use of the function being defined can lead to difficulties. Thus:

maxt(t) = maxt(t)

is acceptable as a proposition, but could not be used as a definition because it provides no way of actually computing a result. What distinguishes the (recursive) uses of *maxt* in the proper definition given above is that they apply to smaller trees. Thus, each time that *maxt* is evaluated it is for smaller trees. This can be illustrated by showing the application of *maxt* to the tree *t* of fig. 12:

maxt(t)
    = *max(maxt(t1), maxt(t2))*
    = *max(max(maxt(t11), maxt(t12)), maxt(t2))*
    = *max(max(1,7), maxt(t2))*
    = *max(7,max(maxt(t21), maxt(t22)))*
    ...
    = *max(7,max(6,max(3,5)))*
    ...
    = *7*

   A recursive definition of a function uses a conditional expression. That expression may contain two or more clauses but at least one clause must specify a simple result computed without the (recursive) use of the function being defined. This defines a ***stopping*** case. The remaining clauses should only use recursive references to the function on values which are closer to the stopping, or end, case.

   In order to write the function *maxt* without the use of recursion, the writer would be forced to simulate the tracing of the trees using some auxiliary data structure such as ***stacks***. Binary trees are themselves recursive in the sense that instances of trees occur within other trees (cf. the definition of ***Bin-tree***). On such data structures, recursive functions are an invaluable tool for obtaining concise and clear function definitions. (The subject of recursion can be studied more deeply in Barron(68).) This part of the book, however, is confined to simple numbers as data types and the use of recursion is less valuable—it is easy to see how simple and efficient iterative programs could be written to fulfil the given specifications.

★ ★ ★

   The technique for proving results about recursive functions is mathematical induction. This is a difficult topic and the material on proving programs correct presents standard lists of results which can be used to check that iterative programs are correct. These lists of results have themselves been justified by proofs using induction but the reader will not have to construct his own inductive arguments. Nevertheless, a background in induction is useful for a better appreciation of some of the later topics.

As an example, consider computing the factorial of a number. The axioms which characterize factorial are:

$0! = 1$
$n! = n * (n-1)!$ for $n \epsilon Nat$

The name *Nat0* is given to the set of natural numbers including zero (i.e. 0, 1, 2,...). The specification of factorial can be given as:

fact: Nat0 → Nat
$post\text{-}fact(n,fn) \triangleq fn = n!$

The function which is to be proved correct is:

$fact(n) \triangleq$
    if $n=0$ **then** 1
    else $n * fact(n-1)$

An evaluation of *fact* is shown in fig. 13.

---

fact(3)
    $= 3 * fact(2)$
    $= 3 * 2 * fact(1)$
    $= 3 * 2 * 1 * fact(0)$
    $= 3 * 2 * 1 * 1$

Figure 13   Evaluation of Factorial

It is required to prove that for all natural numbers:

$pre\text{-}fact(n_0) \Rightarrow post\text{-}fact(n_0,fact(n_0))$

Noting that the left-hand side of this implication is always true indicates that it is required to show:

$post\text{-}fact(n_0,fact(n_0))$

Using the definition of *fact*, this gives, by substitution:

$post\text{-}fact(n_0,$ **if** $n_0=0$ **then** 1 **else** $n_0 * fact(n_0-1))$

Noting that a conditional expression has arisen, The obvious case distinction is to assume:

$n_0 = 0$

which reduces the formula to be proved to:

$post\text{-}fact(n_0,1)$

which, by *post-fact* is

$1 = n_0!$

Given the assumption, this is one of the properties for factorial and this case is therefore concluded.

Remembering that n_0 ranges only over *Nat0* the alternative assumption should be:

$n_0 > 0$

The formula which is to be proved can again be simplified, this time to:

*post-fact(n_0, n_0 * fact(n_0-1))*

Notice that a reference to *fact* is still present. How is this to be handled? If some particular value of n_0 were being considered, the definition of *fact* could be used to derive a value. Thus for, say:

$n_0 = 3$
*post-fact(n_0,n_0 * fact(n_0 -1))*
$\quad \Leftrightarrow$ *post-fact(3,3 * fact(2))*
$\qquad$ ...
$\quad \Leftrightarrow$ *post-fact(3,6)*

which can then be checked against *post-fact* and the properties of factorial. But the whole point of writing a proof is to give an argument for any value of n_0.

★ ★ ★

Induction is the process of concluding general laws from specific observations. Much of science consists of laws derived from observing many instances of events which appear to be linked. ***Mathematical induction*** is a formal technique for proving that properties hold for infinite classes of objects. Obviously, any useful proof must itself be finite. Clearly the proof has been made without observing every object, so there is some reason for calling such proofs inductive—the qualification "mathematical" is normally omitted here.

Proof of a result for a finite class of objects can be performed by enumeration. Proving that there are four prime numbers between ten and twenty requires enumerating and testing the relevant numbers. However, proving that there is no largest prime number is an argument about an infinite set of values. How is one to prove a result for all possible values in an infinite class? The key idea of an inductive proof is to show that a proof could be constructed for any value. Confining the discussion to the natural numbers—if one wishes to prove some result, say *p*, one proves:

p(0)

This is called the ***basis*** of the induction. The next step is to prove that, knowing the property for any value (greater than or equal to zero), one can deduce the property for the next value:

for n≥0: p(n) $\Rightarrow$ p(n+1)

This is called the ***inductive step*** and the, temporary, assumption of p(n) is known as the ***induction hypothesis***. Now it should be clear that a proof for any finite value of *n* could, in fact, be explicitly generated by writing out the proofs:

p(0)
p(1)   *using the proven result for p(0)*
p(2)   *using the proven result for p(1)*

...

p(n-1)   *using the proven result for p(n-2)*
p(n)   *using the proven result for p(n-1)*

So the use of an induction hypothesis in the inductive step is valid. Essentially then, an inductive proof is of the form:

p(0) $\wedge$ *(n≥0*$\wedge$*p(n)* $\Rightarrow$ *p(n+1))* $\Rightarrow$ *(**A**n∈Nat0)(p(n))*

Other forms which can be used are:

p(0) $\wedge$ *(n>0*$\wedge$*p(n-1)* $\Rightarrow$ *p(n))* $\Rightarrow$ *(**A**n∈Nat0)(p(n))*
p(1) $\wedge$ *(n≥1*$\wedge$*p(n)* $\Rightarrow$ *p(n+1))* $\Rightarrow$ *(**A**n∈Nat)(p(n))*

For example, to show that the sum of the first *n* natural numbers is:

sum(n) = (n*(n+1)) / 2

one first proves the basis:

sum(1) = (1*(1+1)) / 2 = 1

The induction hypothesis is:

(n*(n+1)) / 2 = sum(n)

The sum of the first *n+1* natural numbers will be:

sum(n) + (n+1)

but, since:

sum(n+1)
    = ((n+1)*(n+2)) / 2
    = ((n+1)*n)/2 + ((n+1)*2)/2
    = sum(n) + n+1

the induction step has been proved and the property has been proved for all (positive) natural numbers.

Similarly, one can prove that the sum of the first *n* odd numbers is *n**2*.

* * *

Returning to the factorial example, it can be seen that the structure prompted by handling conditional expressions naturally fits the structure of an inductive proof. The first case assumption *(n₀=0)* is exactly the basis of the inductive proof; the second assumption *(n₀>0)* delineates the inductive step. Most importantly, it is now clear that the impasse created by the reference to *fact* in the formula:

post-fact(n₀, n₀ * fact(n₀-1))

can be tackled using an induction hypothesis.

The property being proved is:

$post\text{-}fact(n_0,fact(n_0))$

and the induction hypothesis is therefore:

$post\text{-}fact(n_0\text{-}1, fact(n_0\text{-}1))$

Using the definition of *post-fact* this expands to:

$fact(n_0\text{-}1) = (n_0\text{-}1)!$

Now, substituting this into the formula with the reference to *fact* gives:

$post\text{-}fact(n_0, n_0 * (n_0\text{-}1)!)$

Having disposed of the reference to *fact*, it is appropriate to use the definition of *post-fact*. This gives:

$n_0 * (n_0\text{-}1)! = n_0!$

Using the second property of factorial and the case assumption that n_0 is greater than zero, this can be seen to be true and this case is concluded.

Remembering that the domain of *fact* is *Nat0*, the two cases considered ($n_0=0$, $n_0>0$) can be seen to have covered all possibilities and thus the proof is concluded.

Recapping, the overall proof structure is that of mathematical induction; *fact* has been shown to be correct with respect to the specification embodied in *post-fact* for a zero argument (basis); it has been shown to be correct for any argument value greater than zero under the assumption (induction hypothesis) that it is correct for the value one less than the current argument. The reason that it is then safe to assert that *fact* is correct for all possible arguments in its domain is that a proof for any particular natural number could be constructed from the basis and sufficient repetitions of the inductive step.

★ ★ ★

To illustrate the part played by a pre-condition in an inductive proof, the example of *multp* in the previous section is expanded. From the requirement for a general multiply function, a simplified version was derived which could be used within a conditional expression to fulfil the overall task. This simplified version had the following specification:

$multp\text{: } Int\ Int \longrightarrow Int$
$pre\text{-}multp(x,y) \triangleq x \geq 0$
$post\text{-}multp(x,y,r) \triangleq r = x*y$

The following function is thus adequate:

$multp(x,y) \triangleq$ **if** $x=0$ **then** 0 **else** $y + multp(x\text{-}1,y)$

(Adequate but rather slow.) To prove that *multp* is correct requires showing that:

$pre\text{-}multp(x_0,y_0) \Rightarrow post\text{-}multp(x_0,y_0,multp(x_0,y_0))$

Substituting the definitions of the first predicate and *multp* gives:

$x_0{\geq}0 \Rightarrow post\text{-}multp(x_0,y_0,$**if** $x_0=0$ **then** 0_**else** $y_0+multp(x_0\text{-}1,y_0))$

The presence of a conditional expression prompts the use of a case distinction (the basis of the induction). Assuming:

$x_0 = 0$

The above formula then reduces to:

TRUE $\Rightarrow$ *post-multp(x₀,y₀,0)*

which gives:

$0 = x_0 * y_0$

This follows from the usual laws of multiplication and assumption and concludes the basis of the inductive proof. The inductive step uses the assumption:

$x_0 > 0$

In this case the formula to be proved reduces to:

TRUE $\Rightarrow$ *post-multp(x₀,y₀,y₀+multp(x₀-1,y₀))*

or:

post-multp(x₀,y₀,y₀+multp(x₀-1,y₀))

Now the result being proved is in the form of an implication, i.e.:

pre-multp(x₀,y₀) $\Rightarrow$ *post-multp(x₀,y₀,multp(x₀,y₀))*

and the induction hypothesis must also be so. Thus:

pre-multp(x₀-1,y₀) $\Rightarrow$ *post-multp(x₀-1,y₀,multp(x₀-1,y₀))*

This gives:

$x_0-1 \geq 0 \Rightarrow$ *multp(x₀-1,y₀)*$=(x_0-1)*y_0$

But from the assumption above, the left-hand side of this implication is true so that the right-hand side must also be true. Thus the induction hypothesis has given:

multp(x₀-1,y₀) $= (x_0-1)*y_0$

Using this in what is to be proved yields:

post-multp(x₀,y₀,y₀ $+ (x_0-1)*y_0)$

substituting:

$y_0 + (x_0-1)*y_0 = x_0*y_0$

which follows from the laws of arithmetic. This concludes the case.
    Strictly, one should consider the third case of:

$x_0 < 0$

but the left-hand side of the implication can be seen to be false and thus the implication must be true. In fact, the left-hand side of the implication can be used to limit the case distinctions to the first two.
    The pre-condition has played an important part in both the function

and the proof: if it were ignored, the function *multp* would be undefined for some values in its domain (*Int*); similarly the inductive proof would not have worked. Thinking of the function in programming terms, one would say that:

multp(-1,7)

loops indefinitely. Similarly, a proof of a property, for zero and for the step from any number to the next, does not cover the negative numbers.

Exercise 3.6:   Given the specification:

add: Nat0 Nat0 → Nat0
post-add(x,y,r) ≜ *r = x+y*

prove that:

add(x,y) ≜ **if** *x=0* **then** *y* **else** *1 + (add(x-1,y))*

is correct. As a check, indicate the assumed properties of arithmetic.

Exercise 3.7:   Given the specification:

add: Int Int → Int
pre-add(x,y) ≜ $x \geq 0$
post-add(x,y,r) ≜ *r = x+y*

prove that:

add(x,y) ≜ **if** *x=0* **then** *y* **else** *add(x-1,y+1)*

is correct.

Exercise 3.8:   Given the specification of exponentiation:

exp: Int Int → Int
pre-exp(x,y) ≜ $y \geq 0$
post-exp(x,y,r) ≜ *r = x**y*

prove that:

exp(x,y) ≜ **if** *y=0* **then** *1* **else** *exp(x,y-1) * x*

is correct.

Exercise 3.9:   Given the specification of subtraction:

sub: Int Int → Nat0
pre-sub(x,y) ≜ $x \geq y$
post-sub(x,y,r) ≜ *x = y+r*

prove that:

sub(x,y) ≜ **if** *x=y* **then** *0* **else** *1 + sub(x,y+1)*

is correct. (Use induction on $x_0 - y_0$.)

Notice how the power of the operations can be built up. Exercise 3.7 uses only successor (add *1*) and predecessor (subtract *1*) to define general addition of positive numbers. Similarly *multp* was built up using addition and exercise 3.8 uses multiplication to achieve exponentiation. At each step recursion has been used and the reader is now able to reason about recursive functions whenever they are used. Given a programming language with a realistic set of primitive functions, really complex functions could now be formulated.

*More on Logic

One additional advantage of bounded quantifiers is that they reduce the danger of undefined values. For example, it is standard practice to say that division by zero is undefined. But what then is the meaning of:

$7/0 \leq 7$

Assuming that this proposition is undefined, is

$1 \leq x < 7 \Rightarrow 7/x \leq 7$

defined or not? This comes down to deciding the value of:

FALSE $\Rightarrow$ **UNDEFINED**

Careful use of the constraint part of quantifiers avoids many of these problems. For example:

$(\mathbf{A}x \in \{1:6\})(7/x \leq 7)$

can be thought of as a conjunction, all of whose terms are defined.

The ability to define recursive functions brings with it the danger of undefined expressions. It is clearly stated in the type clause for *fact* that it should not be applied to negative numbers; presumably then:

fact(-1)

is undefined. This is certainly borne out by trying to use its explicit definition to compute the factorial of a negative value. A problem, however, arises with the meaning of logical expressions like:

$(\mathbf{A}x \in Int)(x > 3 \Rightarrow fact(x) > 6)$

For all values of x for which the left-hand side of the expression is true, the right is also. So, one would be tempted to say that the implication is always true. But the constraint part of the quantified expression permits any integers and questions again arise like the meaning of:

FALSE $\Rightarrow$ **UNDEFINED**

This section is essentially concerned with handling those cases which are not covered by quantified expressions. Fortunately, such cases occur infrequently. However, this is an interesting topic for which there is no generally agreed approach and for this reason it is pursued in some detail—albeit in an optional section.

There are several ways out of the problem. In some early work at the IBM Laboratory in Vienna (VDL) the decision was made to extend the meaning of the logical operators to cover three values (**TRUE, FALSE** and **UNDEFINED**). The consequence was that every logical operator had this extended meaning (see Walk(69)). In Dijkstra(76), any operators which require the extended meaning are specially distinguished as *conditional*. In both of these works, the operators themselves are defined by means of conditional expressions. In this book the problem of undefined values is handled by using logical conditional expressions so as to avoid the use of propositional operators with undefined terms.

Remember that:

if *b* **then** *e1* **else** *e2*

was defined as yielding the value of *e1* or the value of *e2* depending on whether the value of *b* was true or false. Thus, the value of the whole expression is defined even if the unused part of the conditional expression is undefined:

if TRUE then TRUE else UNDEFINED   =   **TRUE**

and definitions like:

$p1(x)$ ≜ **if** $x=0$ **then FALSE else** $1103/x > 17$
$p2(x)$ ≜ **if** $x \leq 3$ **then TRUE else** $fact(x) > 6$

yield well defined values:

$p1(0)$ ⟷ **FALSE**, $p1(7)$ ⟷ **TRUE**, $p1(1103)$ ⟷ **FALSE**
$p2(-1)$ ⟷ **TRUE**, $p2(4)$ ⟷ **TRUE**

As an example of how powerful conditional expressions are, one can use them to define the standard (two-valued) propositional connectives, thus:

$\sim a$ ⟷ **if** *a* **then FALSE else TRUE**
$a \lor b$ ⟷ **if** *a* **then TRUE else** *b*

The reader should convince himself that these expressions yield the same result as the agreed truth-tables.

Exercise 3.10:   Provide conditional expression equivalents of:

a) $a \land b$
b) $a \Rightarrow b$
c) $a \Leftrightarrow b$

Since all of the propositional operators can be defined using conditional expressions, it is clear that this one operator (**if then else**) is enough to provide a basis for all logic. Manipulation would, however, become rather tedious and it is far preferable to retain the familiar operators for most purposes.

Having decided that conditional expressions will be used, it is necessary that the reader be able to manipulate them. For example, the two expressions:

if (if *a* **then** *b* **else FALSE) then** *c* **else FALSE**
if *a* **then (if** *b* **then** *c* **else FALSE) else FALSE**

are equivalent and it is necessary to show how this can be proved.

With the propositional operators a list of equivalences was provided (see exercise 2.2) which aids their manipulation; the same is done here. The reader should by now be using some of the logical rules intuitively because their natural readings fit their formal meanings. This will also be true for conditional expressions. Furthermore, the identities for propositional operators can be checked by truth-tables. Here again, a similar approach holds for conditional expressions.

The identities required for conditional expressions are:

let b,b1,etc. be logical expressions
let e,e1,etc. be arbitrary expressions

a)   *b* , **if** *b* **then TRUE else FALSE**

b)   **if TRUE then** *e1* **else** *e2* , *e1*

c)   **if FALSE then** *e1* **else** *e2* , *e2*

d)   **if** *b1* **then (if** *b1* **then** *e1* **else** *e2*) **else** *e3* ,
       if *b1* **then** *e1* **else** *e3*

e)   **if** *b1* **then** *e1* **else (if** *b1* **then** *e2* **else** *e3*) ,
       if *b1* **then** *e1* **else** *e3*

f)   **if (if** *b1* **then** *b2* **else** *b3*) **then** *e1* **else** *e2*,
       if *b1* **then (if** *b2* **then** *e1* **else** *e2*) **else (if** *b3* **then** *e1* **else** *e2*)

A careful reading of these pairs will show that their members have the same meaning. If the reader wishes to check more formally, the following form of truth-table can be constructed ((e) is given as an example):

b1	if b1 then e1 else e3	if b1 then e2 else e3	if b1 then e1 else (if b1 then e2 else e3
TRUE	e1	e2	e1
FALSE	e3	e3	e3

Using the identities one can prove sequences of equivalences such as:

if (if *a* **then** *b* **else FALSE) then** *c* **else FALSE**

from (f):

if *a* then *(if b* then *c* else FALSE)* else *(if* FALSE then *c* else FALSE)*

and, from (c):

if *a* then *(if b* then *c* else FALSE)* else FALSE

Exercise 3.11: Prove the equivalence of the following pairs of conditional expressions:

a)   if *(if a* then TRUE else *b)* then TRUE else *c* ,
      if *a* then TRUE else *(if b* then TRUE else *c)*

b)   if *a* then *(if b* then TRUE else *c)* else FALSE ,
      if *(if a* then *b* else FALSE)* then TRUE
          else *(if a* then *c* else FALSE)*

The example and the two parts of exercise 3.11 correspond to the equivalences:

(a ∧ *b)* ∧ *c* , *a* ∧ *(b* ∧ *c)*
(a ∨ *b)* ∨ *c, a* ∨ *(b* ∨ *c)*
a ∧ *(b* ∨ *c)* , *(a* ∧ *b)* ∨ *(a* ∧ *c)*

Correspond, that is, in the sense that the conditional expressions are the expansions of the propositional expressions using the meanings of the operators given earlier in this section.

Exercise 3.12: Experiment with other identities of exercise 2.2, by expanding them with the conditional expression meanings of their operators, and try to prove the resulting conditional expressions equivalent. Notice which are and which are not equivalent. Terminate the exercise when a clear pattern emerges which permits you to predict whether two expressions will be equivalent.

The results of this last problem are interesting. There is a simple rule which determines whether identities of propositional calculus hold using conditional operators or, as they are also known, *extended logical expressions*. The clue is given by the fact that the conditional operators are not commutative. The rule is that the variables, which must be tested, appear in the same order (cf. McCarthy(63)).

⋆   ⋆   ⋆

With some care in the choice of constraints for bounded quantifiers, virtually all logical expressions in this book can be stated using the standard propositional operators. Where an expression would have some undefined values for its sub-expressions, the use of propositional operators is avoided. Rather, such expressions are written as logical conditional expressions. These are normally used to define a separate predicate and thus localize the use. The rules which have been given for manipulating conditional expressions are intuitively clear and the requirement to resort to their formal use does not exist below. Finally, it should be noted that there is an exact correspondence with the meaning of expressions in programming languages such as ALGOL 60.

Summary

Functions have been used as a basis on which to illustrate correctness proofs. Formal specifications are now providing a major pay-off: rather than testing, functions are being checked by the construction of a proof. Proofs that functions fulfil their specifications have been shown for unconditional, conditional and recursive functions. Simple examples have been chosen for ease of comprehension but the methods for handling such functions are general. In fact, only the framework of such proofs has to be learnt; the basic tools of substitution and simplification were covered in chapter 2. The form of proof for programs is no more complicated. Only the framework has to be expanded to handle programs rather than functions.

Summary Exercises

Exercise 3.13:   Define and prove correct an integer divide function satisfying the following specification:

idiv: Int Int $\longrightarrow$ *Int*
pre-idiv(a,b) $\triangleq$ *b* $\neq$ *0*
post-idiv(a,b,q) $\triangleq$ *b*q* $\leq$ *a* $\land$ *b*(q+1)* > *a*

(Remember how *mult* was tackled.)

Chapter 4

SPECIFYING PROGRAMS

The aim of the rigorous method is the creation of programs. While functions are a convenient vehicle for the introduction of concepts, it is now time to show that precise specifications and proofs apply to the more computer-oriented subject. Since functions are already a part of established mathematics and programs are not, a need to extend what has been presented so far can be anticipated. This chapter builds on chapter 2 and the extension required is small.

An essential introduction is an appreciation of the differences between functions and programs. Consider the expression:

1 + 2 + 3

This expression denotes the number which is usually written:

6

Mathematically, there is no need to discuss order of evaluation or number of computation steps. The same is true, mathematically, for the expression:

fact(3)

(where *fact* is the recursive function shown in the previous chapter). This expression also denotes *6*. While a mathematician is content to read *fact(3)* and *6* as alternative names for the same value, computer programmers are more concerned with how something is computed. Looking at fig. 13 as an evaluation of a recursive procedure, there is a requirement for temporary storage at each recursive call. This is because the expression *n*fact(n-1)* cannot be completely evaluated until the recursive reference has been evaluated. Thus to evaluate the factorial of a value *n* requires an amount of space proportional to *n*. Using recursive programs for tasks where it can easily be avoided is, therefore, wasteful. It becomes unacceptable when larger data structures such as arrays are involved.

Fig. 14 shows an algorithm for computing factorial which uses exactly one temporary variable regardless of the value whose factorial is to be computed. (The use of ¬=, rather than <, for the loop test is a question of program style which is discussed in the section on Input Independence in chapter 22.)

```
C   = 0;
FN  = 1;
DO WHILE (C ¬= N);
  C  = C + 1;
  FN  = FN * C;
END;
```

Figure 14   Program for Factorial

Computers are not built around the concept of functions. Most computer architectures follow the archetypal *von Neumann* machine in their approach to storage: the key characteristic is the storage, or memory, which can be read from and written into, thus re-using a particular storage location to contain different values. The concept of storage has had a dramatic influence on the design of programming languages. Nearly all programming languages have adopted a notion of *variable*. A variable can contain different values at different times. What value a variable contains at some point in time is governed by the most recent assignment. The use of *time* and *most recent* indicates the aspect of programs which distinguishes them from functions.

The essential extension to functions, with which the notation of this chapter must deal, is then the notion of variable. The first section introduces the idea of *states* which are collections of variable values. Programs or their parts are thought of as *operations* and these are explained in the following section. This is followed by a section devoted to the extension of specification by pre- and post-conditions.

States

The sequence of the statements shown in fig. 14 can be extended to a procedure by the addition of the following statements.

FACT: PROCEDURE (N) RETURNS(...);
   DCL (N,FN)...;
              /* N,FN known */

   BEGIN;
   DCL C ...;
              /* N,FN,C known */

     ·
     ·
     ·

   END;
   RETURN(FN);
   END;

Immediately inside the procedure, two variables (N and FN) are known; within the nested block a further variable (C) is known.

The first step in the definition of programs, is to introduce a notation to define states. A **state** is a collection of named values. A class of states defines the (variable) names and the sets from which the values may be chosen. In defining classes of states, a notation is used (abstract syntax) which is fully explained in chapter 14. Here, the use is so restricted that a simple **reading** can be provided. A class of objects can be named and defined by writing the name and its definition separated by a $::$ symbol. A definition contains a list of definition entries where each entry contains an identifier and the name of a set separated by a $:$. Thus:

Sproc:: N: Int FN: Int

The meaning of this formula is that any object in the class of states *Sproc* has exactly two variables; the names of the variables are N and *FN* and they both contain values which are integers. This, then, can be seen as the definition of the class of states which can occur immediately within the procedure for factorial given above. Similarly, the class of states which can occur within the block can be defined by:

Sblock:: N: Int FN: Int C: Int

Notice that *Sblock* is the name of the class of all states just as *Int* is the name of the set of all integers. The definition shows that, in a particular state, the variables will contain a member of the set *Int*.

The names of classes of objects (e.g. *Sblock*) are written with the first letter being upper-case and the succeeding ones as lower-case letters.

Exercise 4.1: Sketch a PL/I program to compute exponentiation (avoiding the recursion of the function shown in exercise 3.8) and define the class of states.

Operations

Much of the remainder of the book is concerned with proving results about, or constructing, programs or parts thereof. Such parts may be single statements in a programming language, sequences of statements or whole programs. The general name of *operation* is used for all of these. Remember what was said about variables and assignment being the essence of programming languages. Operations, as well as accessing the values of variables in a state, may change those values. Noting that the type of a function is given by:

$$f: D \to R$$

one might choose to write the type of an operation (given some defined class *State*) as:

OP: State → State

This would be acceptable but it fails to emphasize an important property of operations. A single statement (e.g. an assignment) can change the values of variables in the state but it cannot change the structure of the state. That is, it cannot introduce or delete variables. The same is true for lists of statements, providing they are *closed*. Thus, while within a block new variables exist, the effect of the whole block is such that, after its execution, the structure of the state is exactly as it was prior to execution. Thus, operations cannot affect the structure of the state. This fact is emphasized by incorporating a new part into specifications. The *states* part specifies the name of the class of states for an operation. Thus:

OP
states: State

A type clause may also be given, and this is discussed in a later section. For the time being, operations are restricted to reading and changing variables in the state.

The meaning of such a state clause is that *OP* is an operation which can be executed in a state of the set called *State*. In general, it accesses values of that state and its execution results in a state with different values. The final state is, however, still of the structure of *State*.

One last point should be made about operations before turning to their specification. For functions (and predicates) the convention for their names is that they are written in lower-case letters; upper-case letters (e.g. *OP*) are used for the names of operations.

Specifying Operations

In addition to the type clause of an implicit function specification, there are two other parts: the pre- and post-conditions. The same information is required for operations. Here, however, the pre-condition is a predicate of a state and the post-condition a predicate of two states. Thus the pre-condition specifies over what subset of all possible states the operation should work, and the post-condition specifies the required relation between initial and final states.

The convention for naming the predicates which are pre-and post-conditions is extended in an obvious way. The convention that **TRUE** pre-conditions are omitted is also followed.

OP
states: State
pre-OP(σ) $\triangleq$ ...
post-OP(σ,σ') $\triangleq$ ...

where:

State :: ...

pre-OP: State $\rightarrow$ *Bool*
post-OP: State State $\rightarrow$ *Bool*

   Figure 15   Implicit Operation Definition

The specification of an operation, then, comprises the three items shown in fig. 15, (cf. fig. 7). The meaning of such a specification can be expressed by:

*(**A**σϵState)(pre-OP(σ)* $\Rightarrow$ *post-OP(σ,exec(OP,σ)))*

That is, for all states, if they satisfy the pre-condition, then executing *OP* on such a state terminates and produces an output state which together with the initial state satisfies the post-condition. Notice that for all states which satisfy the pre-condition, it is required that *OP* terminates.

In order to write predicates of states, it is necessary to decide on notation for constructing and decomposing instances of such states. For the current purposes, a positional notation is used. Suppose a predicate is to be defined over the class *Sblock*:

pred: Sblock $\rightarrow$ *Bool*

If one were to begin the definition of this predicate by writing:

pred(σ) $\triangleq$ ...

the right-hand side of the definition would have to use some notation for selecting the parts of σ. (The full abstract syntax notation defines how the variable identifiers can be used as selectors.) Instead of this, the left-hand side of the definition provides a list of parameter names, one per component of the state, enclosed in pointed brackets ($<>$). Thus:

$pred(<n,fn,c>) \triangleq fn=c! \land c{\leq}n$

The parameter names may be chosen freely. This freedom is used to distinguish between the, upper-case, identifiers of the program and the, lower-case, parameter names. Thus, for example, one might write:

$pred2: Sblock\ Sblock \longrightarrow Bool$
$pred2(<n,fn,c>,<n',fn',c'>) \triangleq ...$

(There is an analogy between the classes of objects defined by $::$ rules and PL/I structures or PASCAL records.)

There are occasions when one does not wish to specify names for individual components. Thus:

$pred3: Sblock\ Sblock \longrightarrow Bool$
$pred3(<n,fn,c>,<n',fn',c'>) \triangleq n'=n \land fn'=fn*c \land c'=c+1$

might be written:

$pred3(<n,fn,c>,\sigma') \triangleq \sigma' = <n,fn*c,c+1>$

A further convention permits the omission of identifiers which are not required. Thus:

$pred4: Sblock \longrightarrow Bool$
$pred4(<n,,>) \triangleq n{\geq}0$

Notice that the commas are retained.

To turn to a concrete example, the specification of the statements in fig. 14 is:

$Sfact:: N:Int\ FN:Int\ C:Int$

$FACT$
$states: Sfact$
$pre\text{-}FACT(<n,,>) \triangleq n{\geq}0$
$post\text{-}FACT(<n,,>,<fn',>) \triangleq fn'=n!$

Notice that the pre-condition only involves the variable N since the others are initialized within the program. Similarly the post-condition only concerns the relationship between one input and one output value.

$\star \quad \star \quad \star$

The reader is now equipped to write specifications of programs in this standard style. Before offering some exercises it is worth returning to the point raised in chapter 2 about how specifications are made shorter than their realizations. The specification of $FACT$, as with the corresponding function, relies on the use of a known operation. Similarly, the technique of using an inverse operation (e.g. addition for subtraction) in the specification of an operation is still available. But now a new alternative exists. Many tasks are relatively simple to specify in terms of (recursive) functions; even if these functions are unacceptably inefficient in computational terms, they can still be used in the specification of an operation. The best examples would again be drawn from richer data structures, but an example can be made of the **Fibonacci numbers**. Suppose the following function is accepted as defining the Fibonacci numbers:

$nfib(n)$ ≜
  if $n=0$ **then** 0
  else if $n=1$ **then** 1
  else $nfib(n-2) + nfib(n-1)$

This would be a hopelessly inefficient basis for a program (try evaluating $nfib(4)$). But it could be used in a specification as follows:

Fibstate:: N: Int R: Int

NFIB
states: Fibstate
$pre\text{-}NFIB(<n,>) ≜ n \geq 0$
$post\text{-}NFIB(<n,>,<,r'>) ≜ r' = nfib(n)$

Exercise 4.2: Write a predicate of the states in exercise 4.1 which requires the value of Y to be greater than or equal to zero.

Exercise 4.3: Define the type of the exponentiation operation introduced in exercise 4.1 and use the recursive function *exp* of exercise 3.8, to complete the specification.

Exercise 4.4: Write a specification for an operation which computes the **greatest common divisor** of the values contained in variables X and Y and leaves this value in variable X.

Exercise 4.5: Write a specification for an operation which works on a state:

Sidiv:: A: Int B: Int Q: Int R: Int

and assigns to Q the quotient and to R the remainder of the integer division of A by B. Limit the operation to positive input values.

It is suggested above that functions can be used in writing specifications. This provides a useful enlargement to the set of tools available and one might be tempted to use programming language statements as a further extension of a specification language. This can be very dangerous. The reason why it is appropriate to use functions is that they are mathematically tractable objects. The whole of the next chapter is concerned with reasoning about the time element of programs. If program constructs like sequencing are used in specifications, there tends to be an over-specification of the order of operations. The following table summarizes the preferences for using implicit or explicit specifications:

	Explicit Definition	Implicit Specification
Functions	if unique result	range of results
Operations	is a program	prefer, avoids ordering

Functions are preferred over operations, except when one must talk about states.

General Operations

Operations may be more general than above. Consider a (non-value-returning) PL/I procedure: because of side-effects on global variables, it certainly has the ability of an operation to change the contents of the state; but, in addition, it can also accept arguments like a function. For such operations, a separate type clause is written. Thus the type of a procedure is specified:

PROC
states: State
type: D1 D2 ... Dn →

The most general case is provided by function procedures which return results. Their type might be:

FN-PROC
states: State
type: D1 D2 ... Dn → R

This general form of operation specification can be read as:

> *FN-PROC* executes in states of *State* and can read and write the values of variables therein; in addition arguments in *D1* to *Dn* are accepted and results in *R* created.

A general operation can be specified by two predicates whose types are:

pre-OP: State D1 D2 ... Dn → Bool
post-OP: State D1 D2 ... Dn State R → Bool

Operations can be classified, depending on their specification, into producers, transformers, and interrogators. **Producers** accept arguments and change the state by storing them—they do not normally rely on the input state. **Transformers** have neither arguments nor results. **Interrogators** have no arguments but produce results—they are normally identities on states.

★   ★   ★

The factorial example can again be used to illustrate these more general operations. The specification of *FACT* is given in terms of a chosen state. A better specification would be one which first defined the function to be performed, thus:

FACT-FN
type: Nat0 → Nat
pre-FACT-FN(n) ≜ *n≥0*
post-FACT-FN(n,fn') ≜ *fn'=n!*

Once this specification is agreed, it is time to decide on a class of states on which one possible program to solve this problem might be based. Setting up the states of the form:

Sfact:: N: Int   FN: Int   C: Int

can be achieved in a programming language by:

```
FACT-FN: PROC(N) RETURNS(...);
        DCL N ...;
        DCL (FN,C) ...;
        /*
          BODY
          states: Sfact
          type: Nat0 → Nat
          post-BODY(,n,,fn') ≜ fn'=n!
        */
END;
```

The transition from a function to an operation with the same domain and range is a simple development step. More interesting is the step to:

```
FACT-FN: PROC(N) RETURNS(...);
      DCL N ...;
      DCL (FN,C) ...;
      /*
        INIT-FACT
        states: Sfact
        type: Nat0 →
        post-INIT-FACT(σ,n,<n',,>) ≜ n'=n */

      /*
      FACT
        states: Sfact
        pre-FACT(<n,,>) ≜ n≥0
        post-FACT(<n,,>,<,fn',>) ≜ fn'=n! */

      /*
        RESULT-FACT
        states: Sfact
        type: → Nat
        post-RESULT-FACT(<,fn,>,σ',r') ≜ r'=fn */
      END;
```

Enclosed in comment brackets (/* */) are three specifications. *INIT-FACT* ignores the starting state (σ) and assigns the value of its parameter to a variable. The values of the other variables are not constrained. The definition of *FACT* is as before. The output function is constrained to deliver the value of the variable *FN* as its result but has no other constraints.

The task of proving that any three operations which fulfil these specifications will satisfy the specification of *FACT-FN* is postponed. Instead, the discussion of general operations is closed by showing an expansion into a program:

```
FACT-FN: PROC(N) RETURNS(...);
      DCL N ...;
      DCL (FN,C) ...;
      /*INIT-FACT is achieved by the
                  semantics of parameter passing */
      /*FACT*/
      C  = 0;
      FN  = 1;
        DO WHILE (C¬=N);
        C  = C+1;
        FN  = FN*C;
        END;
      /*RESULT-FACT*/
      RETURN (FN);
      END;
```

Summary

Programs operate on states. Classes of objects which are to be used as states are defined by rules with $::$ symbols. Thus:

Sfact:: N: Int   FN: Int   C: Int

defines a class of objects:

Sfact = { <*n,fn,c*> | *n,fn,c∈Int* }

The pre-condition for an operation is a predicate of everything it can depend on (i.e. initial state and arguments). The post-condition is a predicate of the input state, arguments, output state, and results.

    The role of the pre-condition should be appreciated. Its basic purpose (i.e. defining the valid range) should be clear. But there is a corollary. Outside the range specified by the pre-condition, a program is free to do anything. Of course, a useful reaction to invalid input is to produce an error message. This can be made part of the specification by widening the pre-condition and showing the required function in the form of a conditional expression. For valid data, the normal processing and, for invalid data, a requirement for error messages is documented. The general topic of design is discussed in chapter 22.

    One aspect of the rigorous method has already been covered. Specifications of a program by predicates not only yield shorter specifications, but also capture those properties on which a user needs to rely. It should now be clear that the first objection to using programming languages for specifications is their inability to say what should be achieved. The purpose of a programming language is, after all, to define sequences of operations.

    The use of post-conditions suggests viewing operations as relations on states. For further information on a relational approach, see Hitchcock(72) and Hitchcock(74).

Summary Exercises

Exercise 4.6: Specify an operation which computes a salary from an argument giving the number of hours worked. The state should contain basic and overtime rates of pay and the number of hours to be treated as basic.

Exercise 4.7: Specify an operation which computes the length of the hypotenuse of a right-angled triangle from arguments giving the lengths of the other two sides.

Exercise 4.8: Discuss the problems of creating a machine architecture which directly implements functions and eschews the idea of rewritable storage. (See also Backus(78).)

Chapter 5

PROOFS IN PROGRAM DEVELOPMENT

It is observed in chapter 3 that the correctness of functions can only be discussed in relation to a specification. The same comment applies equally well to programs. Chapter 4 shows how programs can be specified by means of pre- and post-conditions which are predicates of states. A point has now been reached where it is possible to discuss correctness proofs of programs. This, in itself, would be a huge advance over the current norms of the computing industry. The reader is already able to reason about functions. Programs bring with them concepts of variables and sequence; given a few extra results, they will also be brought within the grasp of mathematical techniques. These results are introduced in this chapter. They are, however, presented in a more useful guise than that of tools for analyzing programs. This chapter moves further into the rigorous method and explains how the ability to reason about programs can be used as an aid in their construction. This point requires some expansion.

Given a precise specification of a program (or system of programs), the question then arises as to what link is to exist between this specification and the code which is alleged to realize the specification. Although a precise specification is extremely valuable in its own right, it would be extravagant to seek precision which could not be used in establishing the correctness of the realization. However, programs are themselves formal objects in the sense that the languages in which they are written are unambiguous. It is therefore conceivable that a link between specification and program could be proved in the same way that theorems in other branches of mathematics are supported. The method introduced by Floyd(67) and Naur(66) shows a style in which this theoretical possibility can be made practical. The so-called *inductive assertion* method of proving programs correct has been the basis of most of the work on program proving in the last decade.

But there is still a fatal flaw in the picture. Fatal, that is, in a practical sense. The plan of development plus proof begs the question of how to create a program as a subject for the proof attempt. This flaw may not affect the toy examples of this part of the book. But with large programs, what will happen in a three-phase development process (specification, development steps, and proof) is that errors will be made during the development steps. The precision of the specification will certainly reduce the frequency of misunderstandings but the development stage is receiving no other assistance and there is thus every reason to expect that errors will still be introduced. These errors, being undetected at the step where they were made, may be present in the final code. Now it is clear that one cannot prove an incorrect program correct. Moreover, attempting to write a proof may not be an efficient way of debugging an incorrect program. More importantly, the impact that errors have on the productivity of the program development process has not been avoided. Errors, in early development steps, which are only located in the final code stage require the reconstruction of large amounts of work which was built on them. For large programs, it is essential that design mistakes are uncovered before further work is based on them.

Thus, in order to make a contribution to programmer productivity, it is necessary to employ the ideas of program proving in a constructive discipline of programming. The flaw alluded to above (i.e. the lack of method to create correct programs) is handled by a stepwise scheme which, in its completely formal version, is as follows:

1.   Precise specification
2.   Formal development
*   2.1 first formal development step*
*   a.   propose realization of specification*
*   b.   prove realization fulfils specification*
*   2.2 second development step*
*   a.   propose realization of specifications from 2.1a*
*   b.   prove realization fulfils specification from 2.1a*

          .
          .
          .

*   2.n development of code*
*   a.   write code for specification from 2.(n-1)a*
*   b.   prove code fulfils specification*

At each intermediate step of development the given specification is being realized in terms of sub-units. Such a realization is a way of achieving the given specification (documented with pre-/post-conditions) in terms of more basic objects. As such, it consists of specifications (again, using pre-/post-conditions) and a proposed way of combining them. The development process terminates when a step occurs whose realization is achieved entirely in terms of available units. Such units may be the statements of the programming language or use sophisticated services from other support software. Each such step of development is referred to as a ***decomposition*** step: the original operation is decomposed into sub-operations for its realization.

The proofs which support such a decomposition step must show that, given any set of modules which satisfy the specifications of the sub-units, combining such modules in the way specified forms a unit which satisfies the given specification.

The importance of a constructive approach to the development of programs has been widely recognized and more recent theoretical work (e.g. Hoare(71), Wirth(71), Jones(72) and Dijkstra(76)) has emphasized how proofs can play a part in such an approach.

The rigorous method makes much less formal use of the results of this chapter. Normally, the lists of properties about programming constructs are used as checklists which remind the programmer of potential errors; only particularly difficult items are proved formally.

★   ★   ★

In view of the formality of the body of this chapter, an example is provided, as an overview, at a less formal level. It is not essential that the reader follow the details of this development.

The choice of examples in this chapter presents a difficulty. Those of chapter 3 are again used, this time as programs. The advantages of a multi-stage development process will, however, become more apparent on larger examples.

Consider the problem of providing a general integer multiplication routine with the specification:

MULT
type: Int Int → Int
post-MULT(x,y,r') $\triangleq r' = x*y$

The first step of design might follow the approach taken in the section on General Operations in the previous chapter. That is, the task is tackled by a program which consists of three parts: store the input values, compute an answer, and deliver that answer. Since this is straightforward, there is no difficulty in going further in this first step. The general task is decomposed to use an operation which is only required to work for positive values of its second argument. This procedure is then used in a conditional statement which achieves the overall task. Thus the first step proposes the following decomposition:

```
MULT:
 PROC(X,Y) RETURNS (...);
 DCL (X,Y) ...;
 DCL R ...;
    MULTP:
     PROC;
      /*
        BODY
        states: Smult
        pre-BODY(<x,,>) ≜ x≥0
        post-BODY(<x,y,>,<,,r'>) ≜ r' = x*y
      */
     END;
 IF X≥0 THEN CALL MULTP;
 ELSE DO;
    X = -X;
    CALL MULTP;
    R = -R;
    END;
 RETURN(R);
 END;
```

Notice the way in which the specification for *BODY* is placed at the point where its eventual realization is needed. This not only provides useful documentation, it also obviates the need to define the state (*Smult*) because it is given by context.

The reader should observe that this program overwrites its input values. It has been agreed that the specification is the complete statement of required conditions and, in this case, there is no requirement that the initial values be preserved. It is, in fact, one of the advantages of using post-conditions of state pairs that they facilitate reasoning about programs which overwrite their input values. With large data structures (e.g. arrays) the freedom to do so is very important.

Given a proposed step of development, it is now necessary to check its correctness. At the level of rigor being used here, such a check would consist of two observations. Firstly, a standard schema has been used for transforming functions into programs; for this no correctness argument is required. Secondly, a conditional construct has been used; this must be justified. The pre-conditions of the statements in both clauses are easily established: both amount to the condition *pre-BODY* and are, therefore, obviously satisfied. The correctness of the overall post-condition is also evident in the case of positive values of X; if X is negative the post-conditions of *post-BODY* and *post-MULT* are not identical and the correctness of the program relies on:

$$-(-x*y) = x*y$$

This argument is only sketched. But, because it is in terms of pre- and post-conditions, it could be formalized and a standard set of rules for such a proof is provided below.

Attention can now be turned to the development of *BODY*. Assuming that such an operation is not available, some loop is required. The loop will have to be preceded by initialization statements. *BODY* can then be developed to:

R = *0*;
DO WHILE (X ⌐= 0);
  /*
    LBODY
    states: Smult
    pre-LBODY(<x,,>) ≜ *x>0*
    post-LBODY(<x,y,r>,<x',y',r'>) ≜ *(r'+x'*y' = r+x*y) ∧ 0≤x'<x*
  */
END;

The choice of the post-condition for the loop body *LBODY* leaves open whether the value of *X* is reduced by only *1* per iteration or whether some faster algorithm is chosen. Informally, the correctness follows from the fact that the value of the expression:

*R + X * Y*

is unchanged. After initialization, this expression has the value of the required result. Therefore the loop terminates (when *X=0*) with the required result in variable *R*. Thus the final result (*post-BODY*) is guaranteed. The termination of the loop follows from the reduction of the (initially positive) value of *X*. Here again, this proof can be formalized.

Attention is now turned to a realization of *LBODY*. Although one possible realization:

X = X-1; R = R+Y;

would be very easy to prove correct, a more complicated solution is offered here. The problem with the easy realization is that it reduces the value of *X* by only *1* per iteration. The number of steps required to compute a result is therefore proportional to the starting value of *X*. Such algorithms are called **linear** because the amount of computation increases linearly with the value of the input. There are, fortunately, algorithms for which the amount of computation increases only in proportion to the logarithm of the input. If one were to microprogram the function multiply, one would want to use one of the logarithmic algorithms.

The basic idea of these algorithms is to use the shifting instructions of a binary machine to achieve multiplication, and (truncation) division, by two. Thus the product:

*1001 * 1111*

is achieved by adding:

0001111

-

-

1111000

rather than *9* additions of *1111*. In the program shown below, the shifting operations are represented by divide and multiply signs; this should not be allowed to obscure the fact that the algorithm uses only simple shifting operations. Here, and later, the equivalence of expressions of the programming language, such as *MOD(X,2)=0*, and more convenient forms for reasoning, such as *is-even(x)*, are used without further justification. (The definitions of *is-odd* and *is-even* are in appendix C.)

Continuing the rigorous development, the effect of *LBODY* is achieved by performing an operation *MKODD*, which leaves the value of *X* as an odd number; this is followed by statements which, among other things, reduce the value of *X* by *1*. Both of these operations leave the value of the expression:

$R + X*Y$

unchanged. Thus:

```
/*
   MKODD
   states: Smult
   pre-MKODD(<x,,>) ≜ x≥1
   post-MKODD(<x,y,r>,<x',y',r'>) ≜ (r'+x'*y'=r+x*y) ∧ 1≤x'≤x
*/
   X = X-1;
   R = R+Y;
```

The justification that this simple composition is correct with respect to the specification of *LBODY* requires only very simple rules.

Finally, the development for *MKODD* gives rise to the loop:

```
DO WHILE (MOD(X,2) = 0);
   X = X/2;
   Y = Y*2;
END;
```

whose function can be proved correct in a similar way to the preceding loop.

The final procedure is shown in fig. 16. The reader should observe some characteristics of this development. Firstly the concept of proof has been used as an integral part of the development process. That is, each step of the decomposition has been supported by an argument of correctness. The second observation concerns the form of these arguments. They are not formal in the sense that they can be checked by a program. They are, in fact, no more than notes towards a proof. But, because a standard list of properties is being used, the little which is recorded provides an adequate basis for the construction of more formal

```
MULT:
 PROC(X,Y) RETURNS (...);
 DCL  (X,Y) ...;
 DCL  R ...;
    MULTP:
     PROC;
       R  = 0;                      /*BODY*/
       DO WHILE (X ¬= 0);
         DO WHILE (MOD(X,2) = 0);  /*MKODD*/ /*LBODY*/
           X  = X/2;
           Y  = Y*2;
         END;
         X  = X-1;
         R  = R+Y;
       END;
     END;
 IF X≥0 THEN CALL MULTP;
 ELSE DO;
     X  = -X;
     CALL MULTP;
     R  = -R;
     END;
 RETURN(R);
 END;
```

Figure 16   Multiplication Program

proofs. Thus, if some step is called into doubt, it is clear what must be done in order to complete the proof. In this way, a framework has been created in which details can be provided as necessary. This can be likened to the way that a large specification is formal in structure, but informal at a detailed level, so that additional details can be inserted without disrupting the structure.

One remaining characteristic of rigorous development should also be noted. The structure of the development is itself an aid to understanding the program. At each step of development it is clear what is to be achieved and what assumptions are being made about sub-components.

Having seen how an example could be presented at a rigorous level of reasoning, it is now necessary to learn how the steps of program proofs can be made more formal. The main sections of this chapter cover ways of combining operations or decomposing problems. Once the formal properties have been understood, they can be used safely as checklists in a less formal but rigorous development method.

Sequential Statements

In a top-down development method, large tasks are decomposed into simpler tasks. The simplest decomposition of a task is achieved by dividing it into two, or more, sub-tasks which are executed one after another. With functions, this would be defined by composition. With operations one writes:

$OP \triangleq OP1; OP2$

to show that operation *OP1* is executed first, followed by operation *OP2*: thus the state after executing *OP1* becomes the starting state for *OP2*. Essentially, this definition asserts that the task specified as *OP* can be realized by the sequential composition of the two operations *OP1* and *OP2*. Remember that the implied meaning of the three-part specification of *OP* is:

$(\mathbf{A}\sigma\epsilon State)(pre\text{-}OP(\sigma) \Rightarrow post\text{-}OP(\sigma, exec(OP,\sigma)))$

Given pre- and post-conditions for *OP* and for the sub-operations, it is straightforward to document which relationships must hold between these predicates for the asserted realization to be correct. Firstly, both *OP1* and *OP2* may only be used on states which are defined to be within their pre-conditions. Thus for *OP1* the formula *da* of fig. 17 must hold. This requires that all states considered valid for *OP* must also be valid for *OP1*. The condition for *OP2* is slightly more complicated because the states in which it will be executed are governed by what *OP1* does to the input states; the condition is stated in rule *db* of fig. 17. It is, lastly, necessary to establish that the states created by the sequence of operations really do achieve the specified result. This is stated in the formula *ra* of fig. 17.

For:

$OP \triangleq OP1; OP2$

to be correct, show:

da. $pre\text{-}OP(\sigma) \Rightarrow pre\text{-}OP1(\sigma)$
db. $pre\text{-}OP(\sigma_1) \wedge post\text{-}OP1(\sigma_1,\sigma_2) \Rightarrow pre\text{-}OP2(\sigma_2)$
ra. $pre\text{-}OP(\sigma_1) \wedge post\text{-}OP1(\sigma_1,\sigma_2) \wedge post\text{-}OP2(\sigma_2,\sigma_3) \Rightarrow post\text{-}OP(\sigma_1,\sigma_3)$

Figure 17   Rules for Sequential Statements

The labels of these rules are chosen to indicate that those beginning with *d* are related to the domain or, more exactly, class of permissible states; those rules whose labels begin with the letter *r*, are concerned with the result to be delivered. This convention is followed in the rules for other forms of statements which follow.

Notice that, although it is a feature of the development method presented here that termination is handled at each step of development, there is no result to be proved with respect to termination. Since each sub-operation is guaranteed to terminate for states satisfying its pre-condition, the composition must terminate.

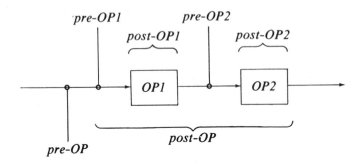

Figure 18   Picture of Sequential Statement

These are the rules which are used for proofs about sequential statements. The reader has some intuitive idea that sequential statements are executed one after another and can check that these rules capture this. The graphic layout of fig. 18 may help to show the essential connections of the predicates in fig. 17. It is also possible to provide a more formal justification of these rules. Appendix A provides a definition of parts of the language used in this book. This is essentially a definition of the *exec* function used above. From this, one can prove that the properties given in fig. 17 are indeed adequate to ensure that *OP1* and *OP2*, executed one after another, satisfy the specification of *OP*. Proofs that the collections of properties are in accord with the language definition are given in appendix D.

In the development shown in the introduction to this chapter the following specification occurred:

Smult:: X: Int   Y: Int   R: Int

LBODY
states: Smult
pre-LBODY(<x,,>) ≜ *x>0*
post-LBODY(<x,y,r>,<x',y',r'>) ≜ $r'+x'*y' = r+x*y \land 0 \le x' < x$

Suppose a linear implementation were acceptable, a realization of *LBODY* might be:

LBODY ≜ *X = X - 1; R = R + Y*

It is obvious that this realization satisfies the specification. But in order to experiment with the list of properties the meaning of the two assignment statements is expressed in terms of predicates. Thus:

LBODY $\triangleq$ *OP1; OP2*

post-OP1(<x,y,r>,σ') $\triangleq$ σ' = <x-1,y,r>

post-OP2(<x,y,r>,σ') $\triangleq$ σ' = <x,y,r+y>

Notice that both assignments are regarded as total (i.e. they have pre-conditions of **TRUE**). In order to check formally that this sequence of assignments satisfies the specification of *LBODY*, the three properties listed in fig. 17 must be proved. But the fact that each operation is total results in the right-hand sides of implications *da* and *db* being true. Such implications are said to be **vacuously true** and require no proof. (cf. tautology (c) in exercise 2.3). This only leaves the result rule *ra* to be checked:

pre-LBODY(σ_1) $\wedge$ post-OP1(σ_1,σ_2) $\wedge$ post-OP2(σ_2,σ_3)
    $\Rightarrow$ post-LBODY(σ_1,σ_3)

This formula can be expanded using the definitions of *pre-LBODY* etc. Such expansion is done in a way which associates the subscripts naturally with the component names of states. Thus:

pre-LBODY(σ_1)

is expanded as though:

pre-LBODY(<x_1,y_1,r_1>)

had been written. The intention to come to a rigorous style can now be used to further simplify proofs. Rather than writing out the literal expansion of *ra*, terms are collected together. Furthermore, terms on the left-hand side of the implication can be omitted if not required (see (i) in exercise 2.3). Expansion via the definitions of the pre- and post-conditions gives:

$x_1>0 \wedge x_3=x_2=x_1-1 \wedge y_3=y_2=y_1 \wedge r_3=r_2+y_2 \wedge r_2=r_1$
    $\Rightarrow r_3+x_3*y_3 = r_1+x_1*y_1 \wedge 0 \le x_3 < x_1$

or:

$0<x_1 \wedge x_3=x_1-1 \wedge y_3=y_1 \wedge r_3=r_1+y_1 \Rightarrow r_3+x_3*y_3 = r_1+x_1*y_1 \wedge 0 \le x_3 < x_1$

The left-hand side of the implication gives:

$r_3+x_3*y_3$
    $= r_1+y_1+(x_1-1)*y_1$

which by the laws of arithmetic gives:

    $= r_1+x_1*y_1$

The implication is therefore true.

When, in the sequel, a logical expression arises whose validity requires only properties of arithmetic, it is marked **immediate**.

$\star$ $\star$ $\star$

To provide a second example of a justification of the sequential decomposition of a task, consider the efficient implementation of *LBODY* introduced earlier. With the specification of *LBODY* unchanged, it is now required to prove correct the realization:

LBODY ≜ *MKODD; MKEVEN*

Where *MKEVEN* is an operation name given to the two assignments shown above. The subsidiary specifications are:

MKODD
states: Smult
$pre\text{-}MKODD(<x,,>) \triangleq x \geq 1$
$post\text{-}MKODD(<x,y,r>,<x',y',r'>) \triangleq$
$\quad (r'+x'^*y'=r+x^*y) \wedge 1 \leq x' \leq x$

and:

MKEVEN
states: Smult
$pre\text{-}MKEVEN(<x,,>) \triangleq x \geq 1$
$post\text{-}MKEVEN(<x,y,r>,<x',y',r'>) \triangleq (r'+x'^*y'=r+x^*y) \wedge 0 \leq x' < x$

The list of properties in fig. 17 can now be checked (for each property, its use in the current context is followed by its simplification):

da.
$pre\text{-}LBODY(\sigma) \Rightarrow pre\text{-}MKODD(\sigma)$
$x>0 \Rightarrow x \geq 1$

which is immediate. To prove that the second operation is used only on states satisfying its pre-condition, requires:

db.
$pre\text{-}LBODY(\sigma_1) \wedge post\text{-}MKODD(\sigma_1,\sigma_2) \Rightarrow pre\text{-}MKEVEN(\sigma_2)$
$x_1 \geq 1 \wedge 1 \leq x_2 \leq x_1 \Rightarrow x_2 \geq 1$

which is again immediate. To establish that the given sequential composition computes the correct result it has to be shown:

ra.
$pre\text{-}LBODY(\sigma_1) \wedge post\text{-}MKODD(\sigma_1,\sigma_2) \wedge post\text{-}MKEVEN(\sigma_2,\sigma_3)$
$\quad \Rightarrow post\text{-}LBODY(\sigma_1,\sigma_3)$

$r_2+x_2^*y_2=r_1+x_1^*y_1 \wedge x_2 \leq x_1 \wedge r_3+x_3^*y_3=r_2+x_2^*y_2 \wedge 0 \leq x_3 < x_2$
$\quad \Rightarrow r_3+x_3^*y_3 = r_1+x_1^*y_1 \wedge 0 \leq x_3 < x_1$

which it requires only simple manipulation to establish.

Exercise 5.1: The development of *MKODD* would use:

MKODD-BODY ≜ *DIVX; MULTY*

where:

MKODD-BODY
states: Smult
pre-MKODD-BODY(<x,,>) ≜ *is-even(x)* ∧ *x>0*
post-MKODD-BODY(<x,y,r>,<x',y',r'>) ≜ *r'+x'*y'=r+x*y* ∧ *1≤x'<x*

and:

DIVX
states: Smult
post-DIVX(<x,y,r>,σ') ≜ *σ' = <x/2,y,r>*

and:

MULTY
states: Smult
post-MULTY(<x,y,r>,σ') ≜ *σ' = <x,y*2,r>*

Prove this step correct.

Exercise 5.2:   An exponentiation program can also be written so that it
works in *log y* steps. Parts of its development would require showing:

a)

Sexp:: X: Int   Y: Int   R: Int

EXP-LBODY ≜ *EXP-MKODD; EXP-MKEVEN*

EXP-LBODY
states: Sexp
pre-EXP-LBODY(<,y,>) ≜ *y≥1*
post-EXP-LBODY(<x,y,r>,<x',y',r'>) ≜
    (r'*x'**y'=r*x**y) ∧ *0≤y'<y*

with:

EXP-MKODD
states: Sexp
pre-EXP-MKODD(<,y,>) ≜ *y≥1*
post-EXP-MKODD(<x,y,r>,<x',y',r'>) ≜
    (r'*x'**y' = r*x**y) ∧ *1≤y'≤y*

EXP-MKEVEN
states: Sexp
pre-EXP-MKEVEN(<,y,>) ≜ *y≥1*
post-EXP-MKEVEN(<x,y,r>,<x',y',r'>) ≜
    (r'*x'**y' = r*x**y) ∧ *0≤y'<y*

b)

EXP-MKODD-BODY ≜ *DIVY; MULTX*

where:

EXP-MKODD-BODY
states: Sexp
pre-EXP-MKODD-BODY(<,y,>) ≜ *is-even(y)* ∧ *y>0*
post-EXP-MKODD-BODY(<x,y,r>,<x',y',r'>) ≜
   (r'*x'**y' = r*x**y) ∧ *1≤y'<y*

DIVY
states: Sexp
post-DIVY(<x,y,r>,σ') ≜ *σ' = <x,y/2,r>*

MULTX
states: Sexp
post-MULTX(<x,y,r>,σ') ≜ *σ' = <x*x,y,r>*

prove that the decompositions (a), (b) are correct.

The above exercises have provided practice in the use of the rules for verifying decomposition to sequential statements. Having seen how they work at this level of detail, it is now possible to use them in a much less formal way.

Observe the way in which assignment statements have been handled so far. The linear version of multiply shown earlier realizes the body of the loop by:

LBODY ≜ *X = X - 1; R = R + Y*

The post-condition which is used to define the first of these assignments is:

post-OP1 (<x,y,r>,σ') ≜ *σ' = <x-1,y,r>*

This condition states that the effect of the assignment statement is to change the value of *X* (by reducing it by *1*) and to leave the values of the other variables unchanged. This would appear to capture the intuitive notion of assignment. But caution must be used when reasoning informally and this is true even with the assignment statement. There is a hidden assumption in the intuitive meaning of assignment that variables do not share storage. Remember that in PL/I there are explicit ways (*DEFINED*, pointer manipulation) of directing that different variable identifiers are to refer to the same location in storage. Any language which permits the passing of parameters by reference can set up storage sharing patterns. Thus the intuitively obvious property of assignment, that it does not change other variables, is only valid under the assumption that nothing has been done to set up storage sharing. Rigorous reasoning can do much to avoid the detail of formal proofs but it will only remain rigorous if such assumptions are understood and borne in mind.

One way to reason more informally is to make the decomposition from an operation specification to a string of assignment statements in a single step. Having understood the translation of simple assignments into post-conditions, sequences of such assignments can be considered. It is obvious that:

$X = X - 1; R = R + Y$

satisfies the post-condition:

$post\text{-}OP(<x,y,r>,\sigma') \triangleq \sigma' = <x\text{-}1,y,r+y>$

But why is this correct? The key observation is again connected with sharing. Providing the right-hand side expressions of the two assignment statements do not refer to variables being changed by the other assignment statement, such combinations are possible. To prove that the combined operation satisfies the specification for *LBODY* it is only necessary to show:

$pre\text{-}LBODY(\sigma) \Rightarrow pre\text{-}OP(\sigma)$
$pre\text{-}LBODY(\sigma_1) \wedge post\text{-}OP(\sigma_1,\sigma_2) \Rightarrow post\text{-}LBODY(\sigma_1,\sigma_2)$

which is simpler than the earlier proof. In fact, this is a special case of sequential composition with only one component. The reader will find that the rules of fig. 17 become an intuitive checklist for decomposition. Only if any of the cases are difficult, is it necessary to write out the details of a proof.

★   ★   ★

In developing a program, one is given a specification; the task is to define some set of units which, when put together in a defined way, will realize the overall objective. The choice of the units is obviously a matter of invention, but some guidance can be given as to how their specifications should be written. The guideline is called *active decomposition*. The idea is to choose specifications for units which separate them from their context. Thus the units should not be described in a way which simply copies the specification of the context. Consider once again the specification of *LBODY*:

Smult:: X: Int   Y: Int   R: Int

LBODY
states: Smult
$pre\text{-}LBODY(<x,,>) \triangleq x>0$
$post\text{-}LBODY(<x,y,r>,<x',y',r'>) \triangleq (r'+x'*y' = r+x*y) \wedge 0 \le x' < x$

Using a sequence of two operations, what is to be the pre-condition of the first operation? From fig. 17 a proof can be made with:

$pre\text{-}OP1(<x,,>) \triangleq x>0$

But, given the function intended in *OP1*, what pre-condition is really required? Clearly, in this simple case, **TRUE** is sufficient. Even in more complicated examples, it is frequently the case that the pre-condition of a unit can be wider than is demanded by the current context. The guideline of active decomposition is to choose the widest pre-condition under which a unit can function and to refrain from simply copying that of the higher level. Units are thereby created which can be used elsewhere. A similar argument applies to determining the pre-condition of *OP2*.

Analogous arguments hold for the post-conditions. The post-condition *post-LBODY* is a relation of two states, but a post-condition for *OP2* could be manufactured which fits the context exactly. For example:

$$post\text{-}OP2(<x,y,z>,<x',y',z'>) \triangleq r'+x'^*y'=r+(x+1)^*y \land x'=x$$

Going further:

$$post\text{-}OP1(<x,y,z>,<x',y',z'>) \triangleq r'+(x'+1)^*y'=r+x^*y \land 0 \leq x'<x$$

Using these two specifications it is easy to prove that *OP1;OP2* is a valid realization of *LBODY*. But the difficulty comes at the next stage of development. The specification is so special to its context that it may be unintelligible to the person who has to develop it. This can significantly complicate the proof of large examples. Here again, the guideline of active decomposition argues for choosing specifications which, like those used earlier, have as little as possible to do with the context. Otherwise the step of development only postpones work to the next step.

Another aspect of the specification of sub-operations is the question of how much freedom can be left open. It has been pointed out that the specification for *LBODY* did not fix the amount by which the value of *X* is to be reduced on each loop iteration. This freedom has subsequently been used to develop both linear and logarithmic implementations. On larger problems it is very important, having decided what a sub-unit should do, to attempt to generalize the specification.

Another issue which arises in developing programs is how much to do at each stage. In general this depends on how much one can safely reason about. However, the reader should be warned against splitting units which properly make more sense together than apart. A case in point is the initialization of iterative constructs. Earlier, a single step proposed the following development of *BODY*:

BODY ≜
  R = 0;
  DO WHILE (X ¬= 0);
  /*
     LBODY
     states: Smult
     $pre\text{-}LBODY(<x,,>) \triangleq x>0$
     $post\text{-}LBODY(<x,y,r>,<x',y',r'>) \triangleq (r'+x'^*y' = r+x^*y) \land 0 \leq x'<x$
  */
  END;

It would have been possible to make this development by splitting into initialization and loop, thus:

$BODY \triangleq INIT; LOOP$

$post\text{-}INIT(<x,y,>,\sigma') \triangleq \sigma'=<x,y,0>$

$pre\text{-}LOOP(<x,,>) \triangleq x \geq 0$
$post\text{-}LOOP(<x,y,r>,<x',y',r'>) \triangleq r' = r+x*y$

The proof can be written without difficulty and the development of
LOOP could then generate the requirement for *LBODY*. There is
nothing wrong with this way of proceeding. However, two steps of
development can easily be combined into one by using the expansion for
initialized iterative statements. Furthermore, because they hang
together, the combination of the two stages is significantly easier to
comprehend than the separated version.

Conditional Statements

After sequential statements, the next simplest way of combining
operations is to use the conditional statement. Since the interest here is
on decomposing tasks, this section reviews how a specified operation can
be realized by sub-operations which are combined by use of a conditional
construct.

In the context of functions, the use of conditional expressions is
discussed in chapter 3. It is possible to extend the proof method used
there to arrive at a way of handling conditional statements. That is, a
way of reasoning by cases could be introduced—this would require some
knowledge of the language definition. Rather than leave the reader to
structure such proofs, a standard checklist of properties is given.

The list of properties for reasoning about conditional statements is
given in fig. 19. A function *e-expr* is used in the rules which check the
domains of the operations. The function computes the value of an
expression in a state:

e-expr: Expr State → Bool

The meaning of this function is assumed to be understood (but see also
appendix A). The fact that this function does not yield a changed state
shows that side-effects are not being considered. Since function
procedures are not used here, the assumption of no side effects is
reasonable. (If the portion of PL/I being used were extended in this
direction, alternative, more complicated, rules would have to be used.)
The correctness of the result delivered is now expressed in two rules (i.e.
ra and *rb*). A graphic view of the rules is shown in fig. 20.

Consider again the multiplication problem using the specification:

For:

OP ≜ IF e THEN OP1 ELSE OP2

to be correct, show:

da. pre-OP(σ) ∧ e-expr(e,σ) ⟹ pre-OP1(σ)
db. pre-OP(σ) ∧ ~e-expr(e,σ) ⟹ pre-OP2(σ)
ra. pre-OP(σ₁) ∧ e-expr(e,σ₁) ∧ post-OP1(σ₁,σ₂) ⟹ post-OP(σ₁,σ₂)
rb. pre-OP(σ₁) ∧ ~e-expr(e,σ₁) ∧ post-OP2(σ₁,σ₂) ⟹ post-OP(σ₁,σ₂)

Figure 19   **Rules for Conditional Statements**

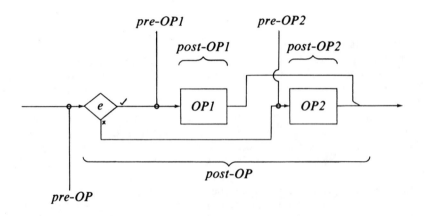

Figure 20   **Picture of Conditional Statement**

Smult:: X: Int   Y: Int   R: Int

MULTB
states: Smult
post-MULTB(<x,y,>,<,,r'>) ≜ r'=x*y

A realization might be made in terms of two sub-operations as follows:

MULTB ≜ IF X≥0 THEN OP1; ELSE OP2;

with the specifications:

OP1
states: Smult
$pre\text{-}OP1(<x,,>) \triangleq x{\geq}0$
$post\text{-}OP1(<x,y,>,<,,r'>) \triangleq r' = x{*}y$

OP2
states: Smult
$pre\text{-}OP2(<x,,>) \triangleq x{\leq}0$
$post\text{-}OP2(<x,y,>,<,,r'>) \triangleq r' = x{*}y$

The rules of fig. 19 can be used to prove this correct.

da.
$pre\text{-}MULTB(\sigma) \wedge e\text{-}expr(x{\geq}0,\sigma) \Rightarrow pre\text{-}OP1(\sigma)$
$x{\geq}0 \Rightarrow x{\geq}0$

db.
$pre\text{-}MULTB(\sigma) \wedge \sim e\text{-}expr(x{\geq}0,\sigma) \Rightarrow pre\text{-}OP2(\sigma)$
$\sim(x{\geq}0) \Rightarrow x{\leq}0$

ra.
$pre\text{-}MULTB(\sigma_1) \wedge e\text{-}expr(x{\geq}0,\sigma_1) \wedge post\text{-}OP1(\sigma_1,\sigma_2)$
$\qquad \Rightarrow post\text{-}MULTB(\sigma_1,\sigma_2)$
$r_2{=}x_1{*}y_1 \Rightarrow r_2{=}x_1{*}y_1$

rb.
$pre\text{-}MULTB(\sigma_1) \wedge \sim e\text{-}expr(x{\geq}0,\sigma_1) \wedge post\text{-}OP2(\sigma_1,\sigma_2)$
$\qquad \Rightarrow post\text{-}MULTB(\sigma_1,\sigma_2)$
$r_2{=}x_1{*}y_1 \Rightarrow r_2{=}x_1{*}y_1$

From this it can be seen that using the list of properties requires the checking of four, trivial, results. Once again, as the reader becomes proficient in their manipulation, these rules become a checklist whose veracity can be checked with little or no writing.

Exercise 5.3: The fact that the post-conditions of *OP1* and *OP2* are the same does not indicate that they are the same operation. To emphasize this point, a realization of *OP2* can be given as:

$OP2 \triangleq X = \text{-}X; OP1; R = \text{-}R$

Write out an extension of the rule in fig. 17 and use it to prove the decomposition correct. Check the clauses at a suitable level of detail.

As a second example, consider a program to compute the **absolute value** of a variable. In order to emphasize that the use of post-conditions of pairs of states handles the destruction of input values without difficulty, the following specification is chosen:

Sabs:: X: Int

ABS
states: Sabs
post-ABS(<x>,<x'>) $\triangleq$ x'≥0 $\wedge$ (x'=x $\vee$ x'=-x)

A possible realization of this specification is:

ABS $\triangleq$ IF X≥0 THEN /* DO NOTHING */; ELSE X = -X;

As a step towards the rigorous method, the definitions of the two clauses are not separately documented. The reader will see their specifications in the proof.
       Referring to fig. 19, it is necessary to prove:

da.
pre-ABS(<x>) $\wedge$ x≥0 $\Rightarrow$ **TRUE**

db.
pre-ABS(<x>) $\wedge$ ~(x≥0) $\Rightarrow$ **TRUE**

both of which implications are vacuously true, and:

ra.
pre-ABS(<x$_1$>) $\wedge$ x$_1$≥0 $\wedge$ x$_2$=x$_1$ $\Rightarrow$ post-ABS(<x$_1$>,<x$_2$>)
x$_1$≥0 $\wedge$ x$_2$=x$_1$ $\Rightarrow$ x$_2$≥0 $\wedge$ (x$_2$=x$_1$ $\vee$ x$_2$ =-x$_1$)

which is immediate, and finally:

rb.
pre-ABS(<x$_1$>) $\wedge$ ~(x$_1$≥0) $\wedge$ x$_2$=-x$_1$ $\Rightarrow$ post-ABS(<x$_1$>,<x$_2$>)
x$_1$<0 $\wedge$ x$_2$=-x$_1$ $\Rightarrow$ x$_2$≥0 $\wedge$ (x$_2$=x$_1$ $\vee$ x$_2$=-x$_1$)

which is again immediate. This concludes the proof of *ABS*.
       The topic of active decomposition should again be discussed in the context of conditional statements. Faced with the specification of *ABS* and wanting to make a step of development, the step could be:

ABS = IF X≥0 THEN OP1; ELSE OP2

with:

pre-OP1(<x>) $\triangleq$ x≥0
post-OP1(σ,σ') $\triangleq$ post-ABS(σ,σ')

pre-OP2(<x>) $\triangleq$ x<0
post-OP2(σ,σ') $\triangleq$ post-ABS(σ,σ')

Nothing has been achieved. It is, of course, trivial to prove correct. But the task of understanding *post-ABS* has been passed on to the developers of *OP1* and *OP2*. Furthermore, the eventual realizations of *OP1* and *OP2* may be capable of performing useful work on a wider class of states than is indicated by their pre-conditions.

Exercise 5.4: Given the specifications:

Smax:: X: Int Y: Int R: Int

MAX
states: Smax
post-MAX(<x,y,>,<,,r'>) ≜ r'≥x ∧ r'≥y ∧ (r'=x ∨ r'=y)

Prove the following realization correct:

MAX ≜ IF X≥Y THEN OP1 ELSE OP2

OP1
states: Smax
post-OP1(<x,,>,<,,r'>) ≜ r' = x

OP2
states: Smax
post-OP2(<,y,>,<,,r'>) ≜ r' = y

Exercise 5.5: Given the specification:

Ssign:: X: Int R: Int

SIGN
states: Ssign
post-SIGN(<x,>,<,r'>) ≜
    (x<0 ⟹ r' = -1) ∧
    (x=0 ⟹ r' = 0) ∧
    (x>0 ⟹ r' = +1)

provide, and prove correct, a realization. Write the operations within the conditional statements as assignment statements and reason at the level of (in)formality used in the *ABS* example above.

There are programs where a useful function can be expressed by a conditional statement with only one clause. In such cases, the general form of fig. 19 must be used as though one of the operations is an identity. Consider the following specification (taken from an alternative logarithmic multiplication program):

Smult2:: X: Int Y: Int R: Int

SETEVEN
states: Smult2
pre-SETEVEN(<x,,>) ≜ x≥1
post-SETEVEN(<x,y,r>,<x',y',r'>) ≜
    *(r'+x'*y'=r+x*y) ∧ 0≤x'≤x ∧ is-even(x')*

Without the last clause of the conjunction in *post-SETEVEN*, the operation could be simply an identity, but it is obviously necessary to do something in the case where the input value of *X* is not even. This suggests a realization of:

$SETEVEN \triangleq IF\ (MOD(X,2)=1)\ THEN$
$\qquad\qquad DO;$
$\qquad\qquad X\ =\ X\text{-}1;$
$\qquad\qquad R\ =\ R\text{+}Y;$
$\qquad\qquad END;$

The modified form of the rules from fig. 19 is:

da.
$pre\text{-}SETEVEN(\sigma) \wedge e\text{-}expr(MOD(X,2)=1,\sigma) \Rightarrow pre\text{-}OP1(\sigma)$

since *pre-OP1* can be **TRUE**, this is vacuously true. There is no equivalent condition to be proved for the *ELSE* clause. For the results:

ra.
$pre\text{-}SETEVEN(\sigma_1) \wedge e\text{-}expr(MOD(X,2)=1,\sigma_1) \wedge post\text{-}OP1(\sigma_1,\sigma_2)$
$\quad \Rightarrow post\text{-}SETEVEN(\sigma_1,\sigma_2)$

$x_1 \geq 1 \wedge is\text{-}odd(x_1) \wedge x_2 = x_1\text{-}1 \wedge r_2 = r_1 + y_1 \wedge y_2 = y_1$
$\quad \Rightarrow r_2 + x_2 * y_2 = r_1 + x_1 * y_1 \wedge 0 \leq x_2 \leq x_1 \wedge is\text{-}even(x_2)$

For the result of the *ELSE clause* it is necessary to check that the identity transformation (notice the second argument for *post-SETEVEN*) achieves the required results:

rb.
$pre\text{-}SETEVEN(\sigma_1) \wedge {\sim}e\text{-}expr(MOD(x,2)=1,\sigma_1) \Rightarrow$
$\quad post\text{-}SETEVEN(\sigma_1,\sigma_1)$
$x_1 \geq 1 \wedge {\sim}is\text{-}odd(x_1) \Rightarrow r_1 + x_1 * y_1 = r_1 + x_1 * y_1 \wedge 0 \leq x_1 \leq x_1 \wedge is\text{-}even(x_1)$

Iterative Statements

Just as recursion is essential for writing interesting functions, the use of iterative statements is a pre-requisite if (short) programs are to evoke useful (i.e. very long) computations. Likewise, as with recursive functions, iterative statements bring a danger with their power: the problem of termination is considered below. In order to prove results about recursive functions, inductive proofs were used. It is possible to prove iterative programs correct by similar inductive arguments. The general lists of rules about iterative programs have themselves been proved by induction. It is, however, one of the virtues of these rules that their use obviates the necessity to construct inductive arguments. The induction has been factored out.

There is more than one set of rules for proving results about iterative statements. The first set of rules appears in fig. 21. (The reason for calling them *Up* rules, alternatives, and their applicability are discussed below.)

In order to provide a meaningful operation, it is normally necessary to precede a loop construct with some initialization. As pointed out earlier, a development which separates the initialization and the loop proper, is likely to be less clear. For this reason, the properties given in fig. 21 apply to the combined effect of initialization and the loop itself.

For:

$OP \triangleq INIT;\ DO\ WHILE(e);\ BODY;\ END;$

to be correct, find:

pre-LOOP: State $\rightarrow$ *Bool*
so-far: State State $\rightarrow$ *Bool*
term: State $\rightarrow$ *Int*

and show:

da. $pre\text{-}INIT(\sigma) \leftrightarrow$ **TRUE**
db. $pre\text{-}OP(\sigma_1) \wedge post\text{-}INIT(\sigma_1,\sigma_2) \Rightarrow pre\text{-}LOOP(\sigma_2)$
dc. $pre\text{-}BODY(\sigma_1) \wedge post\text{-}BODY(\sigma_1,\sigma_2) \Rightarrow pre\text{-}LOOP(\sigma_2)$
dd. $pre\text{-}LOOP(\sigma) \wedge e\text{-}expr(e,\sigma) \Rightarrow pre\text{-}BODY(\sigma)$
ra. $pre\text{-}OP(\sigma_1) \wedge post\text{-}INIT(\sigma_1,\sigma_2) \Rightarrow so\text{-}far(\sigma_1,\sigma_2)$
rb. $so\text{-}far(\sigma_1,\sigma_2) \wedge pre\text{-}LOOP(\sigma_2) \wedge e\text{-}expr(e,\sigma_2) \wedge post\text{-}BODY(\sigma_2,\sigma_3)$
    $\Rightarrow so\text{-}far(\sigma_1,\sigma_3)$
rc. $so\text{-}far(\sigma_1,\sigma_2) \wedge pre\text{-}LOOP(\sigma_2) \wedge \sim e\text{-}expr(e,\sigma_2) \Rightarrow post\text{-}OP(\sigma_1,\sigma_2)$
ta. $pre\text{-}LOOP(\sigma) \Rightarrow term(\sigma){\geq}0$
tb. $pre\text{-}LOOP(\sigma) \wedge term(\sigma){>}0 \Rightarrow e\text{-}expr(e,\sigma)$
tc. $pre\text{-}LOOP(\sigma) \wedge term(\sigma){=}0 \Rightarrow \sim e\text{-}expr(e,\sigma)$
td. $pre\text{-}BODY(\sigma_1) \wedge post\text{-}BODY(\sigma_1,\sigma_2) \Rightarrow term(\sigma_2){<}term(\sigma_1)$

Figure 21   Rules for Initialized Iteration (Up)

As in the preceding two sections, the rules are labelled. Consider, firstly, the domain rules. Rule *da* states that the initialization should be total (work for any states). The remaining three domain conditions involve the predicate *pre-LOOP* which is not one of the pre- /post-conditions which are directly available from either the overall specification (i.e. *OP*) or those of the sub-units (i.e. *INIT* or *BODY*). The predicate *pre-LOOP* must be invented. Since its function is to define the class of states which occur prior to the *DO* construct, it is not usually difficult to find. Rule *db* then specifies that all states in which *OP* can execute should, after execution of *INIT*, yield states which are valid for the *DO* construct. The other states which can arise at this point are those which have been used in the *BODY* of the loop; rule *dc* requires that they also satisfy *pre-LOOP*. The last of the domain rules requires that the limitation chosen for the loop matches the pre-condition for *BODY*.

The three result rules *ra, rb, rc* are expressed in terms of another auxiliary predicate—*so-far*. This predicate is intended to capture the relationship between the state prior to initialization and the state existing after a number of iterations of the body of the loop. Again *so-far* must be invented and this problem is discussed later in this section. The predicate *so-far* is invariant in the sense that it is true after any number of loop iterations. After zero iterations of the loop body, the state is exactly that created by *INIT*; rule *ra* specifies that this must satisfy *so-far*. Given an intermediate state satisfying *so-far*, rule *rb* requires that if a further iteration of the loop is made, another state satisfying *so-far* must be created. Finally rule *rc* requires that a state which satisfies *so-far*, and which is terminal, in the sense that the loop test is false, must also satisfy the post-condition for *OP*.

The reader may find it useful to trace through the rules with the aid of fig. 22: this shows graphically how the predicates relate.

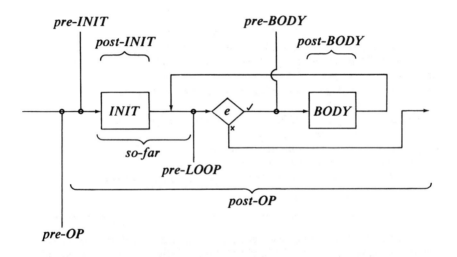

Figure 22   Picture of Initialized Iteration (Up)

The remaining rules are concerned with termination. Before explaining them consider the use of what has so far been covered on the example of addition. Given the specification:

Sta:: X: Int Y: Int R: Int T: Int

pre-ADD(<,y,,>) ≜ *y≥0*
post-ADD(<x,y,,>,<,,r',>) ≜ *r' = x+y*

A decomposition can be made with the following program in mind:

$ADD \triangleq$

    $T = 0;$ $/* INIT */$

    $R = X;$

      $DO\ WHILE\ (T \neg= Y);$ $/* LOOP */$

        $T = T+1;$ $/* BODY */$

        $R = R+1;$

      $END;$

thus:

$pre\text{-}BODY(<,y,,t>) \triangleq t<y$
$post\text{-}BODY(<x,y,r,t>,\sigma') \triangleq \sigma' = <x,y,r+1,t+1>$

The rules of fig. 21 can now be considered one at a time (notice how the definition of *INIT* is derived from the two assignment statements): *da* is true because the initialization requires no pre-condition.
Using:

$pre\text{-}LOOP(<,y,,t>) \triangleq t\leq y$

Then:

db.
$pre\text{-}ADD(\sigma_1) \wedge post\text{-}INIT(\sigma_1,\sigma_2) \Rightarrow pre\text{-}LOOP(\sigma_2)$
$y_1\geq 0 \wedge t_2=0 \wedge y_2=y_1 \Rightarrow t_2\leq y_2$

which is immediate. Also:

dc.
$pre\text{-}BODY(\sigma_1) \wedge post\text{-}BODY(\sigma_1,\sigma_2) \Rightarrow pre\text{-}LOOP(\sigma_2)$
$t_1<y_1 \wedge t_2=t_1+1 \wedge y_2=y_1 \Rightarrow t_2\leq y_2$

which is immediate. Then:

dd.
$pre\text{-}LOOP(\sigma) \wedge e\text{-}expr(t\neq y,\sigma) \Rightarrow pre\text{-}BODY(\sigma)$
$t\leq y \wedge t\neq y \Rightarrow t<y$

which is immediate.

The meaning of the loop can be summarized by the invariant:

$so\text{-}far(<x,y,,>,<,y',r',t'>) \triangleq r'=x+t' \wedge t'\leq y \wedge y'=y$

This can be used to check the three result rules.

ra.
$pre\text{-}ADD(\sigma_1) \wedge post\text{-}INIT(\sigma_1,\sigma_2) \Rightarrow so\text{-}far(\sigma_1,\sigma_2)$
$y_1\geq 0 \wedge y_2=y_1 \wedge t_2=0 \wedge r_2=x_1 \Rightarrow r_2=x_1+t_2 \wedge t_2\leq y_1 \wedge y_2=y_1$

rb.
$so\text{-}far(\sigma_1,\sigma_2) \wedge pre\text{-}LOOP(\sigma_2) \wedge e\text{-}expr(t\neq y,\sigma_2) \wedge post\text{-}BODY(\sigma_2,\sigma_3)$
    $\Rightarrow so\text{-}far(\sigma_1,\sigma_3)$

$r_2=x_1+t_2 \wedge t_2\leq y_1 \wedge y_2=y_1 \wedge t_2\leq y_2 \wedge t_2\neq y_2 \wedge r_3=r_2+1$
    $\wedge x_3=x_2 \wedge t_3=t_2+1 \wedge y_3=y_2$
        $\Rightarrow r_3=x_1+t_3 \wedge t_3\leq y_1 \wedge y_3=y_1$

rc.

$so\text{-}far(\sigma_1,\sigma_2) \land pre\text{-}LOOP(\sigma_2) \land {\sim}e\text{-}expr(t{\neq}y,\sigma_2) \Rightarrow post\text{-}ADD(\sigma_1,\sigma_2)$
$r_2{=}x_1{+}t_2 \land y_2{=}y_1 \land t_2{=}y_2 \Rightarrow r_2{=}x_1{+}y_1$

All three of which are immediate.

Once again, it can be seen that the list of properties has reduced the problem of correctness proof to a series of simple checks.

Notice that, although *so-far* was said to be invariant, this only applies to situations after iterations of *BODY*. There are points within *BODY* where the property does not hold.

$\star \quad \star \quad \star$

The last four rules of fig. 21 have, however, not yet been explained. As has been pointed out, it must be shown that the power of the iterative construct has been used safely. The result proved so far has not shown that the realization terminates for all valid input states. The result which shows only properties for those final states which do arise, is called *partial correctness*. The property to be proved in this book is total correctness which includes termination. Since a stepwise development method is being considered, it is obviously unacceptable to delay the question of termination, for fear that such a delay would result in further development being wasted.

In order to show that the specific *ADD* example will always terminate, it is only necessary to observe that the value of *(y - t)* is always positive and will be decreased each time around the loop. Since, with whole numbers, this cannot go on indefinitely, the loop must terminate sooner or later.

The last four rules of fig. 21 are concerned with a general treatment of termination (hence the names begin with *t*). The proof relies on finding a function from *States* to the integers which (rule *ta*) always yields positive values for states of the loop; decreases (rule *td*) each time the body of the loop is executed; is zero exactly when the loop test expression is false (rules *tb* and *tc*).

Using:

$term({<},y,,t{>}) \triangleq y\text{-}t$

these rules can be checked for the example in hand.

ta.
$pre\text{-}LOOP(\sigma) \Rightarrow term(\sigma){\geq}0$
$t{\leq}y \Rightarrow y\text{-}t{\geq}0$

tb.
$pre\text{-}LOOP(\sigma) \land term(\sigma){>}0 \Rightarrow e\text{-}expr(t{\neq}y,\sigma)$
$y\text{-}t{>}0 \Rightarrow t{\neq}y$

tc.
$pre\text{-}LOOP(\sigma) \land term(\sigma){=}0 \Rightarrow {\sim}e\text{-}expr(t{\neq}y,\sigma)$
$y\text{-}t{=}0 \Rightarrow t{=}y$

td.

$pre\text{-}BODY(\sigma_1) \wedge post\text{-}BODY(\sigma_1,\sigma_2) \Rightarrow term(\sigma_2) < term(\sigma_1)$

$y_2 = y_1 \wedge t_2 = t_1 + 1 \Rightarrow y_2 - t_2 < y_1 - t_1$

all of which are again immediate.

It is worthwhile to understand the role of *term*. In this specific example it is easy to see how it relates to the informal termination argument given above. In general, *term* establishes that the induction is **well-founded**. That is, the induction is over a sequence of values which cannot decrease for ever.

★   ★   ★

In common with the two preceding sections, a table of properties has again been presented to aid with proofs about a programming construct. This set of properties can be proved correct with respect to a definition of the language. The advantage of using this list of properties is that it makes the checking of decomposition into iterative statements more routine than inductive proofs.

Exercise 5.6:   Given the specification for a multiplication program:

Smultt:: X: Int Y: Int R: Int T: Int

MULTT
states: Smultt
$pre\text{-}MULTT(<x,,,>) \triangleq x \geq 0$
$post\text{-}MULTT(<x,y,,>,<,,r',>) \triangleq r' = x*y$

and the realization:

$MULTT \triangleq INIT;\quad DO\ WHILE\ (T\neg=X);\ BODY;\ END;$

with:

INIT
states: Smultt
$post\text{-}INIT(<x,y,,>,\sigma') \triangleq \sigma' = <x,y,0,0>$

BODY
states: Smultt
$pre\text{-}BODY(<x,,,t>) \triangleq t < x$
$post\text{-}BODY(<x,y,r,t>,\sigma') \triangleq \sigma' = <x,y,r+y,t+1>$

Use:

$pre\text{-}LOOP(<x,,,t>) \triangleq t \leq x$
$so\text{-}far(<x,y,,>,<x',y',r',t'>) \triangleq r' = t'*y \wedge x' = x \wedge y' = y$
$term(<x,,,t>) \triangleq x - t$

and fig. 21 to prove the realization correct.

In the last exercise, the three auxiliary predicates were provided—the next exercise asks the reader to find them. The predicate to be found as pre-condition for the loop is normally straightforward: loosely speaking it is the disjunction of the conditions which can be handled by the *BODY* and the negation of the loop test (which ensures that *BODY* is not executed). Thus in the last example:

$t<x \ \vee \ \sim(t \neq x)$

suggests:

$t \leq x$

The invariant *so-far* can be the most difficult to find. In the case of simple loops which count up in a temporary variable, a fairly simple rule suffices to find the core of the invariant. The idea is to develop the invariant from the overall post-condition. The role of the temporary variable is to keep track of how much computation has been done. It is therefore reasonable to substitute the current value of the temporary variable for the name of the variable to which it is compared. Thus:

$r'=x*y$

with *t* running from zero to *x*, this suggests:

$r'=t'*y$

The remaining clauses of the invariant are there to check that everything that should remain constant does so: rules *rb* and *rc* pinpoint any extra terms in *so-far*. In this case *rb* requires knowing that *y* is kept constant; similarly, *rc* requires that *x* still has its initial value. The essential point of the invariant (cf. rule *rc*) is that when it is conjoined with the negation of the loop test it should imply the overall post-condition.

The termination condition is normally obvious and the four rules describe clearly what properties are required.

Exercise 5.7:   Given the specification for an exponentiation program:

Sexpt:: X: Int   Y: Int   R: Int   T: Int

EXPT
states: Sexpt
pre-EXPT(<,y,,>) $\triangleq$ *y≥0*
post-EXPT(<x,y,,>,<,,r',>) $\triangleq$ *r' = x**y*

prove correct the realization:

EXPT $\triangleq$
        R = 1;
        T = 0;
        DO WHILE (T ¬= Y);
            T = T+1;
            R = R*X;
        END;

*More on Iterative Statements

It has been found worthwhile to tailor sets of properties for different forms of iterative statements. The caption of fig. 21 has *Up* in parentheses. Basically, it can be said that this set of rules is applicable where the program to be proved correct has a temporary variable which is incremented up to the initial value of one of the given values. It is a virtue of the system of post-conditions of state pairs that it handles well the situation where input values are overwritten. How are such programs be proved correct? Well, firstly the given schema can be used. It is shown below that using the wrong set of properties has the effect of complicating the proof somewhat—not of making it impossible. There is, however, a special schema for *Down* cases: this is applicable where the value of one of the input variables is decremented to some predetermined value (e.g. *0*). The *Down* rules are given in fig. 23. They are again for the initialized construct.

For:

$OP \triangleq INIT; DO\ WHILE(e); BODY; END;$

to be correct, find:

pre-LOOP: State $\rightarrow$ *Bool*
to-end: State State $\rightarrow$ *Bool*
term: State $\rightarrow$ *Int*

and show:

da. pre-INIT(σ) $\leftrightarrow$ **TRUE**
db. pre-OP(σ_1) $\wedge$ *post-INIT(σ_1,σ_2)* $\Rightarrow$ *pre-LOOP(σ_2)*
dc. pre-BODY(σ_1) $\wedge$ *post-BODY(σ_1,σ_2)* $\Rightarrow$ *pre-LOOP(σ_2)*
dd. pre-LOOP(σ) $\wedge$ *e-expr(e,σ)* $\Rightarrow$ *pre-BODY(σ)*
ra. pre-BODY(σ_1) $\wedge$ *post-BODY(σ_1,σ_2)* $\wedge$ *to-end(σ_2,σ_3)* $\Rightarrow$ *to-end(σ_1,σ_3)*
rb. pre-LOOP(σ) $\wedge$ *~e-expr(e,σ)* $\Rightarrow$ *to-end(σ,σ)*
rc. pre-OP(σ_1) $\wedge$ *post-INIT(σ_1,σ_2)* $\wedge$ *to-end(σ_2,σ_3)* $\Rightarrow$ *post-OP(σ_1,σ_3)*
ta. pre-LOOP(σ) $\Rightarrow$ *term(σ)$\geq$0*
tb. pre-LOOP(σ) $\wedge$ *term(σ)>0* $\Rightarrow$ *e-expr(e,σ)*
tc. pre-LOOP(σ) $\wedge$ *term(σ)=0* $\Rightarrow$ *~e-expr(e,σ)*
td. pre-BODY(σ_1) $\wedge$ *post-BODY(σ_1,σ_2)* $\Rightarrow$ *term(σ_2)<term(σ_1)*

Figure 23   Rules for Initialized Iteration (Down)

The domain (*d*) and termination (*t*) rules require no explanation because they are identical with those of fig. 21. The result (*r*) rules of fig. 23 can be clarified as follows. The purpose of the *to-end* predicate is to summarize what will happen from some given state (which can arise for the loop) until termination of the loop is complete. One special case of such states is, of course, a final state so that rule *rb* states that *to-end* must be true when both arguments are states for which the loop test expression is false. Rule *ra* states that execution of *BODY* followed by execution of the loop has the same effect as executing the loop itself. Rule *rc* requires that execution of *INIT* followed by execution of the loop has the effect required for *OP*. (A supporting picture is given in fig. 24.)

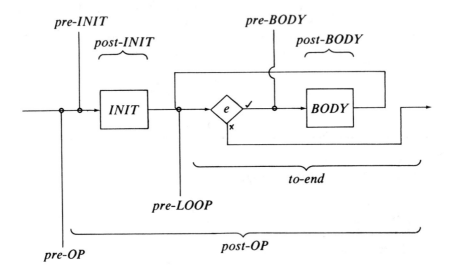

Figure 24   Picture of Initialized Iteration (Down)

With this introduction, the following example shows how the rules are used. Given the specification:

Sadd:: X: Int Y: Int R: Int

ADD
states: Sadd
pre-ADD(<,y,>) ≜ y≥0
post-ADD(<x,y,>,<,,r'>) ≜ r' = x+y

and the realization:

ADD ≜
```
    R  = X;                    /* INIT */
    DO WHILE (Y ¬= 0);         /* LOOP */
      Y  = Y-1;                /* BODY */
      R  = R+1;
    END;
```

thus:

$pre\text{-}BODY(<,y,>) \triangleq y>0$
$post\text{-}BODY(<x,y,r>,\sigma') \triangleq \sigma' = <x,y\text{-}1,r+1>$

The auxiliaries $pre\text{-}LOOP$ and $term$ can be found as before:

$pre\text{-}LOOP(<,y,>) \triangleq y\geq0$
$term(<,y,>) \triangleq y$

The predicate $to\text{-}end$ must be chosen so that it summarizes the rest of loop execution; the overall post-condition is normally a guide and rule rc can be used as a quick check. Here:

$to\text{-}end(<x,y,r>,<,,r'>) \triangleq r' = r+y$

is used.

Proceeding with the proof:

da is immediate

$db.$
$y_1\geq0 \wedge y_2=y_1 \Rightarrow y_2\geq0$

$dc.$
$y_1>0 \wedge y_2 = y_1\text{-}1 \Rightarrow y_2\geq0$

$dd.$
$y\geq0 \wedge y\neq0 \Rightarrow y>0$

$ra.$
$y_2=y_1\text{-}1 \wedge r_2=r_1+1 \wedge r_3=r_2+y_2 \Rightarrow r_3 = r_1+y_1$

$rb.$
$y=0 \Rightarrow r=r+y$

$rc.$
$r_2=x_1 \wedge y_2=y_1 \wedge r_3=r_2+y_2 \Rightarrow r_3=x_1+y_1$

$ta.$
$y\geq0 \Rightarrow y\geq0$

$tb.$
$y>0 \Rightarrow (y\neq0)$

$tc.$
$y=0 \Rightarrow \sim(y\neq0)$

$td.$
$y_2 = y_1\text{-}1 \Rightarrow y_2<y_1$

all of which are immediate.

Exercise 5.8:   Given the specification for multiplication:

Smult:: X: Int Y: Int R: Int

MULT
states: Smult
pre-MULT(<x,,>) ≜ x≥0
post-MULT(<x,y,>,<,,r'>) ≜ r' = x*y

and a realization:

MULT ≜ INIT; DO WHILE(X¬=0); BODY; END;

with:

post-INIT(<x,y,>,σ') ≜ σ'=<x,y,0>

pre-BODY(<x,,>) ≜ x>0
post-BODY(<x,y,r>,<x',y',r'>) ≜ (r'+x'*y' = r+x*y) ∧ 0≤x'<x

Use:

pre-LOOP(<x,,>) ≜ x≥0
to-end(<x,y,r>,<,,r'>) ≜ r' = r+x*y
term(<x,,>) ≜ x

to prove the realization correct.

Exercise 5.9:   Given the specification for exponentiation:

Sexp:: X: Int Y: Int R: Int

EXP
states: Sexp
pre-EXP(<,y,>) ≜ y≥0
post-EXP(<x,y,>,<,,r'>) ≜ r' = x**y

and a realization:

EXP ≜ INIT; DO WHILE(Y ¬= 0); BODY; END;

with:

post-INIT(<x,y,>,σ') ≜ σ' = <x,y,1>

pre-BODY(<,y,>) ≜ y>0
post-BODY(<x,y,r>,<x',y',r'>) ≜ (r'*x'**y' = r*x**y) ∧ 0≤y'<y

Prove the realization correct.

Two sets of rules have been given for reasoning about initialized-iterative statements and it is now appropriate to discuss the selection of the right set for various problems. The key difference between the two sets is the way the induction works. Comparing the essence of rule *rb* of fig. 21 with that of rule *ra* of fig. 23, the former can be pictured as:

```
        so-far                BODY
σ₁-----------> σ₂    -------------> σ₃
 | -------------------------------- |
     gives: so-far
```

while the latter is:

```
        BODY                to-end
σ₁-----------> σ₂    -------------> σ₃
 | -------------------------------- |
     gives: to-end
```

That is, the **Up** rules show that the invariant is preserved if another iteration of the loop body follows it, whilst the **Down** rules show that the effect of one iteration of the loop body followed by the remaining iterations (described by *to-end*) can itself be summarized by *to-end*.

The choice between the two sets of rules, then, is governed by whether it is easier to summarize (by *so-far*) the effect of the first n iterations of a loop, or whether the meaning of all remaining iterations can more easily be described by *to-end*. Consider the two versions of development for multiplication programs which have been given above (viz. *MULTT* of exercise 5.6 and *MULT* of exercise 5.8). In the version using a temporary variable (*MULTT*), the variable T could be used to summarize progress so far with:

$$so\text{-}far(<,y,,>,<,,r',t'>) \triangleq r'=t'*y \land \ldots$$

The development of *MULT* avoids the use of a temporary variable; it functions by adding onto the variable r the product of the current values of X and Y and thus the remaining loop iterations can be summarized with:

$$to\text{-}end(<x,y,r>,<,,r'>) \triangleq r'=r+x*y \land \ldots$$

What happens if the wrong set of rules is selected? In simple examples, the difference is difficult to discern and even on more complicated examples the result is only that the auxiliary definitions become more complex than if the appropriate rules are chosen. The use of **only** in the previous sentence is intended to reassure the reader that a wrong choice will not completely defeat his efforts to construct a proof; it should not prompt careless selection of the rules to be used. What usually happens if the wrong rules are used is that the *so-far* or *to-end* predicate becomes an implication. This can make the checking of the rules more tedious. In the examples of this chapter the actual use of an implication can be avoided but the auxiliary predicates still have to be defined **backwards**. For example, if the *MULTT* development is done using the **Down** rules it is necessary to employ:

$$to\text{-}end(<x,y,r,t>,<,,r',>) \triangleq r' = r+(x-t)*y \land \ldots$$

Comparing this with the *so-far* presented above, one can see that the necessity to state the effect of the remaining iterations of the loop causes $(x - t)$ to be used as a way of showing how many more iterations of the loop body will occur. Similarly, if *MULT* is tackled using the *Up* set of rules, a definition of:

so-far(<x,y,>,<x',,r'>) ≜ *r' = (x-x')*y* ∧ ...

is required. Here, the effect of the iterations thus far can be described only in terms of the difference between the initial and current values of *X*.

Exercise 5.10:   Given the specification for factorial:

Sfact::   N: Int   FN: Int   C: Int

FACTT
states: Sfact
pre-FACTT(<n,,>) ≜ *n≥0*
post-FACTT(<n,,>,<,fn',>) ≜ *fn' = n!*

Prove correct the program:

```
C = 0;
FN = 1;
DO WHILE (C¬=N);
    /*
        BODY
        states: Sfact
        pre-BODY(<,,c>) ≜ c<n
        post-BODY(<n,fn,c>,σ') ≜ σ' = <n,fn*c,c+1>
    */
END;
```

Exercise 5.11:   Given the specification:

Sfactw::   N: Int   FN: Int

FACT
states: Sfactw
pre-FACT(<n,>) ≜ *n≥0*
post-FACT(<n,>,<,fn'>) ≜ *fn' = n!*

Prove correct:

```
/*
  INIT
  states: Sfactw
  post-INIT(<n,>,<n',fn'>) ≜ n'=n ∧ fn'=1
*/
DO WHILE(N¬=0);
  /*
    BODY
    states: Sfactw
    pre-BODY(<n,>) ≜ n>0
    post-BODY(<n,fn>,<n',fn'>) ≜ fn'=fn*n ∧ n'=n-1
  */
END;
```

Exercise 5.12: The reader should now be able to tackle an example using a list of rules as an informal checklist. For the specification:

Ssub:: X: Int Y: Int R: Int

SUB
states: Ssub
pre-SUB(<x,y,>) ≜ x≥y
post-SUB(<x,y,>,<,,r'>) ≜ r' = x-y

The following realization is to be proved correct:

```
BEGIN;
DCL T ...;
T = Y;
R = 0;
    DO WHILE (T¬=X);
    T = T + 1;
    R = R + 1;
    END;
END;
```

Exercise 5.13: Produce a version of a subtraction program which requires the other set of rules than those used in exercise 5.12.

Exercise 5.14: Given the specification:

Sidiv:: A: Int B: Int Q: Int R: Int
IDIV
states: Sidiv
pre-IDIV(<a,b,,>) ≜ a≥0 ∧ b>0
*post-IDIV(<a,b,,>,<,,q,r>) ≜ a=q*b+r ∧ 0≤r<b*

prove correct the decomposition:

```
/*
  INIT
  states: Sidiv
  post-INIT(<a,b,,>,σ') ≜ σ' = <a,b,0,a>
*/
  DO WHILE(B≤R);
    /*
      BODY
      states: Sidiv
      pre-BODY(<,b,,r>) ≜ b≤r
      post-BODY(<a,b,q,r>,σ') ≜ σ' = <a,b,q+1,r-b>
    */
  END;
```

Some time has been spent on these simple examples in order to provide practice with the use of the sets of rules. Some added interest can now be offered by showing that what has been done so far has wider applicability. Recall that the development of the *MULT* algorithm (cf. exercise 5.8) gave rise to a specification for the loop body of:

pre-BODY(<x,,>) ≜ x>0
post-BODY(<x,y,r>,<x',y',r'>) ≜ (r'+x'*y'=r+x*y) ∧ 0≤x'<x

It is now shown that this step of development permits a range of implementations. The interest is to show that the specification, used above for a linear algorithm, also covers fast (logarithmic) solutions. In fact two such programs are presented.

Consider the realization:

BODY ≜ SETEVEN; DIVX

with:

pre-SETEVEN(<x,,>) ≜ x≥1
post-SETEVEN(<x,y,r>,<x',y',r'>) ≜
  (r'+x'*y'=r+x*y) ∧ 0≤x'≤x ∧ is-even(x')

pre-DIVX(<x,,>) ≜ x≥0 ∧ is-even(x)
post-DIVX(<x,y,r>,<x',y',r'>) ≜ (r'+x'*y'=r+x*y) ∧ 0≤x'≤x
  ∧ (x=0 ∨ x'<x)

It is easy to prove this realization correct. Further development of *SETEVEN* and *DIVX* has already been undertaken above and the entire exponential algorithm has been proved correct. Collecting the pieces together gives:

```
R = 0;
  DO WHILE(X ¬= 0);
    IF (MOD(X,2) =1) THEN
        DO;
        X = X-1;
        R = R+Y;
        END;
    X = X/2;
    Y = 2*Y;
  END;
```

This version of a logarithmic algorithm is the traditional approach. It has the odd property that after X has been reduced to zero (by subtracting 1 from 1), a further step (halving of X, doubling of Y) is performed. This irregularity disturbed E.W.Dijkstra and led him to propose an alternative form for such logarithmic algorithms (see Dijkstra(76) where the problem considered is actually exponentiation). The alternative approach is to use a realization of *BODY*:

BODY ≜ *MKODD; DECX*

$pre\text{-}MKODD(<x,,>) ≜ x>0$
$post\text{-}MKODD(<x,y,r>,<x',y',r'>) ≜ (r'+x'{*}y'=r+x{*}y) \land 1≤x'≤x$

$post\text{-}DECX(<x,y,r>,\sigma') ≜ \sigma' = <x\text{-}1,y,r+y>$

Once again, it is obvious that this realization is correct and also to see how *DECX* can be realized by two assignment statements. The interest is in realizing *MKODD*. Consider the realization:

MKODD ≜
```
        DO WHILE(MOD(X,2) = 0);
        X = X/2;
        Y = Y*2;
        END;
```

How is this to be proved correct? The reader should by now have enough practice to expect a **Down** set of rules to be used. But the only rules given so far involve initialized iterative statements. One possibility would be to read the set of rules in fig. 23 as though *INIT* was an identity. It is, however, preferable to have an alternative set of rules tailored to the current problem. This is done in fig. 25. Notice how the roles of *pre-LOOP* and *to-end* of fig. 23 have been usurped in fig. 25 by *pre-OP* and *post-OP*, respectively. Using these new rules on:

$MKODD \triangleq$
    $DO\ WHILE\ (MOD(X,2) = 0);$
    $/*$
        $BODY2$
        $pre\text{-}BODY2(<x,,>) \triangleq x>1\ \wedge\ is\text{-}even(x)$
        $post\text{-}BODY2(<x,y,r>,\sigma') \triangleq \sigma'=<x/2,y*2,r>$
    $*/$
    $END;$

gives:

da.
$x_1>1\ \wedge\ is\text{-}even(x_1)\ \wedge\ x_2=x_1/2 \Rightarrow x_2>0$

db.
$x>0\ \wedge\ is\text{-}even(x) \Rightarrow x>1\ \wedge\ is\text{-}even(x)$

both of which require a little case analysis to check.

ra.
$x_1>1\ \wedge\ is\text{-}even(x_1)\ \wedge\ x_2=x_1/2\ \wedge\ y_2=y_1*2\ \wedge\ r_2=r_1\ \wedge$
$\quad r_3+x_3*y_3=r_2+x_2*y_2\ \wedge\ 1\leq x_3\leq x_2$
$\quad\quad \Rightarrow r_3+x_3*y_3 = r_1+x_1*y_1\ \wedge\ 1\leq x_3\leq x_1$

rb.
$x>0\ \wedge\ is\text{-}odd(x) \Rightarrow r+x*y = r+x*y\ \wedge\ 1\leq x\leq x$

For:

$OP \triangleq DO\ WHILE(e);\ BODY;\ END;$

to be correct, find:

term: State $\rightarrow$ *Int*

and show:

da. $pre\text{-}BODY(\sigma_1)\ \wedge\ post\text{-}BODY(\sigma_1,\sigma_2) \Rightarrow pre\text{-}OP(\sigma_2)$
db. $pre\text{-}OP(\sigma)\ \wedge\ e\text{-}expr(e,\sigma) \Rightarrow pre\text{-}BODY(\sigma)$
ra. $pre\text{-}BODY(\sigma_1)\ \wedge\ post\text{-}BODY(\sigma_1,\sigma_2)\ \wedge\ post\text{-}OP(\sigma_2,\sigma_3) \Rightarrow$
    $post\text{-}OP(\sigma_1,\sigma_3)$
rb. $pre\text{-}OP(\sigma)\ \wedge\ \sim e\text{-}expr(e,\sigma) \Rightarrow post\text{-}OP(\sigma,\sigma)$
ta. $pre\text{-}OP(\sigma) \Rightarrow term(\sigma)\geq 0$
tb. $pre\text{-}OP(\sigma)\ \wedge\ term(\sigma)>0 \Rightarrow e\text{-}expr(e,\sigma)$
tc. $pre\text{-}OP(\sigma)\ \wedge\ term(\sigma)=0 \Rightarrow \sim e\text{-}expr(e,\sigma)$
td. $pre\text{-}BODY(\sigma_1)\ \wedge\ post\text{-}BODY(\sigma_1,\sigma_2) \Rightarrow term(\sigma_2)<term(\sigma_1)$

Figure 25   Rules for Simple Iteration (Down)

This only leaves termination to be proved. Informally, one can argue
that for positive integers the process of dividing by *2* must eventually

yield an odd number. To formalize this argument one can define *term* to be the number of trailing zeros in the binary representation of X.

★　★　★

The topic of active decomposition should again be considered. The reader will remember that, in the first two sections of this chapter, specific advice is given to isolate the sub-units of a development from their context. The same advice is applicable to steps of development involving iterative statements.

Perhaps the easiest, and least desirable, mistake that can be made in such a step is to copy context information into the pre-condition for the body of a loop. This action may be prompted by some vague feeling that the more information the developer of the body has the easier his task will be. This is simply not the case in general. Consider the factorial example used in exercise 5.10. As the specification of *BODY* is presented, its developer need have no knowledge of the properties of factorial; its specification is documented in a way which shows its function without that knowledge. The use of factorial knowledge has been localized to the first step of development. Contrast this with a specification:

BODY
states: Sfact
$pre\text{-}BODY(<n,fn,c>) \triangleq fn=c! \land c<n$
$post\text{-}BODY(<n,,>,<n',fn',c'>) \triangleq n'=n \land fn'=c'! \land c'>c$

The task of the developer of the first step is made easier, although he still needs to know something about factorial. But whoever undertakes the development of *BODY* would, with the revised specification, also have to be conversant with properties of factorial. Although this may not be considered serious with such a trivial collection of knowledge, the danger must be avoided in large examples. A good step of development makes certain decisions and then insulates the successive stages from these decisions by choosing appropriate pre- /post-conditions. In short ***active decomposition***.

★　★　★

The sets of rules for initialized iteration have considerable generality but do not cover every contingency. In some applications above terms on the left of the implication were ignored. This indicates that a set of rules could have been constructed which were more tightly tailored to those applications. There is one point where the above rules have been unnecessarily restrictive. In rule *dc* of figs. 21 and 23 and rule *da* of fig. 25, the first term is:

$pre\text{-}BODY(\sigma_i)$

Consulting rule *dd* one suspects that this clause could be replaced by:

$pre\text{-}LOOP(\sigma_i) \land e\text{-}expr(e,\sigma_i)$

This is true and the appropriate modifications are made in appendix B to widen their generality. Where is this of use? The observant reader will have noted that the pre-conditions of loop bodies were often needlessly strong. While the pre-condition in the multiplication and exponentiation examples was used in verifying the fast (logarithmic) routines, the same is not true, for example, of the subtraction routine whose simple body requires only a pre-condition of **TRUE**. What was happening was that the form of rule *dc* was forcing the knowledge about *pre-LOOP* to be copied into *pre-BODY*. For simple examples this does no harm but it appears worthwhile to document the general rule in the appendix.

Appendix D shows how sets of rules can be proven correct with respect to the language definition. The reader is, however, warned that this is more difficult than the proofs tackled in the body of this book.

Summary

This chapter has introduced sets of rules, for reasoning about programming constructs, which can be used to justify operation combinations. These sets of rules have considered the question of termination and are thus concerned with total correctness. The rules have been presented in a way which makes them of maximum usefulness in a development process. That is, they help present decompositions of operations into realizations where all of the specifications involve post-conditions which are predicates of state pairs.

The sets of rules for each statement type are completely formal but practice with their use makes it possible to use them as checklists. A style of rigorous development then evolves in which a justification consists of sufficient information so that more formal proofs can be constructed in cases of doubt. The constructs which have been covered are the basic ones favored in the construction of structured code.

The principle of active decomposition has been explained as the isolation of sub-units by judicious choice of their specifications.

Concern is frequently expressed by programmers, after first seeing proofs of programs, that errors are as likely (or, at their stage of practice, more likely) to be made in constructing proofs as in writing programs. This is a worry which rapidly diminishes with practice. It is certainly true that errors are made in trying to construct proofs but because they do not match the program some step of the deduction will be impossible. When faced with such a difficulty the mismatch may result from an error either in the program or the proof. The key point is that the probability of a compensating error in a proof hiding one in a program is very small. The assertions force one to look at the program from another point of view. It is precisely such a shift of viewpoint which frequently shows up a bug when seeking assistance from another programmer. The danger of errors remaining unobserved is further reduced by the constructive role proposed for verification within a rigorous development method.

⋆   ⋆   ⋆

The material in this chapter deviates from the standard approach to program correctness proofs. In most expositions (e.g. Floyd(67), Hoare(69), Dijkstra(76)) the equivalent of the post-condition used here is a predicate of the output state alone. (See section *Predicate Transformers in chapter 6) This gives rise to some difficulties with proofs of programs which overwrite their input values. However, the overriding reason for adopting post-conditions of state pairs (cf. Jones(73)) in this book is that they fit more naturally into a development method. Operations are written to realize a required input/output transformation and a notation which handles this properly is more useful when many operations are under consideration.

Furthermore, it must be realized that some of the brevity of the deduction rules for predicates of single states comes from relying on the fact that the predicates (of units and their sub-units) match. Such matches occur infrequently in large problems.

It is interesting to note that Z.Manna, who used the idea of post-conditions of state pairs in his early work, is now using *intermittent assertions* (see Manna(78)). This author believes that much of the simplicity of proofs in this style (or that of *symbolic execution*, see Burstall(74)) is preserved by the approach used here.

A reservation about the use of post-conditions of state pairs is the greater length of the list of properties which must be proved about them. Although the actual results are the same, Hoare's axioms (Hoare(69)) do permit a shorter statement of the properties. Newton's notation for differential calculus was shorter than that of Leibniz, but the latter is used today—it is not always the shortest notation which is best. The shortest rule for proving programs correct is to say "prove programs correct": a longer rule, which indicates useful divisions of the task, can be much more constructive.

The crucial point is that methods which work well on small examples may be at a disadvantage, compared with methods of greater generality, when applied to large problems. This remains true even though the latter may appear cumbersome on small examples.

In closing this chapter, a number of pointers to other pieces of work can be provided. In the bulk of this book, simple assignment statements are regarded as total. This is mainly because the variables are assumed to contain mathematical entities like integers and not to exhibit the unfortunate *OVERFLOW* behavior of computer arithmetic. The problem of checking for these conditions has been called *proof of clean termination* and is tackled in Sites(74) by the inductive assertion method (see also Coleman(79)).

Although some attention has been given to the presentation of fast algorithms, the handling of performance specifications has been ignored. For a coherent extension of formal development methods to this subject, the reader is referred to Wegbreit(76). A further point is concerned with the design of useful programs. With each of the programs developed above, a precise specification of its pre-condition has been given. The fact remains that many of the presented programs will simply loop for invalid data and this makes them dangerous. This topic, among others on design, is returned to in chapter 22.

Another item of further reading, relating to the examples presented in this chapter, is Cooper(66). In that paper, an approach is adopted which relies on the properties (e.g. associativity) of operators.

Summary Exercises

Exercise 5.15:   Specify, develop, and prove correct, a modulus program which requires only two variables in its state.

Exercise 5.16:   Specify, develop, and prove correct a program which performs exponentiation in logarithmic time.

Chapter 6

OTHER ISSUES

Documenting Algorithms

The purpose of this section is to offer some comments on how algorithms can be documented.

An algorithm is a rule for computing some result. For example, there is the well known algorithm, attributed to Euclid, for computing the *greatest common divisor* of two integers. Given such a definition of algorithm it would appear that programs are algorithms. However, while it is certainly true that programs are rules for computing results, they also include much detail which is unnecessary in order to compute a result, for example, defining a fixed order for steps which could be done in any order. In the multiplication program (see fig. 16), both of the pairs of assignment statements:

$X = X/2; Y = Y*2;$
$X = X-1; R = R+Y;$

are independent in the sense that the statements within the pairs can be performed in either order without changing the result of the program. Even in a factorial program (cf. specification in exercise 5.11) the result of the body can be achieved by either:

$FN = FN*N; N = N-1;$

or:

$N = N-1; FN = FN*(N+1);$

It appears, however, that the same algorithm has been used. The necessity to fix the order of assignments is a requirement of the programming language and is not the essence of the rules for computing a result. There are, of course, situations where it might be much more difficult to decide. For example, although they both achieve multiplication in logarithmic time, the author would claim that the two algorithms presented in the previous chapter are different.

There is, then, a concept of algorithm and, for a given algorithm, a class of programs which might be said to embody the algorithm.

It should be clear from what has been said so far that a programming language is not a viable tool for algorithm documentation. The use of such a language forces commitments which are irrelevant to the essence of an algorithm. (Similar observations could be made about data structure commitments.)

What does one hope to achieve by documenting algorithms? For many problems, especially in the area of numeric calculations, proven algorithms already exist. Thus, if one can locate a proven algorithm, it only remains to show that a program embodies the algorithm. It follows, therefore, that algorithms should be documented in a way which makes it straightforward to construct proofs showing that they are embodied in programs.

The technique used in chapter 5 for documenting intermediate stages of development goes some way to satisfying the requirements for algorithm documentation. Thus the algorithm for computing multiplication can be presented as:

$R = 0;$
$DO \ WHILE(X \ \neg= \ 0);$
$\quad /*$
$\quad MKODD$
$\quad states: Smult$
$\quad pre\text{-}MKODD(<x,,>) \triangleq x \geq 1$
$\quad post\text{-}MKODD(<x,y,r>,<x',y',r'>) \triangleq (r'+x'*y'=r+x*y) \land 1 \leq x' \leq x$
$\quad */$
$\quad /*$
$\quad MKEVEN$
$\quad states: Smult$
$\quad pre\text{-}MKEVEN(<x,,>) \triangleq x \geq 1$
$\quad post\text{-}MKEVEN(<x,y,r>,<x',y',r'>) \triangleq (r'+x'*y'=r+x*y) \land 0 \leq x' < x$
$\quad */$
$END;$

This documents the essential decisions without fixing details which may differ in different programs. Most importantly, the above presentation has been proven correct; taken as a starting point for developing a program, the need for reconstructing this argument is obviated.

Thus, given a choice of a level at which one wishes to document an algorithm, a way has been shown in which that level of abstraction can be documented and proven correct. Such a proven and documented solution is then a reference point for alternative programs. The proofs of such programs need only show that the extra (ordering) detail matches the implicitly defined portions of the solution.

In most textbooks, algorithms are documented in some programming language (e.g. MIX in Knuth(68)). In an increasing number of cases such algorithms are supported by proofs. But, if one wishes to make changes to the given program, one must revise the whole proof. Thus a change as simple as the inversion of two assignment statements may force the discarding of much of the work which has been done in developing and proving the algorithm correct. Documentation of something more abstract than the final program provides a better starting point for program development.

For example, a large class of in-place sorting algorithms can be expressed by:

DO WHILE(term ¬= final);
　/*
　BODY
　pre-BODY(σ) ≜ *term(σ)* ≠ *final*
　post-BODY(σ,σ') ≜ *is-permutation(σ',σ)* ∧ *term(σ')<term(σ)*
　*/
END;

Specification

PRIMES
type: Nat → *Nat-list*
post-PRIMES(n,nl) ≜
　elemsnl = {i | 1≤i≤n ∧ is-prime(i)} ∧ is-ordered(nl)

Decomposition

Sprimes = Bool-list

PRIMES ≜
　/*
　　GEN
　　states: Sprimes
　　type: Nat →
　　post-GEN(,n,s') ≜ **len**s'=n ∧ (**A**i∈{1:n})(s'(i)↔is-prime(i))
　*/
　/*
　　OUTP
　　states: Sprimes
　　type: → *Nat-list*
　　post-OUTP(s,,nl) ≜
　　　elemsnl={i | 1≤i≤**len**s ∧ s(i)} ∧ is-ordered(nl)
　*/

Figure 26   Primes Program

As an illustration of how decomposition can be checked by the rules given, an example is introduced which uses notation explained in chapter 9. The specification of a primes program is given in fig. 26. Intuitively, the post-condition requires that the elements in the output list are exactly the primes between *1* and *n* and that the list is ordered. The development chooses a state which is a list of Boolean values. The decomposition is then into operations to generate such a list, corresponding to whether the appropriate index is a prime or not, and to output a list of natural numbers governed by this state. Even though the notation is as yet unexplained, it is possible to follow a correctness argument for this decomposition. Consulting fig. 17, *da* and *db* are vacuously true. Rule *ra* becomes:

$$post\text{-}GEN(,n,s_2) \land post\text{-}OUTP(s_2,,nl) \Rightarrow post\text{-}PRIMES(n,nl)$$

or:

lens_2=n $\land$ (**A**$i\epsilon\{1:n\}$)($s_2(i)\Leftrightarrow is\text{-}prime(i)$) $\land$
    elemsnl={i | $1\leq i\leq$**len**s_2 $\land$ $s_2(i)$} $\land$ *is-ordered(nl)*
        $\Rightarrow$ **elems**nl={i | $1\leq i\leq n$ $\land$ *is-prime(i)*} $\land$ *is-ordered(nl)*

which follows by substituting equal expressions.

★   ★   ★

The use of post-conditions is not a complete solution. In the case of functions, it is observed in chapter 3 that documenting an explicit function rather than a post-condition is acceptable in certain circumstances because function definitions can be easily manipulated. The ease of manipulation comes from the fact that such definitions are mathematical objects. With programs the presence of the notion of time significantly complicates rules for showing that programs are equivalent. A key requirement, then, in documenting algorithms is to minimize the commitment to the order in which things are done. There are programming language proposals which move in this direction. For many simple cases a ***multiple assignment*** construct like:

$$X,Y = X*X, Y/2$$

will help; E.W.Dijkstra has proposed the **guarded command** (see Dijkstra(75)) as a further way of leaving ordering open. But this is still not enough. There are cases where the order of the iterations of a loop is irrelevant. All that is necessary is to specify that the loop is executed once for each possible value of the control variable. For example, the multiplication problem can be solved with:

$Z = 0;$
for all C in 1 to X do
   $Z = Z+Y;$

or the factorial problem with:

$FN = 1;$
for all C in 1 to N do
   $FN = FN*C;$

As before, there are advantages in avoiding the commitment to ordering. Firstly, such algorithms can be proven correct (the rules involve set notation and are not presented here). Secondly, these abstract versions provide documentation for a class of programs which can easily be shown to satisfy the requirements of the algorithm.

*Predicate Transformers

Most of the literature on program correctness proofs uses post-conditions of the final state only (e.g. Alagic(78)). This (optional) section compares the approach of Hoare(69) and Dijkstra(76) with the post-conditions of state pairs used in this book.

Dijkstra(76) uses *predicate transformers* to define the semantics of programs. The meaning of program statements is given by showing how they transform a post-condition into a necessary and sufficient pre-condition. Thus the weakest pre-condition to ensure that a final state has a given value, might be expressed:

$wp(X:=10, X=10) \leftrightarrow$ **TRUE**
$wp(X:=X+1, 0<X) \leftrightarrow 0 \le X$

Notice that the post-condition is a predicate of the final state only. Thus:

pre-OP: State $\rightarrow$ Bool
post-OP: State $\rightarrow$ Bool

The relation between predicate transformers and the approach taken in this book can be compared by considering the sets of rules used for proving results about, say, *IF* statements. Simplifying to post-conditions of single states, the rules of fig. 19 become:
For:

OP ≜ IF e THEN OP1 ELSE OP2

to be correct, show:

da. pre-OP $\land$ e $\Rightarrow$ pre-OP1
db. pre-OP $\land$ ~e $\Rightarrow$ pre-OP2
ra. post-OP1 $\Rightarrow$ post-OP
rb. post-OP2 $\Rightarrow$ post-OP

For any operation, one can assume the predicates are related by:

pre-S $\Rightarrow$ wp(S,post-S)

Are the conditions *da—rb* sufficient to ensure this for conditional statements?
To prove this, assume:

pre-OP

da and *db* show:

(e $\Rightarrow$ pre-OP1) $\land$ (~e $\Rightarrow$ pre-OP2)

Using the relation of the predicates for *OP1* and *OP2*, gives:

$(e \Rightarrow wp(OP1,post\text{-}OP1)) \wedge (\sim e \Rightarrow wp(OP2,post\text{-}OP2))$

There is a general rule for predicate transformers that:

$(p \Rightarrow q) \Rightarrow (wp(S,p) \Rightarrow wp(S,q))$

Using this with *ra* and *rb* gives:

$(e \Rightarrow wp(OP1,post\text{-}OP)) \wedge (\sim e \Rightarrow wp(OP2,post\text{-}OP))$

But, the definition of the predicate transformer for conditional statements is exactly:

$wp(IF\ e\ THEN\ OP1\ ELSE\ OP2,\ post\text{-}OP) \Leftrightarrow$
$\quad (e \Rightarrow wp(OP1,post\text{-}OP)) \wedge (\sim e \Rightarrow wp(OP2,post\text{-}OP))$

Thus it can be seen that, under assumptions *da—rb*, *pre-OP* is sufficient to ensure *post-OP* for conditional statements. In fact the *r* rules cover the problem that the post-conditions of the statements used within the conditional statement do not match those of the overall statement and the *d* rules separate the checks on the pre-conditions.

★   ★   ★

The more important part of the comparison of the two methods concerns their use in program specification and development. One effect of using post-conditions of final states only is the need to use free variables. Thus **greatest common divisor** (cf. exercise 4.4) can be specified by:

OP such that
$x{=}x_0 \wedge y{=}y_0 \Rightarrow wp(OP,\ x{=}gcd(x_0,y_0))$
where:
$gcd(a,b) \triangleq \ldots$

The names x_0 and y_0 are introduced in order to be able to relate the values in the final state to those in the initial state. The manipulation of such variables can become difficult. Moreover, there is a temptation to specify programs which do not change their input values simply to avoid this problem. (Strictly, it is also necessary to prove that they do not change. This is avoided in Dijkstra(76) —pp65-66— by reasoning about *for fixed X ... .*)

To show the sort of problems which occur with the manipulation of the free variables, consider the development of:

OP such that:
$x{=}x_0 \wedge y{=}y_0 \Rightarrow wp(OP,\ z{=}x_0{*}y_0)$

to:

IF $x{\geq}0$ *THEN OP1 ELSE OP2*

where:

$$x{=}x_1 \wedge y{=}y_1 \wedge x{\geq}0 \Rightarrow wp(OP1, z{=}x_1{*}y_1)$$
$$x{=}x_2 \wedge y{=}y_2 \wedge x{<}0 \Rightarrow wp(OP2, z{=}x_2{*}y_2)$$

(Different names have been used for the free variables to make clear what manipulations are required.) Using the predicate transformer rule for conditional statement shown above, gives:

$$wp(OP, z{=}x_0{*}y_0) \Leftrightarrow$$
$$(x{\geq}0 \Rightarrow wp(OP1, z{=}x_0{*}y_0)) \wedge (x{<}0 \Rightarrow wp(OP2, z{=}x_0{*}y_0))$$

But what is:

$$wp(OP1, z{=}x_0{*}y_0)$$

Remembering which variables are free this can be seen to be:

$$x{=}x_0 \wedge y{=}y_0 \wedge x{\geq}0$$

More difficult is the development of:

OP such that:
$$n{=}n_0 \Rightarrow wp(OP,fn{=}n_0!)$$

to:

FN:=1; OP2

where:

$$n{=}n_1 \wedge fn{=}fn_1 \Rightarrow wp(OP2, fn{=}fn_1{*}n_1!)$$

The predicate transformer rule for sequential composition is:

$$wp(OP1;OP2, post\text{-}OP) \triangleq wp(OP1,wp(OP2,post\text{-}OP))$$

Thus:

$$wp(FN{:=}1;OP2, fn{=}n_0!) \Leftrightarrow wp(FN{:=}1,wp(OP2,fn{=}n_0!))$$

How to proceed? Is the next step:

$$wp(FN{:=}1, n{=}n_0 \wedge fn{=}fn_0 \wedge fn_0{=}1)$$

Can this be simplified by omitting the free variables? It appears that the documentation by predicate transformer does not work well for components which must be used in various contexts. The advantage of the predicate transformer rules is their brevity; it would, however, appear that the rules for predicates of state pairs fit better into a development situation.

The above comparison considers the two approaches purely formally. In fact, both methods lend themselves to less formal arguments. Dijkstra uses arguments like **preservation of relation p**. Chapter 5 uses **maintaining the value of expression ...** . Given such rigorous arguments, one should choose the style best fitted to recording the specifications of operations. As is by now clear, post-conditions of state pairs are preferred here. Such specifications can define a range of results, constrain values not to change, or define programs which overwrite values.

It is interesting to note that ALPHARD (see Wulf(76)), the work on *recovery blocks* (see Randell(78)), and some proof checking systems (e.g. EFFIGY—Hantler(75)) all rely on predicates of a pair of states.

Part B

DATA TYPES IN PROGRAM DEVELOPMENT

For programs which are concerned with numbers, it has been shown how precise specifications can be written. Precision is achieved by the use of logic notation. There are three major ways in which conciseness can be achieved: axioms, inverses and recursive functions. Considering the relevance to data processing specifications, axioms are the least useful. The use of inverses is more promising: there is a class of data processing problems which is amenable to this approach. For example, information storage and retrieval problems can be specified by defining that the information retrieved must correspond to that inserted most recently. Specifications which are based on recursive functions are also useful (see for example the *bill of materials* discussed below).

Something, however, is missing. Without some tools to cope with the complexity which results from the structure of the data involved, specifications for data processing problems will be neither concise nor capable of being manipulated. What this part of the book shows is that using the right tools for describing data again makes it possible to write concise specifications and to prove implementations of such specifications correct.

Reverting to the topic of specifications, the class of programs for which formal specifications can be written is now extended from numerical problems to problems of handling non-numerical data (e.g. strings) and on to data-processing problems. The key to this extension is the use of abstract data types (see chapter 7). An ***abstract data type*** is one which cannot be directly implemented in a normal programming language. Tools for defining abstract data types are sets (chapter 8), lists (chapter 9), mappings (chapter 12) and abstract syntax (chapter 14). Abstract data types can be used to shorten the descriptions of data processing problems; a far shorter and more manipulable specification can be written than if it were based on data types available on the machine.

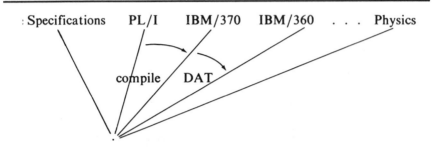

Figure 27   Spectrum of Abstraction

One way of visualizing the purpose of this part of the book is to consider a spectrum of abstraction as shown in fig. 27. On such a spectrum one could place programs written in high level programming languages at some mid-point. The objects (e.g. arrays, structures) which justify this placing are eliminated by a compilation process which creates machine code. Machine code can only use the concrete data types built in the machine architecture, and would thus be towards one end of the spectrum. It is possible to go further in this direction; if the machine supports virtual addressing then there is a dynamic address translation which causes this to work on a more basic machine. This part shows the benefit of moving in the other direction. That is, it shows how using data types more abstract than those available in programming languages can facilitate shorter and clearer specifications.

The form of development which creates realizations of abstract data types is called ***refinement***; this is discussed in chapters 10 and 11.

This part of the book introduces the aspects of the rigorous method related to specification by abstract objects and refinement proofs. This is probably the most important material in the book. Optional chapters (13, 15 and 16) go deeper into aspects of abstract data types. Optional sections discuss induction on data types.

Chapter 7

ON DATA TYPES

The following example shows the effect of data abstraction. A standard data processing problem in the manufacturing industries is **parts explosion**. The task is to determine, for some product which is to be manufactured, what parts will be involved. A database, called a **bill of materials**, is created which reflects the composition of all of the parts used by the manufacturer. A bill of materials stores, for each part number, the set of part numbers which are its components. A product also has a part number so the bill of materials database could be used to find the components of a product. But these components are not, necessarily, basic parts. Thus the interesting aspect of the problem is to describe the way in which the explosion goes on using the database until basic parts are found. Fig. 28 illustrates a possible bill of materials.

---

p1 ———————> { p2,p3,p7 }
p2 ———————> { p4,p5 }
p4 ———————> { }
p5 ———————> { p3,p4 }
p3 ———————> { p4,p6,p7 }
p6 ———————> { }
p7 ———————> { }

Figure 28   Bill of Materials

The non-basic part numbers are linked by an arrow to the set of part numbers which are required in their construction; the basic part numbers are linked to empty sets. Using this particular bill of materials, part number *p1* could be shown to require the following set of part numbers (both basic parts and sub-assemblies are included):

{ *p1, p2, p3, p4, p5, p6, p7* }

while the explosion of *p3* yields:

{ *p3, p4, p6, p7* }

But how is the specification to be written for the whole explosion problem? The data object depicted in fig. 28 is a mapping to sets of part numbers. This is written in formulae as:

Bom = Part-no → Part-no-set

The reader should not have any difficulty understanding the type clause:

expl: Bom Part-no → Part-no-set

That is, the function *expl* creates a set of part numbers from a given bill of materials and a part number to start the explosion. At present the details of the following definition are not important (the meaning of the notation is covered in later chapters) but the reader should note that *expl* is a recursive function and that *bom* is being used like a function (i.e. *bom(p)*):

$$expl(bom,p) \triangleq \{p\} \cup \textbf{union} \ \{expl(bom,c) \mid c\epsilon bom(p)\}$$

Note the brevity of this specification. This is achieved by judicious choice of the data types. The ones chosen match the problem not the implementation. The alternative is to specify the problem in terms of machine data types. Bill of materials information could be included in a database stored on some backing storage. The data types might involve disk addresses, chains of pointers etc. A specification in these terms would be long, opaque and completely beyond the scope of any manipulation.

The specification is not itself an implementation. This fits exactly the approach taken to specifications throughout this book. A propei separation of concerns is to specify in the specification, and undertake design only after the specification is clear. But there is a need to say something about how such design is performed. Chapters 10 and 11 discuss the problem of proving such implementations correct.

* * *

Before coming to the definition of data types, it is necessary to discuss the concept itself. One possible definition of a data type is a set of values. This approach has been common for some time but appears to ignore the essential fact that the usefulness of a data type comes from the manipulations which can be performed with it. Furthermore, two entirely different sets of operations could be associated with the same set of values and create, what would intuitively be viewed as, two distinct data types. A second definition of a data type might, therefore, require that both operations and values are considered.

The view which is adopted here goes further: data types are characterized by their operations alone. This approach is adopted partly to emphasize the way that representations of values can be hidden.

Consider the binary arithmetic of a computer. The data type can be called binary words. Clearly, what one wants to do with binary words is to manipulate them. Typical manipulations might be addition, subtraction etc. Such operators take two values of the type and compute another (binary word) value. Most programmers know how binary words are represented in their machine (e.g. *two's complement* form) but it is not necessary to know this in order to use the data type. The reason for this is that there are instructions for taking binary words and converting them to other data types; in particular, there are instructions for converting them into a printable, decimal, notation.

To return to the view of a data type as being characterized by its operations, the essential information about the operations is their interrelationships. Thus if *1* is added to *2* a value is created which can be printed out as *3*. Thus, the values which are of concern with data types are those of the domains and ranges of operations which convert to or from that data type. The data type itself is like a black box and its representation is of no concern to its user. This situation is pictured in fig. 29. These diagrams are used in Goguen(75). The ovals indicate data types and the arrows their operators. Arrows coming from a data type indicate operand types and the type of the result is shown at the head of the arrow.

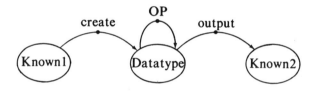

Figure 29   Data Type

If data types are characterized by their operations, one cannot talk about machine data types as though they were integers. Apart from the differences with regard to overflow, one must fix the set of operations. Starting with, say, the binary word data type with addition and subtraction operations, the data type which is similar but has the further operation of integer division is clearly an extension of the original. They are not precisely the same data type because their sets of operations differ. And yet for most purposes they would share one name: binary word. In most of this book, this looseness is tolerated, but when being very formal, the latter data type is spoken of as an *extension* of the former. The reader will see that the whole of part A was concerned with extending·given data types. This part of the book has to address the problem of defining completely new data types. Before coming to this topic in detail, the familiar concept of arrays is used to discuss data types more fully.

Arrays

The programs in the first part of this book were concerned with integers.
To be precise, they were concerned with providing extensions (e.g. an
integer division operator) of a base data type which behaves like some
finite subset of the integers. The most basic data type had operators only
for successor, predecessor and equality test; on this, extensions (e.g.
exponentiation) were provided. From this basis *integer-arrays* can be
considered. Before coming to the subject of arrays as a data type, a
small proof about a program using arrays is given.

The problem is to locate the index of the maximum value in an array
of (machine representations of) integers. Using:

UBD(A)

to determine the upper bound of a (one-dimensional) array *A* (PL/I
definition would be *HBOUND(A,1)*) and assuming that the lower bound
is *1*, the specification might be:

Smaxar:: A: array of Int X: Nat ...

MAXAR
states: Smaxar

$pre\text{-}MAXAR(<a,>) \triangleq UBD(a) \geq 1$
$post\text{-}MAXAR(<a,>,<a',x'>) \triangleq$
   $a'=a \land x' \leq UBD(a) \land (\mathbf{A}k \epsilon \{1:UBD(a)\})(a(k) \leq a(x'))$

Writing a program to fulfil this specification is straightforward.
One such might be:

```
X = 1;
DO I = 2 BY 1 TO UBD(A);
  IF A(I)>A(X) THEN
     X = I;
END;
```

How is such a program to be proved correct? The only form of *DO*
statement discussed so far is the *WHILE* form and the simple iterative
DO/BY/TO form has been ignored. One possibility would be to translate
the given program into one using the *WHILE* form. Thus:

$X = 1;$
$I = 2;$
$DO\ WHILE\ (I{\leq}UBD(A));$
   /*
     BODY
     states: Smaxar
     $pre\text{-}BODY(<a,x,i>)\ \triangleq\ x,i{\leq}UBD(a)$
     $post\text{-}BODY(<a,x,i>,<a',x',i'>)\ \triangleq$
       $a'=a\ \wedge\ i'=i+1\ \wedge$
       if $a(i)>a(x)$ **then** $x'=i$ **else** $x'=x$
   */
$END;$

A proof of the correctness of this program can be constructed using the rules for initialized *WHILE* (see fig. 21). With:

$so\text{-}far(<a,x,i>,<a',x',i'>)\ \triangleq$
   $a'=a\ \wedge\ x'{\leq}UBD(a)\ \wedge\ (\mathbf{A}k\epsilon\{1{:}i'{-}1\})(a(k){\leq}a(x'))$
$pre\text{-}LOOP(<a,x,i>)\ \triangleq\ i{\leq}UBD(a)+1\ \wedge\ x{\leq}UBD(a)$
$term(<a,\ ,i>)\ \triangleq\ UBD(a){-}(i{-}1)$

the items in the checklist of properties are easily verified.

For:

$OP\ \triangleq\ DO\ i\ =\ 1\ BY\ 1\ TO\ u;\ BODY(i);\ END;$

BODY
states: State
type: Int $\rightarrow$

to be correct, find:

pre-LOOP: State Int $\rightarrow$ *Bool*
so-far: State Int State $\rightarrow$ *Bool*

and show:

da. $pre\text{-}OP(\sigma)\ \Rightarrow\ pre\text{-}LOOP(\sigma,l)$
db. $pre\text{-}LOOP(\sigma_1,i)\ \wedge\ i{\leq}e\text{-}expr(u,\sigma_1)\ \wedge\ post\text{-}BODY(\sigma_1,i,\sigma_2)$
   $\Rightarrow\ pre\text{-}LOOP(\sigma_2,i+1)$
dc. $pre\text{-}LOOP(\sigma,i)\ \wedge\ i{\leq}e\text{-}expr(u,\sigma)\ \Rightarrow\ pre\text{-}BODY(\sigma,i)$

ra. $pre\text{-}OP(\sigma)\ \Rightarrow\ so\text{-}far(\sigma,l,\sigma)$
rb. $so\text{-}far(\sigma_1,i,\sigma_2)\ \wedge\ pre\text{-}LOOP(\sigma_2,i)\ \wedge\ i{\leq}e\text{-}expr(u,\sigma_1)$
   $\wedge\ post\text{-}BODY(\sigma_2,i,\sigma_3)$
     $\Rightarrow\ so\text{-}far(\sigma_1,i+1,\sigma_3)$
rc. $so\text{-}far(\sigma_1,i,\sigma_2)\ \wedge\ pre\text{-}LOOP(\sigma_2,i)\ \wedge\ i=e\text{-}expr(u,\sigma_1)+1$
   $\Rightarrow\ post\text{-}OP(\sigma_1,\sigma_2)$

Figure 30   Rules for DO/BY/TO Iteration

But it is clear that it should not be necessary to translate programs in order to discuss their correctness. Furthermore, it can be argued that the *DO/BY/TO* form of iteration is a natural way of manipulating arrays and is thus more likely to be used correctly than the *WHILE* form. Therefore, a set of properties for reasoning about the *DO/BY/TO* form is presented. The rules are given in fig. 30, and a corresponding picture in fig. 31. The validity of these rules depends on a number of assumptions about the way the *DO* loop is used. Specifically, the rules assume that the **control variable** of the loop is a **locally bound constant**. That is, the variable whose identifier occurs after *DO* can be referred to, but not assigned to, within the loop. This is, in fact, the standard meaning of iterative loops in a number of programming languages (e.g. ALGOL 68). Using PL/I it is necessary to impose a discipline on the use of the control variable. (It would be possible to give a set of general rules which did not require this restriction. They would, however, be more difficult to use. Furthermore, preventing assignment to the control variable within the loop will make programs clearer and thus more likely to be correct.)

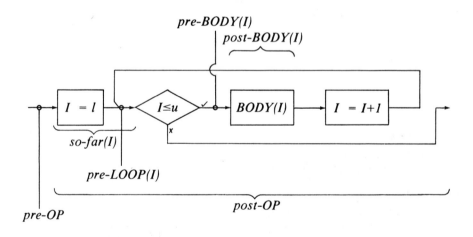

Figure 31   Picture of DO/BY/TO Iteration

There are several things to be noticed about these rules. Firstly, the read-only nature of the control variable has been shown by using it as an argument to *BODY*. Secondly, the limit expression, *u*, is evaluated in the initial state; and finally, there are no termination conditions to be proved.
   Using:

$MAXAR \triangleq$
  $X = 1;$
  /*
    OP
    states: Smaxar
    $pre\text{-}OP(<a,x>) \triangleq UBD(a){\geq}1 \land x{=}1$
    $post\text{-}OP(<a,>,<a',x'>) \triangleq a'{=}a \land (\textbf{A}k\epsilon\{1{:}UBD(a)\})(a(k){\leq}a(x'))$
  */

$OP \triangleq$
  $DO\ I = 2\ BY\ 1\ TO\ UBD(A);$
  /*
    BODY
    states: Smaxar
    $pre\text{-}BODY(<a,x>,i) \triangleq x,i{\leq}UBD(a)$
    $post\text{-}BODY(<a,x>,i,<a',x'>) \triangleq$
       $a'{=}a \land (\textbf{if}\ a(i){>}a(x)\ \textbf{then}\ x'{=}i\ \textbf{else}\ x'{=}x)$
  */

the proof can be constructed with:

$pre\text{-}LOOP(<a,x>,i) \triangleq x{\leq}UBD(a) \land i{\leq}UBD(a){+}1$

$so\text{-}far(<a,x>,i,<a',x'>) \triangleq a'{=}a \land x'{\leq}UBD(a) \land (\textbf{A}k\epsilon\{1{:}i{-}1\})(a(k){\leq}a(x'))$

★ ★ ★

Having discussed how programs using arrays can be proved correct, the array data type itself is examined more closely. The first observation that can be made is that the integer-array data type depends on the integer data type. This dependence is in the sense that the former data type can only be used in a context where the latter is available. In programs, array elements are accessed by referring to the array name followed by a subscript in an expression, e.g.:

$J = ...A(I)...$

Such a subscripted reference extracts an element of the integer data type from one of integer-array data type. Similarly:

$B(I) = ...$

changes the value of a variable of an integer-array data type using one of integer data type. Perhaps this would be clearer if explicit functions were used for converting the values. For instance, using:

access-array: Int-array Subscript $\rightarrow$ *Int*

then

$...access\text{-}array(a,i)...$

could be used. Similarly:

change-array: Int-array Subscript Int $\rightarrow$ *Int-array* could be used to create new array values. Notice that the representation of *Int-array* is completely hidden. In terms of the functions, only *access-array* and *change-array* need be aware of such issues as the order in which array elements are stored.

It is also important to consider how the arguments about the arrays were constructed. In the proofs above, the arguments are informal because the properties of arrays are well-known. If, however, a new data type were being formally introduced one would have to document the properties of its operators. Using the functional form shown above, one would have properties like:

access-array(change-array(a,i,v),i) = *v*

Interpreted in terms of states and operations this would define that the value of the *ith* element of an array immediately after assigning the value *v* to the *ith* position is *v*. Similarly;

i≠j ⟹ *access-array(change-array(a,i,v),j)=access-array(a,j)*

can be interpreted as stating that values other than the *ith* are not affected by assignment to the *ith* position. So far so good, but this is not enough. It is also necessary to constrain the indices used by either operation to be within a valid range.

It is not necessary, at present, to pursue these topics in more detail. Using integer-arrays, a familiar concept, it has been shown how a new data type is dependent on existing ones. The subject of how to define a new data type is addressed in the next section.

One final point can be made about data types in general based on the specific discussion of arrays in this section. What has been discussed here is integer-arrays. One could also have arrays of (machine representations of) real numbers or character strings. There is thus a general concept of forming an array from other data types. Arrays are not alone in this property. There are many similarities between, say, the data type array of integers and that of array of reals. It is therefore useful to think of array as a **parameterized data type**. That is, given some other data type *x*, one can form a data type *array of x*.

Extensions and New Data Types

There is an important difference between providing an extension of an existing data type and defining an entirely new data type. The extensions to the (machine representations of) integers each introduced new operators and these were defined, prior to realization, in two ways. Some new operators (e.g. subtraction, square root) were characterized in terms of their inverses; others (e.g. factorial) by axioms. It was also mentioned earlier that operations on more complex base types can be characterized by recursive functions.

How is one to define a new data type (e.g. *Bom* in the *bill of materials* problem)? If it is new, then there are no existing operators in terms of which inverses can be expressed. The possibility of providing an axiomatic specification is open and must be discussed further. There is also the possibility of providing a *constructive specification*; it is this approach on which most time is spent in the current book.

When an operator is characterized by a recursive function, the idea is that its effect is shown by an equivalent, but possibly inefficient, way of computing the result. Such a specification is intended to state what the result should be and not to prescribe how it should be computed. The recursive function is a convenient definition because it is easy to reason about and can thus be used in a correctness argument for the eventual realization. Similar observations are true of a constructive specification of a new data type. A constructive specification of a new data type provides a way of determining what the effects of its operators are. It is likely to be inefficient in the sense that if a realization was built in the same way then the operators would take a long time to compute. Lastly, the constructive specification uses mathematical concepts. Since these are tractable, it is possible to use the constructive specification to prove a realization correct.

Remember that a data type is taken to be characterized by its operators. A constructive specification of a new data type has to show how to derive the results of all of its (basic) operators. Once the basic type has been defined, extensions can be specified using either inverses or the constructive specification itself. Thus the operation for finding the index of the largest element in an array is an extension of the basic array operations which are specified in the previous section by an implicit specification.

But the question of on what to base the constructive specifications is still open. A number of mathematical concepts can be employed. The concept of sets is an invaluable aid in defining a data type none of whose operators rely on order. The concept of mapping (finite function) is the cornerstone of constructive specifications of data types whose operators use keys to store and retrieve information. These, and other concepts, are introduced below. A tool kit of mathematical concepts is built up. The data types are abstract with respect to the data types of the familiar programming languages. Although PL/I, for example, offers the programmer an array data type which is an abstraction from the (linear) machine storage, it does not go far enough in offering the abstractions required for (constructive) specifications. This, along with the inability to handle implicit specifications, is ground for rejecting programming languages as a tool for writing specifications of the problems tackled in this book.

A new data type, then, is one which is not directly available on the machine. For this reason it is frequently referred to as an *abstract data type*.

★ ★ ★

There is some danger when writing constructive specifications that the specification becomes too like a possible realization. The examples given below avoid this danger, but some specific observations on checking for, and handling, the situation are given in chapter 15. It is, partly, the danger of being over-specific in constructive specifications which makes it attractive to employ axiomatic specifications. Such specifications are referred to as *implicit specifications* of data types. The basic idea is that a specification of a data type can be given by providing axioms which interrelate its operators. The axioms, or accepted statements, then provide a basis for reasoning about uses of the operators. They can also be used as checks to be made of any putative realization of the operators of the data type. For the array example given in the previous section, the rules relating *access-array* and *change-array* are an indication of the sort of axioms which would be required. Axiomatic specifications are certainly attractive in some ways and chapter 16 is devoted to them. They are, however, difficult to construct for complex data types and it is for this reason that constructive specifications are given more prominence in this book.

Models of Data Types

Given a constructive specification of a data type, the next task is to find and prove correct a realization. Here, *realization* is being used as the general term for providing something more concrete which fulfils an abstract specification. Specifically, the term *model* will be used when a realization of a data type is being discussed.

Where a data type is available in a programming language, it will have a number of given operators. If a problem specification requires one of these operators, no work is required in realizing the specification. If, however, a new operator is required (an extension of the data type) the specification must be used to govern a decomposition process which develops a program realization. An entirely new (abstract) data type will not be present in the language; all of its operators will be new. The constructive specification will, in this case, define acceptable realizations. Because such a realization will have to work on the more basic data types of the programming language, it is referred to as a model of the (abstract) data type.

Given a constructive specification, how does one prove a model correct? The model is more concrete in the sense that it has more detail than the abstraction; it must first be proved *adequate* in the sense that it must be possible to represent every value of the abstraction. The remainder of the proof concerns the domains and results of the individual operators and standard sets of rules are provided to check this.

It is important to remember that the constructive specification is a specification and not a proposal for implementation strategy, just as the recursive function definition of Fibonacci series was not a good strategy for writing a program.

Summary

Consider the example of integer-arrays. It has been shown how the introduction of a new data type differs from the extension of an existing data type. A point was made of hiding the representation of the array data type by considering the operations. Thus, only the realizations of the operators of the new data type are concerned with the chosen representation. A new data type can be characterized by a constructive or an implicit specification. It is the former which is of most concern in this book. If the data type is not already part of the language, it is referred to as *abstract* and the last section of this chapter has introduced the problem of finding models and proving them correct.

For a more algebraic approach to data types, the reader is recommended to consult Burstall(77) or Goguen(76).

Chapter 8

SET NOTATION

This chapter introduces the first of the groups of notation which are used in this book for specifying abstract data types. The notation of set theory is presented first because it is, nowadays, widely known. If the reader is familiar with set theory, the section Notation will take only a few minutes to understand; the examples of applying the notation should, however, be followed in detail. This is the whole point of the chapter: set notation makes it possible to write some specifications briefly and clearly. If the reader has difficulty with the description of set notation given here, an introductory text like Lipschutz(64) is recommended.

Before coming to the description of the notation itself, a simple example will be presented. Suppose a program were required which kept track of the names of the students in some given classroom. Various ways of changing and interrogating the recorded data might be required. These would presumably be realized as procedures but they can be thought of as operators on a new data type called *Studc*. Thus the specification of the procedures would rely on a class of states:

Studc

If all the possible student names are in a set called:

Student-name

then the types of the operations can be recorded, using the notation introduced in chapter 4, as follows. The operation which initializes the class status is of the type:

INIT
states: Studc

In other words, it updates the state and requires no arguments to do this; furthermore it delivers no results. The operation for recording that a student has entered the class is of type:

ENTER
states: Studc
type: Student-name $\rightarrow$

that is, it takes an argument of a student name and delivers no result. The operation, which for a given student name returns an answer indicating whether he is in class or not, is of type:

IS-PRESENT
states: Studc
type: Student-name → *Bool*

The specification is proceeding as was foreseen in the last chapter: the required procedures are being viewed as operators on a new data type called *Studc*; these operators enable the data type to be viewed as a black box in the sense that its representation is not exposed. But, the question of how the intended function of the procedures is to be specified is still open.

Consider, for a moment, how the state of the eventual program will be realized. One might choose an array of character strings to hold the student names and an index variable which records the number of entries in the array. Insertion could then be programmed by inserting the new name in the next position of the array and increasing the index by *1*. Removal of a name would be a little more tedious because some other name would have to be moved down into the array position vacated by the removed name. The operation which tests whether a name is in the current status would involve a linear search of the array. But if this last operation were required very frequently, it might be necessary to store the names in an ordered list and program *IS-PRESENT* using a **binary search**. A different approach might be required if many class status variables were required and the maximum number of potential students were high; in this case a **linked-list** approach could be used to avoid reserving maximum size arrays for every class.

Obviously a range of possible representations exists. The point is that, in the specification, it is required to describe what should happen and postpone the design of program data structures. What, then, is to be the description of *Studc* in the specification? The general approach, when faced with a choice of possibilities for implementation, is to find an abstraction of them. That is, a constructive specification of the data type *Studc* is given which possesses only those properties necessary to specify the required results. In this case, the only fact of importance is whether a name is present or not and an appropriate abstraction would be a set of student names. Thus, members of *Studc* are to be defined as objects which can contain a set of values where any of those values must be chosen from *Student-name*. Such a definition is written:

Studc = *Student-name-set*

The suffix -*set*, and the set notation which follows, are defined in the next section.

Notice that *Studc* has been defined with an equals sign. Until now .:: has been used in the definition of states, but in the case of single element states this leads to redundant pointed brackets around single identifiers. The use of equality defines the state without the requirement to use the <> brackets. (More detail on this distinction is given in chapter 14.)

The three procedures can now be specified by means of post-conditions. As earlier, these are predicates of input state, input arguments, output state, and output result. Thus for *INIT*, which takes no argument and delivers no result:

post-INIT: Studc Studc → Bool

is defined as fixing the output state to contain the empty set regardless of the input state:

post-INIT(nms,nms') ≜ *nms'* = { }

The type of *ENTER* requires a post-condition of type:

post-ENTER: Studc Student-name Studc → Bool

which is defined using set union as:

post-ENTER(nms,nm,nms') ≜ *nms'* = *nms* ∪ { *nm* }

The type of the post-condition for *IS-PRESENT* should be:

post-IS-PRESENT: Studc Student-name Studc Bool → Bool

and its definition:

post-IS-PRESENT(nms,nm,nms',b) ≜ *nms'=nms* ∧ *(b* ⇔ *nm∈nms)*

The use of a little notation has made it possible to specify the **students in classroom** problem without being concerned with details of representation for the implementation. The definition of the state alone has said much about the programs. It is the theme of this part that most problems are easy to specify and reason about if their data types are specified in terms of appropriate abstractions.

Further advantages also accrue from the use of such abstractions. It is possible to use the same abstraction for early stages of the design and this again makes reasoning easier—in particular it facilitates the proof that one step is a correct realization of its specification. Furthermore, the use of the abstraction makes it possible to delay the representation decision until enough design work has been done to support that decision.

The essential point about sets is that they are unordered collections where the only property of interest is membership. After the required notation is introduced in the next section, two sections are devoted to providing further examples of its use. Optional sections are also included on induction and the relationship between predicates and sets.

Notation

Set values may be written by explicitly enumerating their members between braces. Thus:

$$\{x_1, x_2, ...\}$$

It is important to bear in mind that neither order nor duplicates make any difference to set values. Thus:

$$\{1,2,3\} = \{3,1,2\} = \{1,2,2,3,1\}$$

although writing duplicates in set values is avoided. A special set is that with no members (the **empty set**). This is written in the obvious way:

$$\{\,\}$$

If set values could only be defined by explicit enumeration, their usefulness would be limited. Fortunately, there are other ways. Set values may be defined implicitly by giving a predicate which limits the selection of members. A notation is adopted which writes the predicate and the variable to be **bound** on the right of a vertical bar; on the left of the bar a function may be specified which is to be applied to each value satisfying the predicate: the whole expression is contained in braces. Thus:

$$\{f(x) \mid p(x)\}$$

Reading the vertical bar as *such that* provides a natural understanding. For example:

$$\{n**2 \mid 0 \leq n \leq 3\} = \{0,1,4,9\}$$
$$\{2**n \mid 0 \leq n \leq 3\} = \{1,2,4,8\}$$

A convenient abbreviation for a subset of integers is:

$$\{i:j\} = \{x \mid i \leq x \leq j\}$$

where i and j must both be integers.

The basic operation on sets is the test for membership:

$$x \in S \Leftrightarrow \textbf{TRUE} \quad \textit{if and only if } x \textit{ is a member of the set } S$$

Obvious extensions like:

$$x,y \in S \Leftrightarrow (x \in S \wedge y \in S)$$

are also used.

Using *is a member*, it is possible to define the three infix operators which yield set values.
Union:

$$S_1 \cup S_2 \triangleq \{x \mid x \in S_1 \vee x \in S_2\}$$

Intersection:

$$S_1 \cap S_2 \triangleq \{x \mid x \in S_1 \wedge x \in S_2\}$$

Difference:

$$S_1 - S_2 \triangleq \{x \mid x \in S_1 \wedge \sim(x \in S_2)\}$$

These operators are shown graphically in fig. 32. Notice that all three of these operators require sets for both operands; if an element is to be handled it must be enclosed in set braces.

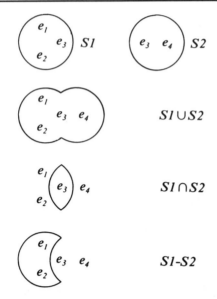

Figure 32   Set Operators

There are occasions where a value which is a set of sets should be collected into a simple set. With SS being a set of sets, the **distributed union** operator is defined:

union $SS \triangleq \{x \mid (\mathbf{E}S\epsilon SS)(x\epsilon S)\}$

Thus:

union$\{\{e_1,e_2,e_3\},\{e_3,e_4\}\} = \{e_1,e_2,e_3,e_4\}$

(Notice that this operator is written as a word rather than as some special symbol. There are languages, notably APL, where all operators are associated with special symbols. Although this can lead to some condensation of formulae, it is not attempted here because of the fact that more than one class of objects is to be considered.)

The two operators for testing whether one set is a subset or proper subset of another are defined:

$S_1 \subseteq S_2 \triangleq x\epsilon S_1 \Rightarrow x\epsilon S_2$

$S_1 \subset S_2 \triangleq S_1 \subseteq S_2 \wedge (\mathbf{E}x\epsilon S_2)(\sim(x\epsilon S_1))$

Notice that these two operators give a Boolean result. Two sets are said to be equal if they contain exactly the same elements. Thus:

$S_1{=}S_2 \triangleq x\epsilon S_1 \Leftrightarrow x\epsilon S_2$

Names have been used above for some special sets:

Bool = {**TRUE,FALSE**}
Nat   = {*1,2,...*}
Nat0 = {*0,1,2,...*}
Int   = {*...,-1,0,1,...*}

Notice that only the first of these four sets contains a finite number of elements. In the others ellipsis points are used to suggest how the enumeration should continue. The sets like *Int* are useful when defining the type clauses of functions or operations. However, most of the sets used are finite. For finite sets an operator is defined which yields the cardinality (i.e. number of elements in a set). This is written:

card*S*

Notice:

card{ } = *0*

   A diagram can be used to indicate the types of the set operators—see fig. 33.

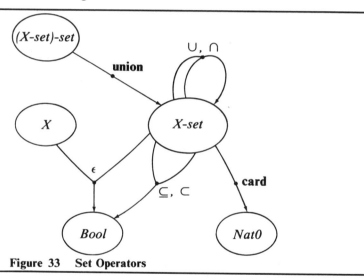

Figure 33   Set Operators

   The notation used in the **students in classroom** problem for defining objects as sets can now be formally explained. Given some set, say *S*, writing:

Ob = *S-set*

defines the class of *Ob* to be all subsets of *S*. Therefore, any object in *Ob* is a subset of the set *S*. Thus:

*ob*ε*Ob* ⟹ *ob*⊆*S*·

In other words *ob* is a set all of whose members belong to *S*. Thus:

{ }ε*Ob* ∧ *S*ε*Ob*

(Readers familiar with set theory will recognize the *-set* as a way of defining power sets.)

Exercise 8.1:   Determine the truth of the following expressions:

a) $7 \in \{3:7\}$
b) $\{4:3\} = \{\}$
c) $25 \in \{x**3 \mid x\in\{1,5,25\}\}$
d) $Nat0 \subseteq Int$
e) $Int \subset Int$
f) $Bool \subseteq Nat0$

Exercise 8.2:   Write the values of:

a) $Nat \cap \{x**2 \mid x\in\{1,3.5,e,\pi\}\}$
b) $\{x**2 \mid x\in Nat\} \cap \{1:20\}$
c) $\{x**2 \mid x\in Nat \wedge 1\le(x**2)\le20\}$
d) $\{x \mid x\in Nat0 \wedge is\text{-}even(x)\} \cup \{x \mid x\in Nat0 \wedge is\text{-}odd(x)\}$
e) **card** $\{x**2 \mid x\in\{-1:+1\}\}$
f) **union** $\{\{1,2\},\{3\},\{3,4\}\}$

Exercise 8.3:   Write expressions for:
a) The integers between *100* and *200* which are exactly divisible by *9*.
b) The set of prime numbers between *200* and *300*.
c) The subset relationships between *Nat*, *Int*, and *Nat0*.

Exercise 8.4:   Check the following useful laws. If they are not obvious, try to construct arguments for their correctness:

a) $S\cup\{\} = S$
b) $S\cap\{\} = \{\}$
c) $\{\} \subseteq S$
d) $S_1\subseteq S_2 \wedge S_2\subseteq S_1 \Rightarrow S_1=S_2$
e) $S_1\subseteq S_2 \wedge S_2\subseteq S_3 \Rightarrow S_1\subseteq S_3$
f) $(x \in \{y \mid p(y)\}) \Leftrightarrow p(x)$
g) $S_1\subseteq S_2 \Leftrightarrow (S_1\text{-}S_2 = \{\})$

Exercise 8.5:   Write out (cf. exercise 2.2):
a) Commutative laws for union and intersection
b) Associative laws for union and intersection
c) Distributive laws for union and intersection

Exercise 8.6:   Define a predicate:

is-disj: Object-set Object-set → Bool

which yields **TRUE** if the two sets have no common elements (i.e. they are disjoint).

It is now time to return to the ***students in classroom*** example and review it in the light of the notation description above. When first presented, the operations had no pre-conditions; since this might make their implementation rather difficult, pre-conditions are now given. Furthermore, there was no operation which foresaw the possibility of a student leaving a classroom (such things do happen); this is now included. The total specification is shown in fig. 34.

$Studc = Student\text{-}name\text{-}set$

INIT
states: Studc
$post\text{-}INIT(nms,nms') \triangleq nms' = \{\ \}$

ENTER
states: Studc
type: Student-name $\rightarrow$
$pre\text{-}ENTER(nms,nm) \triangleq \sim(nm \epsilon nms)$
$post\text{-}ENTER(nms,nm,nms') \triangleq nms' = nms \cup \{nm\}$

EXIT
states: Studc
type: Student-name $\rightarrow$
$pre\text{-}EXIT(nms,nm) \triangleq nm \epsilon nms$
$post\text{-}EXIT(nms,nm,nms') \triangleq nms' = nms\text{-}\{nm\}$

IS-PRESENT
states: Studc
type: Student-name $\rightarrow$ *Bool*
$post\text{-}IS\text{-}PRESENT(nms,nm,nms',b) \triangleq nms'=nms \land (b \leftrightarrow nm \epsilon nms)$

Figure 34   Specification of Students in Classroom Problem

It is important that the reader appreciates what has, and what has not, been determined by such a specification. Notice, firstly, that the data type is closed by its operators in the sense that nothing of its internal representation can be seen (i.e. the data type is a black box). Although a constructive specification has been given, this fixes only the external behavior of the operators. This point is enlarged upon when realizations are considered. Secondly, the pre-conditions have dictated over what range the operators must conform to the post-conditions: outside the specified range, the result of the operators is completely open. The topic of widening pre-conditions is deferred to chapter 22.

⋆   ⋆   ⋆

There are two more points which should be reviewed in connection with the set notation; one is a minor extension to the function notation and the other concerns inductive proofs about sets.

If, in the definition of a function, some computed value is required more than once, it is possible to introduce an abbreviation by using **let**. Thus:

$f(x) \triangleq$
> **let** $t = x + 7$
> $t + 2\ast\ast t$

is an abbreviation for:

$f(x) \triangleq (x+7) + 2\ast\ast(x+7)$

The **let** is introducing a locally named constant. Now, suppose it is required to write a function which applies a simple calculation on every member of a set. It is possible to use the **let** notation and write:

$applys(S,calc) \triangleq$
> **if** $S=\{ \}$ **then** $\{ \}$
> **else** (**let** $e \epsilon S$
> $\{calc(e)\} \cup applys(S-\{e\},calc))$

That is, a recursive function is defined which on each use (with a non-empty set) chooses one element of S and applies the calculation *calc* to it; the result of this calculation is then joined to the set resulting from a recursive call of *applys* with the chosen element of S removed. In this simple case it is possible to write the function more succinctly as:

$applys(S,calc) \triangleq \{calc(e) \mid e \epsilon S\}$

But this is not always possible. One function used below is:

$maxs: Int\text{-}set \rightarrow Int$
$maxs(S) \triangleq$
> **let** $e \epsilon S$
> **if** **card**$S=1$ **then** e
> **else** $max(e,maxs(S-\{e\}))$

*Inductive Proofs on Sets

As with the discussion of mathematical induction, the purpose here is to clarify the foundation of things which are done less formally below. With regard to reasoning about sets, it is worth reconsidering the earlier inductive proofs. In chapter 3, it is shown how a proof, that some property holds for all members of *Nat0*, could be constructed. The key is to prove a basis for the value 0 and to show that the assumption (induction hypothesis) that it holds for some arbitrary value n is sufficient to show that it holds for $n+1$. This is a valid proof technique precisely because any member of *Nat0* is either 0 or can be reached from 0 by the operation $+1$.

Proofs about the natural numbers require the application of induction because there is an infinity of numbers. If proofs are to be constructed about arbitrarily large sets, induction is again required. In fact, induction on sets can frequently be converted into induction on integers by considering the cardinality of the sets. This is not, however, the most natural way of writing inductive proofs about sets. Looking back at the analysis of inductive proofs for the natural numbers, one is led to the question of how all sets can be generated. The answer is simple. All sets come from the empty set or by adding one element to a set. So, if it is necessary to prove that a predicate p of sets holds, one must show:

$p(\{\})$

and:

$e \epsilon S \wedge p(S\text{-}\{e\}) \Rightarrow p(S)$

This can be made less abstract by an example. Suppose it was necessary to write an intersection function. One possibility is:

$intersectf(S_1,S_2) \triangleq$
    if $S_1=\{\}$ **then** $\{\}$
    else
        *(***let** $e \epsilon S_1$
        if $e \epsilon S_2$ **then** $\{e\} \cup intersectf(S_1\text{-}\{e\},S_2)$
        else $intersectf(S_1\text{-}\{e\},S_2))$

It is required to prove that:

$intersectf(S_1,S_2) = S_1 \cap S_2$

This will be done by induction on S_1. Consider as basis the case:

$S_1 = \{\}$

then the definition shows that:

$intersectf(S_1,S_2) = \{\}$

and it is a property of intersection that:

$\{\} \cap S_2 = \{\}$

So the basis is proved.
    Now it is necessary to prove the inductive step, with the assumption:

$S_1 \neq \{\}$

From the definition of intersectf:

$intersectf(S_1,S_2) =$
    *(***let** $e \epsilon S_1$
    if $e \epsilon S_2$ **then** $\{e\} \cup intersectf(S_1\text{-}\{e\},S_2)$
    else $intersectf(S_1\text{-}\{e\},S_2))$

The induction hypothesis is:

$e \epsilon S_1 \wedge (intersectf(S_1\text{-}\{e\},S_2) = (S_1\text{-}\{e\}) \cap S_2)$

Now make a case analysis on e being in S_2; first assume:

$e \epsilon S_2$

Then:

$intersectf(S_1,S_2)$
$$= \{e\} \cup intersectf(S_1-\{e\},S_2)$$
But using the induction hypothesis this gives:
$$= \{e\} \cup ((S_1-\{e\}) \cap S_2)$$
which by the distributive rule is:
$$= (\{e\} \cup (S_1-\{e\})) \cap (\{e\} \cup S_2)$$
But since e is in both S_1 and S_2 this gives:
$$= S_1 \cap S_2$$
which is the required result for this case.

In the other case, assume:

$\sim(e \epsilon S_2)$

then:

$intersectf(S_1,S_2)$
$$= intersect(S_1-\{e\}, S_2)$$
$$= (S_1-\{e\}) \cap S_2$$
which, under the assumption:
$$= S_1 \cap S_2$$
which concludes the inductive proof.

Exercise 8.7:   Write, and prove correct, a function which computes set differences in a way analogous to *intersectf* above.

Exercise 8.8:   Prove that the function:

$subsetf(S_1,S_2) \triangleq$
    if $S_1=\{\}$ **then TRUE**
    else
        $(\textbf{let } e \epsilon S_1$
        if $e \epsilon S_2$ **then** $subsetf(S_1-\{e\},S_2)$
        else FALSE*)*

is such that:

$subsetf(S_1,S_2) \Leftrightarrow S_1 \subseteq S_2$

Use in Specifications

The next specification is for a ***students who do exercises*** problem. Suppose a program is required which permits the recording of students who have, and have not, handed in adequate answers to the exercises set in a course. In this case the states might contain two components: one (*N*) for the students who have not done exercises; the other (*Y*) for students who have done exercises. Thus:

Studx:: N: Student-name-set Y: Student-name-set

Here, as in the **students in classroom** example, the set:

Student-name

is taken as a given, unanalyzed, set.

At the beginning of a course no students are enrolled and therefore both sets of names should be empty. Thus:

INIT
states: Studx
post-INIT(,<n',y'>) ≜ *n' = y' = { }*

A new student who enrols on a course is not expected to have done the exercises so the *ENROL* operation is specified:

ENROL
states: Studx
type: Student-name →
pre-ENROL(<n,y>,nm) ≜ ~*(nm* ϵ*(n∪y))*
post-ENROL(<n,y>,nm,<n',y'>) ≜ *n' = n∪{nm}* ∧ *y' = y*

The successful completion of the exercises is recorded by *COMPL*. Thus:

COMPL
states: Studx
type: Student-name →
pre-COMPL(<n,y>,nm) ≜ *nm* ϵ *n*
post-COMPL(<n,y>,nm,<n',y'>) ≜ *n' = n-{nm}* ∧ *y' = y∪{nm}*

The purpose of the programs is to be able to indicate the students who have passed a course. This can be achieved by an operation which produces as output the appropriate set of names:

RESULT
states: Studx
type: → *Student-name-set*
post-RESULT(<n,y>,<n',y'>,res) ≜ *res=y* ∧ *y'=y* ∧ *n'=n*

It is a consequence of the definition of the operators that the two sets contained in the state must be disjoint. This property is referred to as a **data type invariant** and is considered in more detail in chapter 10. Although the property has not been proved here, its presence has been implicitly acknowledged in the pre-condition for *COMPL*: one might have anticipated a conjoined clause stating:

~*(nm*ϵ*y)*

This situation is, however, already ruled out if *nm* is a member of the set *N* and the two sets are disjoint.

Exercise 8.9: Suppose the state of a program is:

Dict = Word-set

a) Write a specification for a program

SPELLA
states: Dict
type: Word-set → Word-set

which checks whether all of the words in the input word set are in the stored dictionary and produces a set of output words which are not in the dictionary.
b) Define an additional operation for updating the dictionary. (This is the first, and simplest, version of a spelling checking program which could be built up to a realistic system.)

Exercise 8.10: Write a specification for a program which computes *greatest common divisor* (cf. exercise 4.4). Avoid the use of quantifiers by employing set notation.

Exercise 8.11: Consider the following description of the world:

World:: MEN: Name-set
       WOMEN: Name-set
       MARRIED: Name-set

Suppose that a function is available which gives the age of people:

age: Name → Nat0

Specify operations, with state *World*, which·
a) Yield the set of married men
b) Yield the set of unmarried women
c) Yield the set of unmarried women younger than 21
d) Yield the set of married men older than 65

Exercise 8.12: Consider the following abstraction of a school:

School:: STUDENTS: Name-set
      TEACHERS: Name-set
      CLASSA: Name-set
      CLASSB: Name-set
      CLASSC: Name-set

Specify operations which:
a) Check that everyone in a class is either a teacher or a student
b) Check that there are no meaningless duplications of names
c) Check that there is one teacher per class
d) Yield the set of free teachers
e) Compute the average student/teacher ratio

Exercise 8.13: Suppose it is required to specify a program which, for some given natural number, say *n*, produces the set of prime numbers less than or equal to *n*. The specification might regard the task as an operation of type:

PRIMES
states: State
type: Nat $\longrightarrow$ Nat-set

Write a definition of:

post-PRIMES: State Nat State Nat-set $\longrightarrow$ Bool

such that, for example, the following output is considered correct:

PRIMES(12) = { 1,2,3,5,7,11 }

Exercise 8.14: One way to compute the set of prime numbers is by removing the composites (those numbers which can be expressed as a product). This idea is attributed to Eratosthenes and is called a *sieve*. For:

Ssieve = Nat-set

complete the post-conditions in:

```
/*
INIT
states: Ssieve
type: Nat →
post-INIT(,n,s') ≜ ...
*/
DO I = 2 BY 1 TO SQRT(N);
  /*
    BODY(I)
    states: Ssieve
    type: Nat →
    post-BODY(s,n,s') ≜
            if ~(n∈s) then s'=s
            else        s'= ...
  */
```

(A stepwise development of a program for the *sieve of Eratosthenes* is given in Hoare(72d) and a new fast algorithm is developed in Gries(78).)

Recording Equivalence Relations

It is difficult to construct interesting examples with only one abstraction (i.e. sets), because any significant problem is likely to organize various levels of data in different ways. For instance, a set might be an appropriate way of discussing the customer keys of a database system; but then the database itself will be a mapping from keys to records, and the records structured objects.

One example which can be specified in terms of sets alone is the recording of *equivalence relations*. This problem is interesting because its implementation is quite complicated. If, however, the right abstractions are used, it is possible to write a short and precise specification.

Suppose a compiler was to be constructed which, because it had to optimize register allocation, kept track of which variables can share storage. In a language like PL/I, two parameter identifiers might end up referring to the same location if the same argument is passed (by reference) to both. The compiler would need to *EQUATE* the two parameter identifiers to record the fact that they may refer to the same location. When determining which values can be changed, the register allocation part of the compiler would *TEST* whether two locations are equivalent. The result of this test should reflect any chains of equivalence which have been created.

The relation *could share storage* is an equivalence relation and this is one of many problems (see Knuth(68)) which requires a way of recording and testing such relations.

We now review the properties of relations in general and equivalence relations in particular. Here, it is only necessary to consider *two-place* relations: that is, relations between elements of two sets. An example of a two-place relation between two sets of people is *married to*; a two-place relation between a set of people and a set of cars might be *owns*. For a relation which is named R, a way of asserting that two elements, say e_1 and e_2, stand in that relation is:

$R(e_1,e_2)$

Here, interest is restricted to two-place relations between elements both chosen from the same set. The arithmetic relation *less than* is such a relation over integers and one might write:

$lessthan(3,7)$, $\sim lessthan(3,3)$

Of course, a more familiar notation is:

$3<7$, $\sim (3<3)$

Such a two-place relation can be viewed as a set of pairs where both elements are integers. Thus:

$lessthan \subseteq \{<i_1,i_2> \mid i_1,i_2 \in Int\}$

In fact the relation is exactly the set of pairs which satisfy it and it is more precise to write:

$lessthan$
$\quad = \{<i_1,i_2> \mid i_1,i_2 \in Int \wedge i_1<i_2\}$
$\quad = \{<0,1>,<0,2>,...,<1,2>,<1,3>,...\}$

Three properties can be considered for such two-place relations: reflexivity, symmetry and transitivity. These three properties are illustrated by considering relations over the integers which do, or do not, possess the property.

A relation is said to be reflexive if it contains all pairings of elements with themselves. That is:

R(i,i) where i∈Int

The relation ≤ has this property, whereas < does not.

The second property is symmetry. A relation is said to be symmetric if the knowledge that a given pair is in the relation implies that the pair obtained by reversing their order is also contained in the relation. That is:

R(i,j) ⟹ *R(j,i) where i,j∈Int*

Clearly ≠ has, while ≤ does not have, this property.

The last property to be considered is transitivity. A relation is said to be transitive if it follows that two elements are in the relation from the knowledge that there is an intermediate element such that the first and intermediate (pair) and the intermediate and second (pair) are contained in the relation. Thus:

R(i,j) ∧ *R(j,k)* ⟹ *R(i,k) where i,j,k∈Int*

This property is possessed by < but not by ≠.

	Yes	*No*
Reflexive	≤ =	≠ <
Symmetric	= ≠	≤ <
Transitive	= ≤ <	≠

Figure 35   Properties of Relations over Integers

As can be seen from fig. 35, the one relation which possesses all three of the stated properties is equality (=). In general, any relation which satisfies all three of the properties is called an *equivalence relation*. (The reader should appreciate that ⟺ is an equivalence relation on logical expressions.) Everyday examples of equivalence relations are *earns same salary as* between employees, or *lives in same house as*.

Having made clear the concept of equivalence relations, the programming problem can now be stated. What is required is a system for accepting information about pairs of elements which are to be considered equivalent, and then responding to questions as to whether pairs are equivalent. Whenever a question of equivalence is posed, the answer must reflect both the entered pairs and the rules of reflexivity, symmetry and transitivity. Thus, after

EQUATE(a,b)
EQUATE(b,c)

the result of:

TEST(b,a), TEST(d,d), TEST(c,a)

must all be true, and

TEST(d,b)

must be false.

Thus, the new data type has three operators. In order to show the types of these operators something must be said about other objects. To make the programs general (i.e. not restricted to the integers), the elements are taken from some general set:

Element

The class of states of the system will be called *Q*. The initializing operation is of type:

INIT
states: Q

The operation which updates the state to reflect newly equivalenced elements is:

EQUATE
states: Q
type: Element Element →

The operation which tests whether two elements are equivalent is of type:

TEST
states: Q
type: Element Element → Bool

But what is to be the definition of *Q*? In other words, on what is the constructive specification of the operators to be based? It was mentioned above that any relation can be viewed as a set of the pairs which it contains. For equivalence relations there is another possible view. An equivalence relation can be modelled by a (disjoint) partitioning of the base set. That is, a given value of an equivalence relation can be represented by a decomposition of the base set into subsets which have no common elements. For example, suppose the base set were:

Element = {a,b,c,d,e,f}

then one possible equivalence relation could be as shown in fig. 36. Testing whether two elements are equivalent amounts to asking whether they are in the same subset. Thus *a* and *b*, or *d* and *d*, are equivalent while *a* and *d* are not. Notice that this model guarantees the three properties required of equivalence relations; reflexivity and symmetry are obvious; that transitivity is also captured follows from the fact that the sets are disjoint.

Such a model provides an idea for the specification of *Q* because it is easy to make two elements equivalent by uniting the sets of which they are members.

It is necessary, then, to specify that elements of *Q* are made up of sets of sets of *Elements*. Recall that:

S = Element-set

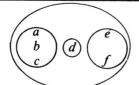

Figure 36   An Equivalence Relation

defines members of *S* to be sets, all of whose members are members of *Element*. What is now required is:

Q = (Element-set)-set

which specifies that members of *Q* are sets, all of whose members are elements of *Element-set*, that is they are subsets of *Element*:

$q \epsilon Q \Rightarrow (\mathbf{A}s \epsilon q)(s \subseteq Element)$

Thus the element of *Q* corresponding to fig. 36 is:

$\{ \{a,b,c\}, \{d\}, \{e,f\} \}$

Having defined the class of states it is now a simple task to specify the three operations. The initialization operation should create the trivial decomposition into unit (i.e. one-element) sets:

post-INIT(,q') $\triangleq q' = \{ \{e\} \mid e \epsilon Element \}$

Making a given pair of elements equivalent affects only the sets which contain the elements; these two sets are united:

post-EQUATE(q,e₁,e₂,q') $\triangleq$
$q' = \{S \mid S \epsilon q \wedge e_1 \sim (e_2 \epsilon S)\} \cup \{S_1 \cup S_2 \mid e_1 \epsilon S_1 \epsilon q \wedge e_2 \epsilon S_2 \epsilon q\}$

It should be observed that if e_1 and e_2 are already equivalent, no change is made. For the test operation the post-condition is:

post-TEST(q,e₁,e₂,q',res) $\triangleq q' = q \wedge (res \Leftrightarrow (\mathbf{E}S \epsilon q)(e_1 \epsilon S \wedge e_2 \epsilon S)))$

All of the operations are total. Fig. 37 illustrates the operations.

It is a property of *INIT* and *EQUATE* that they can only create (disjoint) partitionings of *Element*. Formalizing this notion as a data type invariant:

invq: Q → Bool
invq(q) $\triangleq$
    union$q = Element \wedge$
    $(\mathbf{A}S_1,S_2 \epsilon q)(S_1 = S_2 \vee \text{is-disj}(S_1,S_2)) \wedge$
    $\sim (\{ \} \epsilon q)$

The role of the data type invariant will become clear when implementation proofs are considered.

The system (or new data type) has, then, been specified in terms of sets of sets; it records equivalences of given elements and one can see by inspection that, once entered, an equivalence is never destroyed.

For:

Element = {a, b, c, d, e, f}

Then:

$INIT()() = \{\{a\},\{b\},\{c\},\{d\},\{e\},\{f\}\} = S_1$
$EQUATE(a,b)(S_1) = \{\{a,b\},\{c\},\{d\},\{e\},\{f\}\} = S_2$
$EQUATE(b,a)(S_2) = S_2$
$EQUATE(b,c)(S_2) = \{\{a,b,c\},\{d\},\{e\},\{f\}\} = S_3$
$EQUATE(e,f)(S_3) = \{\{a,b,c\},\{d\},\{e,f\}\} = S_4$
$EQUATE(a,f)(S_4) = \{\{a,b,c,e,f\},\{d\}\} = S_5$
$TEST(a,e)(S_5) =$ **TRUE**
$TEST(d,d)(S_5) =$ **TRUE**
$TEST(a,d)(S_5) =$ **FALSE**

Figure 37   **Recording Equivalence Relations**

It is interesting to consider possible implementation strategies, both in order to see the range and to emphasize how valuable has been the application of abstraction in this specification. Suppose a state were chosen in which all entered pairs were simply recorded: *EQUATE* would execute quickly but the *TEST* operation would be left to do all of the work and would be correspondingly slow. On the other hand one could implement the operations on a state which was a two-dimensional array of truth values (single bits) which represented precisely whether two elements were equivalent. If there is a very large number of elements to be considered, there is an enormous storage requirement. Furthermore, the speed of the equivalence test has been won only at the expense of the enter operation having to compute and enter all equivalences in the array. Algorithms are shown in chapters 12 and 13 which achieve a balance between storage usage and the amount of computation required on insertion/testing.

*Predicates and Sets

This optional section examines the connection between sets and predicates. Denoting the set of elements which satisfies a predicate as:

$set\text{-}of\text{-}pred(p) \triangleq \{x \mid p(x)\}$

then one can observe that if:

$p(x) \Rightarrow q(x)$

then it follows that:

$set\text{-}of\text{-}pred(p) \subseteq set\text{-}of\text{-}pred(q)$

To establish this, the technique of proof by contradiction is used. Suppose the conclusion were not true, then there would be some element x_0 such that:

$x_0 \epsilon set\text{-}of\text{-}pred(p) \; \wedge \; \sim(x_0 \epsilon set\text{-}of\text{-}pred(q))$

but then from the definition of *set-of-pred* it would follow that:

$p(x_0) \; \wedge \; \sim q(x_0)$

Since this contradicts the initial implication, the supposition that the conclusion was false must have been mistaken. It is then established that the subset relation holds.

It can also be shown that:

$set\text{-}of\text{-}pred(p \; \wedge \; q) = set\text{-}of\text{-}pred(p) \; \cap \; set\text{-}of\text{-}pred(q)$

as follows:

$set\text{-}of\text{-}pred(p \; \wedge \; q) = \{ x \; | \; p(x) \wedge q(x) \}$

while:

$set\text{-}of\text{-}pred(p) \; \cap \; set\text{-}of\text{-}pred(q)$
$\quad = \{ x \,|\, p(x) \} \; \cap \; \{ y \,|\, q(y) \}$
$\quad = \{ x \,|\, p(x) \wedge q(x) \}$

Exercise 8.15: Write and prove the relationship between *set-of-pred(p)* and *set-of-pred(q)* when:

$p(x) \Leftrightarrow q(x)$

Exercise 8.16: Document the set expression for:

$set\text{-}of\text{-}pred(p \; \vee \; q)$

Summary

This chapter has introduced the use of set notation as a shorthand for documenting constructive specifications of programs. A technique is now available for describing a class of problems more succinctly than would be possible with the normal data structures of programming languages. No constraints have been put on, or implied about, the implementation and chapter 11 discusses how this freedom is used in development steps. Furthermore, the specification has been recorded in a notation in which it is far easier to make arguments (proofs).

The reader is reminded that, as with logic notation, it is not the intention to use deep results of set theory but rather to adopt a notation as a convenient shorthand.

Abstraction is, in fact, such a familiar part of everyday thinking that there is a tendency to take it for granted. The word *table* conjures up a class of objects which is widely (and immediately) understood. The concept of *table* is, of course, an abstraction in which the key similarities between all objects of this class are recognized and of which the differences (e.g. materials) are ignored. Other abstractions whose role the reader may choose to consider are geographical maps, circuit diagrams, grammars (of natural languages) and, among many possible examples from mathematics, groups.

Summary Exercises

Exercise 8.17: If still in doubt about the advantages of using formal notation, write, in a natural language, a specification for the *recording equivalence classes* problem. Do not assume that equivalence relations are already familiar to readers of the specification. Ask someone else to review the specification looking carefully for ambiguity and incompleteness.

Exercise 8.18: Another category of relations is *partial orders*. They are defined as being:

reflexive: po(x,x)
anti-symmetric: $po(x_1,x_2) \land po(x_2,x_1) \Rightarrow x_1=x_2$
transitive: $po(x_1,x_2) \land po(x_2,x_3) \Rightarrow po(x_1,x_3)$

Identify one of the set operators which is a partial order.

Chapter 9

LIST NOTATION

Lists are ordered collections of arbitrarily many elements which can be accessed by position. Lists, like sets, are an abstract notion in that few programming languages embody the generality of the notation below. Lists can be represented in many ways: at their simplest, it may be possible to model the behavior of a particular list by an array (of fixed size) and a pointer; at the other extreme, a list may have to be realized using linked-list data structures. Lists are, then, abstractions of a wide range of possible realizations.

There is some danger in the choice of name *list* because of the use of the term *list processing* in computing. Because of the danger of confusion, other publications (e.g. Bjorner(78)) have used the term *tuple* or *sequence* for abstract lists. Within this book, the data structures used in list processing are referred to as *linked-lists* (i.e. data plus pointer to next item) and the abstract structures as, simply, *lists*.

The next section introduces the notation itself. An optional section discusses induction on lists. The section on uses of the notation develops some useful auxiliary functions and predicates on lists.

Notation

A distinctive form of bracket (i.e. { }) was chosen to display set values. For lists, the pointed brackets (<>) are used. As with sets, the first item of notation to be introduced is that for the explicit values. These are written:

<el, e2, ..., en>

Unlike sets, the order in which elements appear in a list value is important because of the ability to access their elements by position. Thus:

<1,2> ≠ <2,1>

Furthermore, there is no difficulty with lists containing duplicate elements, so that:

$<1> \neq <1,1>$

The list containing no elements (*empty list*) is written:

$<>$

One way of decomposing lists is by using operators which yield the *head* or the *tail* of a given list. Suppose P is a list of the first six prime numbers:

$P = <1,2,3,5,7,11>$

The head operator yields the first element of a list, thus:

hd$P = 1$

The tail operator yields that list which remains if the head element is removed, thus:

tl$P = <2,3,5,7,11>$

Notice the difference between the results of the operators: **tl** always yields a list whereas **hd** yields an element of the same type as the first element of the list. Thus:

tl$<1,2> = <2>$
hd$<1,2> = 1$

There is no restriction as to what sort of things may be elements of lists—lists of lists etc. are allowed:

hd$<\{1,2\},2> = \{1,2\}$
hd$<<1>,2> = <1>$

Notice also:

tl$<1> = <>$

Both operators have a limited domain in that they may only be applied to non-empty lists. Thus:

hd$<>$, **tl**$<>$

are both undefined in the same sense that:

$3/0$

has no defined value: it is an error to write it and no further computation can be performed with the result.

The length operator yields the number of elements in a list. Thus:

len$P = 6$
len$<> = 0$

It can be defined as:

len*list* $\triangleq$ **if** *list*$=<>$ **then** 0 **else** $1 + $ **len**$(tl$*list*$)$

Notice that the length of a list is the number of elements, including duplicates, in the list to which the operator is applied (counting any elements which are lists as one element), thus:

len$<1, 1, <1,2>, <1,2>, \{1,2\}> = 5$

A particular element of a list may be extracted by indexing (where the value of the index must be between one and the length of the list), thus:

$P(5) = 7$

Indexing can be defined in terms of the more basic decomposition operators as follows:

$list(i) \triangleq$ **if** $i=1$ **then hd**$list$ **else** $(tl\,list)(i-1)$

An (infix) *concatenation* operator can be used to create a list which contains all of the elements of its first operand, followed by all of the elements of the second operand: both operands must be lists. Thus:

$P \mid\mid <13> = <1,2,3,5,7,11,13>$

Concatenation can be defined as:

$list1 \mid\mid list2 \triangleq$
    that list such that:
        len$list =$ **len**$list1 +$ **len**$list2 \wedge$
        $(\mathbf{A}i\epsilon\{1:\mathbf{len}list1\})(list(i)=list1(i)) \wedge$
        $(\mathbf{A}i\epsilon\{1:\mathbf{len}list2\})(list(\mathbf{len}list1+i)=list2(i))$

The need to define something as the unique object satisfying certain properties occurs several times, so a small addition to the logic notation is now proposed. If it is required to assert that there exists exactly one object satisfying a property p, one can write:

$(\mathbf{E}e)(p(e)) \wedge (p(e_1)\wedge p(e_2) \Rightarrow e_1=e_2)$

That is, an assertion is made that some object exists and furthermore, that if e_1 and e_2 satisfy p, they are in fact the same value. Such definitions are required often enough that a special form of the existential quantifier is defined for the purpose:

$(\mathbf{E!}e)(p(e)) \triangleq (\mathbf{E}e)(p(e)) \wedge (p(e_1)\wedge p(e_2) \Rightarrow e_1=e_2)$

The quantifier should be read as *there exists exactly one ...* . It can also be used with a constraint part. Thus:

$(\mathbf{E!}i\epsilon\{12:16\})(is\text{-}prime(i))$

The data type invariant for the *equivalence relation* problem in chapter 8 was defined:

$invq: Q \rightarrow Bool$
$invq(q) \triangleq$
    union$q = Element \wedge$
    $(\mathbf{A}S_1,S_2\epsilon q)(S_1=S_2 \vee is\text{-}disj(S_1,S_2)) \wedge$
    $\sim(\{\} \epsilon q)$

An alternative formulation, which states that each member of *Element* must occur in exactly one subset, would be:

$invq(q) \triangleq$
    $(e \epsilon Element \Leftrightarrow (\textbf{E}S\epsilon q)(e\epsilon S)) \wedge$
    $(\textbf{A}e\epsilon Element)((\textbf{E!}S\epsilon q)(e\epsilon S)) \wedge \sim (\{\ \}\epsilon q)$

If it is established that there exists exactly one element satisfying some property, then it is reasonable to speak about *the unique item such that* ... . A description operator, written as the Greek letter iota, is used to express this in formulae. Thus:

$(\iota x)(p(x))$
$(\textbf{E!}e)(p(e)) \Rightarrow p((\iota e)(p(e)))$

For example:

$(\iota i\epsilon\{12{:}16\})(is\text{-}prime(i)) = 13$
$(\iota list)(list = <1,2> |\ | <3,5>) = <1,2,3,5>$

Given this description operator, the concatenation definition can be rewritten:

$list1\ |\ |\ \ list2 \triangleq$
    $(\iota\ list)$
        $(\textbf{len}list = \textbf{len}list1 + \textbf{len}list2 \wedge$
        $(\textbf{A}i\epsilon\{1{:}\textbf{len}list1\})(list(i)=list1(i)) \wedge$
        $(\textbf{A}i\epsilon\{1{:}\textbf{len}list2\})(list(\textbf{len}list1+i)=list2(i)))$

Analogous to the distributed union on sets, there is a distributed concatenation operator for which:

$\textbf{conc}<<e_1,e_2>,<>,<e_3>> = <e_1,e_2,e_3>$

This operator is rarely used—its definition is given in appendix C.

One final item of notation provides an operator for collecting all of the elements of a list into a set. This is defined:

$\textbf{elems}list \triangleq \{list(i)\ |\ 1{\leq}i{\leq}\textbf{len}list\}$

For example:

$\textbf{elems}P = \{1,2,3,5,7,11\}$
$\textbf{elems}<1,2,1,4,3> = \{1,2,3,4\}$

Exercise 9.1:   What is the value of:

a) $\textbf{tl}<1,2>$
b) $\textbf{len}<<1,2>,<3,4,5>>$
c) $\textbf{hd}<<1,2>,<1,2,3>>$
d) $<<1,2>,<1,2,3>>(2)$
e) $\textbf{elems}<2,2,\{3,4,2\}>$
f) $<1> |\ | <<2>>$

Exercise 9.2:   In each case, what is *list* where:

a) **hd**$list = <1> \wedge$ **hdtl**$list = \{1\} \wedge$ **tltl**$list = <a>$

b) **hd**$list = 1 \wedge$ **len**$list = 3 \wedge$ **tltl**$list = <$**hdtl**$list>$
and sum of the elements of list is 5.

Exercise 9.3:

$(\mathbf{E}list)(\mathbf{len}list \neq \mathbf{card}(\mathbf{elems}list))$

give an example.

A diagram showing the types of the operators is given in fig. 38.

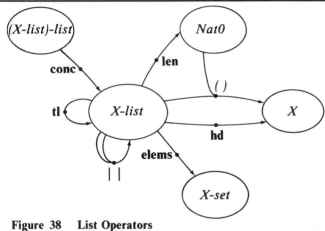

Figure 38   List Operators

Turning now to proving results about lists, it is first necessary to determine what is meant by saying that two lists are equal: they should be of the same length and, for all valid indices, contain the same elements. The definition of what are valid indices is important because indexing a list with an index greater than its length is undefined. Thus:

len$list1 =$**len**$list2 \wedge (1 \leq i \leq$**len**$list1 \Rightarrow list2(i) = list1(i))$

introduces the danger of undefined terms. Remembering the proposal (see *More on Logic in chapter 3) to use conditional expressions, equality can be defined as:

$list1 = list2 \triangleq$
    if len$list1 =$**len**$list2$ **then** $(\mathbf{A}i \in \{1{:}\mathbf{len}list1\})(list2(i) = list1(i))$
    else FALSE

It is intuitively obvious that the empty list should play the same role with concatenation as does 0 with addition. Thus:

$list \mid\mid <> = list$

To see that this is true, use the definition of concatenation to show:

$\textbf{len}(list | \ | \diamondsuit) = \textbf{len}list + 0 \ \wedge$
$(\textbf{A}i\epsilon\{1{:}\textbf{len}list\})((list | \ | \diamondsuit)(i) = list(i))$

And, therefore, from the definition of equality:

$list | \ | \diamondsuit = list$

Concatenation is associative, that is:

$(list1 | \ | list2) | \ | list3 = list1 | \ | (list2 | \ | list3)$

This can be proved by applying the definition of concatenation twice to each side of the equality and reducing both sides to:

$(\iota list)$
$\quad (\textbf{len}list = \textbf{len}list1 + \textbf{len}list2 + \textbf{len}list3 \ \wedge$
$\quad (\textbf{A}i\epsilon\{1{:}\textbf{len}list1\})(list(i) = list1(i)) \ \wedge$
$\quad (\textbf{A}i\epsilon\{1{:}\textbf{len}list2\})(list(\textbf{len}list1+i) = list2(i)) \ \wedge$
$\quad (\textbf{A}i\epsilon\{1{:}\textbf{len}list3\})(list(\textbf{len}list1+\textbf{len}list2+i) = list3(i)))$

Exercise 9.4: Prove, using the given definitions, the following identities:

a) $\diamondsuit | \ | list = list$
b) $\textbf{len}(list1 | \ | list2) = \textbf{len}list1 + \textbf{len}list2$
c) $\textbf{elems}(list1 | \ | list2) = \textbf{elems}list1 \cup \textbf{elems}list2$

*Inductive Proofs on Lists

The key to proofs about arbitrary length lists is again a rule of induction. As with sets, this rule is related to the different creation possibilities. Any list can be created either by taking the empty list or by adding one element on the front of some other list. The induction rule is that, from:

$p(\diamondsuit)$

and (for non-empty lists):

$p(\textbf{tl}list) \Rightarrow p(list)$

it follows that:

$(\textbf{A}list)(p(list))$

Consider a function for reversing the order of a list:

$rev(list) \triangleq$
$\quad \textbf{if } list=\diamondsuit \textbf{ then } \diamondsuit$
$\quad \textbf{else } rev(\textbf{tl}list) | \ | <\textbf{hd}list>$

and suppose it is wished to prove:

$rev(list1\ |\ |\ list2) = rev(list2)\ |\ |\ rev(list1)$

The proof can be made by induction on *list1*. As a basis assume:

$list1\ =\ <>$

then, from a property given above:

$rev(list1\ |\ |\ list2) = rev(list2)$

Since:

$rev(<>) = <>$

from the definition of *rev*, it follows that:

$rev(list2)\ |\ |\ rev(list1)$
$\quad = rev(list2)\ |\ |\ <>$
$\quad = rev(list2)$

which concludes the basis.
For the inductive step, assume:

$list1\ \neq\ <>$

then:

$rev(list1\ |\ |\ list2)$
$\quad = rev(\textbf{tl}(list1\ |\ |\ list2))\ |\ |\ <\textbf{hd}(list1\ |\ |\ list2)>$

Since *list1* is not empty this gives:

$\quad = rev(\textbf{tl}(list1\ |\ |\ list2))\ |\ |\ <\textbf{hd}list1>$

The induction hypothesis is:

$rev(\textbf{tl}(list1\ |\ |\ list2))$
$\quad = rev(\textbf{tl}list1\ |\ |\ list2)$
$\quad = rev(list2)\ |\ |\ rev(\textbf{tl}list1)$

Thus:

$rev(list1\ |\ |\ list2)$
$\quad = (rev(list2)\ |\ |\ rev(\textbf{tl}list1))\ |\ |\ <\textbf{hd}list1>$

and by the associativity of concatenation:

$\quad = rev(list2)\ |\ |\ (rev(\textbf{tl}list1)\ |\ |\ <\textbf{hd}list1>)$

But under the assumption, the parenthesized expression is exactly $rev(list1)$, so:

$\quad = rev(list2)\ |\ |\ rev(list1)$

which concludes the proof.

Exercise 9.5:   Prove:
a)

$\textbf{len}(rev(list)) = \textbf{len}list$

b)

rev(rev(list)) = *list*

Use in Specifications

One remaining item of notation must be introduced. With sets, a way was introduced of specifying objects which were always sets. Once again this is done by a suffix. Thus, given a set of objects:

X

then:

L = *X-list*

defines all elements of *L* to be lists, each of whose elements is taken from *X*. Thus:

$l \epsilon L \implies$ (**A**$i\epsilon$ { *1*:**len***l* })$(l(i)\epsilon X)$

It is sometimes convenient to record that a list has at least one element. A class of non-empty lists can be specified by writing:

L1 = *X-list1*

Thus:

$l \epsilon L1 \implies$ **len***l* ≥ *1* ∧ (**A**$i\epsilon$ { *1*:**len***l* })$(l(i)\epsilon X)$

★   ★   ★

The concept of *stacks* provides an example where the new notation can be put to work. A pushdown stack is a discipline for storing and retrieving data where the access order is last in, first out (LIFO). Stacks are of use in many situations (e.g. expression evaluation) and are generally associated with iterative realizations of recursive processes. The new data type is called:

Stack

Its operations are of the following types. To initialize a stack:

INIT
states: Stack

To place an element on the top of a stack:

PUSH
states: Stack
type: Element →

To access the element on the top of the stack and simultaneously to remove it:

POP
states: Stack
type: → *Element*

To test whether a stack currently contains any elements:

IS-EMPTY
states: Stack
type: → *Bool*

The constructive specification of these four operators is based on *Stack* which, together with the specifications, is shown in fig. 39. Notice that *PUSH* and *POP* work in the expected **LIFO** fashion. One could also observe that a stack is another instance of a parameterized type: there could be stacks of integers, lists etc.

$Stack = Element\text{-}list_{:}$

$post\text{-}INIT(,st') \triangleq st'=<>$

$post\text{-}PUSH(st,e,st') \triangleq st'=<e> \mid\mid st$

$pre\text{-}POP(st) \triangleq st\neq<>$
$post\text{-}POP(st,st',res) \triangleq st'=\mathbf{tl}st \land res=\mathbf{hd}st$

$post\text{-}IS\text{-}EMPTY(st,st',b) \triangleq st'=st \land (b \Leftrightarrow st=<>)$

Figure 39   Specification of Stack

★ ★ ★

Jackson(75) presents the task of printing a ***multiplication table*** in the format:

1
2 4
3 6 9

·

·

·

10 20 30 40 50 60 70 80 90 100

That is, the line with index *i* contains the multiples of *i* from *1* to *i*. The required output can be viewed as a list of lists as follows:

Table = Line-list1
Line = Nat-list1

This output is illustrated in fig. 40.

For normal purposes, such a simple problem could be specified by saying that *table* should be such that:

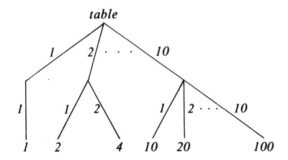

Figure 40   Multiplication Table Viewed as List

MTAB
states:
type: → Table

post-MTAB(,,table) ≜ *is-correct-mtab(table,10)*

is-correct-mtab(table,j) ≜
     len*table=j* ∧ *(**A***i∈{1:**len***table})(is-correct-line(table(i),i))*

is-correct-line(line,i) ≜ **len***line=i* ∧ *is-correct-nos(line,i)*

is-correct-nos(line,i) ≜ *(**A***n∈{1:**len***line})(line(n)=i*n)*

Figure 41   Specification of Multiplication Table Problem

table(i) = <i, i*2, ..., i*i>

A complete, formal, specification is given in fig 41. The separation of subsidiary predicates is useful in the development of this problem in chapter 19.

     Another problem which can be specified using lists is the creation of histograms. Suppose it is required to have sub-programs for initializing a histogram of size *n*:

INIT
states: Histogram
type: Nat →

adding an occurrence of the *ith* observation:

OBS
states: Histogram
type: Nat →

and for computing the relative probability of the *ith* set of occurrences:

PROB
states: Histogram
type: Nat → *Real*

That is, in the terminology of chapter 7, a new data type called *Histogram* is to be defined with three operators. A constructive specification of these three operators can be based on:

Histogram = *(Nat0)-list*

The specifications can be given as:

post-INIT(,n,hist') ≜ len*hist'=n* ∧ *(**A**i∈{ 1:*len*hist'* })(hist'(i)=0)*

pre-OBS(hist,i) ≜ *i* ≤ len*hist*
post-OBS(hist,i,hist') ≜
    len*hist'* = len*hist* ∧
    *(**A**j∈{ 1:*len*hist* })(j≠i* ⟹ *hist'(j)=hist(j))* ∧
    hist'(i)=hist(i)+1

pre-PROB(hist,i) ≜ *i*≤len*hist* ∧ *suml(hist)>0*
post-PROB(hist,i,hist',res) ≜
    hist'=hist ∧ *res* = *hist(i)/suml(hist)*

where:

suml(list) ≜
    if *list*=<> **then** *0*
    else hd*list* + *suml(*tl*list)*

Exercise 9.6: One advantage of a clear specification is that it can be changed easily. Change the ***multiplication table*** specification to:

a) print a square table of the multiples
b) print the multiples of 1 to 10 by 11 to 20

Exercise 9.7: A *queue* is a familiar concept. It is similar to a stack except that it works in a first in, first out (FIFO) order. Define a queue with operators:

INIT, ENQ, DEQ, IS-EMPTY

Exercise 9.8: Define a predicate:

is-disjl: (Object-set)-list → *Bool*

which can be used to test whether all sets in a list of sets are pairwise disjoint. For example:

∼*is-disjl(<{ 1 },{ 2 },{ 1,3 }>)*
is-disjl(<>)

Exercise 9.9:   The first five rows of Pascal's triangle are:

That is, the $i+1th$ row is generated from the ith by adding the elements:

$i1, i2, \quad ... \quad ,in-1, in, \quad 0$
$0, \quad i1, i2, \quad ... \quad ,in-1, in$

Define a function which will generate, for an argument i, the ith row of Pascal's triangle.   (For applications see Knuth(68) on Binomial coefficients.)

Attention is now turned to providing predicates and functions which extend the list notation. All of the definitions are collected together in appendix C. The functions are illustrated in fig. 42.

A useful function for extracting sublists of a list is defined:

$subl(el,i,j)$ ≜ **if** $i=1$ **then** $front(el,j)$ **else** $subl(tlel,i-1,j-1)$
$pre\text{-}subl(el,i,j)$ ≜ $1{\leq}i{\leq}\mathbf{len}el+1 \;\wedge\; 0{\leq}j{\leq}\mathbf{len}el$

where:

$front(el,k)$ ≜ **if** $k>0$ **then** $<hdel>|\;|\;front(tlel,k-1)$ **else** $<>$
$pre\text{-}front(el,k)$ ≜ $k{\leq}\mathbf{len}el$

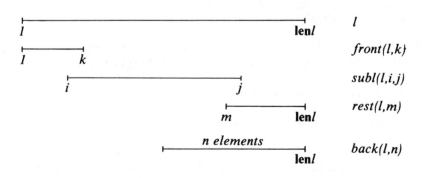

Figure 42   Extended List Functions

The reason for allowing i to exceed the length of the list, and j to be zero, in the pre-condition to *subl* is that zero length sub-lists can then be extracted. Such generalization makes functions more useful. Similar comments apply to the pre-condition of *front*. Examples of results are:

$front(<a,b,c>,1) = <a>$
$front(<a,b,c>,3) = <a,b,c>$
$front(<a,b,c>,0) = <>$

$subl(<a,b,c>,1,1) = <a>$
$subl(<a,b,c>,1,3) = <a,b,c>$
$subl(<a,b,c>,1,0) = <>$
$subl(<x,a,b,c>,2,2) = <a>$
$subl(<x,a,b,c>,4,3) = <>$
$subl(<>,1,0) = <>$

The pre-conditions of these functions are useful for ensuring that functions which use them remain defined over their domains. Strictly, proofs that *front* and *subl* are defined whenever their pre-conditions are true should be given. Such proofs could be made formal by induction on lists. Here, the observation that *front* performs **hd** and **tl** at most **len** el times and that *subl* performs **tl** at most **len** $el-($**len** $el+1)+1$ times will suffice.

The ability to delete elements from lists is given by:

$del(el,i) \triangleq$ **if** $i=1$ **then** **tl** el **else** $<$**hd** $el> | | del($**tl** $el,i-1)$
$pre\text{-}del(el,i) \triangleq 1 \leq i \leq$ **len** el

Notice that:

for $1 \leq i \leq$ **len** el:
  $del(el,i) = front(el,i-1) | | rest(el,i+1)$

Exercise 9.10: Define functions:
a)

rest: Element-list Nat $\rightarrow$ Element-list
$pre\text{-}rest(el,i) \triangleq 1 \leq i \leq ($**len** $el+1)$

which yields (see fig. 42):

$rest(<a,b,c>,3) = <c>$

b)

back: Element-list Nat $\rightarrow$ Element-list
$pre\text{-}back(el,j) \triangleq 0 \leq j \leq$ **len** el

such that (see fig. 42):

$back(<a,b,c>,1) = <c>$

c)

modl: Element-list Nat Element $\rightarrow$ Element-list
$pre\text{-}modl(el,i,e) \triangleq 1 \leq i \leq$ **len** el

which modifies the given list at the *ith* position by inserting *e*.

Exercise 9.11: Define a predicate which indicates whether a list contains any duplicate. Thus:

is-uniquel(<1,2,2>) = **FALSE**

(Many of the remaining functions were inspired by Dahl(78).)

Notice that there has been no analogue, for lists, of implicit set definition. The problem is that such an implicit definition would not fix the order of the elements in the generated list. One can, however, define some useful functions for generating lists. For example a list, of length n, all of whose elements are e can be defined as:

repeat: Element Nat0 $\rightarrow$ *Element-list*
repeat(e,n) $\triangleq$ **if** *n=0* **then** $<>$ **else** $<e>$| | *repeat(e,n-1)*

Exercise 9.12: Define functions which:
a) will generate a list of integers in ascending order. Thus:

interval(2,4) = $<2,3,4>$

b) applies a given function to all elements of a list. Thus:

applyl(<1,2,3>,sq) = $<1,4,9>$

where:

sq(x) $\triangleq$ $x**2$

Three ways of selecting sub-lists of a given list can be defined. Firstly an infix operator is defined which causes selection of those list items which are in a given set. Thus:

list | set $\triangleq$
    if *list=*$<>$ **then** $<>$
    else if **hd***list* ϵ *set* **then** $<$**hd***list>$| | *((tllist) | set)*
    else *(tllist) | set*

A second possibility is to select items from a list if and only if they satisfy a given predicate:

limitl(list,p) $\triangleq$
    if *list=*$<>$ **then** $<>$
    else if *p(***hd***list)* **then** $<$**hd***list>$| | *limitl(***tll***ist,p)*
    else *limitl(***tll***ist, p)*

Finally, there is the possibility of selecting elements from a list by means of a list of indices. Thus:

sel-subl(list,indl) $\triangleq$
    if *indl=*$<>$ **then** $<>$
    else $<$*list(***hd***indl)>$| | *sel-subl(list,***tl***indl)*
pre-sel-subl(list,indl) $\triangleq$ **elems***indl* $\subseteq$ *{ 1:***len***list }*

Summary

This chapter has introduced an abstraction called lists. Lists are rather like sets which are ordered: there are none of the usual computer considerations which make it necessary to fix a maximum size or make it difficult to remove elements from their interior. As such, lists are abstractions of data types available in PL/I. As well as providing specifications, the current chapter has spent some time in developing an extended set of functions and predicates for lists. These permit definitions to be shorter and more readable.

Two groups of notation (i.e. sets and lists) for describing abstract data types have been covered; two more (mappings and abstract syntax) are yet to be discussed. These will be covered following the next two chapters on proving realizations of abstract data types correct.

Further examples of list-like abstractions can be found in the papers on the *CLU* language (see Liskov(77) for references), Burge(75), and Dahl(78).

Summary Exercises

Exercise 9.13:   Define a *stack* (with the operators *INIT*, *PUSH*, *POP*, *IS-EMPTY*) which has a finite maximum size (say 100 elements). To make such a stack usable there should be an additional operator:

IS-FULL
states: Stack
type: → Bool

Exercise 9.14:   Define a finite *stack* with operators *INIT*, *PUSH*, *POP* and *IS-EMPTY* with the property that when an element is pushed onto a full stack the oldest element is lost from the bottom of the stack.

Exercise 9.15:   Exercise 9.7 can be extended to handle priority *queues*. Assume:

Q-item = Nat0

Define an *ENQ* operation which ensures that the queue is kept in order of increasing priority.

Exercise 9.16:   Refer back to exercise 8.9. The assumption that the text would be available as a set of words is rather unreal. Write a specification for:

SPELLB
states: Dict
type: Word-list → Bool-list

with one output per word indicating whether the input word is in the dictionary or not.

Exercise 9.17: Suppose that a *sort* program is specified as:

Sort = Element-list

SORT
states: Sort
post-SORT(els,els') ≜ *is-ordered(els')* ∧ *is-permutation(els',els)*

For normal purposes one might stop at this level; as an exercise in using the list notation:
a) define:

is-ordered: Element-list → Bool

Use ≤ as a relation between *Elements*
b) define:

is-permutation: Element-list Element-list → Bool

c) show that *is-permutation* is an equivalence relation.

Exercise 9.18: *Bit-mask lists* can be used to select items from lists. Define recursive functions:

a) mask-l: Object-list Bool-list → Object-list
b) tally: Bool-list → Nat0

which (a) produces a list containing only those elements of the first argument where the corresponding position of the second argument list is true, (b) which counts the occurrences of true.

Exercise 9.19: Returning to the school theme, suppose a system was required which kept track of students in ten classrooms. The classrooms are numbered from *1* to *10*. The state might be:

Studw = Class-status-list1

where:

Class-status = Student-name-set

The operations must now indicate the room number concerned. Document specifications including reasonable pre-conditions.

Exercise 9.20: One possible basis for a description of *arrays* (e.g. in PL/I) is lists of lists thus:

Array = Array-component-list

Where *Array-components* are either *Elements* or are themselves *Arrays*. Define a function:

index: Array Nat-list → Element

which selects an element of an array.

Exercise 9.21: A formal model of the children's game of *snakes and ladders* can be based on lists. Design an appropriate state and specify some operations.

Exercise 9.22: There is a problem known as *longest ascending sub-sequences*. The idea is to find in some list of integers, the longest chain of increasing values. Thus:

1 2 1 3 1 4   gives   1 2 3 4
1 3 1 2 3   gives   1 2 3

Define a suitable series of functions and predicates to support a clear specification of this problem.

Chapter 10

DATA TYPE INVARIANTS

Two examples in chapter 8 contain comments about data type invariants. This concept is now discussed in detail.

The specification of the **students who do exercises** problem is collected together in fig. 43. What is the meaning of *inv-studx*? The operations are such that the two sets in the state are always disjoint. Putting this in another way, it can be said that there are members of the class of states *Studx* which will never arise. Looking at the formulae one can say that none of the current operations gives rise to overlapping sets; from a knowledge of reality one knows that no meaningful operation would create sets which were not disjoint.

The property *inv-studx* is a data type invariant. In general, a **data type invariant** is a predicate which can be proved to hold for all instances of the states which can be created by the operations of the type. Those states which satisfy the data type invariant are called **valid**.

In the rigorous method, it is normally simple to write the data type invariant and to check, informally, that each of the operations preserves the invariant (i.e. creates only valid states from valid states). The formal rule is presented here and used on a few examples. The general rule is:

pre-OP(σ,args) $\wedge$ *inv(σ)* $\wedge$ *post-OP(σ,args,σ',res)* $\Rightarrow$ *inv(σ')*

Applying this to the current example, the first result required is:

pre-INIT(σ) $\wedge$ *inv-studx(σ)* $\wedge$ *post-INIT(σ,σ')* $\Rightarrow$ *inv-studx(σ')*

The information about the state before initialization is irrelevant and thus the formula reduces to:

n'=y'={ } $\Rightarrow$ *is-disj(n',y')*

which is immediate.

The second result required is:

pre-ENROL(σ,nm) $\wedge$ *inv-studx(σ)* $\wedge$ *post-ENROL(σ,nm,σ')* $\Rightarrow$
  inv-studx(inv-studx(σ')

which reduces to:

$\sim$*(nmϵ(n* $\cup$ *y))* $\wedge$ *is-disj(n,y)* $\Rightarrow$ *is-disj(n* $\cup$ *{ nm },y)*

174

Studx:: N: Student-name-set   Y: Student-name-set
with:

inv-studx(<n,y>) ≜ *is-disj(n,y)*

INIT
states: Studx
post-INIT(,<n',y'>) ≜ *n' = y' = { }*

ENROL
states: Studx
type: Student-name →
pre-ENROL(<n,y>,nm) ≜ ∼*(nm ϵ (n∪y))*
post-ENROL(<n,y>,nm,<n',y'>) ≜ *n' = n∪{nm} ∧ y' = y*

COMPL
states: Studx
type: Student-name →
pre-COMPL(<n,y>,nm) ≜ *nm ϵ n*
post-COMPL(<n,y>,nm,<n',y'>) ≜ *n' = n-{nm} ∧ y' = y∪{nm}*

RESULT
states: Studx
type: → *Student-name-set*
post-RESULT(<n,y>,<n',y'>,res) ≜ *res=y ∧ y'=y ∧ n'=n*

Figure 43   Specification of Students who Complete Exercises Problem

which is again immediate. (Notice how the equalities obtained from
post-ENROL are carried over to the right of the implication.)
    The third result is:

pre-COMPL(σ,nm) ∧ inv-studx(σ) ∧ post-COMPL(σ,nm,σ') ⟹
    inv-studx(σ')

which reduces to:

is-disj(n,y) ⟹ *is-disj(n-{nm},y∪{nm})*

which is immediate. (Notice, here, how terms on the left of the
implication, which are not required for the proof, are simply being
dropped—cf. rule (i) of exercise 2.3. A good rule to guide the selection
of required terms is to write the right-hand side of the implication first.)
    The result for *RESULT* is simple because the operation is an
identity on states.
    Given that the formulae documented in the specification imply the
data type invariant, why should it be necessary to record it? There are
two answers and both relate to the subsequent uses of a specification. The

most immediate problem is proofs of object refinement (see next chapter)—the discovery of appropriate models for abstract data types is greatly facilitated by having a record of the data type invariant. Suppose, in the current example, a realization was sought using a simple vector of bits (one per student—a one-bit could indicate that a student had completed exercises and a zero-bit the opposite situation). Such a realization depends on the fact that no student can ever have both properties: the designer has to rely on the data type invariant.

A second reason exists for recording the invariant. A specification should be extendable, but careless extension could destroy the intent of the original author and one way in which he can document his intent is by recording appropriate invariants. Such information is itself valuable because of the central role of the states in a specification.

Exercise 10.1: Most programming languages require that *arrays* are regular (each sub-array must be of the same shape). Write an appropriate data type invariant for exercise 9.20. But, to simplify the task, assume that the arrays are two dimensional. Thus:

Array = Vec-list
Vec = Element-list

Exercise 10.2: The *equivalence relation* problem presented earlier has a data type invariant. Prove that *inv-q* holds (the operations are collected in fig. 55).

One proves that a data type invariant is satisfied at the end of each operation. It is, however, possible that during an operation the predicate would not hold. For example, suppose the update in the *students who complete exercises* problem is done in two steps the first of which inserts the name in the *Y* set; after this first step the sets overlap but this is remedied prior to the termination of the operation.

The need for data type invariants is due to the fact that the data types in the specification do not mirror reality precisely. Is this inevitable or is it a fault in the definition? The answer varies from case to case. For some problems better (simpler data type invariant) specifications can be found. But data type invariants are often required. That is, for complex problems, reality is often too *ragged* for neat mathematical models. (A context-free syntax description is not capable of defining exactly the class of strings of a programming language. Additional rules must be stated to govern the matching of identifiers etc. In Bjorner(78) such rules are called *context conditions*.)

An example is a state which is to contain *dates*:

Date:: YEAR: Nat MONTH: {Jan, Feb, ..., Dec} DAY: {1:31}

Some constraint has been achieved by carefully selecting the sets for the separate components. To prohibit *1984-Feb-30* is not, however, a question of the set of values of a single field but requires a relationship between fields. A predicate which characterizes the class of valid dates as follows:

$inv\text{-}date(<y,m,d>) \triangleq$
   $(m\epsilon\{Jan,Mar,May,Jul,Aug,Oct,Dec\} \Rightarrow 1 \leq d \leq 31) \land$
   $(m\epsilon\{Apr,June,Sept,Nov\} \Rightarrow 1 \leq d \leq 30) \land$
   $(m=Feb \land \sim is\text{-}leap\text{-}year(y) \Rightarrow 1 \leq d \leq 28) \land$
   $(m=Feb \land is\text{-}leap\text{-}year(y) \Rightarrow 1 \leq d \leq 29)$

Exercise 10.3: Suppose a hotel requires a system which stores information about room numbers:

Room-no.: FLOOR: {1:25} INDEX: {0:64}

Write an invariant which defines valid room numbers to reflect the facts that:

- there is no floor numbered *13*
- level *1* is an open area and has only room number *0*
- the top five floors consist of large suites and these are numbered with even integers.

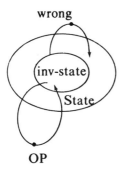

Figure 44   Data Type Invariant

In summary: data type invariants have been introduced as predicates which can be shown to be satisfied by all states created by the operations of a data type. Their major role is in the proofs of refinement but they can also help to document the intent of a specification. Fig. 44 depicts the whole set *State* and the valid subset; *OP* preserves the invariant, the other operation does not.

Chapter 11

DATA REFINEMENT

This part of the book has introduced the abstract object approach to specifications; the advantages of writing a specification as a constructive definition of a data type have been shown to be brevity and ease of manipulation. This chapter deals with the refinement of abstract objects. That is, it shows how a realization can be related to an abstract data type and proved correct. This topic could be deferred until the more interesting tools for defining data types (e.g. mappings) are covered. However, sets and lists suffice to present the idea of one object being a model of another and data refinement is a key part of the rigorous method.

The concept of data refinement can be compared with that of operation decomposition. Both sorts of development are providing realizations of abstractions. Programmers should be familiar with the idea of presenting a development as a (top-down) hierarchy of operations. The discussion of operations began (chapter 4) with implicit specification. Chapter 5, shows that such specifications can be used to facilitate the recording of a correctness argument at each stage of development. In the development process, it is necessary to ask whether an operation possessing the required properties is available via supporting software. If so, the developer's task is completed; if not, the operation is decomposed into a realization built from a number of simpler operations. Each of the subsidiary operations would also be specified and, under the assumption that these specifications are satisfactorily met, a proof can be documented to show that a composition of such units would achieve the overall task.

Abstract data types have been used in specifications. If the programming language possesses the required data types, the developer's task is simple. Usually, however, the data types are more abstract than those available and some further development is required—a realization of the abstraction is to be provided. The process of providing a realization for an abstract data type is called *data refinement* and the term *representation* is used for the more concrete data type of the realization. The operations on the representation are said to *model* those of the abstraction. Here again, the specifications are formal enough to support correctness arguments and also development may be in more than one stage. (See fig. 45.)

	Operations	Data Types
Abstraction	implicit specification	data type
Development process	decomposition	refinement
Realization	realization	representation

Figure 45   Aspects of Stepwise Development

The structure of this chapter is as follows. Firstly a review is given of the range of representations of abstract data types. Then the two concepts of retrieve functions and adequacy are introduced before the main topic of the refinement of operations.

Once again, the approach taken is at first formal so as to convey the theoretical basis of refinement. Once this has been established, the refinement rules can be used as a checklist, only resorting to detailed proofs for critical steps.

Range of Representations

Developing a program in a style which separates the various decisions makes the mental task more manageable. The developer is more likely to produce a correct solution and a later reader will find the work easier to follow. The separation of problems in the case of data is also likely to increase the efficiency of the final program, due to the wide range of possible ways of representing abstract data types. The stepwise development process permits enough development to be done to allow understanding of the operations (and their relative frequencies) on the information content of the data types, before it is necessary to make a decision as to how to represent the data type.

There are reviews of possible ways of representing values of abstract objects in Hoare(72a) and Wirth(76); here a condensed and slightly different list is provided to indicate the range of choice.

The simplest composite value is the Cartesian product of a number of simpler values. Thus, in PL/I, given a number of types, a new type which allows one of each of the sub-types to occur can be achieved by declaring a structure. Each value of the structure type is a collection of values of the given types. The range of choice in representing such combinations is naturally limited but PL/I offers the options of packing into the least amount of storage or of aligning fields on storage boundaries. The decision whether to conserve storage or to achieve faster access can thus be separated from the understanding of the required information content.

In the simplest case an array is dense (i.e. most elements have non-trivial values) and of static size; the implementation maps the collection of elements onto a one-dimensional address space. If one array dimension is to be allowed to vary, it is possible, in PL/I, to avoid reserving storage for the largest possible overall size by having a vector only large enough to contain the maximum size of the varying dimension; and storing into that vector pointers to dynamically allocated storage for arrays of the static dimensions. Rosenberg(74) has studied algorithms for mapping arrays which can expand in more than one dimension. A sparse array (i.e. a large array where less than, say, five percent of the values differ from zero) is best considered as a mapping from its indices to its values (see below).

A one-dimensional array is an acceptable realization of lists only if there is a known maximum length and it is rarely necessary to insert elements. If either of these two limitations do not hold, then it may be necessary to organize the elements in a linked-list structure where each data item is paired with a pointer to the next value.

The range of possibilities for implementing a set is much wider. If, although the range of possible elements is large, the instances of set have a small cardinality, an array may be chosen to store the current elements. But if the class of potential elements is relatively small, it might be worth finding some relationship between the elements and the integers, so that set values can be represented as bit vectors where the bits denote presence or absence of the corresponding element. The presence of suitable bit operations on the machine can lead to very efficient implementations of set operations like union. Finally, if the set on which an operation is defined has no maximum size, it may be necessary to employ linked-list storage.

Chapter 12 introduces mappings from which information can be retrieved by key. Finding suitable representations for abstract data types expressed in terms of mappings is again governed by the likely contents. It may be efficient to regard a map as a set of pairs and then consider how to handle the set. If there is frequent reference to a mapping, the pairs may be better arranged as a list which is ordered on its first elements. An even faster access may be possible, at the expense of storage, if a *hashing* technique is used on the domain element to compute an address where the value may be located.

The problems of finding representations for the tree-like structures which can be described by abstract syntax (see chapter 14) are very varied. The logically simplest implementation might be to allocate a based variable per *node* which contains data and pointers to sub-nodes. But such a realization is unlikely to be acceptable because of excessive storage usage and fragmentation. Arranging trees in a linear order poses two problems. Firstly there is the difficulty of providing sufficient information so that an algorithm can keep track of where it is in the representation. Secondly, operations, which in the tree form may be as simple as looking at the right branch before the left, may become prohibitively slow unless extra cross-referencing mechanisms are built into the representations (cf. the internal representation of PL/I programs which is discussed in Weissenboeck(75)).

Retrieve Functions

A necessary preliminary to proofs of data refinement is the documentation of the relationship between an abstraction and its representation: *retrieve functions* will be used to do this. The abstract data types in a specification are chosen to contain a minimum of information. That is, they contain only information which is required to document the behavior of the operations. Elements of a representation are, then, likely to contain more information than those of the abstraction. This information may be irrelevant as in the case of a list which represents a set, or it may be used to locate information in the representation. An example of this is the information inserted into linear forms of trees to show the tree structure. (This is the role of parentheses in the written form of arithmetic expressions.)

Whatever the purpose of the information in the representation, it often gives rise to a situation where a number of different values of the representation correspond to one abstract value. That is, for each value of the abstract data type there may be several values in the representation data type; these values contain different incidental information. For example, consider an operation which is specified in terms of sets and later realized in terms of lists: fig. 46 shows how different lists correspond to each set value. Contained in each list value is the same information from the set value plus some, in each case different, ordering information which was absent at the more abstract level.

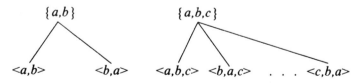

Figure 46   Correspondence of List Representation to Sets

There is then likely to be a one-many relationship between abstract values and their representations. The easiest way of documenting such a relationship is by a function from the latter to the former. That is, a function is written which retrieves the essential (abstract) information. Thus, for the example with lists and sets, the retrieve function would be:

retr-set: X-list → X-set
retr-set(xl) ≜ **elems**xl

Such functions are called *retrieve functions* and are given names which begin with *retr-*.

A retrieve function can be given for the *students in classroom* problem. The abstract specification is given in fig. 34. Suppose it is decided to produce a realization on states which contain lists of names:

Studc1 = Student-name-list

then the retrieve function will be of type:

retr-Studc: Studc1 → Studc

and can be defined as:

retr-Studc(nml) ≜ **elems**nml

Notice that the refinement of *Studc* has been called *Studc1*. In the same way, the realizations of the operations which are to use *Studc1* have the operation names of the specification with suffix *1* (e.g. *INIT1*, *ENTER1*). These new operations are presented when the proofs are considered.

Exercise 11.1:   Present a state for a realization for the *students who do exercises* (see fig. 43) problem. Use two lists and define the retrieve function.

Exercise 11.2:   Using the same problem (fig. 43), write the retrieve function for a realization based on:

Studx1:: NMS: Student-name-list YN: Bool-list

Assume that the two lists are of the same length and that the true entries in the second indicate those students who have done exercises.

Exercise 11.3:   In exercise 8.9 the state of the spelling checker was defined as:

Dict = Word-set

If this is to be represented by ordered lists of words for each possible length, the state would be:

Dict1 = Word-grp-list1
Word-grp = Word-list

Define a retrieve function.

Exercise 11.4:   Present a refinement of exercise 8.11 based on two lists of Boolean values and write the retrieve function.

In the examples presented so far, the retrieve function has been total but it need only be applicable to states which satisfy the data type invariant of the representation.

(Since the subject of equivalence relations has been discussed, it can be mentioned that the retrieve function is defining equivalence classes of the representation values, i.e. the space of representations is partitioned by the abstract element onto which the retrieve function maps them.)

Adequacy

For a representation to be useful, it must be capable of representing every value of the abstract data type. That is, for each (valid) element of the abstract data type there must exist at least one value of the representation which is mapped by the retrieve function onto the abstract value. That there may be more than one has been shown in the last section. Here the intuitive requirement that there must be at least one is formalized as a property called *adequacy*.

A possible representation for the *students in classroom* problem (cf. fig. 34) is:

$Studcl = Student\text{-}name\text{-}list$

the last section has given the retrieve function as:

$retr\text{-}Studc(nml) \triangleq \textbf{elems}nml$

Translating the verbal form of the adequacy requirement into formulae gives:

$(\textbf{A}s\epsilon Studc)(\textbf{E}sl\epsilon Studcl)(retr\text{-}Studc(sl)=s)$

This can be shown informally by pointing out that any set can be laid out in an arbitrary order; this then is a (list) value which is a member of $Studcl$. To formalize this proof one could present an inductive argument on sets.

Basis: suppose the value to be represented is:

$s = \{\}$

Then:

$sl = \Leftrightarrow$

gives:

$retr\text{-}Studc(sl) = s$

For the inductive step, prove that s can be represented where:

$s \neq \{\}$

Choosing some element:

$e\epsilon s$

the induction hypothesis ensures that:

$s - \{e\}$

can be represented. That is:

*(**E**sl')(retr-Studc(sl') = s-{e})*

Therefore *s* can be represented by:

sl' | | <e>

which concludes the proof.

It is not usually necessary to present formal proofs of adequacy. An argument like the earlier constructive one is normally sufficient to show existence. To indicate what happens when a representation is not adequate, suppose one tried to use a representation with:

Studcla = Student-name-listl

This is not adequate because no object of this type can be mapped, by a reasonable retrieve function, onto the empty set. Similarly, if a representation was sought on arrays with an upper bound, then not all sets could be represented.

Exercise 11.5:   Indicate why the representation in exercise 11.3 is adequate.

Exercise 11.6:   For the *students who do exercises* problem (cf. fig. 43), show that the state:

Studxl:: N: Student-name-list Y: Student-name-list

is an adequate representation of:

Studx:: N: Student-name-set Y: Student-name-set

In exercise 11.2 the state, according to the adequacy rule presented so far, is not adequate. This does not indicate that the proposed step of development was mistaken but only that the criteria of adequacy must be made more precise. Chapter 10 introduced the idea of the valid members of a data type being those which satisfy the data type invariant. The problem now is that there are some states which fail to satisfy the data type invariant and for which there is no represention. The full form of the adequacy requirement can then be stated as follows: for some defined abstract data type *State* with data type invariant *inv*, a representation *Statel* with *invl* is said to be adequate if the relevant retrieve function *retr* is such that:

*(**A**σεState)(inv(σ) ⇒ (**E**σlεStatel)(invl(σl) ∧ σ=retr(σl)))*

Thus for exercise 11.2:

inv-studx(<n,y>) ≜ *is-disj(n,y)*

inv-studx1(<nml,bl>) ≜ **len***nml* = **len***bl*

retr-Studx(<nml,bl>) ≜
   <{ *nml(i)* | *1≤i≤***len***nml* ∧ ~*bl(i)* },
    { *nml(i)* | *1≤i≤***len***nml* ∧ *bl(i)* }>

it must be proved:

is-disj(n,y) ⟹
   (**E**<*nml,bl*>∈*Studx1*)(**len***nml*=**len***bl* ∧ *retr-Studx(<nml,bl>)=<n,y>)*

which is clear by construction or by a formal argument of induction on
the two sets.

Exercise 11.7: Show that the refinement presented in exercise 11.4 is
adequate.

Refinement of Operations

The general idea that one data type can be thought of as a refinement of
another is the theme of this chapter. Retrieve functions and the concept
of adequacy have been explained. It is now necessary to consider the
realization of the operations associated with the abstract data type.

   One way of expressing the role of retrieve functions is to consider the
representation as being viewed under the retrieve function. That is, using
the retrieve function as a way of looking at the representation so that it
filters out all of the irrelevant information. Using this point of view, an
important observation can be made about data refinement. In the
students in classroom problem, the abstract state at some point might
contain two names. There are two possible different values for this in the
list representation shown in fig. 47. If a third name is added to the set by
the operation *ENTER* a set of three elements results. Assuming the
corresponding operation on the representation (i.e. *ENTER1*) simply
concatenates names onto the list, two different states will result
depending on the starting state. But, just as with the starting states, when
viewed under the retrieve function, these states look the same (see fig.
47). This observation is the key to proving refinement steps of development correct.

   Remember that operations are normally characterized by pre- and
post-conditions. The use of a predicate to define the input/output
behavior of an operation permits a range of results. For each operation
on the abstract state, there will be a corresponding operation on the
refined state. The new operation will be said to **model** the corresponding
abstract operation if it can be used to fulfil the function of the abstract

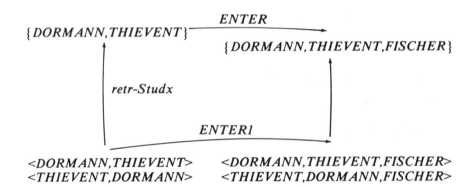

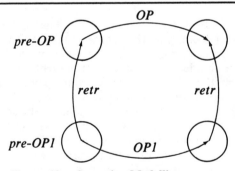

Figure 47   Representations Viewed under Retrieve Functions

operation. To be a model, an operation must have a sufficiently large domain and yield appropriate answers.

To be more precise, consider fig. 48. The operation *OP1* is said to be a model of *OP* if, for any state satisfying the pre-condition of *OP*, the states which are mapped onto it by *retr* also satisfy the pre-condition of *OP1*; and all states in the pre-condition of *OP1* when operated on by *OP1* yield a state which, viewed under the retrieve function, is defined as acceptable by the post-condition of *OP*. Even with the aid of a diagram this is difficult to describe in words; formulae make the situation precise.

Figure 48   Operation Modelling

Two results must be proved about each function. Suppose it is required to prove that *OP1* models *OP*. Given that both operations are specified by post-conditions, a general form of:

$$post\text{-}OP1(s1,s1') \Rightarrow post\text{-}OP(retr(s1),retr(s1'))$$

is to be expected. But it is necessary to clarify over which states *s1* this property must hold. The choice here is to quantify for all states satisfying

the data type invariant of the realization *inv1* and the pre-condition of
OP1. Thus one property required is shown as *ra* (*r* for result) in fig. 49.
It would have been possible to make other choices for the quantification
in *ra* but, given the choice made, it is necessary to prove that if a
retrieved state satisfies the pre-condition of *OP* then the refined state is
within the pre-condition of *OP1*. Because of the data type properties,
this rule can also be restricted by the data type invariant as is shown in
da of fig. 49.

In order to show that OP1 models OP, show

Data Type:

aa. $(\mathbf{A}\sigma1)(inv1(\sigma1) \Rightarrow (\mathbf{E}\sigma)(\sigma=retr(\sigma1)) \wedge inv(retr(\sigma1)))$
ab. $(\mathbf{A}\sigma)(inv(\sigma) \Rightarrow (\mathbf{E}\sigma1)(inv1(\sigma1) \wedge \sigma=retr(\sigma1)))$

Operation

da. $(\mathbf{A}\sigma1)(inv1(\sigma1) \wedge pre\text{-}OP(retr(\sigma1),args) \Rightarrow pre\text{-}OP1(\sigma1,args))$
ra. $(\mathbf{A}\sigma1)(inv1(\sigma1) \wedge pre\text{-}OP1(\sigma1,args) \wedge post\text{-}OP1(\sigma1,args,\sigma1',res) \Rightarrow$
     $post\text{-}OP(retr(\sigma1),args,retr(\sigma1'),res))$

Figure 49   Rules for Proof of Refinement

Apart from the rules *da* and *ra* which have to be proved for each
operation, there are two rules which must be proved about the objects
concerned. Rule *ab* is the adequacy requirement introduced in the
preceding section. Rule *aa* states that *retr* must always be defined for
objects satisfying the data type invariant *inv1* and that, for such objects,
it must yield a state satisfying *inv*.

As with the lists of properties for decomposition, examples are first
given of the formal use of these rules for refinement: the aim is to come
quickly to a rigorous method where they will simply be used as checklists.
(The properties are listed for convenience in appendix B).

A single refined operation can be used to model an operation of the
abstraction. However, a data type normally has more than one operation
associated with it and it is important to see that the proofs for the
individual operations are sufficient to ensure that the collections of
operations relate properly. Remember that the constructs of the
programming language (e.g. *DO*) link operations together. Thus, if the
individual operations model those of an abstraction, so does their
combination. The upper diagram in fig. 50 shows a sequence of individual
operations: as depicted, the arguments and results of the abstract
operations are related to their representations by retrieve functions. But,
if a representation of an initial state is found and processed by *OP1a*, a
state is created which is usable by *OP1b*; it is therefore superfluous to
apply the retrieve function and find another state corresponding to the
resulting abstraction. Thus it is possible to give control entirely to the
operations of the representation—linked by the sequencing constructs of

the programming language. This is shown in the lower part of fig. 50. Of course, when a final (interrogator) operation maps the elements of the states into another data type the answers are identical and do not have to be related by retrieve.

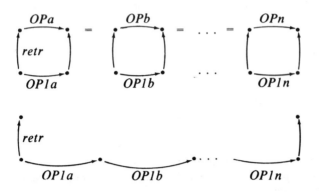

Figure 50   Collections of Operations

Turning now to examples. Consider (for the last time) the *students in classroom* problem (see fig. 34). This is refined to operations using states:

$Studc1 = Student\text{-}name\text{-}list$

in which the possibility of duplicates occurring is excluded. Thus:

$inv\text{-}studc1(nml) \triangleq is\text{-}uniquel(nml)$

The abstract and refined states can be related by:

$retr\text{-}Studc(nml) \triangleq \textbf{elems}nml$

The requirements on the data type can now be considered. Rule *aa* becomes:

$(\textbf{A}nml)(inv\text{-}studc1(nml) \Rightarrow$
$\quad (\textbf{E}nms)(nms=retr\text{-}Studc(nml)) \wedge inv\text{-}studc(retr\text{-}Studc(nml)))$

Since there is no invariant (i.e. it is **TRUE**) for the abstraction, and because **elems** is defined for all lists, this is immediate.

The standard adequacy constraint *ab* has already been proved in the section on Adequacy.

The operations on the refined states are presented in fig. 51 - notice the suffix *1* is being used to show that they are models. Given the operations, it should now be proved that the data type invariant is preserved. This is straightforward and is omitted here. The two required

INIT1
states: Studc1
$post\text{-}INIT1(,nml') \triangleq nml' = <>$

ENTER1
states: Studc1
type: Student-name $\rightarrow$
$pre\text{-}ENTER1(nml,nm) \triangleq \sim is\text{-}present(nml,nm)$
$post\text{-}ENTER1(nml,nm,nml') \triangleq nml'=nml | \; | <nm>$

EXIT1
states: Studc1
type: Student-name $\rightarrow$
$pre\text{-}EXIT1(nml,nm) \triangleq is\text{-}present(nml,nm)$
$post\text{-}EXIT1(nml,nm,nml') \triangleq$
    $(\textbf{let } j=(\iota j)(nml(j)=nm)$
    $nml'=del(nml,j))$

PRESENT1
states: Studc1
type: Student-name $\rightarrow$ *Bool*
$post\text{-}PRESENT1(nml,nm,nml',b) \triangleq$
    $nml'= nml \; \wedge \; (b \Leftrightarrow is\text{-}present(nml,nm))$

where:

$is\text{-}present(nml,nm) \triangleq (\textbf{E}i\epsilon\{1:\textbf{len}nml\})(nml(i)=nm)$

Figure 51   Refinement of Students in Classroom Problem

properties of fig. 49 are now examined for each of the operations.
Consider first *ENTER1*. To show that its pre-condition is sufficiently
wide requires:

da.
$inv\text{-}studc1(nml) \; \wedge \; pre\text{-}ENTER(retr\text{-}Studc(nml),nm) \Rightarrow$
    $pre\text{-}ENTER1(nml,nm)$

$\sim(nm\epsilon\textbf{elems}nml) \Rightarrow \sim(\textbf{E}i\epsilon\{1:\textbf{len}nml\})(nml(i)=nm)$

which is immediate.
    To show that the result is correct requires:

ra.
$inv\text{-}studc1(nml) \; \wedge \; pre\text{-}ENTER1(nml) \; \wedge \; post\text{-}ENTER1(nml,nm,nml') \Rightarrow$
    $post\text{-}ENTER(retr\text{-}Studc(nml),nm,retr\text{-}Studc(nml'))$

$nml'=nml | \; | <nm> \Rightarrow \textbf{elems}nml' = \textbf{elems}nml \cup \{nm\}$

which is immediate.

Exercise 11.8:   Prove results *dₐ* and *ra* for *INIT1* and *EXIT1*

The result for *PRESENT1* is trivial in that both operations are total and are identities on states. For such an (interrogator) operation it must, however, be shown that the correct answer is produced. Thus:

inv-studc1(nml) ∧ pre-PRESENT1(nml) ∧
  post-PRESENT1(nml,nm,nml',b) ⟹
      post-PRESENT(retr-Studc(nml),nm,retr-Studc(nml'),b)

the essential part of which is:

*(b⟺(**E**iϵ{1:**len**nml})(nml(i)=nm))* ⟺ *(b⟺nmϵ**elems**nml)*

which is immediate.

★   ★   ★

This concludes the first example of data refinement using operations. To recap the steps, at some stage of development a solution exists which uses an abstract data type and a set of operations thereon; a model is provided in terms of a representation for the objects and a new set of operations; the representation is related to the abstraction by means of a retrieve function; proving that the representation is adequate and that the new operations model the original ones concludes the development step. The specifications of the new operations may then be subjected to further refinement or decomposition.

The retrieve functions provide the basis of assertions of correctness. The concept of validity conditions for data types has also been introduced; these can be viewed as invariants of the data types and their use can significantly increase the clarity of arguments about data refinement. Just as with the proofs about program decomposition, it is not necessary that large programs be proved correct, even in stages of data refinement, at the level of detail used on the examples given here. In proofs of program correctness, assertions and invariants are used to record the main reasons for a belief in correctness. With data refinement steps, this is achieved by documenting the retrieve and validity predicates.

★   ★   ★

As a second example, consider the problem of implementing **stacks** (see fig. 39). An implementation is given on arrays. But to simplify the task, it is assumed that the arrays can be arbitrarily long. Thus the implementation uses a list and a counter and the refinement proof need only concern itself with the fact that the lists are in reverse order. Thus the realization is based on:

Stack1::   ELS: Element-list CTR: Nat0

with the invariant:

inv1(<ell,n>) ≜ **len**ell ≥ n

The relationship between *Stack* and *Stack1* is shown by the retrieve function:

retr-Stack(<ell,n>) $\triangleq$ *rev(front(ell,n))*

Rule *aa* becomes (the invariant on *Stack* is **TRUE**):

inv1(s1) $\Rightarrow$ *(**E**s)(s=retr-Stack(s1))*

There is a pre-condition for *front* (see appendix C) but its satisfaction is guaranteed by *inv1*.
Rule *ab* requires:

*(**A**stϵStack)(**E**st1ϵStack1)(inv1(st1)* $\wedge$ *st=retr(st1))*

This can be seen by construction. That is, a way of converting a *Stack* into an element of *Stack1* can be defined by reversing the list and putting the length in *ctr*. Notice, however, that there are other elements of *Stack1* which correspond to any given element of *Stack* because the *els* component can have an arbitrary number of elements beyond the *nth*. Existence, however, is proved and not affected by non-uniqueness.
The operations of the realization are:

post-INIT1(,<ell,n>) $\triangleq$ *ell=<>* $\wedge$ *n=0*

post-PUSH1(<ell,n>,e,<ell',n'>) $\triangleq$
   n'=n+1 $\wedge$
   ell'= *(if* *n=lenell* **then** *ell| | <e>* **else** *modl(ell,n',e))*

pre-POP1(<ell,n>) $\triangleq$ *n* $\neq$ *0*
post-POP1(<ell,n>,<ell',n'>,res) $\triangleq$ *ell'=ell* $\wedge$ *n'=n-1* $\wedge$ *res=ell(n)*

post-IS-EMPTY1(<ell,n>,<ell',n'>,b) $\triangleq$ *ell'=ell* $\wedge$ *n'=n* $\wedge$ *(b*$\leftrightarrow$*n=0)*

Considering *INIT1*, property *da* becomes:

inv1(st1) $\wedge$ *pre-INIT(retr-Stack(st1))* $\Rightarrow$ *pre-INIT1(st1)*

which is vacuously true. Property *ra* becomes:

inv1(st1) $\wedge$ *pre-INIT1(st1)* $\wedge$ *post-INIT1(st1,st1')* $\Rightarrow$
   post-INIT(retr-Stack(st1),retr-Stack(st1'))

ell'=<> $\wedge$ *n'=0* $\Rightarrow$ *rev(front(ell',n'))=<>*

which is immediate.
Considering *PUSH1*, property *da* is again vacuously true. Property *ra* becomes:

inv1(st1) $\wedge$ *pre-PUSH1(st1)* $\wedge$ *post-PUSH1(st1,e,st1')* $\Rightarrow$
   post-PUSH(retr-Stack(st1),e,retr-Stack(st1'))

or:

len*ell*$\geq$*n* $\wedge$ *n'=n+1* $\wedge$ *ell'=(if* *n=lenell* **then** *ell| | <e>* **else** *modl(ell,n',e))*
   $\Rightarrow$ *rev(front(ell',n'))* = *<e>| | rev(front(ell,n))*

To show this, consider the case:

$n = \textbf{len}ell$

then:

$ell' = ell| \; | <e> \; \wedge \; n'=n+1$

From these equalities, and the properties of *rev* (see appendix C):

$rev(front(ell',n'))$
    $= rev(ell')$
    $= rev(ell| \; | <e>)$
    $= rev(<e>)| \; | rev(ell)$
    $= <e>| \; | rev(front(ell,n))$

In the other case:

$n > \textbf{len}ell$

Therefore:

$ell' = modl(ell,n',e) \; \wedge \; n'=n+1$

and thus:

$rev(front(ell',n'))$
    $= rev(front(ell,n)| \; | <e>)$
    $= <e>| \; | rev(front(ell,n))$

Considering *POP1*, property *da* becomes:

$inv1(st1) \; \wedge \; pre\text{-}POP(retr\text{-}Stack(st1)) \Rightarrow pre\text{-}POP1(st1)$
$\textbf{len}ell{\geq}n \; \wedge \; (rev(front(ell,n))){\neq}<> \Rightarrow n{\neq}0$
$\textbf{len}ell{\geq}n \; \wedge \; front(ell,n){\neq}<> \Rightarrow n{\neq}0$

which is immediate. Property *ra*:

$inv1(st1) \; \wedge \; pre\text{-}POP1(st1) \; \wedge \; post\text{-}POP1(st1,st1',res) \Rightarrow$
    $post\text{-}POP(retr\text{-}Stack(st1),retr\text{-}Stack(st1'),res)$

or:

$\textbf{len}ell{\geq}n \; \wedge \; n{\neq}0 \; \wedge \; ell'=ell \; \wedge \; n'=n{-}1 \; \wedge \; res=ell(n) \Rightarrow$
    $rev(front(ell',n')) = \textbf{tl}rev(front(ell,n)) \; \wedge \; res = \textbf{hd}rev(front(ell,n))$

Now:

$rev(front(ell',n')) = rev(front(ell,n'))$

But:

$\textbf{tl}rev(front(ell,n))$
    $= \textbf{tl}rev(front(ell,n{-}1)| \; | <ell(n)>)$
    $= \textbf{tl}(rev(<ell(n)>)| \; | rev(front(ell,n{-}1)))$
    $= rev(front(ell,n'))$

thus:

$rev(front(ell',n')) = \textbf{tl}rev(front(ell,n))$

and:

$res = ell(n)$

But:

$ell(n) = \mathbf{hd}rev(front(ell,n))$

thus:

$res = \mathbf{hd}rev(front(ell,n))$

which concludes the argument for *POP1*.

The operations *IS-EMPTY* and *IS-EMPTY1* are both total and identities on states, thus all that has to be shown is:

$n \geq len\,ell \implies (n{=}0 \iff rev(front(ell,n)){=}{<}{>})$

which is immediate. This concludes the proof of the refinement of the stack operations.

Exercise 11.9: Refer back to exercise 11.6 and define operations for that refinement of the *students who do exercises* problem, then prove the refinement correct.

Exercise 11.10: Again using the *students who do exercises* problem, complete and prove the refinement foreseen in exercise 11.2

Summary

It has been shown how stages in a stepwise development process can refine data types. That is, given an abstract data type, its constructive specification can be realized by a more concrete object and a new set of operations thereon. The representation is related to the abstraction by means of retrieve functions and the former is proved adequate. The list of properties in fig. 49 can be used as a checklist in a rigorous development. Fig. 45 shows the relation between the two aspects of stepwise development.

Further examples of refinement occur in the subsequent chapters. The first published work in this area is Milner(70) which speaks of one program *simulating* another. Hoare(72b) takes a similar approach and uses the term *abstraction functions* for, what are called here, retrieve functions. Hoare(73) presents the development of a paging system.

Summary Exercises

Exercise 11.11: Consider the finite *stacks* defined in exercise 9.14. Provide a realization which does have infinite lists and therefore never needs to lose elements; but ensure the same external behavior by storing an additional counter which tracks the bottom of the stack. Prove the refinement correct. (Try using the results as a checklist rather than doing detailed proofs.)

Exercise 11.12: Starting with exercise 9.7 for a specification of *queues*, add a constraint for the maximum length and an operation to test whether queues are full. Then define and prove a realization based on lists and counters.

Exercise 11.13: A *sort* operation was specified in excercise 9.17. Consider a refinement:

Sort1:: ELS: Element-list PERM: Nat-list

SORT1
states: Sort1

with:

$inv1(<els,perm>) \triangleq$ **elems**$perm = \{1:$**len**$els\} \; \wedge \; is\text{-}unique1(perm)$

where:

$post\text{-}SORT1(<els,>,<els',perm'>) \triangleq$
    $els' = els \; \wedge \; is\text{-}ordered(sel\text{-}subl(els',perm'))$

Show that this is a refinement of *SORT* (the definitions of the subsidiary list functions are collected in appendix C).

Exercise 11.14: This and the next two exercises are based on the spelling problem (see exercise 9.16). None of the proofs should be difficult and the reader should experiment with less formal reasoning. In order to make the problem more realistic, extend the specification with an operation *ADDTDIC* which adds one word to the stored dictionary. The first refinement to be proved correct uses a dictionary which is a simple list of words (they would be ordered to facilitate a search, but this property does not yet play a part).

Exercise 11.15: For the second refinement assume the dictionary is organized as a list of lists where each of the individual lists contains words of the same length. Prove this refinement correct.

Exercise 11.16: Finally, assume a refinement where the state is:

Dict1c:: CHARS : Character-list STARTS: Nat-list ENDS: Nat-list

where the *ith* word can be accessed by:

$create\text{-}word(subl(chars,starts(i),ends(i)))$

Chapter 12

MAPPING NOTATION

The value of set and list notation for writing specifications is shown above. Not only are such specifications short but, because they are written in a formal notation, it is also possible to reason about them. Hopefully, the reader has now had sufficient practice with these notations and he can begin to reason safely at a rigorous, non-detailed, level. When writing large specifications, however, it is worth having more tools at one's disposal.

There are many situations where a table-like organization is used for information retrieval via a key (e.g. telephone directory, airline guide, filing cabinet). A mapping provides a natural model for such situations and thus facilitates the construction of specifications which are intuitively clear. Well-chosen concepts will improve the readability of a specification.

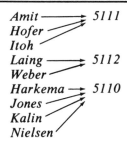

Figure 52   Mapping for Students' Whereabouts

The notation for mappings is again introduced by an example. The problem (*students' whereabouts*) is to be able to determine in which room a student is located. In an implementation of such a system, an array with one element for each possible student might be used; in this element the current room number can be stored. However, this is one possibility among many and there are a number of dangers of basing a specification on an implementation approach. Firstly, it should not be necessary to think so early about how to relate student names and array indices. Secondly, such an array would make some operations very inefficient (e.g. counting the students in a particular room). Clearly then, for the purposes of the specification, it is preferable to try to be more abstract. In a separate phase of development, appropriate refinements can be chosen when the full collection of operators is known. The state of the specification uses a mapping. A mapping between a set of names and a set of room numbers is pictured in fig. 52.

A mapping can be used like a function and much of the terminology for mappings is familiar from functions. But a mapping is more restricted: it has a finite domain. Furthermore, the pairing of domain and range elements for mappings is constructed rather than being defined by an expression. These limitations make it possible to perform operations on mappings which cannot be defined for functions.

One way to picture a mapping is as a table of pairs of values. Thus the table corresponding to fig. 52 is:

Amit	*5111*
Hofer	*5111*
Itoh	*5111*
Laing	*5112*
Weber	*5112*
Harkema	*5110*
Jones	*5110*
Kalin	*5110*
Nielsen	*5110*

(A table, however, is too general because it is a property of mappings that they deliver a unique result for a given argument value. In terms of fig. 52, it could be said that arrows can join, but not divide, going from left to right. The table corresponds to a relation in that one value could appear twice on the left with different values on the right. Given this warning, the table view is used to give an intuitive idea of some of the mapping terminology.)

The set of values in the left-hand column of the table is referred to as the **domain** of the mapping. The mapping can be **applied** to any value in its domain and application yields the corresponding right-hand value. Mappings with disjoint domains could be combined by simply concatenating the two tables. If the domains of the mappings overlap, priority must be given to one of them and an **overwrite** operator is used here to generate a suitable result table.

For the specification of the **students' whereabouts** problem, the state is a mapping:

Studw = Student-name $\rightarrow$ Room-no

(Notice that this notation is the same as for functions. In Bjorner(78) the arrow for mappings was marked with an *m*.)

An initialization operator:

INIT
states: Studw

is defined to set the state to an empty mapping:

post-INIT(,wm') ≜ *wm'*=[]

A student's arrival is recorded by:

ARRIVE
states: Studw
type: Student-name Room-no →

which combines the state with a unit-map containing the appropriate information:

post-ARRIVE(wm,nm,no,wm') ≜ *wm'* = *wm*†[*nm→no*]

A movement is recorded by:

MOVE
states: Studw
type: Student-name Room-no →

which overwrites the current information about a student with the new room number:

post-MOVE(wm,nm,no,wm') ≜ *wm'* = *wm*†[*nm→no*]

The location operation has the type:

LOCATE
states: Studw
type: Student-name → *Room-no*

and is defined by applying the mapping to the student's name:

post-LOCATE(wm,nm,wm',res) ≜ *wm'=wm* ∧ *res=wm(nm)*

Having tried to give a picture of how mappings can be used, it is necessary to define the notation more formally. This is done in the next section. The subsequent section contains some more applications and the remaining sections show refinement steps involving mappings.

Notation

As with both sets and lists, a distinctive form of brackets is used to distinguish mappings ([]). An explicit enumeration of a collection of pairs for a mapping is written:

[*d1→r1,d2→r2, ..., dn→rn*]

Notice that, because a mapping must be single-valued (i.e. many-one), the *di* should be mutually distinct. The order in which the pairs are written is irrelevant, but within a pair the value which is to be in the domain of the mapping must be written to the left of the arrow. The special case of the empty mapping is written:

[]

Mappings, like sets, can be defined implicitly by writing:

$[x \rightarrow f(x) \mid p(x)]$

Thus:

$[x \rightarrow x**2 \mid x \epsilon \{1:4\}] = [1 \rightarrow 1, 2 \rightarrow 4, 3 \rightarrow 9, 4 \rightarrow 16]$

and:

$[x \rightarrow x**2 \mid -1 \leq x \leq 1] = [-1 \rightarrow 1, 0 \rightarrow 0, 1 \rightarrow 1]$

Notice that in this second mapping, two domain elements map onto the same value: it is only the domain elements themselves which must be distinct.

The set of elements for which a mapping is defined, its **domain**, can be determined by an operator:

dom

Using:

$M = [x \rightarrow x**2 \mid 1 \leq x \leq 3]$

then:

dom$M = \{1,2,3\}$

A mapping can be **applied** to any value in its domain. Application yields the second element from the pair which has the argument as the first element. This operator can be viewed as locating a value in a table. Thus:

$M(2) = 4$

For values not in the domain of a map, application is not defined. The **range** (i.e. the set of possible values of a mapping) can be determined by an operator which is defined:

rng$map \triangleq \{map(d) \mid d \epsilon \textbf{dom}map\}$

Thus:

rng$M = \{1,4,9\}$

rng $[x \rightarrow x**2 \mid -1 \leq x \leq 1] = \{0,1\}$

A mapping value can be derived from two others by an **overwrite** operator. Priority is given to pairs of the second operand in cases where the domain elements match. The operator is defined:

$M1 \dagger M2 \triangleq [d \rightarrow r \mid d \epsilon \textbf{dom}M2 \wedge r = M2(d) \vee$
$\qquad\qquad\qquad d \epsilon (\textbf{dom}M1 - \textbf{dom}M2) \wedge r = M1(d)]$

For example:

$M \dagger [3{\to}11, 4{\to}9] = [1{\to}1, 2{\to}4, 3{\to}11, 4{\to}9]$
$[3{\to}11,4{\to}9] \dagger M = [1{\to}1, 2{\to}4, 3{\to}9, 4{\to}9]$
$M \dagger [4{\to}16] = [1{\to}1, 2{\to}4, 3{\to}9, 4{\to}16]$

The last example shows that overwrite can be used to combine two mappings with disjoint ranges.

A mapping can be **restricted** to a given set in the sense that the domain of the resulting mapping is the intersection of the given set and the domain of the original mapping:

$M \mid S \triangleq [d{\to}M(d) \mid d\epsilon(\mathbf{dom}M \cap S)]$

A class of objects can be defined to be mappings by writing:

$M = D \to R$

this defines that the maps m are such that:

$(\mathbf{A}m\epsilon M)(\mathbf{dom}m \subseteq D \wedge \mathbf{rng}m \subseteq R)$

Exercise 12.1:   What is the value of:

a) $[a{\to}5, b{\to}4, c{\to}2, d{\to}1](c)$
b) $[x{\to}2*x \mid is\text{-}prime(x) \wedge 10 \le x \le 15]$
c) $[x{\to}x**2 \mid x\epsilon\{1{:}10\}](9)$
d) $[x{\to}x! \mid x\epsilon\{1{:}10\}](4)$
e) $\mathbf{rng}[x{\to}x**2 \mid x\epsilon\{1{:}3\}]$
f) $([7{\to}a, 2{\to}b] \dagger [3{\to}c])(2)$
g) $([7{\to}a, 2{\to}b] \dagger [2{\to}c, 1{\to}c])(2)$

Exercise 12.2:   Check the following identities; if in doubt construct a proof:

a) $M1 \dagger M2 = [d{\to}r \mid d\epsilon(\mathbf{dom}M1\text{-}\mathbf{dom}M2) \wedge r{=}M1(d)] \dagger M2$
b) $\mathbf{dom}(M1 \dagger M2) = \mathbf{dom}M1 \cup \mathbf{dom}M2$
c) $\mathbf{dom}[x{\to}f(x) \mid p(x)] = \{x \mid p(x)\}$

Exercise 12.3:   Construct an example which shows:

$\mathbf{rng}(M1 \dagger M2) \ne \mathbf{rng}M1 \cup \mathbf{rng}M2$

Fig. 53 shows the types of the operators on mappings.

Equipped with the description of the notation, it is possible to review and complete the definition of the **students' whereabouts** problem—see fig. 54.

In order to drive home the point about not choosing a representation for the implementation too early, suppose that it is necessary to add a further operation which checks (for safety reasons) whether any lecture room is overcrowded. If, say, there is a limit of *50* students per room, it is easy to specify:

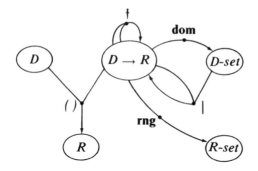

Figure 53   Mapping Operators

Studw = Student-name → Room-no

INIT
states: Studw
post-INIT(,wm') ≜ wm'=[]

ARRIVE
states: Studw
type: Student-name Room-no →
pre-ARRIVE(wm,nm,) ≜ ~(nm∈domwm)
post-ARRIVE(wm,nm,no,wm') ≜ wm' = wm†[nm→no]

MOVE
states: Studw
type: Student-name Room-no →
pre-MOVE(wm,nm,) ≜ nm∈domwm
post-MOVE(wm,nm,no,wm') ≜ wm' = wm†[nm→no]

LOCATE
states: Studw
type: Student-name → Room-no
pre-LOCATE(wm,nm) ≜ nm∈domwm
post-LOCATE(wm,nm,wm',res) ≜ wm'=wm ∧ res=wm(nm)

Figure 54   Specification of Students' Whereabouts Problem

CHECK-SAFETY
states: Studw
type: $\longrightarrow$ *Bool*
post-CHECK-SAFETY(wm,wm',b) $\triangleq$
$\quad$ *(b* $\leftrightarrow$ *(**E**no∈Room-no)(count-studs(wm,no)>50))* $\wedge$ *wm'=wm*
where:

count-studs(wm,no) $\triangleq$ **card**$\{$*nm* | *nm∈domwm* $\wedge$ *wm(nm)=no*$\}$

Although easy to specify at this abstract level, it would be potentially disastrous to implement if the array implementation mentioned above had been chosen. No competent programmer would choose his final data representation until he had a clear idea of the total set of operations. But this should not prevent writing the specification. The specification should use an abstraction which contains only the essential relationships. Thus one can be sure that these will be present, in some form, in the final implementation without prejudging what the representation should be. Indeed, the abstract model is ideal for couching questions like the relative importance of various operations, the answers to which must be determined in order to select a representation which will achieve acceptable performance.

Before moving on to more applications of the mapping notation, it is worth reviewing some of the ways a mapping can be represented. Of course, a mapping could be viewed as a set of pairs (lists of length two) and then the various ways of representing sets can be used. This, however, fails to capitalize on the essential property of a mapping that the domain elements of its pairs are unique. Treating a mapping as a list of pairs makes it possible to order the pairs on the first elements thus making application more efficient. Depending on the frequency of change, the list may be stored either linearly or in a linked-list structure. Direct access to the appropriate range elements can be obtained in most programming languages (if the domain is the integers) by using an array. In PASCAL, the limitation to integers is dropped; however, the domain, as well as being finite, must be a set whose elements are known at compile time. A more general represention, which still allows (almost always) direct access is to use *hashing*. That is, the domain elements are operated on in some way to derive addresses where either the range element or a chain leading to the range element is contained.

Use in Specifications

An interesting example which uses mappings is a *bill of materials*. Suppose a manufacturer builds a number of products each of which is either a base item (no sub-components) or a sub-assembly; sub-assemblies may be made up from a number of components which are themselves either basic or sub-assemblies; and so on. If the only need is to compute the set of component units (basic or otherwise) for a stated unit, the data required is:

$Bom = Part\text{-}no \longrightarrow Part\text{-}no\text{-}set$

An example of this structure is shown in fig. 28. Notice that the basic elements map onto empty sets.

The process of finding all sub-assemblies is called **explosion**. In order for explosion to make sense, the data must not contain any loops. That is, no part which is a (indirect) component of part a can use (indirectly) part a. This can be specified by an invariant:

$inv(bom) \triangleq (\mathbf{A}pn\epsilon\mathbf{dom}bom)(\sim is\text{-}comp(pn,pn,bom))$

where the predicate testing whether a part number is a component of another is defined by:

$is\text{-}comp(pn1,pn2,bom) \triangleq$
$\quad pn1\epsilon bom(pn2) \lor (\mathbf{E}cn\epsilon bom(pn2))(is\text{-}comp(pn1,cn,bom))$

The complete set of sub-components can then be obtained by an explosion operation whose pre-condition requires both inv and that all required part numbers are present:

EXP
states: Bom
type: Part-no $\longrightarrow$ Part-no-set

$pre\text{-}EXP(bom,p) \triangleq$
$\quad inv(bom) \land p\epsilon\mathbf{dom}bom \land ((\mathbf{union\ rng}bom) \subseteq \mathbf{dom}bom)$

$post\text{-}EXP(bom,p,bom',ps) \triangleq bom'=bom \land ps=expl(bom,p)$

where the *expl* function is defined in terms of the distributed union (reducing a set of sets to a set) of a set of recursive calls:

expl: Bom Part-no $\longrightarrow$ Part-no-set
$expl(bom,p) \triangleq$
$\quad$**if** $bom(p)=\{\ \}$ **then** $\{p\}$
$\quad$**else** $\{p\} \cup \mathbf{union}\{expl(bom,c) \mid c\epsilon bom(p)\}$

which, because basic parts are mapped to empty sets, can be simplified to:

$expl(bom,p) \triangleq \{p\} \cup \mathbf{union}\{expl(bom,c) \mid c\epsilon bom(p)\}$

The specification is simple, and not just because the problem is a simplification of that actually faced by manufacturers. What has been ignored is that *Bom* itself may be huge, requiring the design of techniques for retrieval from secondary storage. Furthermore, the *EXP* operation is likely to be required so often that the design of the representation must be governed by considerations of fast access to information on sub-assemblies. Here these problems are deferred until the specification of other operations, such as those for updating *Bom*, have been considered.

The bill of materials problem is a standard example from database work. It is interesting to compare what is being done here, using abstract data type specifications, with database work. Each of the various database approaches uses some particular class of objects to define reality. For instance, the relational database approach uses *n-ary relations* as its basic object, while the hierarchical view is built around a concept very like the mappings used here. These objects are, of course, more abstract than machine addresses and pointers. As such the descriptions are much shorter and clearer than implementations. For each approach, however, there are problems which fit less well than others. This gives rise to discussions about *normal forms* and *storage anomalies*. There are also problems for which relations, for example, are too general and the specification must then limit the choice (cf. data type invariants). For specifications one should not be limited by one or other database approach. The specification can then be refined into a structure which can be represented in the database—see Hitchcock(77).

★   ★   ★

It was observed, for some examples above, that the use of a set abstraction gave rise to the need for a data type invariant. Sometimes, the use of a mapping can eliminate the need. That is, a mapping matches reality better and does not require the extra constraint. This sort of problem is typified by the use of (disjoint) partitionings. Thus if a model suggests itself which can be expressed as a finite number of subsets which are mutually disjoint, then a mapping may prove a more convenient model.

The specification of the *students who do exercises* problem (see fig. 43) is based on a state:

Studx:: N: Student-name-set Y: Student-name-set

It is possible to rewrite the specification based on:

Studxm = Student-name → Bool

where the Boolean value is used to indicate whether a student has done exercises. Such a specification does not require a data type invariant because all possible values of the object can arise in reality.

Exercise 12.4: Write the specifications of the operators *INIT*, *ENROL*, *COMPL* and *RESULT* for the *students who do exercises* problem (see fig. 43) based on the mapping state.

Exercise 12.5: Define a mapping:

Floor → Room-no-set

which shows which rooms are on which floors, for the hotel discussed in 10.3.

Exercise 12.6:   Assume that a state is available which shows the set of possible room numbers and the current occupancy:

Shotel :: ROOMS: Room-no-set
            OCCUPANCY: Room-no → Name

Define some useful operations such as allocating a room, checking out and determining if there are empty rooms.

Exercise 12.7:   Define, for the **bill of materials** problem, a function:

expl-atomic: Bom Part-no → Part-no-set

which yields only the basic parts required in an assembly.

Exercise 12.8:   An extension of the **bill of materials** problem is to be able to determine where parts are used (that is, in which assemblies). Define:

WHERE-USED
states: Bom
type: → Where-used-map

Where-used-map = Part-no → Part-no-set

such that the result on the example in fig. 28 is:

$[p1→\{\ \}$,
$\ p2→\{p1\}$,
$\ p3→\{p1,p5\}$,
$\ p4→\{p2,p3,p5\}$,
$\ p5→\{p2\}$,
$\ p6→\{p3\}$,
$\ p7→\{p1,p3\}]$

Exercise 12.9:   Define an update operation for the **bill of materials** problem:

UPD
states: Bom
type: Part-no Part-no-set →

An interesting concept which is of use in definitions is the **bag** (also called **multi-set**). A **bag** is an unordered collection of elements, but, unlike a set, it can contain duplicates; bags can be thought of as a sort of hybrid of sets and lists. To construct a definition of bags one has to select a basis. It would be possible to base them on lists but, here, their definition is based on mappings.

Bag = Element → Nat0

The basic idea is to map any element, which has been inserted into the bag, onto its multiplicity (i.e. the number of times it is present).

Exercise 12.10: Based on the foregoing definition of *bags*, define operations which:

a) Initialize the bag:

EMPTY-BAG
states: Bag

b) Add an element to the bag:

PLUS-BAG
states: Bag
type: Element →

c) Determine the multiplicity of an element:

MPC-BAG
states: Bag
type: Element → *Nat0*

Exercise 12.11: Define a function which collects the elements of a list into a bag which counts the number of occurrences:

bagol: Element-list → *(Element* → *Nat)*

A functional form of the bag operators is given in appendix C. These operators are useful in handling sorting problems; for example, *is-permutation* can be defined in terms of bags. See also Dershowitz(79) for use in termination proofs.

Data Refinement

The general method of refinement proofs can now be applied to mappings.

The specification, based on a mapping, of the **students who do exercises** problem is:

Studxm = Student-name → *Bool*

INITM
states: Studxm
post-INITM(,rm) ≜ *rm*=[]

ENROLM
states: Studxm
type: Student-name →
pre-ENROLM(rm,nm) ≜ ~*(nm∈domrm)*
post-ENROLM(rm,nm,rm') ≜ *rm'=rm†[nm→***FALSE***]*

COMPLM
states: Studxm
type: Student-name →
pre-COMPLM(rm,nm) ≜
    if *nm∈domrm* **then** *rm(nm)=***FALSE else FALSE**
post-COMPLM(rm,nm,rm') ≜ *rm'=rm†[nm→***TRUE***]*

RESULTM
states: Studxm
type: → *Student-name-set*
post-RESULTM(rm,rm',res) ≜
    rm'=rm ∧ *res={nm | nm∈domrm* ∧ *rm(nm)=***TRUE**}

The specification which was given in fig. 43 can now be viewed as a
putative realization whose correctness is to be proved. Defining:

retr-Studxm: Studx → *Studxm*
retr-Studxm(<n,y>) ≜ *[nm→***TRUE** *| nm∈y]†[nm→***FALSE** *| nm∈n]*

The properties required for a refined object (cf. fig. 49) are firstly *aa*
(note there is no invariant for *Studxm*):

inv-studx(<n,y>) ⟹ *(**E***m∈Studxm)(m=retr-Studxm(<n,y>))*

which is immediate. The second property required of the data (*ab*) is:

*(**A***m∈Studxm)(**E***s∈Studx)(inv-studx(s)* ∧ *m=retr-Studxm(s))*

For this, it is straightforward to define a construction which for any
member of *Studxm* splits the elements of the domain into two sets.

Attention can now be turned to the operations. The operation *INIT*,
now used as a refinement of *INITM*, must be proved correct. Property
da is vacuously true. Property *ra* becomes:

n'=y'={ } ⟹ *([nm→***TRUE** *| nm∈y]†[nm→***FALSE** *| nm∈n'])=[]*

which is immediate.

For *ENROL* property *da* becomes:

is-disj(n,y) ∧ ~*(nm∈dom([nm→***TRUE** *| nm∈y]∪[nm→***FALSE** *| nm∈n]))*
    ⟹ ~*(nm∈(n∪y))*

which is immediate. Property *ra* becomes:

is-disj(n,y) ∧ ~*(nm∈(n∪y))* ∧ *n'=n∪{nm}* ∧ *y'=y* ⟹
    *retr-Studxm(<n',y'>)=retr-Studxm(<n,y>)†[nm→***FALSE***]*

which follows without difficulty. The argument for *COMPL1* is similar.

The operation *RESULT1* is total and an identity on states so it is only necessary to show:

$res=y \Rightarrow res = \{nm \mid (retr\text{-}Studxm(<n,y>))(nm)=\textbf{TRUE}\}$

which is immediate. This concludes the proof that the set model is a refinement of the mapping specification. Chapter 11 contained a proof that a list model was a refinement of the set description. Thus a two-stage refinement has been made.

Exercise 12.12: Staying with the *students who do exercises* problem, prove correct a refinement based on:

Studx1c:: NUMBS: (Student-name → Nat) INDS: Bool-list

Exercise 12.13: Define a data type to model *arrays*, including a data type invariant and *ACCESS* and *CHANGE* operations.

Exercise 12.14: Recall the *students' whereabouts* problem (see fig. 54). Suppose a state were chosen:

Studw1:: INDEX:(Student-Name→Student-no) ROOM:Room-list
Room = Room-no | **NIL**

Write down the conditions for *Studw1* to be adequate; a retrieve function; and the new operations complete with correctness proof.

Recording Equivalence Relations

As a further example of refinement of data types the problem of *equivalence relations* is developed further (see fig. 55 for the specification). This specification cannot itself be taken as an implementation because the language being used here does not have sets as a data type. Given such a specification, then, some refinement is necessary. The refinement here is not directly to a program but rather to a data type defined by a mapping; chapter 13 carries the development through to programs.

It was observed earlier that, when a specification is presented in terms of a partitioning of a set, it may be advantageous to employ a mapping instead. This is now done. The basic idea is to represent the partitioning by a mapping from the set *Element* to some set *Key*. Thus:

$Qm = Element → Key$

$Q = (Element\text{-}set)\text{-}set$

$invq(q) \triangleq$
   $(\mathbf{union}q = Element \; \wedge$
   $(\mathbf{A}e\epsilon Element)((\mathbf{E}!S\epsilon q)(e\epsilon S)) \; \wedge \; \sim(\{\,\}\epsilon q)$

$INIT$
states: Q
$post\text{-}INIT(,q') \triangleq q' = \{\{e\} \;|\; e\epsilon Element\}$

$EQUATE$
states: Q
type: $Element\; Element \rightarrow$
$post\text{-}EQUATE(q,e_1,e_2,q') \triangleq$
   $q' = \{s \;|\; s\epsilon q \; \wedge \; is\text{-}disj(\{e_1,e_2\},..s)\} \; \cup \; \{s_1 \cup s_2 \;|\; e_1\epsilon s_1\epsilon q \; \wedge \; e_2\epsilon s_2\epsilon q\}$

$TEST$
states: Q
type: $Element\; Element \rightarrow Bool$
$post\text{-}TEST(q,e_1,e_2,q',b) \triangleq q'=q \; \wedge \; (b\leftrightarrow(\mathbf{E}s\epsilon q)(e_1\epsilon s \; \wedge \; e_2\epsilon s))$

Figure 55   Specification of Equivalence Relation Problem

Instead of the rather complex data type invariant on Q, it is now only necessary to require that every member of *Element* is present. Thus:

$invm(qm) \triangleq \mathbf{dom}qm = Element$

A partitioning into groups is now represented by a mapping which maps all items of one group onto the same key and each group onto a different key. Thus, the test for equivalence between two elements is now based on:

$qm(e_1) = qm(e_2)$

The operations are illustrated in fig. 56.

     Before coming to the actual descriptions of the operations, the adequacy properties can be checked (cf. fig. 49). The relationship between Qm and Q is documented by:

$retr\text{-}Q(qm) \triangleq groups(qm,\mathbf{rng}qm)$

$groups\text{:}\; (D \rightarrow R)\; R\text{-}set \rightarrow (D\text{-}set)\text{-}set$
$groups(m,rs) \triangleq \{group(m,r) \;|\; r\epsilon rs\}$

$group\text{:}\; (D \rightarrow R)\; R \rightarrow D\text{-}set$
$group(m,r) \triangleq \{d \;|\; d\epsilon\mathbf{dom}m \; \wedge \; m(d)=r\}$

That is, a set of sets is created with one set corresponding to each *Key* which occurs in the range of the mapping. The set corresponding to a key is simply the elements which are mapped to that key. One way of

Element = {a, b, c, d, e, f}
Key   = {ka, kb, kc, kd, ke, kf}

INITM() = [a→ka,b→kb,c→kc,d→kd,e→ke,f→kf] = m_1
EQUATEM(a,b)(m_1) = [a→ka,b→ka,c→kc,d→kd,e→ke,f→kf] = m_2
EQUATEM(b,a)(m_2) = m_2
EQUATEM(b,c)(m_2) = [a→ka,b→ka,c→ka,d→kd,e→ke,f→kf] = m_3
EQUATEM(e,f)(m_3) = [a→ka,b→ka,c→ka,d→kd,e→ke,f→ke] = m_4
EQUATEM(a,f)(m_4) = [a→ka,b→ka,c→ka,e→ka,f→ka,d→kd] = m_5
TEST(a,e)(m_5) = **TRUE**
TEST(d,d)(m_5) = **TRUE**
TEST(a,d)(m_5) = **FALSE**

Figure 56   Recording Equivalence Relations

looking at this is to say that the keys induce the equivalence classes over the domain of the mapping.

The first requirement (*aa*) is:

invm(qm) ⟹ *(**E**q∈Q)(q=retr-Q(qm)) ∧ invq(retr-Q(qm))*

The totality of *retr-Q* does not even require the hypothesis of the implication. To establish that *retr-Q* creates only elements which satisfy *invq* it is necessary to observe:

- *qm* contains a domain entry for every *Element* (*invm*)
- *qm* maps any given *Element* onto exactly one key (*qm* is a map)
- no element key in the range of *qm* has zero elements mapped onto it

Therefore the three conditions (existence, uniqueness and no empty set) of *invq* are established. The second requirement (*ab*) becomes:

invq(q) ⟹ *(**E**qm)(invm(qm) ∧ q=retr-Q(qm))*

This can again be shown by a constructive argument. For some given *q* a mapping can be built up as follows. For each set in *q* choose one element of the set (which, is immaterial) to be the key. Construct a mapping by joining the mappings from the subsets to their chosen keys. The keys are distinct because the subsets were disjoint and for the same reason the individual mappings for each subset have disjoint domains. Each chosen key is a range element of the mapping and is used by *retr-Q* to reconstitute the original set.

Notice that the data type invariant is not essential for the original specification. There it was a useful comment which helped the reader (and writer) understand the intent of the definition. However, for refinement stages it becomes crucial. Not only is it not possible to model overlapping sets with the *Qm* states, but the exclusion of empty sets is also required. (Look back at the constructive argument for adequacy. It would not be possible to **choose one element ...** from an empty set.) This has, of course, exposed a potential problem in the development method. While it is fairly obvious to record the first part of *invq* for *Q*, the exclusion of the empty set might well have been overlooked. Only when a step of refinement is reached is it found that there are elements, supposedly in the abstract data type, which cannot be modelled by a chosen representation. Is this a flaw in the method? The answer would only be affirmative if it were crucial to the method that it proceed strictly top-down with no back-tracking. This has never been claimed. The aim is to arrive at top-down documentation for a development, not to regulate thinking. An attempt should be made at any stage of development to document a reasonably tight validity constraint. If, during refinement, it is found that a narrower definition is required (in order to prove a representation is adequate) it is necessary to back-track and try to prove that the new condition really is an invariant. Provided this proof is successful, refinement can then continue based on the new invariant.

The operations on *Qm* are now defined and justified. Since they are all total, their pre-conditions are omitted. Firstly:

INITM
states: Qm
post-INITM(,qm) $\triangleq$
  domqm=*Element* $\land$ (**A**$e_1,e_2\epsilon$*Element*)(e_1=e_2 $\lor$ $qm(e_1)\neq qm(e_2)$)

Notice that this post-condition does not fix the actual choice of the keys, it only states that they must all be distinct. Consulting fig. 49 it is noticed that *da* is vacuously true because *INITM* is total (the same is true for the other two operations below). Rule *ra* becomes:

invm(qm) $\land$ *pre-INITM(qm)* $\land$ *post-INITM(qm,qm')* $\Rightarrow$
  post-INITM(retr-Q(qm),retr-Q(qm'))

domqm'=*Element* $\land$ (e_1=e_2 $\lor$ $qm'(e_1)\neq qm'(e_2)$) $\Rightarrow$
  groups(qm',**rng**qm'*) = { {e} | $e\epsilon$*Element* }

which, since the keys are distinct, becomes:

domqm'=*Element* $\Rightarrow$ { {e} | $e\epsilon$**dom**qm'} = { {e} | $e\epsilon$*Element*}

which is immediate.

For the operation which is to model *EQUATE*, one might use:

post-EQUATEM(qm,e_1,e_2,qm') $\triangleq$
  qm' = qm † [$e\rightarrow qm(e_2)$ | $qm(e)$=$qm(e_1)$]

Although perfectly correct, this makes an arbitrary decision as to which key is to be used for the combined map. A more general condition is:

EQUATEM
states: Qm
type: Element Element →

$post\text{-}EQUATEM(qm,e_1,e_2,qm') \triangleq$
  domqm' = **dom**$qm \wedge$
  $(\mathbf{A}e\epsilon\mathbf{dom}qm)(\sim(qm(e)\epsilon\{qm(e_1),qm(e_2)\})) \Rightarrow qm'(e)=qm(e)) \wedge$
  $(\mathbf{A}e\epsilon\mathbf{dom}qm)(qm(e)\epsilon\{qm(e_1),qm(e_2)\} \Rightarrow qm'(e)\epsilon\{qm(e_1),qm(e_2)\}) \wedge$
  $(\mathbf{A}d,e\epsilon\mathbf{dom}qm)(qm(d),qm(e)\epsilon\{qm(e_1),qm(e_2)\} \Rightarrow qm'(d)=qm'(e))$

This condition is rather lengthy but its meaning is not difficult to grasp.
The terms of the conjunction require:

- the domain of the mapping remains unchanged
- all elements which did not map to the keys of either e_1 or e_2 in qm still map to the same key in the output map.
- elements which did map to either the key of e_1 or the key of e_2 still map to one of those keys (but not necessarily the same one as before) in the result map.
- all elements which mapped to the key of e_1 or the key of e_2 are mapped by the result mapping to one and the same key.

Property *ra* becomes:

$invm(qm) \wedge post\text{-}EQUATEM(qm,e_1,e_2,qm') \Rightarrow$
  $post\text{-}EQUATE(retr\text{-}Q(qm),e_1,e_2,retr\text{-}Q(qm'))$

Now, assuming:

$post\text{-}EQUATEM(qm,e_1,e_2,qm')$

and using the definition of *retr-Q*:

$retr\text{-}Q(qm')$
  $= groups(qm',\mathbf{rng}qm')$
  $= groups(qm',(\mathbf{rng}qm'-\{qm'(e_1)\})) \cup \{group(qm',qm'(e_1))\}$

the clauses of *post-EQUATEM* give:

  $= groups(qm,(\mathbf{rng}qm-\{qm(e_1),qm(e_2)\})) \cup$
    $\{group(qm,qm(e_1)) \cup group(qm,qm(e_2))\}$

But:

$retr\text{-}Q(qm) = groups(qm,\mathbf{rng}qm)$

Thus:

$post\text{-}EQUATE(retr\text{-}Q(qm),e_1,e_2,q')$

requires:

$q' = \{s \mid s\epsilon retr\text{-}Q(qm)\wedge is\text{-}disj(\{e_1,e_2\},s)\} \cup$
  $\{s_1\cup s_2 \mid e_1\epsilon s_1 \wedge e_2\epsilon s_2 \wedge s_1,s_2\epsilon retr\text{-}Q(qm)\}$

or, combining this with the definition of *retr-Q*:

$q' = groups(qm,(\mathbf{rng}qm-\{qm(e_1),qm(e_2)\}))\ \cup$
    $\{group(qm,qm(e_1))\ \cup\ group(qm,qm(e_2))\}$

Thus:

$post\text{-}EQUATE(retr\text{-}Q(qm),e_1,e_2,retr\text{-}Q(qm'))$

follows.

The operation:

TESTM
states: Qm
type: Element Element $\rightarrow$ *Bool*
$post\text{-}TESTM(qm,e_1,e_2,qm',b) \triangleq qm'=qm\ \wedge\ (b{\leftrightarrow}qm(e_1)=qm(e_2))$

is, like *TEST*, an identity on states. It is thus only necessary to show:

$(b{\leftrightarrow}qm(e_1)=qm(e_2))\ \Rightarrow\ (b{\leftrightarrow}(\mathbf{E}s\epsilon retr\text{-}Q(qm))(e_1\epsilon s \wedge e_2\epsilon s))$

or:

$qm(e_1)=qm(e_2)\ \Rightarrow\ (\mathbf{E}s\epsilon groups(qm,\mathbf{rng}qm))(e_1\epsilon s\ \wedge\ e_2\epsilon s)$

which is immediate.

Now that the definitions of all of the operations on *Qm* are available, it is easy to check that *invm* really is an invariant.

*Arbitrary Sets Modelled on Regular Arrays

Both of the models of *arrays* which have been proposed (cf. exercises 9.20 and 12.13) require a data type invariant. The reason for preferring that based on a mapping can now be shown. An array is often visualized as a list of lists; in particular arrays of more than two dimensions cannot be drawn easily and are normally presented as a series of planes. However, this gives an asymmetrical view. In fact, it is as easy to view one plane (by fixing an index) as to view any other plane of an array. The following model is therefore adopted:

$Array = Nat\text{-}list1 \rightarrow Value$

$inv\text{-}array(a) \triangleq (\mathbf{E}rank\epsilon Nat\text{-}list1)(\mathbf{dom}a = gen\text{-}sscs(rank))$

$gen\text{-}sscs: Nat\text{-}list1 \rightarrow (Nat\text{-}list1)\text{-}set$
$gen\text{-}sscs(rank) \triangleq$
    $\{ssc\ |\ \mathbf{len}ssc = \mathbf{len}rank\ \wedge\ (\mathbf{A}i\epsilon\{1\text{:}\mathbf{len}rank\})(1{\leq}ssc(i){\leq}rank(i))\}$

This section develops a way of representing arbitrary sets on such arrays. It is straightforward to represent simple sets of values on arrays—especially on arrays, like those of APL, whose length can vary dynamically. However, the regularity constraint of arrays makes it difficult to represent sets which can have sets as their members.

The details of the representation can be hidden in a series of functions:

create-elemrep: Int → Set-rep

is-elemrep: Set-rep → Bool
is-elemrep(create-elemrep(i))

create-emptyset: → Set-rep

put-set: Set-rep Set-rep → Set-rep
pre-put-set(sr,er) ≜ ~is-in(er,sr)

is-proper-setrep: Set-rep → Bool
is-proper-setrep(create-emptyset())
is-proper-setrep(put-set(sr,er))

card: Set-rep → Nat0
pre-card(sr) ≜ is-proper-setrep(sr)
*card(sr) = **card**(retr-set(sr))*

select-item: Set-rep Nat → Set-rep
pre-select-item(sr,n) ≜ 1≤n≤card(sr)
select-item(sr,n) ε retr-set(sr)

Exercise 12.15: Define a representation for sets on regular arrays. Elementary values, say integers, are represented by a vector of length two with a flag and the value. Sets of objects will be arrays with one plane storing the cardinality in its first position and the representations of the contained objects in its subsequent planes. Thus:

$\{v1,v2\}$

is represented by:

2	-
-1	v1
-1	v2

Remember that a set may contain objects of different *set depths*. Document a data type invariant and a retrieve function (from the representation to sets).

Exercise 12.16: In terms of the above operations, program:

is-in: Set-rep Set-rep → Bool
is-in(sr,er) ⇔ retr-set(er)εretr-set(sr)

is-eq: Set-rep Set-rep → Bool
is-eq(sr,sr') ⟺ retr-set(sr) = retr-set(sr')

is-subs: Set-rep Set-rep → Bool
is-subs(sr,sr') ⟺ (retr-set(sr) ⊆ retr-set(sr'))

These functions can be mutually recursive. Discuss why this is well defined. Prove the functions correct with respect to the set notation specifications.

Exercise 12.17:   Assume an operation:

addset: Set-rep Set-rep → Set-rep

which is like *put-set* except that it does not require a pre-condition. Define (in terms of set notation), program (in terms of the above operations), and prove correct programs for union, distributed union, intersection, difference, and proper subset. Then do the same for:

restrict-set: Set-rep Predicate → Set-rep
retr-set(restrict-set(s,p)) = {e | e∈retr-set(s) ∧ p(e)}

mod-set: Set-rep Function → Set-rep
retr-set(mod-set(s,f)) = {f(e) | e∈retr-set(s)}

(The development described here was done in collaboration with J.Hicks as part of an APL package written to simulate the data types described in this book.) In connection with this problem, the reader is referred to Gull(79).

Summary

This chapter has introduced the notation for defining objects as mappings. The value of this notation is that it captures many of the ways in which data is organized in reality. Examples of refinement have been shown whose correctness would be difficult to establish without formal tools. For the problem of **recording equivalence relations** some complex solutions are presented in chapter 13.

Only one more group of notation remains to be introduced. In fact much of it has already been used, and the chapter which covers abstract syntax notation does little more than pull together and formalize what has been used in the description of states. There is, then, very little essential material to be covered before the rigorous method can be presented and applied in C.

Summary Exercises

Exercise 12.18: Over a hundred years ago, Lewis Carroll proposed a *telegraph cipher* based on the table:

	A	B	C	. . .	Z
A	a	b	c	. . .	z
B	b	c	d	. . .	a
C	c	d	e	. . .	b
.	.	.	.	. . .	.
.	.	.	.	. . .	.
.	.	.	.	. . .	.
Z	z	a	b	. . .	y

Given a keyword, a message is coded by repeating the keyword above it as many times as necessary—blanks are ignored throughout. The letters of the keyword are used to indicate which column of the table is to be used as a substitute for the corresponding letter of the message. Thus:

keyword: vigilancevigila
message: meetmeontuesday
coded: hmkbxebpxpmylly

Specify an operation:

CODE
states:
type: Letter-list1 Letter-list → Letter-list1

which accepts a non-empty keyword and a message and produces the coded output. A check on how well the original definition has been structured is to see how much can be used in defining the *DECODE* operation.

Exercise 12.19: (Example from Guttag(77).) A *compiler dictionary* is a structure for recording information about the attributes of identifiers. When declarations are processed, the type information is recorded in the dictionary; when the identifiers are used their attributes can be looked up in the dictionary to check that the use matches the declared type. In a block structured language like PL/I the declaration information from different blocks must be kept separate and information retrieved from the most recent declaration of an identifier. Define an appropriate data type:

Symbol-table

with operators:

EMPTY-ST
states: Symbol-table

ENTER-BLOCK
states: Symbol-table

ADDINF
states: Symbol-table
type: Id Attribute-list →

LEAVE-BLOCK
states: Symbol-table

IS-IN-BLOCK
states: Symbol-table
type: Id → *Bool*

LOOKUP
states: Symbol-table
type: Id → *Attribute-list*

Exercise 12.20: Decide on some extensions to the student tracking problem (e.g. which courses students are enrolled on, which teacher teaches which course) and specify appropriate operations in terms of sets, lists and mappings.

Exercise 12.21: Lists can be viewed as mappings from *Nat* to the type of their elements. Define, and prove correct, list operators based on such mappings.

Exercise 12.22: Define a function:

reachable: D M → *D-set*

where:

$M = D \rightarrow D$

which yields the set of elements of *D* that can be reached by applying the argument mapping one or more times to the argument element. Be careful to avoid the function becoming undefined (looping).

Exercise 12.23: Define the **transitive closure** of a mapping, that is, the mapping from all domain elements to the set which can be reached from them.

Exercise 12.24: A slightly different form of explosion problem arises with program libraries. Suppose information about the use of components (programs, macros etc.) by components is stored as:

Useage: Component-name → *Component-name-set*

Define the function which determines the impact of a change of a component:

affected: Useage Component-name → Component-name-set

But remember that, because of recursion, loops may arise (i.e. the data type invariant differs from that for *bill of materials*).

Exercise 12.25: Write definitions of tape and direct access files to show their essential difference.

Exercise 12.26: Show that mappings can be represented by sets using:

Mapm = Pr-set
Pr:: D R

and:

retr-map: Mapm → (D→R)

Define functions like:

map-union: Mapm Mapm → Mapm

such that:

retr-map(map-overwrite(mn1,mn2)) = retr-map(mn1)†retr-map(mn2)

Exercise 12.27: One way of implementing maps is by *hashing* the domain element and storing the range elements in a list (indexed by the hashed value). Specify insert and lookup operations for such a model.

Exercise 12.28: The storage of a computer can be pictured as a mapping from addresses to values. *Virtual store* has extended this to give each user an abstract machine with an address space as large as, or larger than, that of the whole machine. Provide a definition, on more than one level of abstraction, which explains this concept.

Exercise 12.29: Show, and argue the correctness of, a refinement of the *recording equivalence relation* problem onto a representation using an array of bits.

Chapter 13

*THEORIES OF DATA TYPES

The techniques introduced in chapters 10 and 11 apply to any development step using data refinement. Such proofs will be straightforward for specifications in terms of, say, single sets. More interesting specifications will, however, be built up from quite complex combinations of objects and proofs could become long and opaque because there are no established results about the objects. Whereas there is an established algebra of set notation, one must be developed for new data types.

This chapter considers the separate development of a *theory* of a data type. This will lead to shorter proofs for problems involving the data type. Such proofs will be more intuitive and the collection of results presents a body of knowledge which can be used in other developments. The creation of theories is illustrated here around the *equivalence relation* problem. The various versions of the problem and their development are pictured in fig. 57.

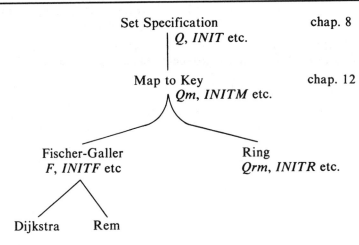

Figure 57   Versions of Equivalence Relation Problem

Problem Description

The *equivalence relation* problem has been discussed in earlier chapters. The point of departure for the current development is shown in fig. 60. (An example is given in fig. 56.) The problem of choosing a data structure for the program has been mentioned. The programs shown here offer a balance between storage requirement and performance even for very large sets of elements.

Forests

It would be simple to construct an algorithm which satisfies the specification in fig. 60 by storing the mapping *Qm* in an array. However, in such an implementation the *EQUATE* operation would be inefficient because it would have to search the whole array to locate all of the elements with one key which had to be changed to the other. A more efficient representation for the mapping from *Elements* to *Keys* uses an array to store what might be called a *forest*. A forest is a collection of trees and, in this example, a key is located at the root of a tree.

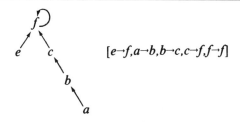

$[e{\rightarrow}f,a{\rightarrow}b,b{\rightarrow}c,c{\rightarrow}f,f{\rightarrow}f]$

Figure 58   A Tree

With mappings which use the same set as both domain and range, a variety of structures can be represented. If there are no *rings* (i.e. sequences of elements which chain into a loop), such a mapping can be used to represent trees. Each element will be mapped into the node closer to the root of the tree and roots are identified by making them map to themselves. An example of a tree is pictured in fig. 58. From the fact that a mapping is a many-one relationship, it follows that nodes may come together, but not diverge. Formally:

$F = Element \longrightarrow Element$

and:

$is\text{-}root: Element\ F \longrightarrow Bool$
$is\text{-}root(e,f) \triangleq f(e){=}e$

The data type invariant must exclude, among other things, rings. This is done by using the mapping function *reachable* (see appendix C). Thus:

invf(f) ≜
    domf = *Element* ∧
    (**A**e∊**dom**f)(is-root(e,f) ∨ ~(e∊reachable(f(e),f)))

The roots of trees can be found by:

root: Element F ⟶ *Element*
root(e,f) ≜ **if** *is-root(e,f)* **then** *e* **else** *root(f(e),f)*
pre-root(f) ≜ *invf(f)*

A way of gathering together all elements with a common root (i.e. the set of elements in a tree) in given by:

collect: F Element ⟶ *Element-set*
collect(f,r) ≜ {e | e∊**dom**f ∧ root(e,f)=r}
pre-collect(f,r) ≜ *invf(f)* ∧ *is-root(r,f)*

So far the data type has been introduced in the familiar way: constructive type and functions. It is now possible to develop a theory (i.e. collection of results) about forests. Each of the properties shown is fairly obvious and only an indication of its proof is given.

Property *F1* shows that a forest defines a disjoint partitioning of its domain; each partition is obtained by using the *collect* function:

F1. for invf(f) ∧ *is-root(r1,f)* ∧ *is-root(r2,f)*:
    r1=r2 ∨ *is-disj(collect(f,r1),collect(f,r2))*

This result follows immediately from the fact that *root* is a (single-valued) function. It also provides the clue to the representation of equivalence relations using forests: the elements of each partition are arranged as a single tree.

It will obviously be necessary to update the data structures; under what circumstances is validity preserved? Two cases are required below. Firstly, no ring can be introduced providing no element is made to map onto an element from which it can be reached:

F2. for invf(f) ∧ *d,e∊Element*:
    ~(d∊reachable(e,f)) ⟹ *invf(f†[d→e])*

A second condition states that validity will be preserved when anything is made to map onto a root. The only case which is not already covered by *F2* is the root itself and in this case the data structure is unchanged:

F3. for invf(f) ∧ *d,e∊Element*:
    is-root(e,f) ⟹ *invf(f † [d→e])*

The next problem is to consider the effect of validity preserving changes on the represented value. A preliminary result is:

F4. for invf(f) ∧ *e∊Element*:
    reachable(e,f) ⊆ *collect(f,root(e,f))*

Elements retain their same key if none of their reachable elements is changed. Thus:

F5. for invf(f) $\wedge$ eϵElement:
  f| reachable(e,f) = f| reachable(e,f) $\Rightarrow$ root(e,f')=root(e,f)

which can be proved by induction. On the other hand, if one of the reachable elements of an element is changed, its root will be defined by:

F6. for invf(f) $\wedge$ d,eϵElement $\wedge$ ($\sim$(dϵreachable(e,f)) $\vee$ is-root(e,f)):
  *(**A**cϵElement)(dϵreachable(c,f) $\Rightarrow$ root(c,f†[d$\rightarrow$e]) = root(e,f))*

These properties will more than suffice for the proof of the basic Fischer-Galler algorithm.

Fischer-Galler Algorithm

The Fischer-Galler algorithm achieves space and speed efficiency by storing elements of equivalence classes in trees. In the initial state, all trees consist of a root alone:

INITF
states: F
post-INITF(,f) $\triangleq$ *f* = [e$\rightarrow$e | eϵElement]

It is immediate from the definition of *invf* that such a state is a valid forest because all trees are roots.

To update a forest in such a way as to equate e_1 and e_2 it is only necessary to graft the root of one tree (say that for e_1) onto some point in the other. It is essential that the root of e_1 is found in order to ensure that all elements equivalent to e_1 are also affected. The decision to graft onto the root of e_2 is partly an efficiency consideration: minimizing the depths of the trees reduces the number of steps required by subsequent root operations. Thus:

EQUATEF
states: F
type: Element Element $\rightarrow$
post-EQUATEF(f,e_1,e_2,f') $\triangleq$ *f'* = *f* † [root(e_1,f)$\rightarrow$root(e_2,f)]

To see that this operation preserves *invf* (the data type invariant), it is only necessary to observe that:

is-root(root(e_2,f),f)

and to refer to *F3*—it has been shown that anything (even the root itself) can be grafted onto a root without destroying the forest property.

In order to determine whether two elements are equivalent it is only necessary to compare their roots:

TESTF
states: F
type: Element Element → Bool
post-TESTF(f,e_1,e_2,f',b) ≜ f'=f ∧ (b ⇔ root(e_1,f)=root(e_2,f))

Once again an example can be used to give an intuitive picture of the algorithm:

INITF() = [a→a,b→b,c→c,d→d,e→e,f→f] = f1
EQUATEF(a,b)(f1) = [a→b,b→b,c→c,d→d,e→e,f→f] = f2
EQUATEF(b,a)(f2) = f2
EQUATEF(b,c)(f2) = [a→b,b→c,c→c,d→d,e→e,f→f] = f3
EQUATEF(e,f)(f3) = [a→b,b→c,c→c,d→d,e→f,f→f] = f4
EQUATEF(a,f)(f4) = [a→b,b→c,c→f,d→d,e→f,f→f] = f5
TEST(a,e)(f5) = **TRUE**
TEST(d,d)(f5) = **TRUE**
TEST(a,d)(f5) = **FALSE**

(See also fig, 59.)

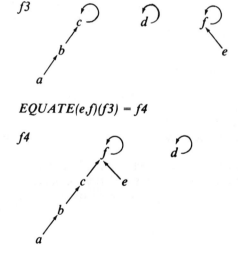

f3

EQUATE(e,f)(f3) = f4

f4

Figure 59   Effect of Operation

Faced with a specification and an implementation it is necessary to show that the latter satisfies the former. Firstly, the relationship between the two representations is documented by a retrieve function:

retr-Qm: F → Qm
retr-Qm(f) ≜ [e→root(e,f) | e∈domf]

Having made precise the relationship between the two sets of states, the question of adequacy can be checked. Referring to fig. 49, rule *aa* gives:

$(\mathbf{A}f)(invf(f) \Rightarrow (\mathbf{E}m)(m=retr\text{-}Qm(f)) \wedge invm(retr\text{-}Qm(f)))$

The fact that *retr-Qm* is defined follows from the fact that the only pre-condition for *root* is *invf*; *invm* requires only an adequate domain which follows immediately from *invf*. Rule *ab* requires:

$(\mathbf{A}m)(invm(m) \Rightarrow (\mathbf{E}f\epsilon F)(invf(f) \wedge m=retr\text{-}Qm(f)))$

This can be shown by construction with *Key* being the same as *Element*; a tree in which each element is mapped directly to its root can then be constructed by selecting an arbitrary element of each set as the root.

Qm = Element $\rightarrow$ Key

invm(qm) $\triangleq$ **dom**qm = Element

INITM
states: Qm
post-INITM(,qm) $\triangleq$
    domqm=Element $\wedge$ $(\mathbf{A}e_1,e_2\epsilon\text{Element})(e_1=e_2 \vee qm(e_1)\neq qm(e_2))$

EQUATEM
states: Qm
type: Element Element $\rightarrow$
post-EQUATEM(qm,e_1,e_2,qm') $\triangleq$
    domqm' = **dom**qm $\wedge$
    $(\mathbf{A}e\epsilon\mathbf{dom}qm)(\sim(qm(e)\epsilon\{qm(e_1),qm(e_2)\}) \Rightarrow qm'(e)=qm(e)) \wedge$
    $(\mathbf{A}e\epsilon\mathbf{dom}qm)(qm(e)\epsilon\{qm(e_1),qm(e_2)\} \Rightarrow qm'(e)\epsilon\{qm(e_1),qm(e_2)\}) \wedge$
    $(\mathbf{A}d,e\epsilon\mathbf{dom}qm)(qm(d),qm(e)\epsilon\{qm(e_1),qm(e_2)\} \Rightarrow qm'(d)=qm'(e))$

TESTM
states: Qm
type: Element Element $\rightarrow$ Bool
post-TESTM(qm,e_1,e_2,qm',b) $\triangleq$ qm'=qm $\wedge$ $(b\leftrightarrow qm(e_1)=qm(e_2))$

Figure 60   Equivalence Relation Problem: Map to Key

Each of the operations is total providing *invf* is true and the preservation of this invariant has been proved. It is, then, only necessary to consider the result rule (*ra*) for each operation in order to complete the proof that the forest operations model those of fig. 60.
For the initialization operation:

$post\text{-}INITF(f') \Rightarrow post\text{-}INITM(,retr\text{-}Qm(f'))$

follows immediately from the definitions.

In both versions, the test operation is an identity on states and thus it is only necessary to show:

$invf(f) \Rightarrow (root(e_1,f)=root(e_2,f) \leftrightarrow retr\text{-}Qm(f)(e_1)=retr\text{-}Qm(f)(e_2))$

which is again immediate.

The interesting problem is the equate operation for which it must be shown:

$invf(f) \wedge post\text{-}EQUATEF(f,e_1,e_2,f') \Rightarrow$
$post\text{-}EQUATEM(retr\text{-}Qm(f),e_1,e_2,retr\text{-}Qm(f'))$

Firstly note:

$f' = f \dagger [root(e_1,f) \rightarrow root(e_2,f)]$

and introduce the names:

$rm = retr\text{-}Qm(f)$
$rm' = retr\text{-}Qm(f')$

Proceeding by cases, consider those e such that:

$root(e,f) \neq root(e_1,f)$

From this and property *F1* conclude:

$is\text{-}disj(collect(f,root(e,f)),collect(f,root(e_1,f)))$

From *F4* this shows:

$is\text{-}disj(reachable(e,f),reachable(e_1,f))$

and since:

$root(e_1,f) \in reachable(e_1,f)$

it follows:

$\sim(root(e_1,f) \in reachable(e,f))$

Having established that the only element changed by *EQUATEF* is not in the reachable set of the e being considered, *F5* gives:

$root(e,f') = root(e,f)$

But the definition of *retr-Qm* shows for such e:

$rm(e) \neq rm(e_1)$
$rm'(e) = rm(e)$

Therefore:

$(\mathbf{A}e \in Element)(rm(e) \neq rm(e_1) \Rightarrow rm'(e)=rm(e))$

Now for the other case, consider e such that:

$root(e,f) = root(e_1,f)$

Then the definition of *reachable* shows:

$root(e_1,f) \in reachable(e,f)$

from which *F6* gives:

$root(e,f')$
$\quad = root(root(e_2,f),f)$
$\quad = root(e_2,f)$

Again using the definition of *retr-Qm* shows that for the *e* now under consideration:

$rm(e) = rm(e_1)$
$rm'(e) = rm(e_2)$

Therefore:

$(\mathbf{A}e\epsilon Element)(rm(e)=rm(e_1) \Rightarrow rm'(e)=rm(e_2))$

Combining the conclusions of the two cases, gives:

$rm' = rm \dagger [e{\rightarrow}rm(e_2) \mid rm(e)=rm(e_1)]$

This is, in fact, the more restrictive (asymmetric) version of *post-EQUATEM* shown in chapter 12; the more general version of the post-condition in fig. 60 follows as an immediate consequence.

This concludes the proof of the implementation on forests. A program using these operations can now be shown. So far nothing has been fixed about the nature of *Element*. It is necessary to define some relationship to the integers. This could be done by introducing a one-one mapping between *Element* and some subset of the integers—Correll(78) is followed here in assuming that *Element* is identical with such a set:

$Element = \{1:n\}$

In the following program, the mapping *F* is stored in a vector *A* which is indexed from *1* to *n* and is capable of holding values *1* to *n*. Thus in an environment with:

DCL A(1:N) FIXED BIN(15);

the individual procedures are:

```
INIT:
 PROC;
 DCL T FIXED BIN(15);
  DO T = 1 TO N;
   A(T) = T;
  END;
 END;
```

```
ROOT:
 PROC(E) RETURNS(FIXED BIN(15));
 DCL E FIXED BIN(15);
 DCL T FIXED BIN(15);
  T = E;
  DO WHILE(A(T)¬=T);
   T = A(T);
  END;
  RETURN(T);
 END;

EQUATE:
 PROC(E1,E2);
 DCL (E1,E2) FIXED BIN(15);
 DCL (R1,R2) FIXED BIN(15);
  R1 = ROOT(E1);
  R2 = ROOT(E2);
  A(R1) = R2;
 END;

TEST:
 PROC(E1,E2) RETURNS(BIT(1));
 DCL (E1,E2) FIXED BIN(15);
  RETURN(ROOT(E1)=ROOT(E2));
 END;
```

What has been achieved so far? An efficient program has been developed from a specification. While the specification is obvious, or intuitively acceptable, it is difficult to grasp the intent of the program itself. The development process, however, has shown reasons for believing the program to be correct, and the reasoning has been easy to follow. In trying to increase confidence in a program, one possibility is to create or check a proof by machine. In contrast to this approach (though not to its exclusion) proofs can be presented which are built up of convincing steps. The reason the steps have been easy to follow is that properties of the data type have been separated from the proof of the algorithm.

More about Forests

The shape of the trees created by the basic Fischer-Galler algorithm depends on the order in which elements are equated. Thus the sequence of equates:

<a,b>, <c,b>, <d,c>, <e,d>

forms a short fat tree, whereas:

$<a,b>$, $<b,c>$, $<c,d>$, $<d,e>$

generates a tall thin one (see fig. 61). The number of steps required by the *root* function depends on the height of tree and, because this function is used by both the equate and test operations, the height of the trees should be reduced whenever possible. The next section shows several different ways of tackling this problem.

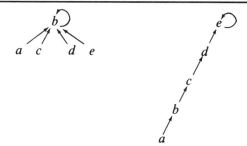

Figure 61   Alternative Trees

This section is concerned with extending the theory of the forest data type. An obvious property states that, if one element is in the reachable set of another, they must share the same root:

F7. for invf(f) $\wedge$ *d,eϵElement:*
   eϵreachable(d,f) $\Rightarrow$ *root(d,f)=root(e,f)*

The depth of a tree can be defined by:

depth: Element F $\rightarrow$ *Nat0*
depth(e,f) $\triangleq$ **if** *is-root(e,f)* **then** *0* **else** *depth(f(e),f)+1*
pre-depth(,f) $\triangleq$ *invf(f)*

About this function, a new property can be given:

F8. for invf(f) $\wedge$ *d,eϵElement:*
   eϵreachable(d,f) $\Rightarrow$ *depth(e,f)$\leq$depth(d,f)*

The proof follows by comparing the reachable elements of *d* and *e*.

Cleaning up Forests

The process of transforming trees to equivalent but shorter (less deep) ones will be called *cleaning up*. An operation which makes some chosen element, and all elements reachable from it, point directly to the root can be specified:

CLEANUP
states: F
type: Element →
post-CLEANUP(f,e,f') ≜
    $f' = f † [d \rightarrow root(e,f) \mid d\epsilon reachable(e,f) \wedge d \neq root(e,f)]$

(The first tree in fig. 61 can be obtained by performing *CLEANUP(a)* on the second.)
    It is easy to show that this operation preserves validity of the forest representation:

invf(f) ∧ *eϵElement* ∧ *post-CLEANUP(f,e,f$_i$)* ⇒ *invf(f')*

because:

depth(root(e,f)) = 0

thus:

$(\mathbf{A}d\epsilon(reachable(e,f)-\{root(e,f)\})))(depth(root(e,f))<depth(d))$

and property *F8* then shows:

$(\mathbf{A}d\epsilon(reachable(e,f)-\{root(e,f)\})))(\sim(d\epsilon reachable(root(e,f),f)))$

which property *F2* shows to be sufficient for the preservation of validity.
    It is only slightly more complicated to show that *CLEANUP* does not change the equivalence classes:

invf(f) ∧ *eϵElement* ∧ *post-CLEANUP(f,e,f')*
    ⇒ *retr-Qm(f')* = *retr-Qm(f)*

The proof proceeds by considering three possible cases. Firstly, for *c* such that:

is-disj(reachable(c,f),reachable(e,f))

Property *F5* shows that:

root(c,f') = *root(c,f)*

In the second case, consider *c* such that:

c = *root(e,f)*

Then it is immediate from *post-CLEANUP* that:

root(c,f') = *root(c,f)*

The third, and last, case is:

cϵreachable(e,f) ∧ *c≠root(e,f)*

From which, it follows:

root(c,f')
    = *root(root(e,f),f)*
    = *root(e,f)*

but from *F7*:

$root(e,f) = root(c,f)$

and thus (and now in all three cases):

$root(c,f') = root(c,f)$

which is the required result of *retr-Qm*.

A *CLEANUP* procedure could be run as a cooperating process with the basic Fischer-Galler procedures. Since *CLEANUP* can be interrupted very easily, no delay would occur for the main procedures. However, cooperating processes are beyond the scope of this book and this approach is not pursued here.

The algorithm for this problem in Dijkstra(76) is presented here using slightly simpler code than the original.

In the basic Fischer-Galler algorithm, the decision to make the equate operation graft the e_1 tree onto the root of the e_2 tree tends to keep trees short. It also avoids the danger of creating a ring if the two elements are already equivalent. The equate operation can compact trees which have grown tall (deep). Essentially, the idea in the algorithm by E.W.Dijkstra is to clean up the trees for the two elements which are equated. For the e_2 element this can be done while the root is being sought; for the other element, finding the root and cleaning up are performed in two separate scans over the tree. With this explanation, the following code should be easy to grasp:

```
EQUATE:
 PROC(E1,E2);
 DCL (E1,E2) FIXED BIN(15);
 DCL (R1,T1,T2) FIXED BIN(15);
 R1  = ROOT(E1);
 T1  = E1;
 DO WHILE(T1¬=A(T1));
    A(T1)  = R1;
    T1  = A(T1);
 END;
 T2  = E2;
 DO WHILE(T2¬=A(T2));
    A(T2)  = R1;
    T2  = A(T2)
 END;
 A(T2)  = R1
 END;
```

This version of *EQUATE* cleans up as much of the forest as it has access to; trees can, however, still grow arbitrarily deep. In Dijkstra(76), dissatisfaction is expressed with the asymmetric treatment necessary for the two nodes. An algorithm (attributed to Rem) is then shown which traces both paths to the roots of the two nodes together, compressing the trees as it goes. The compression is performed by making one tree point to the other. There is, of course, a danger of creating rings if the equated elements are already in the same tree and some criterion must be used which avoids this danger. The depth of the tree would be adequate but would require pre-tracing of the tree. What is done in Rem's algorithm is to use an auxiliary ordering system.

The extension to the forest theory to handle this problem is very simple. Suppose a one-one mapping:

order: Element → Nat

then:

($\textbf{A}e\epsilon Element$)(order(e) ≥ order(f(e)))

can be conjoined to the data type invariant for forests. Equality only occurs at roots because *order* is one-one. It should then be clear that:

F9. for d,e∈Element: e∈reachable(d,f) ⟹ order(d)≥order(e)

The new equate operation must preserve this property—the representation must also be shown to be adequate. Rem's algorithm has an anomaly and is not shown here.

Rings

Figure 62   Rings

The next section presents an alternative to the Fischer-Galler algorithm; here the data type to be used is introduced. A mapping with equal domain and range can be used to represent a collection of rings. Thus:

R = Element → Element

invr: R → Bool
invr(r) ≜
   dom*r=Element* ∧
   *($\textbf{A}e\epsilon$**dom***r)(e∈reachable(r(e),r))*

The number of rings is between one and the cardinality of *Element* (see fig. 62). The first observation is that there is a simpler way of stating that *invr* holds: it is only necessary that the mapping is one-one:

R1. for **dom***r=Element:*
   ($\textbf{A}e\epsilon Element$)(($\textbf{E}!d\epsilon Element$)(r(d) = e)) ⟹ invr(r)

The key property for the *equivalence relation* problem is the ability to represent a disjoint partitioning; this can be stated formally:

R2. for invr(r), d,e∈Element:
$\sim$ *(d∈reachable(e,r))* $\Rightarrow$ *is-disj(reachable(d,r),reachable(e,r))*

The data type invariant is preserved providing the one-one property holds. Below only the following case is used:

R3. for d,e∈Element:
invr(r) $\Rightarrow$ *invr(r † [d→r(e),e→r(d)])*

The changes to the data structure made in the next section are always joining rings (corresponding to the merging of equivalence classes). The property showing this merging is:

R4. for invr(r), c,d,e∈Element:
$\sim$ *(d∈reachable(e,r))* $\wedge$ *r' = r † [d→r(e),e→r(d)]* $\Rightarrow$
reachable(d,r') = reachable(d,r) $\cup$ *reachable(e,r)* $\wedge$
($\sim$(c∈reachable(d,r')) $\Rightarrow$ *reachable(c,r')=reachable(c,r))*

Although not required below, the property for splitting rings is presented because of its pleasing symmetry:

R5. for invr(r), c,d,e∈Element:
d∈reachable(e,r) $\wedge$ *r' = r † [d→r(e),e→r(d)]* $\Rightarrow$
reachable(d,r') $\cup$ *reachable(e,r') = reachable(d,r)* $\wedge$
($\sim$(c∈reachable(d,r)) $\Rightarrow$ *reachable(c,r')=reachable(c,r))*

Ring Algorithm

The approach here is to use two representations of the stored equivalence relations: a direct map (as in fig. 60) for the test, and a ring representation for updating the mapping. Obviously these two representations must be kept in step. (This algorithm would only be attractive if *TEST* were used much more frequently than *EQUATE*.)

The data structure, then, is:

Qrm:: M: Element → Element   R: Element → Element

invqrm(<m,r>) $\triangleq$ *invr(r)* $\wedge$ *(**A**e∈Element)(reachable(e,r)=group(m,m(e)))*

Its adequacy poses only the minor problem of showing that rings can be found which match the equivalences of the mapping specification of fig. 60.

The operations do what is shown in fig. 60 plus the updating of the rings. Thus:

INITR
states: Qrm
post-INITR(,<m,r>) $\triangleq$ *m=r=[e→e | e∈Element]*

EQUATER
states: Qrm
type: Element Element $\longrightarrow$
post-EQUATER($<m,r>,e_1,e_2,<m',r'>$) $\triangleq$
    if $m(e_1)=m(e_2)$ **then** $m'=m \wedge r'=r$
    else
        $(m' = m \dagger [e{\rightarrow}m(e_1) \mid m(e){\epsilon}reachable(e_2,r)] \wedge$
        $r' = [e_1{\rightarrow}r(e_2), e_2{\rightarrow}r(e_1)])$

TESTR
states: Qrm
type: Element Element $\longrightarrow$ *Bool*
post-TESTR($<m,r>,e_1,e_2,<m',r'>,b$) $\triangleq$
    $m'=m \wedge r'=r \wedge (b \Leftrightarrow m(e_1)=m(e_2))$

The correctness property for these operations is simple because the data structure of fig. 60 is being maintained in an almost identical fashion. The only real work, then, is to establish that the operations preserve validity.

In an environment with:

DCL M (1:N) FIXED BIN(15);
DCL R (1:N) FIXED BIN(15);

the individual procedures are:

INIT:
 PROC;
 DCL T FIXED BIN(15);
  DO T = 1 TO N;
      R(T) = T;
      M(T) = T;
  END;
 END;

```
EQUATE:
 PROC(E1,E2);
 DCL(E1,E2,T,RE2) ...;
    IF M(E1) = M(E2) THEN /*SKIP*/;
    ELSE DO;   /* UPDATE M*/
       T  = E2;
          DO WHILE (TRUE);
          M(T)  = M(E1);
          IF R(T)=E2 THEN LEAVE; ELSE T  = R(T);
          END;

             /*UPDATE R*/
       RE2  = R(E2);
       R(E2)  = R(E1);
       R(E1)  = RE2;.
       END;
 END;

TEST:
 PROC(E1,E2);
 DCL(E1,E2) ...;
    RETURN (M(E1) = M(E2));
 END;
```

Summary

Several different algorithms based on two different data structures have been developed from one specification (see fig. 57). In each case the correctness of the final algorithm has been made plausible by the steps of its development. As familiarity with the formal basis grows, the steps of reasoning are becoming larger but they remain rigorous because intermediate steps can be filled in as required. In this chapter, there has been an important contribution to making the arguments more intuitive: the collection of results about data structures has provided key notions for seeing why the algorithms work.

The collection of results about data types has the additional value that they will be of use in the development of other problems. It is hoped that this chapter will stimulate the collection of such sets of properties. The task of building such collections requires a more mathematical approach (e.g. analyzing various sets of properties and seeking generalization) but they make it far easier for others to employ a rigorous approach.

The material presented in this chapter is derived from Jones(76b) and Jones(79a). The *equivalence relation* problem has been tackled by a number of authors (e.g. London(72), Morris(72), Dijkstra(76)).

Correll(78) provides a more axiomatic approach which is discussed in chapter 16. The trees handled in this chapter are traced from the nodes back to the root; in chapter 14 tree-like objects which can be traced from the root to the tips are considered. Further reading on the topic of data type theories is given in Reynolds(78), Dahl(78) and Burstall(77). The last of these papers presents the creation of theories in an algebraic way. Further references on data structures are Hall(75) and Berztiss(75).

Summary Exercises

Exercise 13.1:   Write out the formal statements of each of the required results (cf. fig. 49) for the ring algorithm.   Prove the preservation of validity by *EQUATER*.

Exercise 13.2:   Study a group of related algorithms (perhaps in Knuth(68)) and identify the key data types; develop a theory of the data types and use the properties to prove the correctness of the algorithms.

Chapter 14

ABSTRACT SYNTAX

Three different notations for describing abstract data types have been defined so far: sets, lists, and mappings. The more interesting specifications have employed combinations of the objects (e.g. mappings to sets). There are, however, some gaps to be filled in. For example, there is no formal way of saying that an object will take one of two different forms, or that an object is to be built up from a fixed number of components of different sorts. Some of the gaps have been filled by using notation (e.g. for state descriptions) which has not yet been formally introduced. This chapter formalizes the notation used already and introduces some extensions. The relatively few new ideas, however, will dramatically increase the range of problems which can be conveniently specified.

The notation to be described is called *abstract syntax* notation. This terminology is explained in terms of something with which the reader is certainly familiar. If the reader consults a manual on a programming language, he will find, for most constructs in the language, a definition of how the construct can be built up. That is, there is a description of its structure before any discussion of its meaning is undertaken. For example, the PL/I manual (ref. IBM(a)) contains the following information about *IF* statements:

General format:

> IF element-expression THEN unit-1 [ELSE unit-2]

Syntax rules:

1. Each unit is either a single statement (except DO, SELECT, END, PROCEDURE, BEGIN, DECLARE, DEFAULT, FORMAT, or ENTRY), a do-group, a select-group, or a begin block.
2. The IF statement itself is not terminated by a semicolon; however, each *unit* specified must be terminated by a semicolon.
3. Each *unit* may be labelled and may have condition prefixes.

General rules:

1.   ...
2.   IF statements may be nested; that is, either *unit*, or both, may itself be an IF statement. Since each ELSE clause is always associated with the innermost unmatched IF in the same block or do-group, an ELSE with a null statement may be required to specify desired sequence of control. ...

In the **General format**, the upper-case letters denote things which actually occur in the text while the names written in lower-case letters stand for strings of text which must be generated from some other rules. Enclosing an item in square brackets means that valid occurrences of the whole construct can be made with or without text corresponding to the enclosed description. A more complex case, which uses vertical stacking to show options, is the **General format** description of the alternative forms of the *DO* statement. This is shown in fig. 63.

Type1. DO;

Type2. DO $\begin{Bmatrix} WHILE\text{(element-expression)} \, [UNTIL\text{(element-expression)}] \\ UNTIL\text{(element-expression)} \, [WHILE\text{(element-expression)}] \end{Bmatrix}$

Type3. DO $\begin{Bmatrix} pseudovariable \\ variable \end{Bmatrix}$ = *specification* [,*specification*]...,

where specification has the form:

expres-sion1 $\begin{bmatrix} TO\ expression2[BY\ expression3] \\ BY\ expression3[TO\ expression2] \\ REPEAT\ expression6 \end{bmatrix}$ $\begin{matrix} [WHILE\text{(expression4)}]' \\ [UNTIL\text{(expression5)}]; \end{matrix}$

' The WHILE and UNTIL options may appear in either order.

Figure 63   DO Statement Concrete Syntax

In the study of natural languages, the term syntax refers to the structure of a language. For example, sentences can be analyzed (parsed) to show that they are made up of a subject, verb, object etc. The same terminology has been adopted for the study of programming languages (see Zemanek(66)). Here, the term *concrete syntax* is used for a set of rules which defines how to produce the strings of a language.

There are several different ways of writing down the sets of rules

and one of the other forms may be more familiar. For example, in BNF
(Backus-Naur Form) notation the above definitions would be written:

<if statement>::=
  IF <element expression> THEN <unit> ELSE <unit> |
  IF <element expression> THEN <unit>

<do statement>::=
  DO; |
  DO <while until clause>; |
  DO <iterative clause>;

<while until clause>::=
  WHILE(<element expression>) |
  WHILE(<element expression>) UNTIL(<element expression>) |
  UNTIL(<element expression>) |
  UNTIL(<element expression>) WHILE(<element expression>)

<iterative clause>::= <target reference> = <specification list>
<target reference>::= <pseudovariable> | <variable>

<specification list>::=
  <specification> , <specification list> |
  <specification>

<specification>::= <expression><iterative part><while until clause>
etc.

The effect of BNF on language development is most encouraging. It
was first used in the definition of ALGOL 60. This language set a new
norm for the regularity of its constructs and the tightness of its
definition. All subsequent languages have used some notation for syntax
description. Not only has this greatly improved the structure of these
languages but it has also made possible the automation of the production
of parsers (front-ends) for their compilers.

Another syntax notation was introduced by N.Wirth and used in the
description of PASCAL (see Jensen(76)); it is favored by some people
because of its visual clarity. It is essential to realize that all of these
notations are equivalent: each collection of rules describes the same set of
strings. Which form of rules is preferred is a matter of taste.

The starting point then is concrete syntax notation. But, the real
interest here is to define the meaning of the commands etc. Again
borrowing terminology from the study of natural languages, the term
semantics is used to refer to the meaning of the constructs of a language.
For a relatively small language or system, it is quite practical to base a
definition of the semantics of its constructs on a concrete syntax. For
more complex systems, however, it is preferable to introduce an abstract
syntax.

Rather than describe a set of strings, an abstract syntax defines a set of objects. A convenient way of viewing these objects is as trees. The use of the word syntax conveys that the concern is still with structure and not with meaning. As the name suggests, these objects are more abstract than strings of characters. In order to convey how an abstract syntax is abstract, it is easier to show the ways in which a concrete syntax is too concrete.

Looking back at the concrete syntax of *DO* statements, it can be observed that some of the length of the set of rules comes from the necessity to permit things to be written in different orders. This is considered useful freedom for the programmer but there is no difference in the meaning of statements which differ only in the order in which the clauses are written. It is therefore more abstract to have a form in which information is located in some way which does not depend on written order. Another problem with strings is that information location is not easy (consider, for example, locating the first identifier in the right-hand side of an assignment statement). Here, a tree-like structure permits direct selection of components. Other problems, such as the need to use sets to show that collections of things can appear in any order, are illustrated below.

An abstract syntax, then, describes the structure of a class of abstract objects each of which is an abstraction of many different strings (as defined by the concrete syntax). A description of a system based on an abstract syntax is, therefore, shorter and more readable. (The relationship between the concrete and abstract objects can be documented by a retrieve function. This topic is taken up in the section On Interfaces in chapter 17.) Even in informal descriptions of systems, the simultaneous description of how a command must be written, and its essential content, is confusing. Remembering the effect of BNF on the development of languages, the use of abstract syntax should lead to the design of much more usable systems.

Notation

The abstract syntax notation is defined in terms of sets. That is, for each form of rule, the set of denoted objects is defined. While this is the formal base, it is also helpful to picture the rules in terms of trees; this is also done below.

An abstract syntax description consists of a set of rules. The purpose of each of these rules is to identify a defined set of objects. The simplest form of syntax rule defines a new name for a set which is already named. The two names become synonyms in the sense that their members cannot be distinguished. For example:

$A = B$

defines the class of objects A such that:

$x \epsilon A \Leftrightarrow x \epsilon B$

The set B may have been defined elsewhere by an abstract syntax rule or may be a given set like *Bool*.

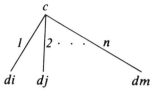

Figure 64   A List

Many other forms of = rule have been used in earlier chapters. For example, chapter 9 uses:

$C = D\text{-}list$

to define C to be the name of a set of objects which are lists. Using *LIST* to be a name for the set of all possible lists, the elements of C are such that:

$(\mathbf{A}c\epsilon C)(c\epsilon LIST \wedge (\mathbf{A}i\epsilon\{1\text{:}\mathbf{len}c\})(c(i)\epsilon D))$

This is shown in fig. 64. From the intended use of a list it may be known that it must always contain at least one element. This can be shown by writing:

$E = F\text{-}list1$

which, in addition to the properties for standard lists, shows:

$e\epsilon E \Rightarrow e \neq <>$

It is important to appreciate that objects of an abstract syntax class retain the structure of their creation. Thus if:

$List2 = List1\text{-}list$
$List1 = Element\text{-}list$

then:

$list \epsilon List2$

might be represented as in fig. 65. Thus it is possible to write:

$list(2)(3) = list(1)(1)$

Another form of equality rule used above is for the definition of sets in chapter 8: defining:

$G = H\text{-}set$

gives:

$g\epsilon G \Rightarrow g \subseteq H$

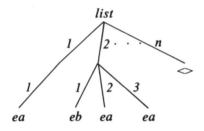

Figure 65   A Two-Level List

Also used above (chapter 12) is:

$K = L \rightarrow M$

which, using MAP as a name for all possible mappings, defines:

$(\mathbf{A}k\epsilon K)(k\epsilon MAP \wedge \mathbf{dom}k \subseteq L \wedge \mathbf{rng}k \subseteq M)$

Coming to some new items of notation which can be expressed by equality rules, it may be necessary to define a set to be the union of two given sets. Since this can be thought of as defining the elements to be from one set or the other, the vertical bar of BNF is adopted. Thus:

$P = Q \mid R$

defines:

$p\epsilon P \leftrightarrow p\epsilon Q \vee p\epsilon R$

A special case of an optional rule is where one possibility is that the element is absent. Again a notation is borrowed from concrete syntax:

$S = [T]$

This is taken to be the same as:

$S = T \mid \mathbf{NIL}$

that is:

$s\epsilon S \Rightarrow (s\epsilon T \vee s=\mathbf{NIL})$

The object **NIL** is a unique object chosen to mark that an optional element is not present. Thus, given:

$S = [T]$
$T = \{t_1, t_2\}$

then:

$S = \{t_1, t_2, \mathbf{NIL}\}$

The introduction of **NIL** brings up the topic of elementary objects. The objects so far introduced are composite in the sense that they have structure. Thus, for example, the elements of a list can be selected. In contrast to this, there are occasions where elementary objects are required which have no structure. To be more precise, an elementary object is one whose structure is of no interest but which can be compared with other objects for equality. As well as **NIL**, the objects **TRUE** and **FALSE** have been used above. Elementary objects are written as a sequence of, capital letters. Any two different sequences denote objects which are unequal. When an elementary object is used in a rule, it is taken to mean the unit set containing the object. Thus:

Input = Nat | INVALID

gives:

$in \epsilon Input \Leftrightarrow in \epsilon Nat \vee in \epsilon \{INVALID\}$

Another form of abstract syntax rule has been used for the definition of states: the situation to be captured is where an object is required with a fixed number of components which may be of different types. Thus chapter 8 used:

Studx:: N: Student-name-set Y: Student-name-set

The rules which use a ::, then, introduce a class of structured objects. The elements of a set defined by such a rule are like lists of a pre-determined length; they contain members of the defined sets but, instead of being anonymous lists, are considered to have been created by a constructor function. Thus an object $state_0$ of *Studx* is represented in fig. 66. The role of the constructor function is essentially to distinguish otherwise similar elements. The constructor can be thought of as adding a flag for this purpose. Thus one can write a seemingly ambiguous description like:

Object = Option1 | Option2 | Option3 | Option4

Option1:: Basic1 Basic2
Option2:: Basic1
Option3:: Basic1 Basic2
Option4:: Basic2

defining the options in terms of the sets *Basic1* and *Basic2*, and still be able to decide for any given:

obj ϵ Object

to which of the option sets it belongs. This is very useful, for example, in a system definition where commands contain the same information and only the keyword distinguishes the required function.

Formally, then, a rule:

W:: X Y

defines the set *W* as:

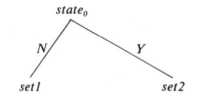

$state_0$

N

Y

$set1$ $set2$

Figure 66   A Constructed Object

$\{mk\text{-}W(x,y) \mid x \epsilon X \wedge y \epsilon Y\}$

The constructor (or make) functions are named by prefixing the name of the set being defined with *mk-*. The properties of the constructor functions are obvious and, for most purposes, of no real concern. Formally, they can be characterized by saying that they are functions with the following uniqueness property:

$mk\text{-}a(b1,b2,...,bn) = mk\text{-}a'(b1',b2',...,bn')$
$$\Leftrightarrow a'=a \wedge b1'=b1 \wedge b2'=b2 \wedge ... \wedge bn'=bn$$

Given:

$x_0 \epsilon X \wedge y_0 \epsilon Y$

an element of W can be formed by:

$w_0 = mk\text{-}W(x_0,y_0)$

An extension of this is to use the constructor, in what would normally be a naming situation, to define the names of sub-components. Thus writing:

let $mk\text{-}W(first,second) = w_0$ ...

has the same effect as writing:

let $first = x_0$
let $second = y_0$ ...

Similarly (because it is also a naming position) for a function:

$f\colon W \rightarrow R$

one can write:

$f(mk\text{-}W(erste, zweite)) \triangleq$ ...

The elucidation of a convention used throughout this book is now only one step away. Pointed brackets are used in situations like:

Studx:: N: Student-name-set Y: Student-name-set

$inv\text{-}studx(<n,y>) \triangleq is\text{-}disj(n,y)$

The elements of states are not simply lists; it is now clear that:

Studx = {*mk-Studx(n,y)* | *n,y* ⊆ *Student-name*}

The convention is that where the constructor to be used is obvious from context (as it was for *inv-studx*) it may be replaced by the list brackets.

There is another way of decomposing a constructed object and that is to use the names introduced in the definition. Thus for elements of *Studx*, as defined above:

let *premiere* = *N(w)*
let *deuxieme* = *Y(w)* ...

has the same effect as:

let *<premiere,deuxieme>* = *w*

The so-called *selector* names can be depicted as in fig. 66. It is entirely optional whether selector names are given or not and what they are called. Thus:

W:: XPT:X OTHERPT:Y

defines the same class of objects as the previous rule without selectors. If present they may be used as follows:

$(\mathbf{A}x \epsilon X, y \epsilon Y)(w{=}mk{-}W(x,y) \Rightarrow XPT(w){=}x \wedge OTHERPT(w){=}y)$

Obvious extensions to the forms of rules are permitted. For example:

A:: B S:C TH:D-set E→F LAST:G-list1

It is frequently convenient to retain suggestive names for elements of a defined set (e.g. a parameter name of stated type). It is, however, essential to distinguish between members of the sets and the sets themselves. Names with lower-case letters are used for the former and names whose first character is a capital letter for the sets themselves. Thus:

prog ∈ *Prog*

The problem of finding representations for the tree-like objects which can be defined by abstract syntax rules is more difficult than with sets etc. Even with an example as simple as expressions, a compiler designer must choose between many different linear forms of the essential tree structure being represented. For a glimpse of the full scale of the problem the reader is referred to Weissenboeck(75) where part of the internal text of an actual PL/I compiler is related to the abstract syntax of the language.

Use in Specifications

As an example of the use of the slightly expanded abstract syntax notation which is now available, the problem known as **Cantor's enumeration** (see Jackson(75)) is used. The problem is based on an idea of the nineteenth century mathematician Georg Cantor. A simple intuitive idea of two sets of things having the same number of elements is to test whether there is a one-to-one correspondence between the two sets. Thus, a shepherd who could not count beyond two could check the number of sheep returning to the fold each evening by having a pile of stones with one for each sheep that went out in the morning. He checks by picking up one stone each time a sheep goes into the pen; while there are stones remaining on the floor there are still sheep to return. Cantor's idea was to extend the idea of a one-to-one correspondence to infinite sets. He argued that if a one-to-one correspondence could be created between two sets, then they were equally numerate. Now there is an obvious correspondence between:

{1,2,3,...}

and:

{0.5, 1.5, 2.5, ...}

and thus the two sets, although both infinite, can be said to have the same number of elements. One says that they are of the same order of infinity. Surprisingly, some sets are of the same order of infinity as proper subsets of themselves. Thus there is a one-to-one correspondence (i.e. multiply by 2) between:

{0,1,2,...}

and:

{0,2,4,...}

Intriguingly there are infinite sets of higher degree. For example, no one-to-one correspondence exists between the natural numbers and all functions over the natural numbers. The same is true for the real numbers (i.e. numbers like sqrt(2) and π).

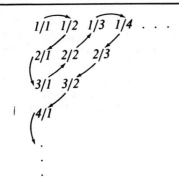

Figure 67   Rational Numbers

There is, however, a simpler class of numbers called the rationals. Rational numbers are those which can be expressed as a fraction of two natural numbers (e.g. 71/100, 1000001/1000000). It is therefore of interest to determine to which order of infinity the rational numbers belong. Cantor set up a way of enumerating the rational numbers so that a one-one correspondence with the natural numbers can be established. The idea is to lay out all of the rational numbers in a doubly infinite table as in fig. 67. Reading either horizontally or vertically, no numbers in the other planes will ever be reached. Cantor proposed to work up and down diagonally reading off the numbers in the order:

1/1, 1/2, 2/1, 3/1, 2/2, 1/3, 1/4, 2/3, 3/2, 4/1, ...

In this way, any given rational will be reached eventually. Thus the rational numbers are of the same order of infinity as the natural numbers.

M.Jackson specified a program which was to zigzag through the rationals in just this order and to print all of the numbers up to *100/1*. This specification is given in fig. 68. (The subsidiary predicates on sublists are divided up for use in the program development below.)

Zigzag:: ZIG:Rat-list ZAG:Rat-list
Rat:: NUM:Nat DEN:Nat

RATS
type: → *Zigzag-list*
post-RATS(,zzl) ≜ *is-correct-zig-zag-list(zzl,50)*

is-correct-zig-zag-list(zzl,n) ≜
    len$zzl = n$ ∧
    *(**A**z∈{1:n})(is-correct-zig-zag(zzl(z),z))*

is-correct-zig-zag(<zig,zag>,z) ≜
    is-correct-zig(zig,z) ∧ *is-correct-zag(zag,z)*

is-correct-zig(rl,z) ≜ *is-correct-zig-list(rl,2*z-1)* ∧ **len**$rl=2*z-1$

is-correct-zig-list(rl,i) ≜
    *(**A**t∈{1:**len**rl})(rl(t) = mk-rat((i - t + 1),t))*

is-correct-zag(rl,z) ≜ *is-correct-zag-list(rl,2*z)* ∧ **len**$rl=2*z$

is-correct-zag-list(rl,i) ≜
    *(**A**s∈{1:**len**rl})(rl(s) = mk-rat(s,(i - s + 1)))*

Figure 68   Specification of Rational Numbers Problem

⋆　⋆　⋆

One reason that abstract syntax definitions are so useful is the fact that they can be defined recursively. That is, the definition of an object can use that object on the right-hand side. The reader should think back to the discussion of recursive functions in chapter 3. With (the explicit definition of) recursive functions, the name of the function being defined could also occur on the right-hand side of the definition symbol ($\triangleq$). Since that point, many recursive functions have been encountered, but they have all exhibited the essential feature that there is always a way of stopping the recursion. Normally this is by means of a conditional expression one of whose clauses does not require recursion. An analogous situation exists with recursive abstract syntax rules. There is normally a rule which is non-recursive. Recall the definition of **binary trees** given in chapter 3:

Bin-tree = Int | Node
Node:: LEFT:Bin-tree RIGHT:Bin-tree

Another example of a recursive abstract syntax description can form the basis of a realization of **stacks** (cf. fig. 39). Here the stopping rule is given implicitly by the brackets denoting that the clause is optional (i.e. may be **NIL**). Thus:

Stack1 = [Stack-level]

Stack-level:: TOP:Element REST:Stack1

with the operations being defined as:

INIT1
states: Stack1
*post-INIT1(,st1') $\triangleq$ st1'=***NIL**

PUSH1
states: Stack1
type: Element $\rightarrow$
post-PUSH1(st1,e,st1') $\triangleq$ st1' = mk-Stack-level(e,st1)

POP1
states: Stack1
type: $\rightarrow$ Element
*pre-POP1(st1) $\triangleq$ st1$\neq$***NIL**
post-POP1(st1,st1',res) $\triangleq$ st1'=REST(st1) $\land$ res=TOP(st1)

IS-EMPTY1
states: Stack1
type: $\rightarrow$ Bool
*post-IS-EMPTY1(st1,st1',b) $\triangleq$ st1'=st1 $\land$ (b $\Leftrightarrow$ st1=***NIL***)*

The reader should understand that a recursive definition defines an infinite class in the sense that it contains elements which are generated by any number of recursions. There is no maximum size for the elements of the set but each element in the set is of finite size. It is important to understand this distinction: the elements, just like the natural numbers themselves, are of unbounded but finite size.

Exercise 14.1:   Using the definition:

Tree:: LEFT:[Tree] RIGHT:[Tree]

define a predicate:

test-tips: Tree Tree → Bool

which is satisfied if the tips of the two trees have the same values in the same order; the structure of the trees should not affect the outcome.

Exercise 14.2:   Write an abstract syntax for a book (like this one) where the text is a mixture of references and items, and a bibliography is included which maps references onto publication information.

Exercise 14.3:   Write an abstract syntax for the overall structure of a book start from:

Book :: FRONTMATTER: ... BODY: ... BACKMATTER: ...

and work down through chapters, paragraphs etc..

*Defining the Abstract Syntax of a Language

This section covers a particular use of abstract syntax notation. It is not, however, so special as the title might suggest. In fact most large systems (e.g. database systems) can be viewed as processing a language. So, although the discussion here is limited to the abstract syntax of the programming language used in this book, it should be read by any reader who plans to define large systems.

Many programming languages permit a wide range of alternative representations of programs. That is, many different ways exist of writing character strings of the language which have the same meaning. PL/I has many such options and defaults. Basing a discussion of the language on the concrete syntax forces much repetition. Of particular interest here is the problem of defining the meaning of the language. By using an abstract syntax there are far fewer objects whose semantics must be fixed. The abstract syntax provides a sort of normal form for the language. (See Urschler(69b) on the question of relating abstract and concrete syntax.) There is another advantage of using the abstract syntax as the basis of a language definition: location and manipulation of parts of the program text via a linear string of characters can be very difficult. For this reason a compiler usually has phases concerned with tokenization and parsing of the linear text. In contrast, the tree-like objects (see fig. 69) are easier to manipulate.

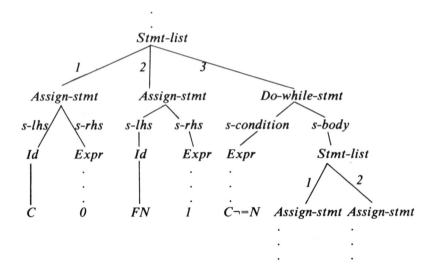

Figure 69   Abstract Form of Factorial Program

The concrete form of the programs in this book might allow declarations to be intermixed with statements. This has, however, no semantic significance and the abstract programs can group the declarations. Furthermore, since the order of the declarations is unimportant, they can be treated as a set. Thus the first abstract syntax rule defines programs as:

Program:: s-dcls:Declaration-set s-body:Stmt-list

The form of declaration is not considered further. Each statement (*Stmt*) which occurs in such a statement list may be of one of several kinds:

Stmt = Compound-stmt | If-stmt | Do-while-stmt |
*   For-stmt | Assign-stmt*

Whenever an abstract syntax rule introduces alternatives in this way, it is necessary to ensure that the sets are disjoint. This is easy to achieve because all that is necessary is to ensure that constructors are used for each set: this is done by making each of the defining rules a *::* rule. Thus the rule for compound statements is:

Compound-stmt:: Stmt-list

The rule for *IF* statements is:

If-stmt:: s-condition:Expr s-then:Stmt s-else:Stmt

Notice how the selector names serve a useful mnemonic role. The simple *DO WHILE* used here can be defined:

Do-while-stmt:: s-condition:Expr s-body:Stmt-list

and the iterative *DO/BY/TO* form:

For-stmt:: s-control-var:Id s-init:Expr s-limit:Expr s-body:Stmt-list

and finally assignment statements:

Assign-stmt:: s-lhs:Id s-rhs:Expr

It is interesting to compare (see figs. 14 and 69) the concrete and abstract forms of a program. Not only have the symbols like = been removed in the abstract program (its purpose was only to make the concrete linear text unambiguous), but also the structure is now recorded as a tree.

The design of a language (or system) can be an enormous undertaking; the design of concrete syntaxes which are unambiguous is an intricate task. The two tasks should not be undertaken at the same time. A division into more manageable problems can be made by designing the semantics based on the abstract content of constructs and then, separately, designing an unambiguous way of expressing this information content. It could also be observed that the descriptions of many systems would be far clearer if this dichotomy were followed. The abstract syntax for ALGOL 60 is given in Henhapl(78) and that for PL/I in Bekic(74).

Exercise 14.4: Provide abstract syntaxes for the PL/I *IF* and *DO* statements as described in the earlier extracts from the language manual. Assume classes:

targ-ref   target reference
expr
ex-unit   statement with prefix names etc.

have been defined. Discuss the problems which are resolved by this abstract syntax.

Exercise 14.5: This exercise concerns the conversion between tree forms of (abstract) expressions and a (linear) ***reverse Polish*** form. Consider the abstract syntax:

Expr = Var | Bin-expr
Bin-expr :: Expr Op Expr

One definition of the linear form is:

Rep-expr = Token-list
Token = Var | Op

But, the idea of reverse Polish is that the representation conforms to the concrete syntax:

Rep-expr ::= Var | Rep-bin-expr
Rep-bin-expr ::= Op Rep-expr Rep-expr

Write the functions:

rep-expr: Expr → Rep-expr
retr-expr: Rep-expr → Expr

*Structural Induction

This optional section discusses proof by induction. To make formal proofs about the tree-like objects which can be described by abstract syntax rules requires the use of **structural induction**. This is a technique proposed by R.M.Burstall (see Burstall(69)) for dealing with trees of unbounded size. In fact, then, it is only objects defined by recursive rules which are of concern.

Consider the example of the *maxt* function given in chapter 3:

Bin-tree = Int | Node
Node:: LEFT:Bin-tree RIGHT:Bin-tree

maxt(t) ≜
    if *t∈Int* **then** *t*
    else *max(maxt(LEFT(t)),maxt(RIGHT(t)))*

Suppose a specification of this function had been given in terms of a collection of the tree elements into a set (*maxs* is defined in appendix C). Thus:

post-maxt(t,v) ≜ *v=maxs(gather(t))*

where:

gather(t) ≜
    if *t∈Int* **then** *{t}*
    else *gather(LEFT(t)) ∪ gather(RIGHT(t))*

The proof that *maxt* satisfies this specification requires that a result is proved about all possible trees satisfying the syntax. Like the earlier induction rules the induction concerns the way the objects are built up; in fact **structural induction** is just induction over this structure.

The rule, then, is to prove the required property for the basic elements, then to assume it as an induction hypothesis for elements of the non-basic elements and to prove it for objects which contain them. This last is the inductive step. Thus, for the syntax in question, if:

p(n) for n∈Int

and:

$p(t_1) \wedge p(t_2) \Rightarrow p(mk\text{-}Node(t_1,t_2))$ *for* $t_1,t_2\epsilon Bin\text{-}tree$

then:

$p(t)$ *for all* $t\epsilon Bin\text{-}tree$

Thus, for the problem in hand, assume for the basis:

$t\epsilon Int$

From which:

$maxt(t)$
   $= maxs(gather(t))$
   $= maxs(\{t\})$
   $= t$

This concludes the basis.
   For the inductive step, assume:

$t\epsilon Node$

Then:

$maxt(t) = max(maxt(LEFT(t)),maxt(RIGHT(t)))$

But by induction hypothesis:

$maxt(LEFT(t)) = maxs(gather(LEFT(t)))$
$maxt(RIGHT(t)) = maxs(gather(RIGHT(t)))$

Thus:

$maxt(t)$
   $= max(maxs(gather(LEFT(t))),maxs(gather(RIGHT(t))))$
   $= maxs(gather(LEFT(t)) \cup gather(RIGHT(t)))$

But this is exactly:

$maxs(gather(t))$

which concludes the proof.

Exercise 14.6:   Prove by structural induction that:

$collect(revt(t)) = rev(collect(t))$

where:

$t \epsilon Bin\text{-}tree$
$revt(t) \triangleq$
   if $t\epsilon Int$ **then** t
   else $mk\text{-}Node(RIGHT(t),LEFT(t))$

$collect(t) \triangleq$
   if $t\epsilon Int$ **then** $<t>$
   else $collect(LEFT(t))$ $||$ $collect(RIGHT(t))$

Data Refinement

The example which is used to introduce the new application of refinement concerns *inverted files*. This is a well known data processing problem which is introduced informally at the same time as the formulae of the specification and refinement are given.

Following Hall(75), the description is based on a telephone directory problem. A normal telephone directory is built up of entries which contain three items of information: a name, an address, and a telephone number. Suppose it is required to automate access to this directory. The most frequent form of access is via name. (The reader can no doubt imagine many sophistications for such a system: approximate spellings, display of all duplicate names with addresses for further selection etc. The purpose here can be served by a simpler specification.) But sometimes access via telephone number is also required. The telephone number is regarded as a secondary key while the name is referred to as the primary key. There is no great difficulty in supporting access by one key but inverted files are used for implementing the access by the secondary key.

First, however, the specification must be fixed. The basic state could be regarded as a mapping with *Names* as its domain. But, since names are not unique, the range of the mapping would have to be sets of information. In short, it is really a relation which is being modelled and a better model will be found by basing the definitions on sets of entries. Thus:

Directory = Entry-set
Entry:: NAME:Name   Address   NUMB:Number

For the current purposes, the structure of the sets *Name*, *Address* and *Number* are of no concern. The operation for providing new information is simple to specify:

ADD-ENTRY
states: Directory
type: Entry →
post-ADD-ENTRY(dir,e,dir') ≜ *dir'=dir* ∪ {*e*}

Location of information via the primary key is defined as:

LOC-NAME
states: Directory
type: Name → *Number-set*
post-LOC-NAME(dir,nm,dir',res) ≜
      dir'=dir ∧
      res={*NUMB(entry)* | *entry*∈*dir* ∧ *NAME(entry)=nm*}

For the specification there is no difficulty in defining access via the secondary key:

LOC-NUMB
states: Directory
type: Number → *Name-set*
post-LOC-NUMB(dir,no,dir',res) ≜
    dir'=dir ∧
    res={*NAME(entry)* | *entry∊dir* ∧ *NUMB(entry)=no*}

How is an efficient realization to be found? Clearly it cannot be based on an unordered collection of entries because then each locate operation would have to search, on average, a half of the number of entries. Whenever information has to be located by key, an obvious strategy is to store it in order on that key. It may then be possible to use a binary search strategy to locate information. Here, the presence of the *ADD-ENTRY* operation suggests that a linear list may be impractical and that the entries will have to be ordered in a linked-list structure. But it is still possible to provide fast access by, for example, a decoding tree which divides the search space. Depending on the size of the directory there would be one or more auxiliary lists which could be used to locate a starting point for a linear search. The actual method of locating the information is not covered here. This is not an oversight, rather it is an important part of the general method being proposed that separable problems should be separated. The location of items in ordered lists is certainly a separable problem.

What cannot be separated is the difficulty that there are two different keys by which this problem is to locate information. Clearly, a list cannot be kept in two orders at once; this is where the idea of a secondary index comes in. Logically a second list is kept which is in order on the secondary key. The items in this list provide a way of locating entries. This can be done by storing the primary key or, more likely, pointers to the entries themselves. Again coding lists would be used to access this list and, if the secondary key is used infrequently, these may sacrifice some speed in order to economize on storage space. A file with a secondary index is said to be *inverted* with respect to the secondary key.

Logically then, the realization is based on the following inverted directory structure:

Inv-dir:: PRIM: Entry-list SEC: Nat-list

with invariants which specify that the file is ordered appropriately:

inv1 (<entryl,secl>) ≜
    is-ordered-name(entryl) ∧
    *is-permutation(secl,interval(1,***lenentryl***))* ∧
    is-ordered-number(sel-subl(entryl,secl))

(For *sel-subl* etc., see appendix C.) The problem of actually preserving these ordered lists in linked list storage is left to the next stage of development.

The relationship between this representation and the specification is trivially described by:

retr-Directory(<entryl,>) ≜ **elems***entryl*

Similarly, the adequacy properties (*aa* and *ab* in fig. 49) are obviously fulfilled.

    In order to define the models of the location operations (without getting involved in those things which are being deliberately postponed to the next step of development) a general search function is defined. The function:

search: Compound-item-list Key ⟶ *Compound-item-list*

relies on *Compound-items* being ordered on the key. It will search, in an efficient way, for all items in the list with the appropriate key and return these as a list.

    The model of the operation which locates information by *Name* is then:

LOC-NAME1
states: Inv-dir
type: Name ⟶ *Number-set*
post-LOC-NAME1(inv-dir,nm,inv-dir',res) ≜
    inv-dir' = inv-dir ∧
    *(***let** *resl = search(PRIM(inv-dir),nm)*
    res = {NUMB(resl(i)) | *1≤i≤***len***resl})*

Since this operation is total, the property *da* is immediate. Since it is an identity on states, the bulk of *ra* is redundant; only the computation of *res* is in doubt. Providing *search* performs in an obvious way this result is also immediate. The model of LOC-NUMB is similar.

    Notice how informally this proof has been conducted. It is an essential part of the rigorous method that lists of properties are used simply as checklists. If doubt arises one can go back and fill in the details of the various definitions and conduct the proof more formally.

Exercise 14.7: Prove that the recursive tree form of *stack* specified in the Use in Specifications section of this chapter is a valid realization of the list version specified in fig. 39.

Summary

This chapter has introduced the last of the collections of notation which are used, in the rigorous method, for describing abstract data types.

    The requirements for specifications, given in fig. 5, led to the use of specification languages which are formal, with natural language only being used for self-contained parts within an overall framework. As well as introducing the use of pre- and post-conditions for specifying programs, the idea of using abstract data types in writing specifications has been explained and illustrated. Since this is the end of this particular avenue, some general comments on the description of abstract data types are made.

Firstly, the question of the generality of the notation introduced is considered. The basic notations introduced here are those described in Bjorner(78). In the form of a systems specification language this notation has been applied to programming languages (e.g. PL/I in Bekic(74)), database systems (e.g. Hansal(76), Nilsson(76)) and other systems including complex machine architectures. There is, then, no doubt that it is of wide applicability. It is not, however, claimed to be universal. In particular, if an application is envisaged for some area which makes extensive use of special data structures, (such as relations) it would be advisable to develop notation and results for this. In fact, there are occasions when it is worth tailoring a class of objects very precisely to a particular application. This can be done using implicit methods as discussed in chapter 16.

The approach taken here to the development of abstract data types is aimed at tackling complex problems. There is another approach which will become part of the general development method but which has narrower applicability. The best way of contrasting the two approaches is by way of an analogy. E.W.Dijkstra (in Dijkstra(76)) makes the point that a specification, like that for *greatest common divisor* (cf. exercise 8.10) could be used as the basis of an implementation. That is, the greatest common divisor could actually be computed by generating two lists of divisors, finding the common elements and then taking the highest. Given Euclid's algorithm this would be foolish in the extreme. But this is not a criticism of the specification; it states what is required, not how it is to be computed. This can be related to abstract data types by considering the set-oriented definitions of the *recording equivalence relations* problem in chapter 8. This specification could be used as a plan for an implementation if the set-like objects were available in a language. One way, then, of constructing a program is to realize the set operations. But, again, this is confusing the roles of specification (what is to be done) and realization (an efficient way to do it).

There is a part to be played in program development by the direct implementation of abstractions. This topic is taken up in the section on Language Support for Abstract Data Types of chapter 17.

It is also worth considering whether abstract data types should be added to programming languages. Remember that current high-level languages are already offering data types which abstract from details of the machine. But even with the simple example of an array, the implementation is not straightforward. A naive implementation is likely to be unacceptably inefficient; one which attempts to discern patterns in the programmer's indexing through arrays is faced with the problem of optimization across sequences of statements (this sort of optimization is known as *strength reduction*). Some of the objects introduced above could be implemented in a programming language. However, the scope for inefficiency would be huge and the implementation would have to do complex optimization. Work is going on in this area. For example the language *SETL* (see Schwartz(73)) has an implementation for finite sets, see also Katzenelson(79).

Although the use of abstraction is a proper tool for specifications, it is a fundamental part of the programmer's task to find representations which fit the particular operations he requires.

Summary Exercises

Exercise 14.8: Exercise 8.11 presented a rather restricted view of the world. Define a new data type capable of recording such facts as age, parentage, spouse, and nationality; define data type invariants and some functions for extracting census information.

Exercise 14.9: Exercise 12.20 proposed that the reader experiment, with the tools then at hand, in the definition of a student tracking system. A project can now be made of describing a school recording system. Design the model around a situation from your own experience but include enrolments on courses, advisors, and student marks.

Exercise 14.10: (Example derived from the description of *Tables* in Hall(75).) There are many ways of representing mappings in a computer. Find appropriate abstractions for the following three storage organizations and prove them correct as refinements. The proposed operations are: *INSERT* (key and item), *UPDATE* (at key with item), *DELETE* (key), *LOOK-UP* (item from key), and *OUTPUT* (list of keys/items, in order of key). To illustrate the data structures assume the following sequence of data:

Key   *Item*

Key	Item
2	Bopp
8	Earl
14	Rusdal
4	Bridgett
6	Di Bene
10	Gambke
12	Rey Marcos
16	Schimpf
18	Zingg

The three organizations to be defined are:
a) a list of objects each of which can contain a *Key* and an *Item*. The pairs are stored in the order they are inserted.
b) The second structure uses the same state but this time the elements are kept in order of their key. Thus the final structure contains:

2	4	6	. . .	18
Bopp	Bridgett			Zingg

c) To avoid the movement on insert, use a linked-list with a third component which contains the index of the next element. After five items have been inserted, the situation is:

2	8	14	4	6
Bopp	Earl	Rusdal	Bridgett	Di Bene
4	3	-	5	2

Exercise 14.11: Write a specification for a *bill of materials* system which counts the number of required components. Obviously, the basic data type must include the number of components per part. Furthermore, the required number of parts must be computed by multiplying the number of assemblies required by the number of components. This, and the requirement to sum such counts, will best be achieved by developing some theory of mappings.

Exercise 14.12: One way of explaining a *binary search* is to define it as an operation on binary trees and then to show how these trees can be represented by linear lists. Provide such an abstract definition and use it to develop a correct binary search algorithm.

Exercise 14.13: *B-trees* are a generalization of binary trees: they offer an efficient structure for storing large mappings (e.g. from keys to addresses). Efficiency is achieved by keeping the keys in order within the tree. At each node of the tree there are pointers to sub-trees; but, between each such pointer there is at least one key/data pair—this allows the search algorithm to know which sub-tree to search (see Comer(79) or Knuth(75) for more details). Abstractly the aim is to provide a representation of a mapping.
a) Write an abstract syntax of the data structure and list the required operations.
b) Write a definition of the insert operation and prove it correct as a refinement of the specification.

Exercise 14.14: Set operations can be defined on trees which build up a representation of the defining expressions without performing any evaluation for union, intersection, or difference. The definition of the membership predicate over such representations must search the left and right trees of each expression representation. Define a collection of set operations on this representation and prove them correct.

Exercise 14.15: Exercise 14.5 introduced linear representations of expressions. Define expression evaluation on trees and reverse Polish forms and prove that the latter is correct with respect to the former.

Chapter 15

*ON BEING SUFFICIENTLY ABSTRACT

In choosing between various abstract models, the guideline has been proposed that only the required properties should be reflected in the abstraction. This notion must be made more precise.

Some Alternative Specifications

The main example used in this chapter is that of *stacks*. In order to use the same example throughout this and the next chapter, the operators on stacks are defined as functions rather than (state changing) operations. A first specification, using abstract syntax rules is:

Stack1 = [*Stack-level*]
Stack-level:: *TOP: Element REST: Stack1*

NEWSTACK1: → *Stack1*
NEWSTACK1() = **NIL**

PUSH1: *Stack1 Element* → *Stack1*
PUSH1(st,el) ≜ *mk-stack-level(el,st)*

INSPECT1: *Stack1* → *Element*
INSPECT1(mk-stack-level(el,st)) ≜ *el*
pre-INSPECT1(st) ≜ *st*≠**NIL**

REMOVE1: *Stack1* → *Stack1*
REMOVE1(mk-stack-level(el,st)) ≜ *st*
pre-REMOVE(st) ≜ *st*≠**NIL**

IS-EMPTY1: Stack1 → Bool
IS-EMPTY1(st) ≜ st=NIL

An alternative specification (omitting the type clauses and pre-conditions) based on lists would be:

Stack = Element-list

NEWSTACK() = <>

PUSH(st,el) ≜ <el>| | st

INSPECT(st) ≜ hdst

REMOVE(st) ≜ tlst

IS-EMPTY(st) ≜ st = <>

Another possibility is to base a specification on:

Stack2:: ST: Element-list CTR: Nat

with the operations:

NEWSTACK2() ≜ mk-stack2(<>,0)

PUSH2(mk-stack2(st,c),el) ≜
     mk-stack2((if lenst=c then st| | <el> else modl(st,c+1,el)),c+1)

INSPECT2(mk-stack2(st,c)) ≜ st(c)

REMOVE2(mk-stack2(st,c)) ≜ mk-stack2(st,c-1)

IS-EMPTY2(mk-stack2(st,c)) ≜ c=0

Notice that the *REMOVE2* operation does not destroy any information in the list; only the counter is reduced.

     The relationship between these various specifications can now be considered. The reader should have no trouble proving that the following modelling relationships hold.

Exercise 15.1:   With the above specifications, prove that the following relationships hold:
a) *Stack1* and its operations model *Stack*
b) *Stack* and its operations model *Stack1*
c) *Stack2* and its operations model *Stack*
d) *Stack2* and its operations model *Stack1*

Implementation Bias

In exercise 15.1, it is easy to write the retrieve function because the specification chosen as the starting point contained, in each part, no information which was lacking in the specification taken as realization. The starting point possessed only required properties. The situation would be very different if the *Stack2* specification were taken as the starting point. These functions preserve information which is not necessary (cf. *REMOVE2*). As far as the specification is concerned, exactly the right results are prescribed. Furthermore, any implementation which preserves as much information can still be proved correct. But the *Stack2* specification is **biased** towards such implementations. It is explained below that it is possible to prove other implementations correct but, if they do not preserve as much information, this would be more difficult.

One interpretation of ***possessing only the required properties*** is that retrieve functions can be constructed for reasonable implementations. In practice this is quite a good test but a theoretical test can be given which does not simply shift the problem to the meaning of **reasonable**.

A characterization of sufficient abstractness (lack of bias) can be given by requiring that equality of the states of the specification should be testable in terms of the operators defined. Thus, for *Stack*, it is straightforward to define:

eq: Stack Stack → Bool
eq(s,s') ≜
    if *IS-EMPTY(s)* ∧ *IS-EMPTY(s')* **then TRUE**
    else if *IS-EMPTY(s)* ∨ *IS-EMPTY(s')* **then FALSE**
    else *(INSPECT(s)=INSPECT(s')* ∧ *eq(REMOVE(s),REMOVE(s')))*

This predicate is true in exactly the cases where the actual representations are identical.

The fact that the *Stack2* specification is storing irrelevant information is now disclosed by the fact that:

eq2: Stack2 Stack2 → Bool

cannot be written in the same way. This is because there are representations which differ, but the difference cannot be determined by any sequence of the stack operators because the difference is beyond the counter.

An indication of how the appropriateness of the representation varies with the set of operators can be given by removing some of the latter. Suppose the *INSPECT* operator was deleted; is the *Stack* approach without bias? No! Having lost the ability to interrogate the actual elements, their storage has become redundant. Instead:

Stackr = Nat0

NEWSTACKR() ≜ *0*

PUSHR(n) ≜ *n+1*

REMOVER(n) ≜ *n-1*

IS-EMPTY(n) ≜ *n=0*

can be shown to be without bias using:

eqr: Stackr Stackr → Bool
eqr(n,n') ≜
    if *IS-EMPTY(n)* ∧ *IS-EMPTY(n')* **then TRUE**
    else if *IS-EMPTY(n)* ∨ *IS-EMPTY(n')* **then FALSE**
    else *eqr(REMOVER(n),REMOVER(n'))*

Furthermore, if the operator *REMOVE* is deleted, even tracking the length of the stack is unnecessary and therefore biased. So that equality of *Stackr* representations cannot be decided with a reduced set of operators.

Exercise 15.2:   Define a predicate in terms of the stack operators:

eq1: Stack1 Stack1 → Bool

which tests for the equality of that representation.

Exercise 15.3:   Design an unbiased specification for the operators *NEWSTACK, PUSH, IS-EMPTY* and define an equality test in terms of these operators.

Exercise 15.4:   An implementation can be designed which can be proved correct with respect to *Stack2*. Consider a list of pairs where each pair contains an element and the stack depth; this list and a depth counter can be used to define the stack operations. Complete the operator definitions and prove the refinement correct.

    The key property required of specifications is that the retrieve functions can be constructed. An argument can be constructed that the bias test given here is necessary and sufficient (see Jones(77b)).

Dictionary Example

Another example is the ***compiler dictionary*** problem as given in Guttag(78). The operators required are:

NEWDICT: → *Dict*

ENTERBLOCK: Dict → *Dict*

ADDID: Dict Id Attributes → *Dict*

LEAVEBLOCK: Dict → *Dict*

ISINBLOCK: Dict Id → *Bool*

LOOKUP: Dict Id → *(Attributes |* **UNDEFINED***)*

A constructive specification can be based on:

Dict = Block-info-list1
Block-info = Id → *Attributes*

as follows:

NEWDICT() ≜ ◁[▷

ENTERBLOCK(dict) ≜ ◁[▷ | | *dict*

ADDID(dict,id,attr) ≜ <**hd***dict* † *[id→attr*▷ | | **tl***dict*

LEAVEBLOCK(dict) ≜ **if len***dict=1* **then** ◁[▷ **else tl***dict*

ISINBLOCK(dict,id) ≜ *id*∈**domhd***dict*

LOOKUP(dict,id) ≜
    if *id*∈**domhd***dict* **then hd***dict(id)*
    else if len*dict=1* **then UNDEFINED**
    else *LOOKUP(***tl***dict,id)*

(Notice that *Dict* is a stack of *Block-infos*. This shows how the concept of parameterized types can be useful: if a general treatment of representing stacks of unequal length elements had been given, it could now be used to provide dictionary representations.)

To show that *Dict* is not biased, it is necessary to define:

eqdict: Dict Dict → *Bool*

in terms of the dictionary operators. Here a problem arises. Because of the paucity of the operator set, the equality test can only be partially decidable. That is, in the case of non-equality it will be located but two equal representations will be tested forever. The difficulty arises from the lack of an *IS-EMPTY* type operator. The non-constructive form of *eqdict* is not of concern since it is only being sought as a bias test. Thus:

$eqdict(d,d') \triangleq \sim(\textbf{E}n)(\sim eqdict2(d,d',n))$

$eqdict2(d,d',n) \triangleq$
    if $n=0$ **then** $eqblinfo(d,d')$
    else $eqdict2(LEAVEBLOCK(d),LEAVEBLOCK(d'),n-1)$

$eqblinfo(d,d') \triangleq$
    $(ISINBLOCK(d,id) \leftrightarrow ISINBLOCK(d',id)) \wedge$
    $(ISINBLOCK(d,id) \Rightarrow LOOKUP(d,id) = LOOKUP(d',id))$

Difficult Refinement Steps

What is to be done if it is discovered that a specification is biased? If the implementation to be proved correct fits with the bias no immediate harm results (but a delayed penalty may occur if another implementation is undertaken). If discovered early enough, the specification might be reworked. It is one of the advantages of the bias test that it can be tried independently of and prior to the implementation.

But the danger of an over-defined specification must still be accepted. One approach is to use a relation to express the connection between the representation and the abstraction. If the operations concerned are expressed as functions:

$a\text{-}fn\colon Abs \rightarrow Abs$
$r\text{-}fn\colon Rep \rightarrow Rep$

then the correctness argument revolves around:

$rel\colon Abs\ Rep \rightarrow Bool$
$rel(a,r) \Rightarrow rel(a\text{-}fn(a),r\text{-}fn(r))$

If the abstract operations were specified by post-conditions, this would bring in another relational argument and the proofs become unwieldy.

An alternative approach is to bring in a more abstract specification as a sort of bridge between the two concrete but differing representations. A third possibility is to use **ghost variables**. These can be used to construct the mechanism of the starting definition in that of the implementation. The implementation now contains more information and the retrieve function can be written. In a last step the ghost variables are shown to be irrelevant and are dropped. The idea of ghost variables was introduced in Lucas(68).

Summary

The specifications given in this book contain only the information essential to the problem in hand. If this is not done, the specification becomes biased towards certain implementations. A definite test for avoidance of bias is whether a predicate can be defined, solely in terms of the external operators, such that it is equivalent to equality of the objects used in the specification.

Chapter 16

*IMPLICIT DEFINITION OF DATA TYPES

The approach of this part of the book has been based on the constructive specification of data types. That is, the definitions of the operators have been built around objects defined explicitly in terms of sets, lists etc. There is another, implicit, approach in which the operators are characterized solely by properties relating them to one another. This optional chapter provides an introduction and offers some comments on the implicit approach.

The form of the **stack** used in the last chapter provides a convenient example. The specification in Guttag(78) consists of two parts; the first is a syntax part which is similar to the type clauses used in this book.

NEWSTACK: → Stack
PUSH: Stack Element → Stack
INSPECT: Stack → (Element | **UNDEFINED***)*
REMOVE: Stack → Stack
IS-EMPTY: Stack → Bool

In a constructive specification, the meaning of the operators is given in terms of some defined objects. Here, no objects are defined but the operators are linked by equations:

REMOVE(NEWSTACK()) = NEWSTACK()
REMOVE(PUSH(st,el)) = st
INSPECT(NEWSTACK()) = **UNDEFINED**
INSPECT(PUSH(st,el)) = el
IS-EMPTY(NEWSTACK()) = **TRUE**
IS-EMPTY(PUSH(st,el)) = **FALSE**

The truth of these equations should be fairly obvious. All of the operators have been made total: attempting to remove an element from an empty stack is defined as yielding an empty stack and the range of the inspect operator has been extended to include a specific indicator for the case of an empty stack. Implicit specifications are normally presented as algebras and it is because of the relative ease of dealing with total algebras that operators are normally extended in this way (cf. the use of pre-conditions in this book).

The avoidance of objects in an implicit definition is its key advantage over constructive specifications—there is no danger of choosing a specification which uses objects with a bias. There are, nevertheless, different styles of implicit definitions and their usefulness in proofs must be considered. Here, the comments are concentrated on developing refinements of abstract objects, although it is in the area of using defined objects to implement something else that the implicit definitions are most useful.

The only requirement to show that an implementation of the operators is valid is to show that the above equations hold. If the appropriate extensions (e.g. *REMOVE* tests for an empty stack) are made, both *Stack* and *Stack1* of chapter 15 can be shown to satisfy such an implicit specification without difficulty. There is, however, a problem with a proof of *Stack2*. The difficulty is with the rule:

$$REMOVE(PUSH(st,el)) = st$$

Read literally, this property is not true of the stack representation used. In consequence, a technique like retrieve functions must also be employed in proofs from this style of implicit definition.

Constructive specifications were chosen for this book because there is a practical objection to implicit specifications—correct implicit specifications are not easy to construct. There is, for instance, a danger of writing an inconsistent specification. That is, the list of properties might contain two which contradict in some way. This fact may only be discovered when an implementation is considered. There is also a risk of leaving unintentional freedom. In fact, some of the risks of natural language specifications are again run. There are some rules which give guidance in the construction of implicit specifications. For example, Guttag(75) proposes a way of generating a checklist of the left-hand sides of the equations. Thus the danger of leaving unintentional freedom is reduced. J.V.Guttag's specification of the ***compiler dictionary*** example of the last chapter becomes:

$$\qquad Syntax$$
$$NEWDICT: \rightarrow Dict$$
$$ENTERBLOCK: Dict \rightarrow Dict$$
$$ADDID: Dict\ Id\ Attributes \rightarrow Dict$$
$$LEAVEBLOCK: Dict \rightarrow Dict$$
$$ISINBLOCK: Dict\ Id \rightarrow Bool$$
$$LOOKUP: Dict\ Id \rightarrow (Attributes\ |\ \textbf{UNDEFINED})$$

Semantics

$LEAVEBLOCK(NEWDICT()) = NEWDICT()$
$LEAVEBLOCK(ENTERBLOCK(dict)) = dict$
$LEAVEBLOCK(ADDID(dict,id,attr)) = LEAVEBLOCK(dict)$
$ISINBLOCK(NEWWDICT(),id) = $ **FALSE**
$ISINBLOCK(ENTERBLOCK(dict),id) = $ **FALSE**
$ISINBLOCK(ADDID(dict,id,attrs),id') = id'{=}id \lor ISINBLOCK(dict,id')$
$LOOKUP(NEWDICT(),id) = $ **UNDEFINED**
$LOOKUP(ENTERBLOCK(dict),id) = LOOKUP(dict,id)$
$LOOKUP(ADDID(dict,id,attrs),id') = $
    if $id'{=}id$ **then** *attrs* **else** $LOOKUP(dict,id')$

Again, it would be possible to show that the constructive specification of the previous chapter is a realization of this implicit definition. Considering them as alternative specifications, one contrast becomes clear. Having chosen the basic object for a constructive specification of *Dict*, the individual operators can be specified one at a time; while in an implicit definition, it is precisely the combinations of the operators which capture the meaning.

Another familiar example is the *equivalence relation* problem. Correll(78) gives the following axioms:

$INIT: \rightarrow Q$
$EQUATE: Q \ Element \ Element \rightarrow Q$
$TEST: Q \ Element \ Element \rightarrow Bool$

$TEST(INIT(),i,j) \Leftrightarrow i{=}j$

$TEST(EQUATE(q,i,j),k,l) \Leftrightarrow$
    $TEST(q,k,l) \lor$
    $(TEST(q,i,k) \land TEST(q,j,l)) \lor$
    $(TEST(q,i,l) \land TEST \ (q,j,k))$

Exercise 16.1: Prove that the various implementations of the *equivalence relation* problem:
a) fig. 43
b) fig. 55
c) chapter 13
satisfy the implicit specification.

What is the role of implicit specification in the rigorous development method? Firstly, there are certain times when an implicit specification is the only possibility. Such cases are analogous to operations whose post-condition (cf. *sqrt*) leave open a range of possible results. For example, it was one of the intended freedoms of the PL/I language that certain things about the storage mapping should be left unconstrained. The way in which the storage properties were documented is discussed in Bekic(71). Most of the implicit specifications in the literature are, however, constrained to give a single result. Implicit specifications require more mathematical skill while constructive ones are easier for someone experienced in writing programs (see Kapur(79)). Large problems like database definitions have normally been constructive (e.g. Hansal(76), Nilsson(76)).

Implicit definitions might then be most useful for isolated data types where a greater degree of mathematical sophistication can be applied to their construction. There is also no difficulty in the development of complementary specifications (implicit and constructive, proved to correspond) in the way envisaged for programming languages in Hoare(74). Rules for reasoning about the use of data types have, here, been provided by developing a theory of the data type.

There was a difficulty observed above with the requirement of an identical stack after *REMOVE* of *PUSH*. This can be overcome by identifying the set of operators which can generate all distinct stacks and then observing that other equivalencies are meant in the sense of not being able to observe differences with any operator sequence. This approach is discussed in Hitchcock(72) and Hitchcock(74). There is extensive interest in the subject of implicit data type definition. Apart from the references above, Liskov(75), Burstall(77), Goguen(75) and Goguen(76) all take an algebraic view of the problem.

Part C

THE RIGOROUS
METHOD

This part of the book shows how the rigorous method can be applied to large problems. The *rigorous method* employs the techniques covered in the first two parts. The method does not present a fixed algorithm for developing programs, but rather indicates a general order in which the techniques should be applied.

Chapter 17 contains an overview of the method; it is probably best to scan this material and then study it in more detail after having covered some of the examples given chapters 18, 20, and 21. One way to approach the examples is to work on them in groups—if one person studies a specification or development step in detail, he can then play the part of author in a subsequent review.

There is, in this part, less explanation of formulae; the reader should now be able to read them.

Minor extensions to the techniques covered so far are given in chapter 19 and sections of chapter 17. Finally, chapter 22 takes up the topic of design.

For further reading on the application of the specification techniques to large problems such as programming languages see Bekic(74), Henhapl(78); for database systems see Nilsson(76), Hansal(76), Bjorner(79). Outlines of how to apply the general method to the specific problem of compiler construction are given in Jones(79b), Jones(71), and Lucas(73). (One reason why compiler design was chosen for early application is the reliance that all other programs have on the processors of their languages.)

Chapter 17

OVERVIEW OF THE RIGOROUS METHOD

Computers are being applied to increasingly difficult problems. The attendant increase in software complexity can only be handled by new development methods. Such systems as those for banking or airline seat reservation have a large number of different functions. This inherent diversity is magnified enormously by the wealth of detail which surrounds each function. The only possible way of tackling such tasks is to decompose them. Thus it has been argued that clarification of an abstract syntax should precede the details of the concrete syntax. Furthermore, it has been a feature of the whole approach in this book that the documentation of a specification can, and should, be done without reference to design. The techniques which have been described in the first two parts all aim at the isolation of problems. What this part shows is how these separate techniques can be brought together into a coherent method for tackling large problems.

The method shows in what order the various techniques should be used. Developing a program in a style which separates decisions makes the subsequent tasks more manageable and, therefore, more accurate. Here, there is less formality than above. The skills learnt in the earlier exercises now allow the reader to outline informal correctness arguments. But this does not mean that the reader will now be encouraged to use a development style identical with that used before the formal material was tackled. Two crucial changes have been made.

Firstly, the reader is now aware of the possibility to document a correctness argument. However informal this may be, the mere process of trying to formulate why something is believed to be correct is an excellent way of locating errors. The second strength which has been developed is related: if necessary, the reader knows how to formalize the steps relating to the techniques covered so far.

The idea of having some group meeting to evaluate stages of a developing project is now fairly common (see Weinberg(71) and Fagan(76)). Suppose that any stage of development which was to be considered at such a review were required to be supported by a

273

correctness argument where the developer could choose the level of (in)formality which he considered appropriate. If there were a challenge to the validity of the argument, everybody conversant with the techniques in this book would know how to construct a more formal argument. In this way, either errors would be uncovered or the reviewers be reassured. Typical items which might be useful notes when outlining a correctness argument are the invariants for loops or retrieve functions.

A third change will follow from this chapter as the isolated techniques are fitted into an overall framework which guides the sequence and size of each step of development.

Each of these three benefits for the developer offer corresponding advantages for those who seek, after the fact, to understand a documented development. Decomposition and some understanding of why the author believes his work to be correct are crucial to any reader's comprehension.

Apart from greater accuracy, it can also be argued that implementations with better performance are created by a rigorous design method. Although the performance of any completed system can be improved marginally by various tricky techniques, the really important decisions which affect performance are on a much higher level. In order to bring these within intellectual grasp, they must be shorn of detail. Thus, precisely the approach of using abstractions, which is necessary to make proofs manageable, also makes it possible to handle performance questions. This is particularly true in the area of data structure design where there is a wide range of possible ways of representing abstract data types.

The next section provides a top-down review of the method and its parts; the various techniques that have been covered are fitted into a framework. Other sections expand on special points which have not been covered in the first two parts.

A Top-Down View of the Method

A High-Level View of the Method

At the highest level, most proposals for development methods are broadly similar. Fig. 70 gives an overview of the rigorous method. This shows the separation of the documentation of the specification and that of the development. Whether an improvement phase is undertaken is optional and more is said on this in the relevant sub-section below.

In fig. 71 the specification begins with a conscious check as to whether some useful material is already available. The word *algorithm* is used here rather loosely; some software houses now sell designs for software; they are then not committed to any one machine and the customer is free to fill in details which match his particular environment. If a properly documented solution is available, it is clearly better to use it

Phase	Produces
Specification	Specification
Development	Design Documentation Code
Improvement	(revised) Specification Design Documentation Code

Figure 70   Overall View of Rigorous Method

Phase

Specification if an algorithm is known
             then start from *properly* documented algorithm
             else
                 create specification:
                     choose *data type* to *match* problem
                     document *data type invariant*
                     show *validity* preserved
                     develop *theory*
                     prove properties match *intuitive* view

Development repeat
             either *refine* data types
             or *decompose* operations
          until program

Improve

Figure 71   The Rigorous Method

than to start from scratch. The key point is that it must be properly documented. A solution which is described at too low a level of detail will be very difficult to fit into a new environment. The observations on how algorithms can be documented (see chapter 6) bear some resemblance to the idea of using *pseudo-code*. The similarity stems from the common use of program sequence connectives (e.g. *DO*). The difference is that pseudo-code relies on the use of suggestive phrases to record what sub-components should do whereas the proposal here is that a precise, though abstract, specification should be given.

This book is concerned mainly with the other possibility shown in fig. 71: the situation where a specification must be created and a system developed to fulfil this specification. The material related to such specifications is covered in chapters 2, 4, 7- 9, 12 and 14.

The development phase is shown in fig. 71 as being an iterative process of providing realizations which are progressively more concrete. The final output of this process is a program, written in some language, for a particular environment using certain available software—a design should aim to use as much existing software as possible. The iterated search for realization uses two methods: decomposition (covered in chapter 5) and refinement (see chapters 10, 11, 12 and 14). These two areas are analyzed in their respective sub-sections.

The whole process is top-down. That is, the aim is to provide a documentation of the design of a system which relates the various levels in a hierarchy. This does not imply a straitjacket on thought—there are occasions where it is wise to sketch far ahead and there are occasions where something which was thought finished must be revised. This means that a preparedness to discard work is essential. Once an earlier decision is seen as erroneous, a revision must be worked out and prior efforts may have to be consigned to the waste-paper basket. To try to proceed without making the changes to the earlier design history will make this latter less than worthless.

When faced with a choice of which sort of development step to do first it is preferable to give priority to refinement. Decomposition tends to fix the order of operations and this is usually done best after representation questions have been addressed. On large problems there is a tendency to alternate between development steps of the two kinds.

It is important to avoid trying to do too much in one stage of development. If a stage requires some essential change in the representation then the consequences of this should be understood before proceeding to decompose the operations. Similarly, if a new algorithm is introduced at a stage of decomposition, it is more likely to be correct (and comprehensible) if further refinement of data structures is deferred.

Creating a Specification

In order to choose a data type, one must know how they are characterized—this topic was discussed in chapter 7. The choice criterion proposed in fig. 71 is that it should match the problem in hand and this can best be judged by the extent to which it minimizes the need for data type invariants. But such invariants are, for large problems, still necessary and they are discussed in chapter 10. The next item in fig. 71 is the development of a theory of the data types and operations special to a problem area. It was shown in chapter 13 that the development of a collection of auxiliary definitions and results could make a development shorter and clearer and provide a body of recorded knowledge which could be of use in future problems.

The last item on the list of specification topics shown in fig. 71

concerns the match of the specification with the intuitive view of its function. This is a new subject. One advantage of writing a specification in an informal way is that it is easy to state properties of a system. This enables the user to gain some confidence that the specification he is authorizing really defines the system he wants. His confidence is often sadly misplaced. A specification written in natural language and based partly on realizations and partly on properties is likely to be both incomplete and contradictory. Furthermore, the resolution of ambiguities and contradictions by a developer is rarely in the direction that the user requires. With a formal specification, the user can gain confidence in its fit to his requirements from properties proved about its consequences. Although, it is not possible to prove that the specification fits exactly what the user has in mind (this is inherently non-formalized and proofs can only deal with things which can be formalized), one can propose expected properties of a system and then see whether they follow from the specification. This was done, for example, with PL/I in Izbicki(75).

There are several general comments which can be made about constructing a specification. Firstly, there should be a consistent effort to generalize; this can often result in a system whose lifetime is greatly extended (see also chapter 22). Secondly, abstraction (a recurrent theme in this book) will shorten and clarify the specification (as an example, see the discussion on abstract versus concrete syntaxes in chapter 14). From the first draft of a specification, it is often possible to see a further step of abstraction which leads to a clearer specification. This may, in turn, suggest new approaches to implementation. The third general point about specifications is that they should be split up into small meaningful functions.

The subject of specifications is illustrated in more detail in fig. 72. The major distinction is whether the data type is known or is new. Chapter 7 discussed this distinction on small examples. The reader must now appreciate that, in a large example, the data type might be a whole database. The distinction then is whether that database is given or is to be designed. The case of extending a given data type is relatively straightforward.

If a new data type is to be specified, a decision has to be made between a constructive and an implicit definition (see chapter 16). Given a name for the data type, the types of the main operations should be recorded. Next suitable objects should be chosen. Perhaps more than anywhere else, abstraction is vital here. The design of the state of a definition will determine the level of abstraction of the whole specification. If objects can be chosen which minimize the need for complex data type invariants (see chapter 10), the specification will be easier to comprehend. If bias (see chapter 15) can be minimized, the specification will leave more scope to the designer in his search for efficient implementations. Here is a place where preparedness to discard imperfect solutions will pay large dividends. Once the data type and its invariants are understood and documented in outline, the detailed specifications of the operations can be filled in.

be *abstract*
choose *data type* to *match* problem
if known data type
   then
      extend data type:
         use pre- and post-conditions
         post-conditions using:
            —(recursive) functions
            —inverses, axioms etc.
   else
      define *new* data type:
         either *constructively*:
            types of operations
            define data type using sets, lists etc.
            minimize *bias*
            define operations
         or *implicitly*
document *data type invariant*
develop *theory*
prove properties match *intuitive* view
      Figure 72   Creating a Specification

Development using Refinement

choose *representation*
relate to abstraction by *retrieve* functions
show *adequate*
realize operations:
   if changes algorithm
      then true *refinement*:
         specify new operations
         show they model abstract operations
            domain
            range
            use properties
   else
      simulate abstract operations in language
use small steps
      Figure 73   Refinement

An overview of the material on refinement (covered in part B) is given in fig. 73. The topics relating to representations, retrieve functions and adequacy are covered in chapters 10, 11, 12 and 14. When choosing the representation, not only the current operations should be considered if, for example, the data is to be part of a large database for several projects. In this case the potential operations should also be visualized. When it comes to presenting realizations of the operations there is another decision to be made. If the development is already at a detailed stage, it may be possible to simulate the abstract operations in the language being used. Earlier work in this area was presented in terms of SIMULA (see Hoare(72b))—a section of this chapter on such simulation discusses how it can be achieved in other languages. Starting from a specification, true *refinement* handles the general case where the change of representation causes a change of algorithm. As described in chapter 11, this consists of specifying operations to model those of the abstraction and using lists of required results to check that they really are models (the properties are documented in appendix B). In writing the proofs, the properties developed in a theory should be used.

Development using Decomposition

---

either functions to operations

or

    decompose operations:
        specify sub-operations
        define control
        show *realize* abstract operations
            domain
            range
            use properties
        active decomposition
    Figure 74   Decomposition

Fig. 74 develops the techniques related to decomposition. The split here acknowledges that functions may have been used in the development and that a step to operations can be straightforward decomposition (cf. section on General Operations in chapter 4). The other case is the decomposition of things which are already specified as operations.

The actual decomposition involves specifying the sub-operations and showing how they will be controlled (*DO, IF* etc.). The results required (see appendix B) can then be proved. This material was covered in detail in chapter 5. The rule of active decomposition requires that the detailed specifications should isolate it from its context.

It is important to check that operations are only used over their valid domains—this is largely ensured by the rules relating to pre-conditions. A further step in this area is the handling of **UNDEFINED** by conditional logical expressions (cf. *More on Logic in chapter 3); these match the *IF THEN ELSE* constructs in programming languages.

For both decomposition and refinement stages, rigorous correctness arguments could be presented at a group review. Doubts can then be resolved by providing an argument at a greater level of formality. The rules presented in appendix B are the formal basis on which such design steps are justified.

Improvement of Solution

Having completed a development, it should be reviewed for possible improvement. Apart from better performance, can the domain of a system be extended to make it do something in more cases? Generality has been put forward as a virtue and it may still be possible to extend this without significant development cost. One way in which a system can be made more usable is by widening its pre-condition (see chapter 22) and providing defined results for erroneous input.

The incorporation of modifications into a system which has been developed using the rigorous method is an altogether more scientific matter (see chapter 18 and Jones(73)) than where design documents are inadequate.

Language Support for Abstract Data Types

There is a growing interest in the design of programming languages that make it possible to write programs which introduce new data types (i.e. ones not in the base language).

The basic idea (see Hoare(72a) and Hoare(72b)) is to use some new scope-defining construct such as a *class* which, while somewhat like a procedure differs from it in important ways. Fig. 75 shows how a *class* extension to PL/I might look. A class would define its own variables (i.e. *M, A*) to be local just as in a procedure. Other variables could then be declared to be of type *SET* (the name of the class), but their representations in terms of arrays would be hidden. The representation, however, can be manipulated by the operations within the class (in this case: *INSERT, REMOVE,* and *HAS*). What distinguishes a class from existing scope-defining constructs is that the names of these procedures are known outside the class. (The statement marked *INITIALIZATION* is executed when objects are created.) Thus it is possible to write a program in terms of sets, such as:

```
SET:
 CLASS;
 DCL M, A(100);

 INSERT:
  PROC(I);
  DCL (I,J);
  DO J = 1 TO M;
   IF A(J) = I THEN RETURN;
  END;
  M = M + 1;
  A(M) = I;
  END;

 REMOVE: ...

 HAS:
  PROC(I) RETURNS(BOOLEAN);
  DCL (I,J);
  DO J = 1 TO M;
   IF A(J) = I THEN RETURN(TRUE);
  END;
  RETURN(FALSE);
  END;

 M = 0;            /* INITIALIZATION */
END;
```

Figure 75   Class-like Construct

```
DCL N SET, Y SET;
COMPL:
   PROC(STNM);
   IF HAS(N,STNM) THEN
           DO;
           INSERT(Y,STNM);
           REMOVE(N,STNM);
           END;
   ELSE /* ERROR */ ;
   END;
```

The representation, and access thereto, is completely restricted to within the class and checking of types can be performed at compile time.

There are a number of languages or language proposals which embody class-like constructs (e.g. Clusters in CLU—see Liskov(77); Forms in ALPHARD—see Wulf(76); CLEAR—see Burstall(77); Ada—the U.S. department of defence language which is described in the

ACM SIGPLAN notices of June 1979). These languages offer varying degrees of sophistication - including the important concept of parameterized data types. The most important bonus from languages designed with abstract data types in mind, is the fact that complete type checking can be performed at compile time.

The most obvious way to provide such features in standard programming languages is via the procedure mechanism. Unfortunately, this is not possible in most languages because the names of the class operations cannot be *exported*. B.Liskov has, however, explained how PL/I's secondary entry points can be used to simulate examples like *SET* above. A special entry point is required which allocates *BASED* variables for the representation. Given a PL/I implementation which checks pointer types, this provides most of the security of a genuine class feature.

There may be performance penalties associated with procedures, or indeed with classes. Another approach which yields better performance is to use a macro-language. The penalty here is the loss of the absolute security of representations. However, an approach with very low execution overhead may be more generally applied. For example, it can be used for simple insulation from control block layouts. The author was involved in a project which used macros in this way; for many years he made the claim that the representations of the control blocks could have been changed without touching the basic system; recently he was told that, several years ago, this had indeed been done by the people who had taken over the project.

A way of using macros is described in Hansal(74). The example used there is the processing of graphs. The abstract definition is:

Graph = Edge-set
Edge:: Node-id Node-id

Three operations are defined and an abstract algorithm written in terms of them. Three different PL/I representations are then provided and running programs created by macro-expansion.

The danger of the macro approach is potential name clashes. It is easy to create conventions (e.g. all variable names introduced by macros begin with the name of the class) but the representations are no longer completely safe from change - accidental or otherwise.

The example of chapter 18 uses macros for a range of purposes. At one extreme, as simple readability aids like:

BOOLEAN   *for*   *BIT(1)*
TRUE   *for*   *'1'B*

and at the other, to hide very complicated representations.

There is one limitation of the programming language approach. The fact that a specification is written in terms of an abstraction (e.g. sets) which can be simulated in a language, does not suggest that this is a valid implementation strategy. The distinction is between true refinement—where refinement changes the algorithm—and simulation (see fig. 73). This point is developed in chapter 18.

On Interfaces

A new system must often interface with one or more existing systems. Where these are not documented in a rigorous style, there is a danger that this will subvert the effort to use rigorous methods on the new system. This brings up the question of interfaces and their control. The first observation to be made is not unique to the rigorous method. It is essential that such interfaces are kept as narrow as possible. That is, the interaction with the existing systems should, within the new one, be localized. Furthermore, the argument lists to the interface modules should be as short as possible. These recommendations should be followed even if they prevent access to all of the function or performance of the underlying software. If for no other reason, the localization of interface modules will pay off in migration to other systems—or versions of the basic one.

There is another proposal for controlling existing interfaces. Throughout this book, representations have been designed via abstractions. But even if the representation exists, it is still worth documenting the abstraction; complexity can only be controlled by abstraction. The relationship of the representation to the abstraction can then be documented by retrieve functions. An example of this approach is given in chapter 21. A large application of this approach was forced on the author when he was working on a compiler project. The specification of the translator process had been developed based on abstract (PL/I) programs; the actual interface was to be the output from the parser of an existing compiler - complete with many devices to represent trees in linear form. An indication of how the problem was tackled is given in Weissenboeck(75); a miniature version of the problem is shown in exercise 14.5. The abstract documentation got the interface under control and the necessary retrieve functions lead to the development of the basic scanning techniques required in the final program.

Limitations

It would be unfair to terminate this chapter without some review of the limitations of the rigorous method.

What should be done if only a small part of an existing system is to be changed—is a retroactive definition of the whole system really justified? If only one such change is to be made in the rest of the system's life then the answer is probably no. It is, however, far more likely that the change in hand is one of many and that, integrated over the life of the system, the effort to properly document an existing system will pay off.

A general area not addressed in this book is distributed and parallel systems. There is certainly work being done in this area (see Kahn(79)). But it is fair to say that there is not yet the same sort of consensus as there is about the specification and development of non-parallel systems.

Chapter 18

*EARLEY'S RECOGNIZER

Readers will have come in contact with parsing because of the part it plays in compiling. Formal descriptions of both parsing and recognition are given below and used as the basis of a large-scale application of the rigorous method.

This development provides a good illustration of the rigorous method because of the key role played by abstract data types and their refinement. The problem is that of table-driven recognition; the solution developed is that of J.Earley (see Earley(70)). The algorithm is developed from the specification. This raises the question of what would be the starting point for program development. Given the style of documenting algorithms proposed in chapter 6, the given (i.e. Earley's) algorithm could be documented as in the third step of development below and this should be the starting point for the development of a program.

A word of caution is in order about this example. The algorithm presented is sophisticated and its correctness not obvious. It should be pointed out that the first (non-rigorous) development of a program from Earley's paper took many weeks and even then resulted in a program with errors. The reader should not expect to read this chapter at a single sitting.

Although the program developed in this chapter is almost exclusively concerned with data manipulation, it is clearly in the class of algorithmic, rather than data processing, problems. Readers from the data processing environment can get a picture of the more general points by scanning the sections Grammars and Parsing, Program and Modifications.

Grammars and Parsing

The concept of parsing is familiar from natural languages. Fig 76 shows the parsing of a simple English sentence. When a sentence in a natural language, or a formula in a formal language, is written, it is essentially a linear or one-dimensional string of characters. In order to make strings comprehensible, some extra symbols, which are not part of what is being expressed, must be included. In natural languages the most used *delimiter* is the humble blank; but punctuation, such as commas and semicolons, is also indispensable for complex sentences.

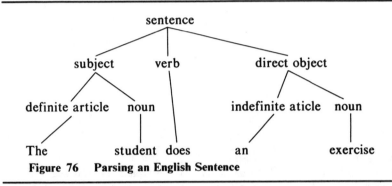

Figure 76 Parsing an English Sentence

Natural languages and programming languages developed in different ways. The former had been used for millennia before their grammar was deduced and documented, whereas the best programming languages were designed via a grammar. Attention is now turned to formal languages. Chapter 14 has already discussed concrete syntax. The syntax of a language is described by its grammar and parsing can only be discussed in relation to a particular grammar. (The sentence of fig. 76 could be parsed against other grammars than that used.) So, before coming to the topic of parsing, a more careful definition of grammar must be developed.

<root> ::= <expr>
<expr> ::= <term> | <expr> + <term>
*<term> ::= <primary> | <term> * <primary>*
<primary> ::= a

Figure 77 Grammar for Expressions

An example of a possible grammar for expressions is given in fig. 77. It has been written in the *BNF* notation. The grammar can be seen to be made up of a collection of rules; the left-hand side of each rule is a name; on the right of the ::= symbol there are a number of alternatives separated by | symbols. The alternatives are made up of two types of objects: names and symbols which stand for themselves. The names are called ***non-terminals*** because the grammar must again be used to determine how their strings are constructed; other rules can be found in the grammar with these names on the left. The (***terminal***) symbols show that exactly that symbol is required. Thus a *term* can be built up from any *term* and *primary* but these are always separated by the * symbol.

An abstract syntax of the structure of a grammar can now be given:

Grammar = Non-terminal ⟶ Right-hand-set
Right-hand = Right-hand-el-list
Right-hand-el = Non-terminal | Symbol
Non-terminal is not further specified
Symbol is not further specified

For a grammar to be useful, all of the non-terminal names which are used must be defined. This can be specified by:

is-complete-grammar(g) ≜ *non-terminals-used(g)* ⊆ **dom**g

The auxiliary function is probably obvious but can be formalized

non-terminals-used: Grammar ⟶ Non-terminal-set
non-terminals-used(g) ≜
    union { *non-terminals-used-rhs(rhs)* | *rhs∈rng g* }

non-terminals-used-rhs(rhs) ≜
    union { *non-terminals-used-rh(rh)* | *rh∈rhs* }

non-terminals-used-rh(rh) ≜ { *rhel* | *rhel∈elems rh* ∧ *rhel∈Non-terminal* }

The simplest way of discussing the strings which are valid with respect to a grammar is to view it as a recipe for producing strings. If a string of *Right-hand-els* contains a *Non-terminal*, for example:

<primary> + a

it is said to ***directly produce*** a string in which the *Non-terminal* is replaced by one of the *Right-hands* given in the grammar, thus:

a + a

Formally:

direct-prod: Right-hand-el-list Right-hand-el-list Grammar ⟶ Bool
direct-prod(t1,t2,g) ≜
    len $t2$ ≥ **len** $t1$ ∧
    (**E**i∈{ 1:**len** $t1$ })
        (*front(t2,i-1) = front(t1,i-1)* ∧
        *back(t2,***len***t1-i) = back(t1,***len***t1-i)* ∧
        (**if** ~*(t1(i)∈Non-terminal)* **then FALSE**
        else *subl(t2,i,***len***t2-(***len***t1-i))* ∈ *g(t1(i)))))*

Notice the use of the conditional logical expression. This is required because:

tl(i)ϵNon-terminal ∧ subl(...)ϵg(tl(i))

could be undefined, (cf. *More on Logic in chapter 3).

The general concept of (indirect) production is the transitive closure of *direct-prod*. That is, it is defined by a predicate which is true if one string can be obtained from the other by zero or more steps of direct production. Formally:

prod: Right-hand-el-list Right-hand-el-list Grammar → Bool
*prod(tl,t2,g) ≜ t2=tl ∨ (**E**t3)(direct-prod(tl,t3) ∧ prod(t3,t2))*

In the remainder of this chapter the *Grammar* is normally obvious from context, in which case the argument *g* is omitted. Some obvious properties hold:

prod(t,t) including the special case: prod(<>,<>)

prod(tl,t2) ∧ prod(t3,t4) ⇒ prod(tl | | t3,t2 | | t4)

When it is claimed that some string, say *str*, is an *expr*, what is being said is that, using the appropriate grammar, *str* can be produced from the *Non-terminal*. Thus:

prod(<expr>,str)

Having clarified the notions of grammar and production, that of parsing can now be made precise. Given a grammar and a string, parsing can be thought of as discovering how the string was produced from the grammar. There is, of course, a subsidiary question of whether it is at all possible to produce the string from the grammar—this task is called **recognition** and is returned to below.

Fig. 76 shows the parse tree for an English sentence; that for a logical expression is in fig. 78. In the simple cases, the way a parse tree corresponds to a grammar and the produced string should be obvious. It is, however, necessary to be more formal because there are a number of complications. The first problem is that grammars can be ambiguous. That in fig. 77 avoids ambiguity, but the same set of strings would be described if each of the recursive rules were changed to a symmetrical form. An ambiguous grammar results, for example, from:

<expr> ::= <term> | <expr> + <expr>

A further problem arises with empty lists of elements on the right of a rule: it may be possible to use such a rule an arbitrary number of times in a production.

To make the notion of parsing more precise, parse trees are first defined by an abstract syntax:

Parse-tree:: s-nt:Non-terminal Right-hand-parse
Right-hand-parse = Right-hand-el-parse-list
Right-hand-el-parse = Parse-tree | Symbol

There are two essential facets of a parse tree, both of which can be

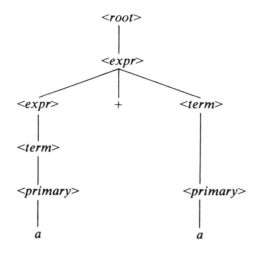

Figure 78   Parse Tree of a Logical Expression

formalized by functions. Firstly, the string whose parse is presented can be determined by the function:

symboll: Parse-tree → Symbol-list
symboll(mk-parse-tree(,rhepl)) ≜ **conc** *applyl(rhepl,symboll-of-el)*

symboll-of-el(e) ≜ **if** *eϵSymbol* **then** *<e>* **else** *symboll(e)*

Secondly, the correspondence between a parse tree and a grammar is defined by:

is-v-ptree: Parse-tree Grammar → Bool
is-v-ptree(<nt,rhepl>,g) ≜
    *(**E**rhϵg(nt))*
        (if **len***rh* ≠ **len***rhepl* **then** FALSE
        else *(**A**iϵ{ 1:***len***rh })(is-v-ptree-el(rhepl(i),rh(i),g)))*

is-v-ptree-el(e,rhe,g) ≜
    if *rheϵSymbol* **then** *e=rhe*
    else *s-nt(e)=rhe* ∧ *is-v-ptree(e,g)*

The concept of parsing a string can now be made precise by requiring that a valid parse tree is created whose *symboll* is the original string and which corresponds to the given grammar. This is formalized in the next section (where the approach to ambiguity is also discussed).

Notice that a specification on the lines indicated gives no clue as to how to construct a parsing algorithm. Given that parsers play a key role in compiling, their performance is important. Unfortunately, the simplest algorithms can be very inefficient (time grows proportional to the cube of the length of the string to be parsed). Special classes of grammars have been identified which can be parsed in less (preferably linear) time. The algorithm in this chapter is due to J.Earley (see Earley(70) or Earley(68)); it is general in the sense that it does not rely on special properties of the grammar and it also performs well (i.e. linear time) on grammars which do possess special properties.

The task of recognizing involves determining whether a string could have been produced by a grammar; it does not require the production of a parse tree. On the other hand, much of the work is common to both tasks. Indeed, a parser must be equipped to handle invalid strings. What is actually developed in this chapter is a recognizer using Earley's ideas.

Specification

This specification is given so that the whole development of Earley's algorithm can be presented. The section Third Development Step contains the algorithm and this should be thought of as the specification of the program to be written. A simple function which parses valid strings with respect to some given grammar and specified *root* can be specified as:

parse: Grammar Non-terminal Symbol-list → Parse-tree-set
pre-parse(g,rt,) ≜ *is-complete-grammar(g)* ∧ *rt∈domg*
post-parse(g,rt,sl,parses) ≜
     parses = {p | symboll(p)=sl ∧ is-v-ptree(p,g) ∧ s-nt(p)=rt }

The actual program developed here only handles the recognition task, so the specification for this is now presented. To make the program usable, it is necessary to be able to read (once) the grammar and root indication and then to process a number of strings. The specification is therefore split up into a number of operations, each of which can be specified. These operations work on a basic state:

Sbasic:: g: Grammar1   root: Non-terminal

Grammar1 is a modification of *Grammar* which uses *Right-hand1* instead of *Right-hand*, where:

Right-hand1 = Right-hand-el-list1

Notice that, in the parse tree, the presence of rules with empty lists as alternatives could introduce infinite sets. Here, the problem of empty lists as alternatives in rules is being eliminated. In fact, much of the development which follows could be done before this restriction plays any part. It is brought in here to shorten the exposition. Notice that this has the effect that:

nt∈Non-terminal ∧ *prod(nt,sl)* ⟹ **len***sl≥1*

The top level view of the problem can be presented as:

INPUT-GRAMMAR;
DO WHILE (input file not empty);
  RECOGNIZE-STRING;
END;

With:

INPUT-GRAMMAR
states: Sbasic
type: Grammar1 Non-terminal →
pre-INPUT-GRAMMAR(,g,rt) ≜ *is-complete-grammar(g)* ∧ *rt∈***domg**
post-INPUT-GRAMMAR(,g,rt,<g',rt'>) ≜ *rt'=rt* ∧ *g'=g*

RECOGNIZE-STRING can be defined more usefully if it is first decomposed:

RECOGNIZE-STRING ≜
        INPUT-STRING;
        EARLEY;
        PRINT-ANSWER;

These three subsidiary operations use an extended state:

Srec:: g: Grammar1 root: Non-terminal
        string: Symbol-list answer: Bool

With:

INPUT-STRING
states: Srec
type: Symbol-list →

PRINT-ANSWER
states: Srec
type: → Symbol-list Bool

The specifications of these operations are straightforward. Of interest here is:

EARLEY
states: Srec
pre-EARLEY(<g,rt,,>) ≜
    is-complete-grammar(g) ∧
    (if ∼*(rt∈***domg***) then* **FALSE** *else* **card***(g(rt))=1)*
post-EARLEY(<g,rt,sl,>,<g',rt',,ans'>) ≜
    g'=g ∧ *rt'=rt* ∧
    ans'⟺*prod(<rt>,sl)*

The pre-condition for *EARLEY* has a clause which was not in the pre-condition for *INPUT-GRAMMAR*. Thus the input routine would have to insert a dummy rule if the existing root rule had multiple alternatives. The advantage gained from the restriction is slight and might not be made in the real development, but it permits the use of abbreviations such as (for root rule):

$rr(rt,g) \triangleq (\iota rh)(g(rt)= \{ rh \})$

Several observations can be made about this specification. Much of it has been sketched: formality has only been applied (e.g. the definition of *prod*) to the difficult parts. Furthermore the specifications are very short. How has this been achieved? The technique employed for *parse* has been to use essentially an inverse; for *EARLEY* inverses and recursive functions have been combined. Looking at fig. 72, the data type *Grammar1* has been taken and extended with the operation *EARLEY*.

First Development Step

The specification of the recognition task has been written via the inverse production concept. This has given a short specification and is certainly in the spirit of the approach proposed for specifications. It is not, however, much help as far as design goes. It is now necessary to propose a more constructive approach to recognition, and to show that it matches the specification.

The way of defining the recognition process is to define two, mutually recursive, functions for recognizing strings of symbols which may have been produced from either a *Non-terminal* or a *Right-hand1*. Each of these functions relies on the *Grammar1* and *Symbol-list*, but, since these arguments remain constant, they are not shown in the argument list. To present the fully formal functions each argument and parameter list must be extended with *,g,sl*. The index parameter (named *i*) to the functions indicates the position (in the string) after which recognition should be attempted (i.e. the first to *ith* characters have been recognized already). If there were no problems of ambiguity, these functions could yield the index of the last position which would be produced; here a set of such indices is returned, the empty set providing a convenient way of indicating no recognition.

recn: Nat0 Non-terminal $\rightarrow$ *Nat0-set*
pre-recn(i,) $\triangleq$ *i*≤len*sl*
recn(i,nt) $\triangleq$ **union**{*recrh(i,rh,0)* | *rh*ϵ*g(nt)*}

recrh: Nat0 Right-hand1 Nat0 $\rightarrow$ *Nat0-set*
pre-recrh(i,rh,j) $\triangleq$ *i*≤len*sl* $\wedge$ *j*≤len*rh*
recrh(i,rh,j) $\triangleq$
    if *j*=len*rh* **then** {*i*}
    else
      if *rh(j+1)*ϵ*Symbol* **then**
        if *i*<len*sl* **then**
          if *rh(j+1)*=*sl(i+1)* **then** *recrh(i+1,rh,j+1)*
          else { }
        else { }
      else union{*recrh(i',rh,j+1)* | *i'*ϵ*recn(i,rh(j+1))*}

To gain an intuitive picture of how these functions work, an evaluation is presented on the grammar of fig. 77. The grammar must now be read as an object of *Grammar*; furthermore the names of the *Non-terminals* have been abbreviated to their first letters. The string to be parsed is:

a + a

The following equations have been ordered for compactness, the reader should notice the order in which the values are actually generated. (What is shown is the least fixed point of the equations.)

recn(0,r)
    = **union**{*recrh(0,rh,0)* | *rh*ϵ*g(r)*}
    = *recrh(0,<e>,0)*
    = {*1,3*}

recrh(0,<e>,0)
    = **union**{*recrh(i',<e>,1)* | *i'*ϵ*recn(0,e)*}
    = *recrh(1,<e>,1)* $\cup$ *recrh(3,<e>,1)*
    = {*1,3*}

recn(0,e)
    = **union**{*recrh(0,<t>,0),recrh(0,<e,+,t>,0)*}
    = **union**{{*1*},{*3*}}
    = {*1,3*}

recrh(0,<t>,0)
    = **union**{*recrh(i',<t>,1)* | *i'*ϵ*recn(0,t)*}
    = *recrh(1,<t>,1)*
    ={*1*}

$recn(0,t)$
    $= \textbf{union}\{ recrh(0,<p>,0),recrh(0,<t,*,p>,0)\}$
    $= \textbf{union}\{ \{1\},\{\}\}$
    $= \{1\}$

$recrh(0,<p>,0)$
    $= \textbf{union}\{ recrh(i',<p>,1) \mid i' \epsilon recn(0,p)\}$
    $= recrh(1,<p>,1)$
    $= \{1\}$

$recn(0,p)$
    $= recrh(0,<a>,0)$
    $= \{1\}$

$recrh(0,<a>,0)$
    $= recrh(1,<a>,1)$
    $= \{1\}$

$recrh(0,<t,*,p>,0)$
    $= \textbf{union}\{ recrh(i',<t,*,p>,1) \mid i' \epsilon recn(0,t)\}$
    $= recrh(1,<t,*,p>,1)$
    $= \{\}$

$recrh(1,<t,*,p>,1) = \{\}$

$recrh(0,<e,+,t>,0)$
    $= \textbf{union}\{ recrh(i',<e,+,t>,1) \mid i' \epsilon recn(0,e)\}$
    $= recrh(1,<e,+,t>,1) \cup recrh(3,<e,+,t>,1)$
    $= \{3\} \cup \{\} = \{3\}$

$recrh(1,<e,+,t>,1)$
    $= recrh(2,<e,+,t>,2)$
    $= \{3\}$

$recrh(2,<e,+,t>,2)$
    $= \textbf{union}\{ recrh(i',<e,+,t>,3) \mid i' \epsilon recn(2,t)\}$
    $= recrh(3,<e,+,t>,3)$
    $= \{3\}$

$recn(2,t) = \ldots = \{3\}$

$recrh(3,<e,+,t>,1) = \{\}$

This shows that complete expressions, as defined by the grammar, are recognized up to the first position and up to the third position of the string.

   Given *recn*, it is possible to realize the overall recognition task by:

$EARLEY \triangleq answer = (\textbf{len}string \; \epsilon \; recn(0,root));$

where the proposition on the right of the assignment is true if and only if the whole of *string* can be produced by *<root>*.

It is now necessary to establish that this (recursive) function approach satisfies the specification. The first thing to do is to check that the functions do not become undefined by, for example, indexing outside *sl* or using *g* outside its domain. (Notice how the conditional expressions are used to guard against this.) In order to aid this check, pre-conditions have been given for the two functions. Furthermore it is claimed that:

$i' \epsilon recn(i,nt) \Rightarrow i < i' \leq \text{len}sl$
$i' \epsilon recrh(i,rh,j) \Rightarrow i \leq i' \leq \text{len}sl$

These results, and the fact that pre-conditions are not violated, can be proved by induction. There is, however, still the problem of termination. Basically, the functions are always defined because of the ban on zero length right-hand sides. (To prove formally this and other results in this section is easiest by *fixed point induction*—see Park(70). This technique can be thought of as induction over the referencing structure of the functions. This is not covered because an alternative proof approach is presented below.)

Given that the functions are defined, do they compute the required results? Again it is possible to see that:

for $0 \leq i \leq i' \leq \text{len}sl$, $0 \leq j \leq \text{len}rh$:
$\quad i' \epsilon recrh(i,rh,j) \Leftrightarrow prod(rest(rh,j+1),subl(sl,i+1,i'))$

for $0 \leq i < i \leq \text{len}sl$:
$\quad i' \epsilon recn(i,nt) \Leftrightarrow prod(<nt>,subl(sl,i+1,i'))$

From these results, it is clear that the test used in the realization:

$\text{len}sl \ \epsilon \ recn(0,rt)$

is equivalent to:

$prod(<rt>,sl)$

which is in accord with the specification of *EARLEY*.

(In the development which was performed in 1971 of a program for this task, the presentation of Earley(70) was followed in that the whole algorithm was explained in terms of *state-sets*. This is what is presented in Third Development Step below. The development shown here gives a deeper insight into why the algorithm works.)

Second Development Step

The recognition process has been described by a recursive function; the next section shows how this can be realized by a more efficient process: this process employs Earley's *state-sets*. Before going on to this, some optimizations are considered. The first of these was used in the actual program that was developed in 1971, the second was used by J.Earley to establish performance bounds for his algorithm—it was not used in the program because of the storage requirement.

The idea behind the first optimization is very simple. If parsing paths which lead to a dead-end can be avoided, performance improves without affecting the result. The way chosen to spot such rules is a look-ahead symbol added to a rule: if such a symbol is present, it indicates that any production of that rule must begin with that symbol. Thus the definition of a grammar is now:

Grammarle = Non-terminal $\longrightarrow$ Right-handle-set
Right-handle:: s-rh:Right-hand-el-list1 s-lk:[Symbol]
Right-hand-el = Non-terminal | Symbol

Clearly the look-ahead symbols must match the grammar. This can be expressed formally in the following condition:

(Arhsϵrngg)(A<rh,lk>ϵrhs)
   (if lk=NIL then TRUE
    else prod(rh,st) $\Rightarrow$ st(1)=lk))

The functions *recn* and *recrh* must be modified to take the revised grammar into account—the essential change is:

recn2(i,nt) $\triangleq$
   union*{ recrh2(i,rh,0) |*
        <rh,lk>ϵg(nt) $\wedge$
        (if i<lensl then lk=NIL $\vee$ lk=sl(i+1)
        else FALSE)}

Notice that a check must again be put on the range of *i* to avoid indexing outside *sl*. The correctness of this optimization follows from the property, relating *recn* and *prod*, which shows that under the grammar assumption no output index would have been generated in the case where the reference to *recrh* is now avoided.

The technique proposed in Earley(70) is to avoid passing back parse indices which are such that a continuation from that point is impossible; in order to determine this, a set of strings must be given as an additional argument to, modified, recognition functions; this set represents all possible continuations of the production and can be compared with the actual characters present beyond the index to which recognition has been successful.

Third Development Step

A (proven) recursive function is available from the second development step. How is this to be realized by a program? Given the implementations of recursion in many compilers, simply programming the recursion will not be efficient. Moreover, some refinement would have to be done to obtain a representation for the sets of integers which are given as the results of the functions. But, in fact, the crux of Earley's algorithm has not yet been presented and the development in this step performs this task. As was stated in the introduction to this chapter, this step (without the justification) should be regarded as the proper starting point for the development of the program. What has passed till now, and what is given here as a justification, is all work in the theory of parsing and has been presented only to convey an understanding of the problem.

The algorithm by Earley essentially performs all (top-down) parses of a string in parallel: that is, all decisions based on one character of the string to be parsed are made at one time before moving on to the next character. The clever part is keeping track of all of the active parses. As has been stated, concern is limited here to the task of recognition. The objects used to keep track of the recognition process contain four components:

Rec-inf:: s-nt: Non-terminal
        s-rh: Right-hand-el-list1
        s-rh-ind: Nat0
        s-start-ind: Nat0

In order to show why the algorithm is correct, a minor change to the functions already developed is first shown. This change does not affect the results but extends the argument lists so that the generation of recognizer information can be explained. The change consists of passing extra arguments to *recrh*, which note the *Non-terminal* whose rule is being used, and the string index where the parsing of this rule began. Thus the two functions become:

recn3: Nat0 Non-terminal $\rightarrow$ *Nat0-set*
recn3(i,nt) $\triangleq$
    union$\{$ *recrh3(i,nt,rh,0,i)* $\mid$
            $<rh,lk> \epsilon g(nt)$ $\wedge$
            *(if i<lensl then lk=***NIL** $\vee$ *lk=sl(i+1)*
            else FALSE*)$\}$

recrh3: Nat0 Non-terminal Right-hand-el-list1 Nat0 Nat0 $\rightarrow$ *Nat0-set*
recrh3(i,nt,rh,j,f) $\triangleq$
    if *j=*len*rh* **then** $\{i\}$
    else
        if *rh(j+1)*ϵ*Symbol* **then**
            if *i<*len*sl* **then**
                if *rh(j+1)=sl(i+1)* **then** *recrh3(i+1,nt,rh,j+1,f)*
                else $\{\}$
            else $\{\}$
        else union$\{$ *recrh3(i',nt,rh,j+1,f)* $\mid$ *i'*ϵ*recn3(i,rh(j+1))*$\}$

As can be seen by comparing these functions with the earlier versions, no change has been made to their result and therefore their correctness is obvious. The change does, however, make it possible to show the collection of recognizer information to be built up. Formally, given:

Status = *Nat0* → *Rec-inf-set*

which is initialized to a mapping:

$[i \mapsto \{ \} \mid 0 \leq i \leq \text{len} sl]$

Then:

$<nt,rh,j,f>$

is united into the set mapped to by *i*, if a reference of the form:

recrh3(i,nt,rh,j,f)

is evaluated. That is, *Status* is made to record the arguments of all *calls* of *recrh3*. (This could be made completely formal by adding arguments and results to the functions; but they are already unwieldy and a move from functions to operations is due.) The overall proposition for testing whether recognition is successful can now be written:

$<rt,rr(rt,g),\text{len}(rr(rt,g)),0> \epsilon \ status(\text{len} sl)$

So far, nothing has changed. But the collection of recognizer information is sufficient to permit changes in the order in which elements are generated. This is because all information about calls is captured. Changing the order in which the elements of *Status* are generated amounts to changing the order of calls to *recrh3*. The idea is to make iteration through the elements of *Status* govern the calls rather than the recursive structure of a function. Thus an iterative algorithm will select the next recognizer information and process it—possibly generating new elements. There are obviously some constraints on valid orders since all calls must be evaluated. Here, it is shown that a left-to-right order is adequate. That is, order of increasing index to the domain of the *Status* map. That this is possible at all comes from the retention of *start-ind* in each *Rec-inf*; that it is valid follows from the fact that the recognizer information is always generated for an index greater than or equal to the current one. Formalizing this argument requires the property that production from a *Non-terminal* must generate a non-empty string.

The iterative algorithm can now be described. It works on states:

Searley::
    g: Grammar1e
    root: Non-terminal
    string: Symbol-list
    answer: Bool
    status: Nat0 → *Rec-inf-set*
    consid: Rec-inf-set

The algorithm is:

EARLEY ≜
  /*INIT
  status = [0→{ <*rt,rr(root,g),0,0>* }] ∪ [*i*→{ } | *1≤i≤***len***string*];
  */
  DO i = 1 TO **len***string;*
    consid = { };
    DO WHILE (consid≠status(i));
      /*
      pre ≜ *status(i)≠consid*
      let *ri∈(status(i)-consid)*
      EXTEND(ri)
      */;

      consid = *consid* ∪ {*ri*};
    END;
  END;
  /*TEST
    answer =
      *(<root,rr(root,g),***len***(rr(root,g)),0>* ∈ *status(***len***string));*
  */

Before giving the formal definition of *EXTEND*, Earley's three operations (prediction, scanning and completion) are introduced by means of an example. This is again built around the parsing of:

a + a

using the grammar of fig. 77. Processing begins with *status* as:

[0→{ <*r,<e>,0,0>* },1→{ },2→{ },3→{ }]

Each element of *Rec-inf* records the status of a parse. If the value of the *rh-ind* is *j* and the *j+1th* element of the *rh* is a non-terminal, a parse of a *Non-terminal* is required: the operation called **prediction** is used to generate new elements of status which record the right-hand sides of all relevant rules. Thus:

[0→{ ...,<*e,<t>,0,0>,<e,<e,+,t>,0,0>* },...]

and again using prediction:

[0→{ ...,<*t,<p>,0,0>,<t,<t,*,p>,0,0>* },...]
[0→{ ...,<*p,<a>,0,0>* },...]

No more entries will be created by prediction. One of the *j+1th* entries is a *Symbol*: this is checked by the **scanning** operation which adds a *Rec-inf* to the next position in *status* if the *Symbol* in the input string matches that in the rule. This causes:

[0→{ ... },1→{ <*p,<a>,1,0>* },...]

Now this new *Rec-inf* has *j* equal to the length of the rule; which shows that the parse using this rule has been successful. It is now necessary to trace back and find *Rec-infs* which required this parse. This is done by the operation of **completion**. The start indication (*s-start-ind*) shows which element of status is to be searched and the *Non-terminal* which element has been completed. This gives rise to:

$$[0\rightarrow\{...\},1\rightarrow\{...,<t,<p>,1,0>\},...]$$

and again by completion:

$$[0\rightarrow\{...\},1\rightarrow\{...,<t,<t,*,p>,1,0>,<e,<t>,1,0>\},...]$$

Continuing to apply these three operations gives a final status of:

$$[0 \rightarrow \{<r,<e>,0,0>,\ <e,<t>,0,0>,\ <e,<e,+,t>,0,0>,$$
$$<t,<p>,0,0>,\ <t,<t,*,p>,0,0>,\ <p,<a>,0,0>\},$$
$$1 \rightarrow \{<p,<a>,1,0>,\ <t,<p>,1,0>,\ <t,<t,*,p>,1,0>,$$
$$<e,<t>,1,0>,\ <e,<e,+,t>,1,0>,\ <r,<e>,1,0>\},$$
$$2 \rightarrow \{<e,<e,+,t>,2,0>,\ <t,<p>,0,2>,\ <t,<t,*,p>,0,2>,\ <p,<a>,0,2>\},$$
$$3 \rightarrow \{<p,<a>,1,2>,\ <t,<p>,1,2>,\ <e,<e,+,p>,3,0>,$$
$$<t,<t,*,p>,1,2>,\ <r,<e>,1,0>\}]$$

which the overall test for success shows to be a correct parse.

The outline of the algorithm above has fixed the order of operations only as required by Earley's algorithm; sets have been used to ensure against over-specification. Care is, however, necessary with *EXTEND* and it is specified by a post-condition:

EXTEND
states: Searley
type: Rec-inf →
post-EXTEND(<g,,string,,status,>,<nr,rh,j,f>,<,,,,status',>) ≜
    if *j≠*len*rh* **then**
        if *i≠*len*string* **then**
            if *rh(j+1)ϵSymbol* **then**
                status'=unionm(status,i+1,scan(string(i+1),<nt,rh,j,f>))
            else *status'=unionm(status,i,predict2(g,i,rhs(j+1),string(i+1)))*
        else *status'=status*
    else *status'=unionm(status,i,complete(status(f),nt))*
    ∧ *other state components unchanged*

with:

unionm: (D→R-set) D R-set → (D→R-set)
unionm(map,d,rs) ≜ map†[d→map(d)∪rs]

scan: Symbol Rec-inf → Rec-inf-set
pre-scan(,<,rh,j,>) ≜ j<lenrh
scan(sym,<nt,rh,j,f>) ≜ {<nt,rh,j+1,f> | rh(j+1)=sym}

predict2: Grammar1 Nat0 Non-terminal Symbol → Rec-inf-set
predict2:(g,i,nt,sym) ≜
    {<nt,rh,0,i> | <rh,lk>εg(nt) ∧ (lk=NIL ∨ sym=lk)}

complete: Rec-inf-set Non-terminal → Rec-inf-set
complete(ris,nt) ≜
    {<nt',rh',j'+1,f> |
        <nt',rh',j',f>εris ∧ j'≠lenrh' ∧
        (if rh'(j'+1)εNon-terminal then rh'(j'+1)=nt
        else FALSE)}

*Alternative Proof

The presentation of Earley's algorithm has been justified by a chain of argument from the specification. Because the problem is in an area which has a well-developed theory, it is possible to present a more direct proof. This section outlines a proof which is interesting because of the approach of giving bounds to the collection of recognizer information.

The plan is to implicitly state constraints on the contents of *Status*; from the way these are stated it is obvious that *TEST* delivers the correct answer; it is also easy to see that the algorithm in the previous section satisfies the constraint. But, this is only one algorithm with this property: the constraint leaves much freedom. The constraint consists of a lower and an upper bound. For given:

g, rt, str

a valid *status* must satisfy the upper bound:

domstatus={0:lenstr} ∧
(**A**iεdomstatus)(**A**riεstatus(i))(is-valid-rec-inf(ri,i,g,str,rt))

where:

is-valid-rec-inf(<rt,rh,j,f>,i,g,str,rt) ≜
  if 0≤j≤lenrh ∧ rhεg(nt) ∧ 0≤f≤i
    then
        prodf(<rt>,front(str,f) | | nt) ∧
        prod(front(rh,j),subl(sl,f+1,i))
    else FALSE

$prodf(t1,t2,g) \triangleq (\mathbf{E}t3\epsilon Right\text{-}hand\text{-}el\text{-}list)(prod(t1,t2 \mid \mid t3,g))$

Two lower bound constraints must also be satisfied:

$<rt,rr(rt,g),0,0> \epsilon status(0)$

$(\mathbf{A}i,f)$
    $(0{\leq}f{\leq}i{\leq}\mathbf{len}str \wedge$
    $(\mathbf{if}\ prod(<rt>.front(sl,f) \mid \mid nt \mid \mid rest(str,i+1)) \wedge$
          $rh\epsilon g(nt) \wedge 0{\leq}j{\leq}\mathbf{len}rh$
    then
        $\mathbf{if}\ prod(front(rh,j),subl(sl,f+1,i))$
                  $\mathbf{then}\ <nt,rh,j,f>\epsilon status(i)$
        else TRUE
    else TRUE*)*

For formal proofs that these constraints are adequate and met by the algorithm of the preceding section see Jones(72) sections 4 and 5.

Fourth Development Step

The third step of development has removed one of the aspects of the *rec* solution which made it unsuitable as an implementation: the recursion. The problem of the use of abstract data types is, however, still present. In fact, the mappings used in the iterative algorithm look somewhat more forbidding than the sets of integers used earlier. In addition there is still the problem of the (very abstract) grammar. Having documented the main lines of the algorithm, it is now time to do some refinement of the data types. In this step the overall structure of the program data types is shown, but shown still in terms of abstract objects like mappings - this makes them easy to reason about. The step to PL/I data types is straightforward because the objects at this stage have been chosen with the subsequent transition in mind.

The overall state is called *Spli*. Thus, the part of the state concerned with representing the grammar is:

Spli:: GR_NTL: Rhs-ptr-list
     RHS_DICT: Rhs-ptr → Gr-rhs
     GR_REL: Gr-rel-list
     GR_SYML: Gr-syml-list
     GR_STL: Symbol-list

     ...
Rhs-ptr is not further specified
Gr-rhs:: RULES: Rules-list
Rules:: ST: Nat LN: Nat
Gr-rel:: TYPE: {T | N} N: Nat
Gr-syml:: ST: Nat

The idea behind representing the grammar is that all of the rule information is collected into one long vector (*GR_REL*). Both terminal and non-terminal symbols are represented by natural numbers. For terminals this is an index into the array variable *GR_SYML*; this is in turn an index into *GR_STL* (the generality, made possible by this indirection, to have strings of different length, is not used in this version). *Non-terminals* are represented by natural numbers which are indexes to *GR_NTL*. The actual sets of alternatives for rules are stored in *BASED* storage (cf. ALGOL 68 heap storage). The individual *Gr-rhs* are located by looking up the appropriate pointer in *GR_NTL*. The element *RHS_DICT* is simply the storage in which the pointers can be used. A *Gr-rhs* is a list of *Rules* and, as foreseen, this is a pair of indices into *GR_REL*. This description can be conveyed formally by writing the relevant retrieve function (selector names are now being used to decompose the state - see chapter 14):

retr-grammarle: Spl1 → Grammarle
retr-grammarle(s) ≜
    [*i→retr-rhs(GR_NTL(s)(i),s)* | *1≤i≤***len***(GR_NTL(s))*]

retr-rhs(rhs-ptr,s) ≜
    let *rhl = RULES(RHS_DICT(s)(rhs-ptr))*
    { *retr-rh(rhl(j),s)* | *1≤j≤***len*** rhl* }

retr-rh(<st,ln>,s) ≜
    mk-right-handle(applyl(subl(GR_REL(s),st,(st + ln - 1)),
                                  retr-rh-el),
       retr-lk(retr-rh-el(GR_REL(s)(st - 1),s)))

retr-rh-el(<tp,ind>,s) ≜
    if *tp=T* **then** *retr-sym(ind,s)* **else** *mk-non-terminal(ind)*

retr-sym(ind,s) ≜ *(GR_STL(s))(ST((GR_SYML(s))(ind)))*

retr-lk(c) ≜ **if** *c=' '* **then** **NIL** **else** *c*

Notice that the look-ahead symbol is stored at the **zeroth** element of the rule list.

    The *root* component of *Searley* can be chosen abitrarily, the choice here is:

retr-root(s) ≜ *mk-non-terminal(1)*

The following data type invariant applies to the representation of the grammar.

is-v-gr-rep: Spli → Bool
is-v-gr-rep(s) ≜
    elems(*GR_NTL(s)*) ⊆ **dom**(*RHS_DICT(s)*) ∧
    *(**A**el∊elems(GR_REL(s)))*
        ((TYPE(el)=N ⟹ *1≤n(el)≤***len**(*GR_NTL(s)*)*)) ∧*
        (TYPE(el)=T ⟹ *1≤n(el)≤***len**(*GR_SYML(s)*)*))) ∧*
    *(**A**symi∊***elems**(*GR_SYML(s)*))*)(1≤ST(symi)≤***len**(*GR_STL(s)*)*))*

The string component is unchanged in its representation:

Spli:: ... STRING: Symbol-list ...

This only leaves the representation of *status* and *consid*. They are represented by the components:

Spli:: ...
        RI_S_PTRL: Nat0 → Ri-tp-s-ptr
        RI_DICT: Ri-tp-s-ptr → Ri-s

Ri-tp-s-ptr is not further specified
Ri-s:: info: Info-list
Info:: nt: Rhs-ptr
        rhi: Nat
        j: Nat
        f: Nat

Once again the variable size structure is put into *BASED* variables (pointers *Ri-tp-s-ptr* and storage as *RI_DICT*). *RI_S_PTRL* is represented by an array indexed from zero. Thus:

retr-status(s) ≜
    let *riptrs* = *RI_S_PTRL(s)*
    *[i→retr-rec-inf-set(riptrs(i),s) | i∊***dom***riptrs]*

retr-rec-inf-set(ptr,s) ≜
    let *ris* = *RI_DICT(s)(ptr)*
    *{retr-rec-inf(ris(i),s) | 1≤i≤***len***info(ris)}*

retr-rec-inf(<nt,rhi,j,f>,s) ≜
    let *rhs-ptr* = *GR_NTL(s)(nt)*
    let *rhs'* = *RULES((RHS_DICT(s))(rhs-ptr))*
    mk-rec-inf(nt,retr-rh(rhs'(rhi),s),j,f)

An obvious data type invariant applies to the representation of *status*. Adequacy can be verified, for each of the representations.

Program

The development here has been concerned only with the recognizer itself. (The routines for reading the grammar etc. are of similar size—although simpler.) The code for the recognizer uses macros in a way which makes the macro program look very like the algorithm presented in the third step above. The details of the representation are hidden in the macros (see chapter 17). The actual PL/I code for the recognizer is about *130* statements.

Modifications

Changes to specifications are a normal part of a development project. In the original report (Jones(72)), the initial development was performed ignoring optimizations and then a change simulated by introducing the look-ahead idea. Although this made some useful points, it was unfair because the design had already been thought out with the change in mind.

Some time after the report was produced, there was a requirement for a real modification. When applying the parser to a large grammar for PL/I, the performance had become unacceptable. Insertion of counters confirmed that the loop in the procedure which inserts states into state sets was being executed an enormous number of times. It was decided to use a hash vector to determine if a *Rec-inf* was definitely not present. The modification was thought out and documented in terms of the development documentation before coding.

Summary

One of the interesting points about this application of the rigorous method is the effect of the choice of development steps. Proper use of abstraction, especially of data, has given rise to a development whose very structure is a major influence on its comprehensibility. It would, on the other hand, be impossible to understand the final program faced only with the specification and the PL/I text. The third step of development provides a documentation of the overall algorithm in a way which could be used as a base for many different programs.

This example is large enough to clarify the distinction between two different uses of abstract data types in program development. Although the early stages use objects (e.g. sets) for which it would be easy to provide simulations, this would not yield a realistic implementation. These abstractions must be seen as specifications and not as abstract algorithms. The role of true *refinement* steps is to introduce different data structures which require different algorithms.

Summary Exercises

Exercise 18.1: Study Earley(70) and formulate the original optimized recognition process shown there as recursive functions like *recn* and *recrh*.

Exercise 18.2: Study Earley(70) then specify, design, and code the parsing algorithm in a style similar to that used in this chapter.

Exercise 18.3: As an experiment in modification, remove the restriction on rules being non-empty.

Chapter 19

INPUT/OUTPUT STATEMENTS

A number of language features (e.g. blocks and assignment statements) have been introduced informally above. Because of the importance to data processing of input/output statements, a more formal treatment is given. The presentation of the formal rules does not, however, commit all developments to a high degree of formality and subsequent examples show that intuitively clear, but rigorous, reasoning is quite practical. In view of their acknowledged importance, it may be surprising that so much of this book has succeeded in avoiding the use of input/output statements. Inspection of the examples above discloses that this has been achieved by splitting problems into operations concerned with input, process, and output. The core of the program has been developed from a post-condition for the process part; the input and output operations have not been developed.

The presentation of a formal treatment for input/output is divided over two sections concerned with the definition of, and proof rules about, operations which either consume input or produce output.

Definition

The need to consider input/output statements above was reduced by the presentation of (general) operations which take arguments and create results (i.e. they have a type clause in their definition). There is a close analogy between a list as argument and input; also between a list as result and output. This analogy gives a clue as to the structure of the style of definition for operations which perform input/output.

The *production of primes* example (cf. fig. 26) is presented in terms of input/output operations in fig. 79. The three operations shown are each concerned with input and/or output. The overall specification (i.e. *PRIMES*) both reads input and produces output. Additional clauses are added to the specification of the operations to show the input and output behavior. As would be anticipated from the treatment of arguments and

Specification

PRIMES
states: Sprimes
input: Nat-list
output: Nat-list
pre-PRIMES(,il) ≜ **len**il=1
post-PRIMES(,il,,ol) ≜
   let n = **hd**il
   elemsol = { i | $1 \le i \le n \land$ *is-prime(i)* } $\land$ *is-ordered(ol)*

Decomposition

Sprimes = *Bool-list*

PRIMES ≜ /*
   GEN
   states: Sprimes
   input: Nat-list
   pre-GEN(,il) ≜ **len**il=1
   post-GEN (,il,s') ≜
      let n = **hd**il
      lens' = $n \land$
      $(\textbf{A}i\epsilon\{1{:}n\})(s'(i) \leftrightarrow$ *is-prime(i))*
/;
/*
   OUTP
   states: Sprimes
   output: Nat-list
   post-OUTP(s,,ol) ≜ *is-op(s,ol)*
*/

is-op(s,ol) ≜ **elems**ol = { i | $1 \le i \le$ **len**$s \land s(i)$ } $\land$ *is-ordered(ol)*

Figure 79   Primes Example as Input/Output Operations

results, the pre-condition thus becomes a predicate of the input state and the input file. Both input and output files are viewed as lists even when, as here, only single values are required. Thus the overall pre-condition is of type:

pre-PRIMES: Sprimes Nat-list → *Bool*

Similarly, the post-condition must constrain the relation between the starting state, input file, the output state, and output file. Thus the overall post-condition is of type:

post-PRIMES: Sprimes Nat-list Sprimes Nat-list → *Bool*

The actual definitions of the pre- and post-conditions show the use of input, and the contribution to the output, of the individual operations. By convention, an operation which has no output clause (e.g. *GEN*) is considered to produce an empty list of output values.

Exercise 19.1: Write a specification of the *multiplication table* example (cf. fig. 41) as an operation which produces output.

Exercise 19.2: Write a specification of the *rational numbers* example (cf. fig. 68) as an operation which produces output.

It should be remembered that the specification of an operation shows, via predicates, its input/output behavior. In writing, for example, a pre-condition concerned with input, it is possible to write logical expressions concerning the length of the list. Such expressions are not, of course, a part of the programming language. Furthermore, operations with wider pre-conditions would be more usable and, in developing such operations, the language features which test for end-of-file etc. would have to be employed.
(It is possible to avoid the introduction of new notation for input/output statements by introducing appropriate components—containing the files—of the state; the statements themselves then become rather like assignment statements for the extended state. However, this approach is not recommended because it fails to model the essential growing property of the output file.)

Proofs

The rules for reasoning formally about combinations of operations which are concerned with output statements are straightforward. (Those for input are slightly complicated by the pre-conditions.) The nature of output statements is to extend the output file. Thus the rules shown in fig. 80 are the natural extension of those given in fig. 17 for sequential statements. A simple application of these rules is to show that the composition of *GEN* and *OUTP* in fig. 79 is valid (remember that operations with no output clause are considered to create an empty list as output).
Of more interest are the rules for dealing with iterative combinations of output-producing operations. A number of different iterative constructs are used in this book. The form most commonly used with output-producing operations is *DO/BY/TO* and the appropriate rules are presented in fig. 81.
A first application of this set of properties is to prove correct an

For:

OP ≜ OP1;OP2

to be correct, show:

da. pre-OP(σ) ⟹ pre-OP1(σ)
db. pre-OP(σ₁)∧ post-OP1(σ₁,σ₂,ol₂) ⟹ pre-OP(σ₂)
ra. pre-OP(σ₁) ∧ post-OP1(σ₁,σ₂,ol₂) ∧ post-OP2(σ₂,σ₃,ol₃) ⟹
    post-OP(σ₁,σ₃,ol₂| | ol₃)

Figure 80   Rules for Sequential Statements with Output

For:

OP ≜ DO i = l BY 1 TO u; BODY(i); END;

BODY
states: State
output: Out-list
type: Int →

to be correct, find:

pre-LOOP State Int → Bool
so-far: State Int State Out-list → Bool

and show:

da. pre-OP(σ) ⟹ pre-LOOP(σ,l)
db. pre-LOOP(σ₁,i) ∧ i≤e-expr(u,σ₁) ∧ post-BODY(σ₁,i,σ₂,ol₂)
    ⟹ pre-LOOP(σ,i+1)
dc. pre-LOOP(σ,i) ∧ i≤e-expr(u,σ) ⟹ pre-BODY(σ,i)
ra. pre-OP(σ) ⟹ so-far(σ,l,σ,<>)
rb. so-far(σ₁,i,σ₂,ol₂) ∧ pre-LOOP(σ₂,i) ∧
    i≤e-expr(u,σ₁) ∧ post-BODY(σ₂,i,σ₃,ol₃)
       ⟹ so-far(σ₁,i+1,σ₃,ol₂| | ol₃)
rc. so-far(σ₁,i,σ₂,ol₂) ∧ pre-LOOP(σ₂,i) ∧ i=e-expr(u,σ₁)+1
    ⟹ post-OP(σ₁,σ₂,ol₂)

Figure 81   Rules for Iteration with Output

OUTP operation according to the specification given in fig. 79. A
straightforward implementation of this output function is:

OUTP ≜
  DO I = 1 BY 1 TO **lens***;*
      /*
        OUTOP
        states: Sprimes
        type: Int →
        output: Nat-list
        pre-OUTOP(s,i) ≜ *i*≤**lens**
        post-OUTP(s,i,s',ol') ≜
            s' = s ∧
            ol' = **if** *s(i)* **then** *<i>* **else** *<>*
      */
  END;

This can be proved correct using:

pre-LOOP ≜ **TRUE**
so-far(s,i,s',ol') ≜ *s'=s* ∧ *is-op(front(s,i-1),ol')*

The reader should check the list of properties mentally and if any look
difficult they should be checked on paper.

   A multi-stage development of the **rational number** example (see
exercise 19.2) can be presented as follows. The first stage of development is:

DO z = 1 TO 50 ;
/*
  ZIG-ZAG
  states:
  type: Int →
  output: Zigzag-list
  post-ZIGZAG(,z,,ol) ≜ **len***ol=1* ∧ *is-correct-zig-zag(***hd***ol,z)*
*/

This can be proved correct using:

pre-LOOP ≜ **TRUE**
so-far(,z,,ol') ≜ *is-correct-zig-zag-list(ol',z-1)*

   The next stage of decomposition is into the sequential composition of
two operations:

ZIG-ZAG ≜
  /*
    ZIG
    type: Int →
    output: Rat-list
    post-ZIG(,z,,ol) ≜ *is-correct-zig(ol,z)*
  */;
  /*
    ZAG
    type: Int →
    output: Rat-list
    post-ZAG(,z,,ol) ≜ *is-correct-zag(ol,z)*
  */

Remembering that the extra structure of the output (cf. *Zigzag* in fig. 68) is only an abstraction, this composition can be proved using the rules of fig. 80.

The last stage of development expands each of *ZIG* and *ZAG* into loops. Considering *ZIG*, a state is defined

Szz:: s: Int t: Int

and:

ZIG ≜ *s* = *2*z-1;*
  DO t = *1 TO s ;*
    /*
      ZIG-RAT
      states: Szz
      out: Rat-list
      post-ZIG-RAT(<s,>,t,<s',>,ol) ≜ *s' = s-1* ∧ *ol = <mk-Rat(s,t)*
    */
  END;

This can again be proved correct, using the properties of fig. 81 with:

pre-LOOP ≜ **TRUE**
so-far(<s,>,t,<s',>,ol') ≜
    is-correct-zig-list(ol,t - 1) ∧ **len***ol=t-1* ∧ *s' = s-(t-1)*

and factoring in the initial assignment.

Summary

The way in which reasoning about output-producing programs can be formalized should now be clear. This chapter has provided the necessary formal rules. The subsequent use of output-producing programs is rigorous rather than formal.

Summary Exercises

Exercise 19.3: Develop a program according to the specification for exercise 19.1. At each stage of development give adequate details of a correctness argument so that it is clear how it can be completed.

Exercise 19.4: Develop the input/output parts of the program discussed in chapter 18.

Chapter 20

JOSEPHUS RINGS

An earlier exercise (12.18) addresses the topic of cryptography. Another technique, which can be combined with letter substitution, is to code a message by transposing its letters. One way of performing such a rearrangement is by counting round a *Josephus* ring at some defined interval as in fig. 82. The important point to note is that once a letter is located it is not only generated as the next output symbol, but it is also dropped from the ring. Thus, for a counting interval of two, fig. 83 illustrates the sequence of rings.

ring:

interval	gives
1	$<a,b,c,d,e,f>$
2	$<b,d,f,c,a,e>$
3	$<c,f,d,b,e,a>$
7	$<a,c,f,b,d,e>$

Figure 82   Josephus Rings

ring	output
$a\ b\ c\ d\ e\ f$	b
$c\ d\ e\ f\ a$	d
$e\ f\ a\ c$	f
$a\ c\ e$	c
$e\ a$	a
e	e

Figure 83   Josephus Rings with Counting Interval of Two

The problem is to write a program which, for a given sequence of characters, produces the characters in the sequence derived by counting round a Josephus ring at a specified interval. This problem requires many parts of the rigorous method in its solution. Among other techniques, it is useful to establish theories for some data types; informal use is made of reasoning about input/output statements and the specification is checked by establishing some properties. A variety of data structures can be employed to solve this problem (those shown below are taken from Gerhart(76) which also stimulated the choice of the example).

The first section studies the data type circle; the remaining sections cover the specification and various approaches to its implementation.

Circles

Fig. 72 indicates that the specification of a problem should be based on a suitable data type. *Circle* is a new data type and this section provides a constructive specification. Given the data type:

Circle

a cursory inspection of the problem in hand suggests that operators are required such as:

rotate: Circle Nat0 $\rightarrow$ Circle
circle-el: Circle Nat $\rightarrow$ Sym
circle-len: Circle $\rightarrow$ Nat0

The most pressing question is the class of objects on which the (constructive) specification is to be based. A reasonable proposal would appear to be:

Circle = Sym-list

Such a representation necessitates rearrangement of the list (cf. fig. 83) when it is rotated. However, the mechanics of this rearrangement are hidden in the functions concerned with circles. The fact that this representation does not require a validity constraint suggests that it is well chosen—it can be shown that this representation has no implementation bias (see chapter 15).

Having selected the representation, the operations can be defined:

rotate: Circle Nat0 → Circle
rotate(c,i) ≜
    (ιc')
    (circle-len(c')=circle-len(c) ∧
    (Ak∈{1:circle-len(c)})(circle-el(c',k)=circle-el(c,i+k)))

circle-el: Circle Nat → Sym
pre-circle-el(c,) ≜ *c≠<>*
circle-el(c,i) ≜ *c(count-round(c,i))*

where:

count-round: Sym-list Nat → Nat
pre-count-round(sl,) ≜ **len**sl≥*1*
count-round(sl,i) ≜ *index-mod(i,***len**sl)*

index-mod: Nat Nat → Nat
index-mod(i,j) ≜ *((i-1)***mod**j)+1*

    It would be possible to hide the representation of *Circles* completely by defining further functions. Here, list operators are used directly on circles in order to minimize the length of formulae. Thus:

for: *use:*

circle-len	**len**
is-circle-empty(c)	*c=<>*
circle-hd	**hd**
circle-rest	**tl**

    Some theory can be developed about circles which relates the operators to each other. These properties *(C1—C6)* might be useful in the development of other programs concerned with *Circles*. The given properties should be obvious and can be easily proved.

C1. *1≤count-round(c,i)≤***len***(c)*
    follows from: 1≤index-mod(i,j)≤j

C2. *index-mod(index-mod(i,k)+j,k) = index-mod(i+j,k)*

C3. *for* **len***(c') = ***len***(c):*
    count-round(c',count-round(c,i)+j) = count-round(c,i+j)
    follows from C2

C4. *for 0≤i, 1≤j≤***len***c, c≠<>:*
    circle-el(rotate(c,i),j) = circle-el(c,i+j)

C5. *rotate(rotate(c,i),j)=rotate(c,i+j)*
    follows from C4

C6. *for 1≤j≤***len***c:*
    tl*rotate(c,j-1) = rotate(del(c,j),(***if*** j=***len***c then 0 else j-1))*

Specification

Based on the data type *Circle*, it is possible to specify the operation:

JOSL
input: Sym-list Nat
output: Sym-list

A completely formal specification could be given in terms of a recursive function. In the rigorous method, it is worth going further. There is a standard equivalence between such (simple) recursive functions and iterative programs which suggests documenting the specification as:

Sjosl:: C: Circle M: Nat

Notice that this implies that m≥1.

JOSL ≜
   /*
     IN
   */
   DO WHILE (C≠<>);
    /*
     NEXT-LETTER
     states: Sjosl
     output: Sym-list
     pre-NEXT-LETTER(<c,m>) ≜ *c≠<>*
     post-NEXT-LETTER(<c,m>,<c',m'>,ol) ≜
       m'=m ∧
       *(***let** rc = rotate(c,m-1)*
       *ol = <***hdrc***> ∧ c' = ***tlrc***)*
    */
   END;

The problem has been specified by making some commitment to order: input is done before output; the output elements are produced one at a time. But this does not constrain the details of *NEXT-LETTER* and thus does not violate the advice of chapter 6. It would be straightforward to prove that this specification satisfied one based on a recursive function using a rule for *WHILE* which covered output statements. At the current level of rigor, however, this is not necessary.

In Gerhart(76), the proposal is made to develop alternative specifications and to prove their equivalence. In chapter 17, it was proposed that a specification could be checked by proving that intuitively obvious properties hold. This can reduce the danger of creating a specification which is precise but does not define the system required by the user.

Some properties, which can be deduced about running *JOSL* with inputs *il* and *m* to produce *ol*, are:

$il=\diamond \Rightarrow ol=\diamond$

Then for:

$il \neq \diamond$

it follows from property *C4*:

hd$ol = circle\text{-}el(il,m)$
tl$ol = JOSL($**tl**$rotate(il,m\text{-}1),m)$

and it can also be shown that:

is-permutation(ol,il)

Exercise 20.1: Specify the inverse (decoding) operation which converts the output of *JOSL* back to the original symbol list.

Non-Rotation Algorithms

The specification has, via the data-type *Circle*, kept track of the current position in a circle by rearranging the order of the elements. Such movement is inefficient and the key to the non-rotation algorithms is to leave the elements alone and to track the current position with an additional pointer. Thus:

Circlea:: L: Sym-list P: Nat

with the data-type invariant:

is-v-circlea(<l,p>) $\triangleq$ $1 \leq p \leq$ **len**l $\lor$ $l=\diamond$

the relationship to the original data type is expressed by:

retr-circle: Circlea $\longrightarrow$ *Circle*
retr-circle(<l,p>) $\triangleq$ **if** $l=\diamond$ **then** $\diamond$ **else** *rotate(l,p-1)*

The part of the specification state storing the value of the interval is unchanged, thus:

Sjosla:: C: Circlea M: Nat

Consulting fig. 73, the next step is to show that the new representation is adequate. The adequacy of the whole state (*Sjosla*) follows from that of the *C* component and it is clear that any *Circle* can be represented as a *Circle* by setting the *P* pointer to *1*, and storing the given circle as the *L* component. To formalize this, use rules *aa* and *ab* of fig. 49.

The input operation on *Sjosla* should be obvious (the *P* component is set to *1*). The loop test can now test the *L* component for emptiness rather than the whole *Circle*. The correctness of both of these refinements should be obvious. The real interest lies in the refinement of:

NEXT-LETTERA
states: Sjosla
output: Sym-list
pre-NEXT-LETTERA(<<l,p>,m>) ≜ l≠<>
post-NEXT-LETTERA(<<l,p>,m>,<<l',p'>,m'>,ol) ≜
       m'=m ∧
       (let j = count-round(l,p+m-1)
       ol=<l(j)> ∧ l'=del(l,j) ∧
       p' = if j≤len l' then j else 1)

The proof that the domain of this operation is large enough (*da*) is immediate because both *NEXT-LETTER* and *NEXT-LETTERA* rely on non-empty lists and this property is preserved by *retr-circle*. For states (rule *ra*) the argument is as follows:
consider:

<l,p>ϵCirclea

then *NEXT-LETTERA* creates *<l',p'>* such that:

j = count-round(l,p+m-1)
l' = del(l,j)
p' = if j≤len l' then j else 1

Thus, from *C1*:

retr-circle(<l',p'>) = rotate(del(l,j),if j=len l then 0 else j-1)

Compare this with the circle part of the state after *NEXT-LETTER* is applied to *retr-circle(<l,p>)* (use *C5*, *C1*, and *C6*):

tl*rotate(retr-circle(<l,p>),m-1)*
    *= **tl**rotate(rotate(l,p-1),m-1)*
    *= **tl**rotate(l,p+m-2)*
    = rotate(del(l,j),if j=len l then 0 else j-1)

Noting that *m* is preserved in both concludes the proof.
    The output created by *NEXT-LETTERA* is a list containing:

l(j)

and by *NEXT-LETTER*:

hd*rotate(l,p+m-2) = circle-el(rotate(l,p+m-2),1)*

which are equal by property *C4*.
    It would be possible to realize the deletions shown in the above algorithm by means of linked-list storage. The next two sub-sections offer alternative approaches which avoid dynamic storage management.

Bit-Mask Lists

One way to model the deletion of elements shown in *NEXT-LETTERA* is to have an additional vector which indicates whether elements have been deleted or not. Thus:

Circleaa:: S: Sym-list B: Bool-list P: Nat

with the data-type invariant:

is-v-circleaa(<s,b,p>) ≜ **len***b*=**len***s* ∧ *(1≤p≤***len***s* ∨ *s=<>)*

The relationship to the earlier lists, where elements are really deleted, is expressed by:

retr-circlea(<s,b,p>) ≜ *<mask-l(s,b),p>*

(See appendix C for the auxiliary functions.) The adequacy of *Circleaa*, for representing elements of *Circlea*, is immediate from the observation that the *B* component can be set to:

*repeat(***TRUE**,**len***l)*

The same technique applies to the model of the input operation.

The test operation, which previously tested the length of a list, must now use another of the operations defined in the extended list notation, thus:

testaa(<<s,b,p>,>) ≜ *tally(b)≠0*

This development is continued in the exercises.

Exercise 20.2: Develop operators for *bit-mask lists* (in particular an operator for counting round). Define and argue the correctness of *NEXT-LETTERAA* which uses:

Sjoslaa:: C: Circleaa M: Nat

Exercise 20.3: The actual coding of bit-mask lists is very language dependent. Choose some programming language and code the algorithm developed so far. If possible, hide the details of the language features by using macros. The task may be simplified by assuming that the input symbol list is an ascending sequence of natural numbers, thus:

interval(1,n)

Exercise 20.4: Develop (from the specification in exercise 20.1) an inverse operation using bit-mask lists.

Count Trees

Counting round bit-mask lists is tedious. If they are very large, the bit counting will be very slow. What is required is a way of stepping across many elements at a time. Such a possibility is given by *count trees*. An example of a count tree is shown in fig. 84.
In general the structure is:

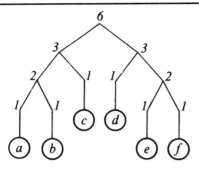

Figure 84   A Count Tree

Count-tree :: Sym-node | Branch-node
Sym-node :: s-n:Nat0 s-sym:Sym
Branch-node :: s-n:Nat0 s-1:Count-tree s-2:Count-tree

with data type invariant:

is-v-count-tree(t) ≜
    if *t∈Sym-node* **then** $s\text{-}n(t)=0 \lor s\text{-}n(t)=1$
    else
        *(**let** $<n,t1,t2> = t$*
        is-v-count-tree(t1) $\land$ *is-v-count-tree(t2)* $\land$
        $s\text{-}n(t1)+s\text{-}n(t2) = n)$

Some useful functions are:

count-tree-el: Count-tree Nat → *Sym*
pre-count-tree-el(t,i) ≜ *is-v-count-tree(t)* $\land$ $1\leq i\leq s\text{-}n(t)$
count-tree-el(t,i) ≜
    if *t∈Sym-node* **then** *s-sym(t)*
    else
        *(**let** $<,t1,t2> = t$*
        if $i\leq s\text{-}n(t1)$ **then** *count-tree-el(t1,i)*
        else *count-tree-el(t2,i - s-n(t1)))*

count-tree-del: Count-tree Nat → *Count-tree*
pre-count-tree-del(t,i) ≜ *is-v-count-tree(t)* $\land$ $1\leq i\leq s\text{-}n(t)$
count-tree-del(t,i) ≜
    if *t∈Sym-node* **then** *mk-sym-node(0,s-sym(t))*
    else
        *(**let** $<n,t1,t2> = t$*
        if $i\leq s\text{-}n(t1)$ **then**
            mk-branch-node(n - 1,count-tree-del(t1,i),t2)
        else
            mk-branch-node(n - 1,t1,count-tree-del(t2,i - s-n(t1)))

count-tree-len(t) ≜ *s-n(t)*

Some obvious properties of count-trees can be given:

CT1.   *count-tree-el is total (over its defined domain)*
CT2.   *count-tree-del is total (over its defined domain)*
CT3.   *count-tree-del preserves validity*
CT4.   *count-tree-len(count-tree-del(t,i)) = count-tree-len(t) - 1*

These properties can be formally proved by structural induction.
     The realization of *JOSL* in this sub-section is, then, to be based on:

Sjoslab::   C: Circleab   M: Nat

Circleab::   T: Count-tree   P: Nat

with:

is-v-circleab(<t,p>) $\triangleq$ *is-v-count-tree(t)* $\wedge$ *(1$\leq$p$\leq$s-n(t)* $\vee$ *s-n(t)=0)*

This is an alternative model of the *NEXT-LETTERA* version, so the relationship is expressed by:

retr-circlea: Circleab $\rightarrow$ *Circlea*
retr-circlea(<t,p>) $\triangleq$ *<count-tree-col(t),p>*

where the collection of elements into a list is defined by:

count-tree-col(t) $\triangleq$
     if *s-n(t)=0* **then** *<>*
     else if *tϵSym-node* **then** *<s-sym(t)>*
     else *count-tree-col(s-1(t))|* | *count-tree-col(s-2(t))*
pre-count-tree-col(t) $\triangleq$ *is-v-count-tree(t)*

From this it is possible to prove (by structural induction):

CT5.   *count-tree-col is total over its defined domain*

CT6.   *for is-v-count-tree(t):*
       count-tree-len(t) = **len***count-tree-col(t)*

CT7.   *for 1$\leq$i$\leq$count-tree-len(t):*
       count-tree-col(t)(i) = count-tree-el(t,i)

CT8.   *for 1$\leq$i$\leq$count-tree-len(t):*
       count-tree-col(count-tree-del(t,i)) = *del(count-tree-col(t),i)*

     In order to show that *Circleab* is adequate to represent all elements of *Circlea*, the two rules are considered. For rule *aa* the totality of *retr-circlea* is given by *CT5* and, given *is-v-circleab*, the validity of the result by *CT6*. As usual, a constructive argument is the best way of showing that *ab* holds. The easiest such construction creates unbalanced trees where every *s-1* branch contains a *Sym-node*.
     The input operation can create any valid count tree for which *count-tree-col* yields the given list of symbols. The actual choice of trees is then a performance issue.

The loop test is:

testab(<<ct,p>,>) ≜ count-tree-len(ct)≠0

The model of *NEXT-LETTERA* is:

NEXT-LETTERAB
states: Sjoslab
output: Sym-list
pre-NEXT-LETTERAB(<<t,p>,>) ≜ count-tree-len(t)≠0
post-NEXT-LETTERAB(<<t,p>,m>,<<t',p'>,m'>,ol) ≜
   m'=m ∧
   (**let** *j = index-mod(s-n(t),p+m-1)*
   ol = <count-tree-el(t,j)> ∧
   t' = count-tree-del(t,j) ∧
   p' = **if** *j≤s-n(t')* **then** *j* **else** *1*)

Given the properties which have been established, the argument that *NEXT-LETTERAB* is a model of *NEXT-LETTERA* is simple: the domain part (rule *da*) is immediate; for the states use *CT8*; and for the output use *CT7*.

Exercise 20.5: This step of development could also be shown to be correct with respect to the **bit-mask list** realization. Write the retrieve function and sketch the correctness argument.

Exercise 20.6: Count trees could be reorganized in order to increase the efficiency of scanning. What are the correctness criteria for such a reorganizing routine?

Exercise 20.7: Develop an inverse operation using count trees from the specification in exercise 20.1.

Pseudo-Rotation Algorithms

It is pointed out above that rotation should be avoided for efficiency reasons. It is possible to avoid actual rotation, while preserving the semblance thereof, by using linked-list storage. An abstract way of presenting a linked-list containing symbols is by a **ring** which contains a pointer and a mapping for each symbol to the next. Thus:

Ring:: PTR: [Sym] MAP: Sym → Sym

is-v-ring(<p,m>) ≜ **if** *p=NIL* **then** **TRUE** **else** *is-in-loop(m,p)*

where:

is-in-loop(m,p) ≜ p ε reachable(m(p),m)

It is now possible to design an implementation, of the original specification, based on **rings**. Rotating a ring is actually achieved by moving the *PTR*, thus:

ring-rotate(<p,m>,i) $\triangleq$
    if *i=0* **then** *<p,m>* **else** *ring-rotate(<m(p),m>,i-1)*

and removing parts of a *Ring* by simple changes to the mapping component.

Exercise 20.8:   Complete the development of *NEXT-LETTERB* and argue its correctness with relation to the specification.

Exercise 20.9:   Code an implementation of the algorithm of the previous exercise. Assume that the input is:

interval(1,n)

Chapter 21

TELEGRAM ANALYSIS

The *telegram analysis* problem has become a classic case study for program development methods. The problem was originated by P.Henderson as an example of structured programming methods. When presenting his development to a group of students one of them, R.A.Snowdon, discovered an error. Henderson(72) offers a natural language specification and a plausible development of a program. Only after this is the reader made aware of the error found and the remainder of the paper reviews how the error originated.

The style of exposition has prompted a number of subsequent papers (also a chapter of Jackson(75)) in which authors have tried to show that the error would not have occurred using their method. As with the Earley example, this author's attempt to prove the (corrected) program correct became unwieldy. Producing the rigorous development shown here resulted in an emphasis on data structure refinement (and the location of two further errors in the corrected program—see Jones(76b)).

There has been some criticism levelled at Henderson's specification but it is, in fact, as good as most starting points for data processing problems. In the development shown here, the lack of clarity is resolved by presenting an abstract specification. The way in which this abstraction is developed towards the actual representation presents an interesting facet of the rigorous method.

Henderson's Specification

The specification given in Henderson(72) is:

A program is required to process a stream of telegrams. This stream is available as a sequence of letters, digits and blanks on some device and can be transferred in sections of predetermined size into a buffer area where it is to be processed. The words in the telegrams are separated by sequences of blanks and each telegram is delimited by the word ZZZZ. The stream is terminated by the occurrence of the empty

325

telegram, that is a telegram with no words. Each telegram is to be processed to determine the number of chargeable words and to check for occurrences of overlength words. The words *ZZZZ* and *STOP* are not chargeable and words of more than twelve letters are considered overlength. The result of the processing is to be a neat listing of the telegrams, each accompanied by the word count and a message indicating the occurrence of an overlength word.

Exercise 21.1:   Read the specification carefully and generate a list of points which could be considered unclear. Discuss whether all such questions could be resolved by a specification in natural language.

Abstract Specification

There are two sorts of problem with the specification. Firstly, there are questions of what processing is required (e.g. are overlength words to be charged in the same way as normal words?); secondly, there are the problems caused by the representation of the information content. The approach here is to separate these problems. This section presents an abstract specification which shows the processing required on the information itself. The questions about the representation (delimiters etc.) are dealt with in subsequent sections.

At an abstract level, the input file can be viewed as a list of telegrams. These are the real (i.e. information holding) telegrams and the *empty telegram* is only considered later as a delimiter for the representation. Similarly the delimiting word is not present in the telegrams. Thus the specification is:

TAN
input: Telegram-list
output: Report-list
$post\text{-}TAN(,tgml,,repl) \triangleq repl = applyl(tgml,analyze\text{-}telegram)$

Telegram = Word-list1
Word = Character-list1
Character = Letter | Digit

with a property for each individual *tgm*:

$\sim(zw\epsilon\textbf{elems}tgm)$

where:

$zw = <Z,Z,Z,Z>$
$stopw = <S,T,O,P>$

and:

Report:: tel: Telegram charge-count: Nat0 ovlen-flag: Bool

Given such an abstract view of the files being handled, it is straightforward to formalize the function which maps single telegrams into single reports:

analyze-telegram(tgm) ≜
   mk-report(tgm,charge-words(tgm),check-words(tgm))

charge-words(wdl) = **card**$\{j \mid 1 \leq j \leq$**lenwdl** $\wedge$ *wdl(j)≠stopw*$\}$

check-words(wdl) = *(***E***j∈*$\{1:$**lenwdl**$\}$*)(***len***(wdl(j))>12)*

In writing this formal specification, a number of interpretations of the original specification have been made. For example:

- overlength words are charged as normal words
- the overlength words are not modified (e.g. truncated) for output
- the given definition of overlength states that only letters should be considered, this is assumed to be an oversight and digits are also included in the count of *check-words*
- a simple flag (rather than a count) is used to indicate the occurrence of one or more overlength words
- the delimiting word (i.e. *zw*) is not transferred to the output
- similarly the delimiting empty telegram gives rise to no report

It is certainly possible to argue with some of these decisions. This is precisely the problem with natural language specifications: they are open to various interpretations. A wrong interpretation is not an error, just a symptom of the weakness of the starting point. The strength of the approach adopted here is that the attempt to formalize the specification is uncovering the problems before program development begins. The questions derived above can be resolved with the user much earlier than would otherwise be possible.

If it was necessary to resolve all questions about the specification before proceeding, the representation could now be brought in (see Second Development Step below) and the relationship between the representation and the abstraction documented by a retrieve function. This is, in fact, the way the problem was tackled in Jones(76b). This process exposes the questions about the specification which concern the representation. The development of the actual data structure is shown here (along with the interpretations) in the next two sections.

First Development Step

In a formal development, this stage might only introduce a *DO* construct with an appropriate *BODY* and prove that this fulfils the abstract specification. It is, however, possible to do more than this in one stage of development and still retain rigor. Here, a refinement of the input data structure is also presented. In combining this refinement with the decomposition to an iterative statement, the option is preserved of showing a more formal development if the step is considered to be unclear.

This first refinement removes one aspect of the abstraction: here the input is treated as a list of *Words* with the delimiter word *zw* marking the end of each telegram. The new facet of this refinement step is that it is forced to consider a predefined representation rather than, as before, being the designer's choice. The necessity to work to given representations is fairly common (cf. section On Interfaces in chapter 17.)

The state of the algorithm would be:

Stan.:: WORD_COUNT: Nat0
          CHARGE_COUNT: Nat0
          OVLEN_FLAG: Bool
          WORD: Character-list1

The processing of a file of words (both real and occurrences of *zw*) is defined by:

DO UNTIL (WORD_COUNT = 1);
 /*INIT*/
 DO UNTIL (WORD = ZW);
  /*READ*/
  /*HANDLE - INCLUDING OUTPUT WORD*/
 END;
 IF WORD_COUNT ¬= 1 THEN
 /*OUTPUT CHARGE_COUNT OVLEN_FLAG*/
END;

(The PL/I *DO UNTIL* evaluates the test at the foot of the loop.)

Each of the named operations could be formally specified. In fact, PL/I is high-level enough to make this unnecessary. The above state and schema are therefore expanded directly into PL/I statements in fig. 85. The only point which may need clarification is the use of *GETWORD*: this is explained in the next section.

An interesting point arises with this step of development. It can be illustrated by noting that, to formalize the refinement step, the following retrieve function would be used:

retr-telegrams: Word-list → Telegram-list

retr-telegrams(wdl) ≜
     let $j = locate(wdl,zw)$
     if $j=1$ **then** <>
     else <mk-Telegram(front(wdl,j-1))> | | retr-telegrams(rest(wdl,j+1))

It is clear that for this function to be defined, there must be an *empty telegram*; the program requires a similar pre-condition. The abstract

```
TAN:
PROC;
   DCL ZW CHARACTER INIT('ZZZZ');
   DCL STOPW CHARACTER INIT('STOP');
   DCL WORD_COUNT FIXED BIN(15);
   DCL CHARGE_COUNT FIXED BIN(15);
   DCL OVLEN_FLAG BOOL;
   DCL WORD CHARACTER(...) VARYING EXTERNAL;
   DCL GETWORD ENTRY EXTERNAL;

   DO UNTIL (WORD_COUNT = 1);
                             /* INIT */
      CHARGE_COUNT  = 0;
      OVLEN_FLAG  = FALSE;
      WORD_COUNT  = 0;

      DO UNTIL (WORD = ZW);

         CALL GETWORD;              /* READ */
                             /* HANDLE */
         IF (WORD¬=STOPW) & (WORD¬=ZW) THEN
            CHARGE_COUNT  = CHARGE_COUNT+1;
         IF LENGTH(WORD)>12 THEN OVLEN_FLAG  = TRUE;
         IF WORD¬=ZW THEN /* WRITE(WORD) */;
         WORD_COUNT  = WORD_COUNT + 1;

      END;

   IF WORD_COUNT ¬= 1 THEN
      /* WRITE(CHARGE_COUNT,OVLEN_FLAG) */;

   END;
END;
```

Figure 85   Telegram Analysis: Main Program

program has no need of this requirement; it has been acquired in moving closer to the representation. This acquired pre-condition appears to be dangerous. The lack of data checking is tolerated here to permit comparison with other solutions to the problem. But, although the given specification does not require any checking, this topic is reviewed below.

Second Development Step

The purpose of the statement *CALL GETWORD* in the procedure *TAN* is that each time it is called the (external) variable *WORD* is set to contain the next word from the input. By writing a procedure call, rather than the specification of an operation, the approach of this section has already been disclosed.

The actual program which is to be created should accept input as defined by:

input: Block-list1
Block = Symbol-list1
Symbol = Character | Blank

Had the process of obtaining words been defined as an operation, it could have been expanded into one which built words by obtaining one symbol at a time. (Although PL/I *list directed input* would make this possible, it should be clear that handling the *Blocks* is an essential part of the problem. In a sense, the problem is to build the buffer handling software.) Given that the task of building up words is non-trivial, it is here split off as a procedure. It has been made a separate external procedure because it might be of use to other parts of a telegram handling system. This also indicates how procedures can be used as a part of the abstraction process; *TAN* can be understood as a procedure working on a (fictitious) *Word* file.

But there is a problem with constructing the *GETWORD* procedure. It must deliver the next word each time it is called; however, some special processing will be required the first time the procedure is called (e.g. opening the input file). The problem here is, in fact, a simple case of a general need for two routines to cooperate. Procedure calls are a rather limited way of linking two collections of code. The case in hand needs *GETWORD* to execute from a different point on calls after the first. One language feature aimed at permitting this is the *co-routine* of SIMULA (see Dahl(72b)). The problem with *GETWORD* can be handled by a *STATIC* first-entry switch, but it is easier to understand this if it can be seen as an implementation of some more abstract synchronizing device.

The main point of *GETWORD* is to set up the variable *WORD*. In addition the procedure makes certain assumptions about its own internal variables (these must be true for all calls other than the first). Thus the post-condition acquires the extra constraint that the value of *BUFFER_COUNT* is less than or equal to the length of the buffer.

A PL/I procedure to achieve the required function is given in fig. 86.

Here again a number of interpretations of the specification have been made. One of these can be seen by noting how this refinement step would be formalized. The relationship of the input to the earlier abstraction could be expressed by a function:

```
GETWORD:
  PROC;
    DCL WORD CHARACTER(...) VARYING EXTERNAL;
    DCL BUFFER CHARACTER(...) VARYING STATIC;
    DCL BUFFER_COUNT FIXED BIN(15) STATIC;
    DCL FIRST_ENTRY STATIC INIT(TRUE);

    IF FIRST_ENTRY THEN
      DO;
      FIRST_ENTRY = FALSE;
      /* OPEN etc. */
      /* read to BUFFER */
      BUFFER_COUNT = 1;
      END;

    DO WHILE (SUBSTR(BUFFER,BUFFER_COUNT,1) = ' ');
      IF BUFFER_COUNT < LENGTH(BUFFER)
        THEN BUFFER_COUNT = BUFFER_COUNT + 1;
        ELSE DO;
           /* read to BUFFER, on eof error */
           BUFFER_COUNT = 1;
           END;
    END;

    WORD = '';
  W : DO WHILE (SUBSTR(BUFFER,BUFFER_COUNT,1) ¬= ' ');
      WORD = WORD || SUBSTR(BUFFER,BUFFER_COUNT,1);
      IF BUFFER_COUNT<LENGTH(BUFFER)
        THEN BUFFER_COUNT = BUFFER_COUNT + 1;
        ELSE DO;
           /* read to BUFFER, on eof LEAVE W */
           BUFFER_COUNT = 1;
           END;
    END;
END;
```

Figure 86   Telegram Analysis: Subroutine

retr-wordl: Block-list1 → Word-list

which concatenated all of the blocks into one list of *Symbols* before splitting it into words. Thus it has been decided that the specification does not require that words are terminated by the end of a buffer. Furthermore, it has been assumed that any *Block* has at least one character. But, as before, these assumptions are being made explicit by the use of rigorous development style. Notice that encountering an end-of-file after the last word—no trailing blanks—is handled by a comment. In full PL/I an appropriate *ON unit* would be used.

Summary

The steps in the development of this example have not been formal, but a rigorous structure has been preserved and the missing details (e.g. the retrieve functions) could be filled in to make a formal proof. The increased confidence in the development has been achieved here more by the choice of stages than by the writing out of details of the formal proof. What has guided the choice of stages is the formal material presented earlier in the book.

The difficulties of natural language specification have been illustrated. Furthermore, it has been shown how an existing interface can be accommodated during a development.

Summary Exercises

There are a number of ways in which this program can be improved—two possibilities are shown as exercises.

Exercise 21.2:   One of the most glaring weaknesses of the specification is the part relating to the output listing. Decide on a *neat* format and develop a suitable program.

Exercise 21.3:   Chapter 22 discusses how to widen a pre-condition to make a program safer to use. Apply the technique to this problem and aim to produce meaningful error messages for invalid input files.

Chapter 22

ON DESIGN

The question of what is good or bad design has not been addressed earlier in this book. It is not, for example, claimed that any of the algorithms shown here are the best known. Rather, this book shows how a designer can develop the solution of his choice in a rigorous way.

Of course, the subject of design is of crucial importance and in this chapter a number of design proposals are explored, all of which are related to the formal techniques described so far; references to other publications are given.

Programs and Their Data

Designing Programs from Data Structure

The use of the structure of data as a guide to the structure of a program for processing that data is mentioned in chapter 1. For data manipulation problems, Jackson(75) has shown this to be a useful guide.

There is a close link between the (data) structure diagrams of Jackson and the abstract syntax descriptions used here. The structure diagrams can be thought of as drawing the abstraction on top of the representation. The interpretation of most of Jackson's design rules with abstract syntax descriptions is not difficult. There are, however, a few points which should be borne in mind. Only in the *telegram analysis* problem (chapter 21), has a given representation been used. Elsewhere, the starting point has been the abstraction, and the choice of representation has been part of the design process.

Some of the abstractions (e.g. sets) used in this book could provide extensions of Jackson's proposals: Thus it can be seen that a program processing:

File = Record-list

is likely to be batch oriented while:

File = Key → Record

gives the possibility of an on-line system.

There is a difficulty with the derivation of program structure, from that of data—the choice of the starting point for *data analysis* is not always uniquely determined. The difficulty can be shown on the *rational number* problem of chapter 14. The specification given is based on:

Rats = Zigzag-list
Zigzag:: Rat-list Rat-list

and this results (see chapter 19) in a program with two consecutive loops nested within a third. But either:

Rats = Diag-list
Diag = Rat-list

or even:

Rats = Rat-list

could be used as a basis for the specification and would give rise to different program structures.

A particularly interesting topic in Jackson(75) is the identification and resolution of *structure clashes*. The *telegram analysis problem* shows that at least the *boundary clash* problem is handled well by abstraction.

Another facet of the data analysis work which appears to be handled well by abstraction is the topic of erroneous data. If perfection is considered to be an abstraction, then the refinement to a representation which includes the reality of bad data can be handled in the normal way.

For a description of data analysis work, Jackson(75) is highly recommended reading; see also Warnier(74).

Making Programs Table-Driven

Obviously, programs should never be written which contain data like salaries or rates of taxes. The fact still remains that much of the huge burden of program maintenance could be done by non-programmers if more thought were given to the program design.

Consider, for example, the problem of stating the discount rates for customers. The most wasteful solution is to store these as constants in each customer record: any discount policy change requires amendment of many records. There is another solution which, however, puts changes in the hands of programmers. If the discount rate is determined by combinations of various properties of customers (e.g. turnover) the rates for all customers can be changed by changing the program. But, having identified the properties these could be built into a table which specified the combinations and their respective discount rates; such a table could be stored in a database and updated by clerical staff (using a utility program). For an insight into the effect that such an approach can have on a large data processing organization see Lucas(79).

A related approach is the use of finite state machine descriptions in the development of programs. If an algorithm can be described by such a diagram, then a very clear (and thus reliable) program can be generated from the table. An interesting example of a program created in this way is a version (see North(77)) of the *ELIZA* program (described in Weizenbaum(67)); the number of executable PL/I statements required to interpret the table is only eighty.

Variables and Flow

A trade-off can be made between complexity of program sequence constructs (flow) and data (variables).

Consider the following two programs:

```
IF P THEN
    DO;
    /*A*/;
    /*D*/;
    /*E*/;
    END;
ELSE
    DO;
    /*B*/;
    /*D*/;
    /*F*/;
    END;

IF P THEN
    DO;
    SW = TRUE;
    /*A*/;
    END;
ELSE
    DO;
    SW = FALSE;
    /*B*/;
    END;
/*D*/
IF SW THEN  /*E*/,
ELSE /*F*/;
```

If the comments indicate blocks of code, that on the right might occupy less store. Even if the *D* block changes the value of *P*, they are equivalent providing *SW* is a new variable. This can be expressed, and proved, formally using a post-condition either by localizing *SW* within a block or by simply not constraining the transformation on *SW*.

Another, similar, example is the pair of programs:

```
IF X<0 THEN
    DO;
    Z  = MULT(-X,Y);
    Z  = -Z;
    END;
ELSE
    Z  = MULT(X,Y);

IF X<0 THEN
    DO;
    M  = -1;
    X  = -X;
    END;
    ELSE M  = +1;
Z  = MULT(X,Y);
Z  = Z*M;
```

Yet another example arises with exit from the middle of a *DO*
iteration. Rather than use a *GOTO*, many structured coding addicts will
set and test a switch which causes the loop to terminate.

What conclusion can be drawn from using formal methods on such
examples? In general, it is more difficult to reason about data than
about flow. This runs counter to some of the conventional structured
coding dogma. The problem with variables is that, in most programming
languages, the places where they are safe from change are not clearly
marked. It is therefore necessary to check that much of the generality
introduced by using variables will never be used. In contrast, the flow of
control tends to show only what can happen. This is not, of course, an
argument for undisciplined use of *GOTO*—proofs then become
unmanageable—but a simple *DO* exit is easier to reason about than the
corresponding switch. Clearly, rather than encoding flow of control into
variables, the best solution is a restructuring of the algorithm.

Another topic which should be mentioned in this section is
optimization. Compare the first part of the algorithm shown in Cleaning
up Forests of chapter 13 with the structure of the original given in
Dijkstra(76):

```
T1  = E1;
DO WHILE (T1¬=A(T1));
  A(T1)  = R1;
  T1  = A(T1);
END;

T1  = E1;
T2  = A(E1);
DO WHILE (T1 ¬= T2);
  A(T1)  = R1;
  T1,T2 = T2,A(T2)
END;
```

These portions of code can be shown to satisfy the same post-condition. But the purpose of the longer code is to reduce duplicate evaluation of the array reference. This is a task which should be within the scope of an optimizing compiler (some would fail because of the structure).

The general design advice is to question the use of extra variables. In fact, there are three uses made of variables:

1. Variables are introduced as abbreviations.
2. Variables eliminate common sub-expressions—as above.
3. A recursive solution is avoided by developing successive values in a variable (true assignment).

It is not the intention to argue against all (superfluous) variables. There are some problems where slight changes to the data significantly simplify a program. Most programmers are, for example, aware of the efficacy of placing some extra *high* values beyond the end of a vector to be sorted (e.g. see examples R5.1 and R5.2 in Naur(74) or chapter 4 of Hall(75)). Alternative ways of storing tree structures can also have a dramatic influence on performance. For example, having parent pointers as well as child pointers in nodes may be the only way of supporting the location of information from parent nodes. Such decisions must be weighed carefully. For further discussion see Hall(75).

Anticipating Change

The necessity to change specifications is a common feature of program development projects. The design method presented has been based on formal specifications and its applicability in a changing environment must be shown.

It should be remembered that the very process of abstraction provides an insulation against certain changes of detail. Furthermore, the ability to perform many stages of design without fixing, for example, details of interface representations, will reduce the incidence of change.

However, there will still be changes which are imposed from outside a project. When first presented with a specification, it is normally possible to form some judgment of the relative firmness of its parts. An attempt should then be made to document the formal specification and design work in a way which isolates the less firm parts. If, for example, an interactive compiler is to be built for a new programming language, it would pay to concentrate on the interactive part, thus anticipating that the details of the language will continue to evolve.

The splitting of the specification can be quite formal in that post-conditions might be expressed as conjunctions of predicates some of which are incomplete. In this way, it may also be possible to design a more general program where alternative modes of use are permitted even in the final program.

One area where such flexibility is very important is in the design of databases. When making steps of refinement from an abstract data description, it should be remembered that a database will be accessed by more than one program. The representation should therefore be chosen more for flexibility than for performance in one particular case (see Hitchcock(7.7) for further discussion).

The proposal, then, is to leave open what is not essential. Even having done this there will, in some projects, be changes to the specification in areas which have influenced the design. This is true for any design method. The rigorous method, however, makes it possible to form a detailed estimate of the impact of a change (see discussion in chapter 18 on modifications).

The work of a student who attended a course on the rigorous method might be used to conclude this section. In the workshop period which followed the lectures, the students were invited to specify and design a problem of interest to themselves. The student in question chose his example because, as he gleefully explained to the class, *it could not be specified in advance*. The challenge being presented was genuine: how is a data gathering problem to be specified where the final choice of analysis to be made will be determined by the early results?

The input was to be an automatic log tape from a computer, so the student readily accepted the usefulness of documenting its structure at both abstract and concrete levels. This was so successful that he considered that maximum advantage had been derived from the rigorous method. He was, however, eventually convinced that his internal table structure could usefully be documented (at an abstract level) and, furthermore, that the input routine could be specified at this abstract level. Now firmly convinced that he had derived much advantage, he was finally prepared to document one analysis as an example of how the tables could be used to create the output.

Given that some problems cannot be specified completely before starting development, there is no reason to abandon rigorous methods.

Input Independence

Many of the programs developed in this book, have pre-conditions which are very restrictive. It is now necessary to consider the task of widening pre-conditions in order to make programs less dependent on their input. It must be remembered that, outside its pre-condition, a program is not constrained at all.

There are two ways in which pre-conditions can be widened. One way is to generalize. Thus the multiplication operation which does not rely on positive arguments is a generalization of that which does. The post-conditions of the two versions are the same. Generalization is probably not the best way to handle the square root operation. Here, a second technique is used—the pre-condition is widened and a check will be made on the input. The results of such a check must be reflected in the post-condition which might, for example, define the creation of an (output) diagnostic if the test fails.

This section is concerned with the widening of pre-conditions for checking input assumptions. Excessive internal checking of assumptions must be avoided. However, where input values are coming from outside the system, stringent checks must be applied. In particular programmers should make the minimum of assumptions about data coming from a user. Here, it must be remembered that the type clause is also a hidden assumption which a user may be able to violate (e.g alphabetic characters in a numeric field).

Some input checking can be performed in an *IF* statement which tests, for example, that a number is positive: the algorithm for handling correct data can then become the *THEN* clause while production of a diagnostic becomes the task of the *ELSE* clause.

Fig. 14 is one of many examples in this book where the test condition is such that the program loops for invalid data. The pre-condition can be widened by changing the test. The cost then becomes clear: the post-condition must be extended to cover the answer created for input outside the range of the original pre-condition. (Cf. Dijkstra(76).)

There are, however, cases where the input checking is nearly as complex as the algorithm to be performed. Take, for example, a search routine. A somewhat simpler solution can be constructed with a pre-condition which states that the sought element is in a table. If this pre-condition is to be relaxed, there is little point in constructing a conditional statement which first searches the table to permit the production of a diagnostic. Clearly, the search algorithm itself should be extended to reflect the possibility of missing elements.

Here, a word on the design approach should be interjected. The section on &@hnum3.Designing Programs from Data Structure has already proposed viewing perfection (i.e. freedom from errors) as an abstraction of reality. Thus an overall algorithm might be designed which handles only valid data. The normal refinement process (retrieve functions etc.) will be used, but the question is what structure will the modelling algorithm have? The ideal is to preserve the overall structure as far as possible.

In Bron(76) and Fokkinga(77), it has been shown how the structure of the basic algorithm can best be preserved by handling exceptions with a language construct which has the ability to cause abnormal exit. Using such a language construct, it is possible both to represent the main algorithm clearly and imbed the checking in a way which is efficient. The full version of the meta-language used here includes such an exit construct (see Bjorner(78)). Thus the design proposal is to design first the main processing, then incorporate error checking using an exit construct and finally to achieve the same flow of control in the chosen programming language. This approach is facilitated by the proof rules for exit given in Fokkinga(77).

Environment Independence

Given the poor quality of some software, it is a matter of debate whether a program has more need of insulation from its input data or from the supporting software with which it must run. The wisest course would appear to be to check both. The technique of *recovery blocks* (see Randell(75)) permits the recording and checking of assumptions about operations to be used.

The basic idea is to associate a test condition with any piece of software which is to be checked. Such a test is like a post-condition in that it is a predicate of the starting and final states. It differs, however, in two important ways. Firstly, it is intended to be tested dynamically (i.e. at run time) and secondly it might be an incomplete test. Thus, for a sort routine the test-condition might check that the result vector is in an appropriate order and that some simple check-sum of the input and output values matches. This, then, is a fairly cheap test which can be evaluated after the sort. What is to be done if the test indicates failure? In the ideal situation an alternative (perhaps slower) sort routine might be available. Switching to the *alternate* must of course, be preceded by restoring the initial values. (The Newcastle group have proposals for hardware assistance.) There may, however, be no (further) alternative and in this case failure is signalled to the calling level. Which units should be recovery blocks (i.e. have test-conditions)? The whole scheme extends in a natural way to a hierarchy of nested recovery blocks.

Clearly, for any piece of code which has been formally defined, a possible test-condition is already available. Is it worth using recovery blocks with rigorous development? The answer depends on the environment but it should be recalled that rigorous development has aimed at *increased confidence*. Even with the relative certainty of machine-checked proofs, the test-conditions could trap hardware or compiler errors. Clearly, for some critical systems, the ideas of recovery blocks should be employed in conjunction with rigorous methods, and the reader is strongly recommended to read Randell(75) or Randell(78).

Summary

The design proposals covered in this chapter have a common aim: they make programs easier to understand, modify, and use. Underlying them all is a formalism like the one developed in the body of this book.

On the subject of design, Kernighan(74) and Kernighan(76) are recommended.

Appendix A

*LANGUAGE DEFINITION

The basis of the formal proofs in this book are the properties of the language constructs (collected in appendix B). These have not, as in Hoare(72c), been taken as an *axiomatic definition* of the programming language, but, rather, alternative rules have been provided for different circumstances. The meaning of the programming language itself must then be fixed in some other way. Here, a functional definition is used (for a review of alternative definition methods, see Lucas(78)); from the given definition, examples of how properties can be proved correct are shown in appendix D.

The abstract syntax, of the language constructs, is explained in chapter 14. Collecting it together gives:

Program:: s-dcls: Declaration-set s-body: Stmt-list
Stmt = Compound-stmt | If-stmt | Do-while-Stmt |
*   For-Stmt | Assign-stmt*
Compound-stmt:: Stmt-list
If-stmt:: s-condition: Expr s-then: Stmt s-else: Stmt
Do-while-stmt:: s-condition: Expr s-body: Stmt-list
For-stmt:: s-control-var: Id s-init: Expr s-limit: Expr s-body: Stmt-list
Assign-stmt:: s-lhs: Id s-rhs: Expr
Declaration, Expr, Id are not further specified

This abstract syntax would be satisfied by many programs to which it would not be possible to give a meaning (e.g. ones which use variables which are not declared). Following chapter 10, the class of *Programs* can be restricted by a data type invariant. This is not written out formally here; items which would have to be covered include the appropriate declaration of variables and a restriction that *s-condition* expressions always evaluate to a Boolean value.

Since the main interest here is in the flow of control constructs, little need be said about the states which record the values of variables. It is sufficient for this fragment of definition to know that:

State = Id ⟶ Value

The general approach to defining the meaning of statements is to define functions like:

i-stmt: Stmt State → State

Here *i* is an abbreviation for *interpret* and indicates that the function interprets the given statement in the given state by fixing the resulting state. Thus:

i-compound-stmt(<body>,σ) ≜ *i-stmt-list(body,σ)*

i-stmt-list(stl,σ) ≜
    if *stl=<>* **then** *σ*
    else
        *(***let** *σ' = i-stmt(**hd**stl,σ)*
        *i-stmt-list(**tl**stl,σ'))*

Using *e-expr* (*e* for *evaluate*) which is discussed below:

i-if-stmt(<c,th,el>,σ)
    let *b = e-expr(c,σ)*
    if *b* **then** *i-stmt(th,σ)*
    else *i-stmt(el,σ)*

i-do-while-stmt(<c,body>,σ) ≜
    let *b = e-expr(c,σ)*
    if *b* **then**
        *(***let** *σ' = i-stmt-list(body,σ)*
        i-do-while-stmt(<c,body>,σ'))
    else *σ*

i-for-stmt(<cv,init,limit,body>,σ) ≜
    let *initv = e-expr(init,σ)*
    let *limitv = e-expr(limit,σ)*
    let *σ' = iterate-for(cv,limitv,body, σ†[cv→initv])*
    σ'| **dom**σ

iterate-for(cv,limitv,stl,σ) ≜
    if *σ(cv)≤limitv* **then**
        *(***let** *σ' = i-stmt-list(stl,σ)*
        iterate-for(cv,limitv,stl,σ'†[cv→σ(cv)+1]))
    else *σ*

i-assign-stmt(<l,r>,σ) ≜ *σ†[l→e-expr(r,σ)]*

The function which evaluates expressions is of type:

e-expr: Expr State → Value

Furthermore, it must ensure that Boolean expressions return values in *Bool*.

Because the input/output parts of the language are not shown, the interpretation of programs is:

i-program: Program →
i-program(<dcls,body>) ≜
    let σ = *create-state(dcls)*
    let σ' = *i-stmt-list(body,σ)*

where:

create-state: Declaration-set → State

Notice that all of the functions are defined explicitly—the need for specifying a range of result states, by a post-condition, does not arise in this simple language.

Appendix B

DEDUCTION RULES FOR PROOFS

The rules introduced for decomposition and for refinement are collected here for ease of reference.

Decomposition Steps

SEQ (see fig. 17)
For:

$OP \triangleq OP1; OP2$

to be correct, show:

da. $pre\text{-}OP(\sigma) \Rightarrow pre\text{-}OP1(\sigma)$
db. $pre\text{-}OP(\sigma_1) \wedge post\text{-}OP1(\sigma_1,\sigma_2) \Rightarrow pre\text{-}OP2(\sigma_2)$
ra. $pre\text{-}OP(\sigma_1) \wedge post\text{-}OP1(\sigma_1,\sigma_2) \wedge post\text{-}OP2(\sigma_2,\sigma_3) \Rightarrow post\text{-}OP(\sigma_1,\sigma_3)$

★ ★ ★

IF (see fig. 19)
For:

$OP \triangleq IF\ e\ THEN\ OP1\ ELSE\ OP2$

to be correct, show:

da. $pre\text{-}OP(\sigma) \wedge e\text{-}expr(e,\sigma) \Rightarrow pre\text{-}OP1(\sigma)$
db. $pre\text{-}OP(\sigma) \wedge \sim e\text{-}expr(e,\sigma) \Rightarrow pre\text{-}OP2(\sigma)$
ra. $pre\text{-}OP(\sigma_1) \wedge e\text{-}expr(e,\sigma_1) \wedge post\text{-}OP1(\sigma_1,\sigma_2) \Rightarrow post\text{-}OP(\sigma_1,\sigma_2)$
rb. $pre\text{-}OP(\sigma_1) \wedge \sim e\text{-}expr(e,\sigma_1) \wedge post\text{-}OP2(\sigma_1,\sigma_2) \Rightarrow post\text{-}OP(\sigma_1,\sigma_2)$

★ ★ ★

IWHILEUP (cf. fig. 21)
For:

$OP \triangleq INIT; DO WHILE(e); BODY; END;$

to be correct, find:

pre-LOOP: State → Bool
so-far: State State → Bool
term: State → Int

and show:

da. pre-INIT(σ) ↔ **TRUE**
db. pre-OP(σ$_1$) ∧ post-INIT(σ$_1$,σ$_2$) ⇒ pre-LOOP(σ$_2$)
dc. pre-LOOP(σ$_1$) ∧ e-expr(e,σ$_1$) ∧ post-BODY(σ$_1$,σ$_2$) ⇒ pre-LOOP(σ$_2$)
dd. pre-LOOP(σ) ∧ e-expr(e,σ) ⇒ pre-BODY(σ)
ra. pre-OP(σ$_1$) ∧ post-INIT(σ$_1$,σ$_2$) ⇒ so-far(σ$_1$,σ$_2$)
rb. so-far(σ$_1$,σ$_2$) ∧ pre-LOOP(σ$_2$) ∧ e-expr(e,σ$_2$) ∧ post-BODY(σ$_2$,σ$_3$)
    ⇒ so-far(σ$_1$,σ$_3$)
rc. so-far(σ$_1$,σ$_2$) ∧ pre-LOOP(σ$_2$,i) ∧ ~e-expr(e,σ$_2$) ⇒ post-OP(σ$_1$,σ$_2$)
ta. pre-LOOP(σ) ⇒ term(σ)≥0
tb. pre-LOOP(σ) ∧ term(σ)>0 ⇒ e-expr(e,σ)
tc. pre-LOOP(σ) ∧ term(σ)=0 ⇒ ~e-expr(e,σ)
td. pre-BODY(σ$_1$) ∧ post-BODY(σ$_1$,σ$_2$) ⇒ term(σ$_2$)<term(σ$_1$)

★   ★   ★

IWHILEDN (cf. fig. 23)
For:

$OP \triangleq INIT; DO WHILE(e); BODY; END;$

to be correct, find:

pre-LOOP: State → Bool
to-end: State State → Bool
term: State → Int

and show:

da. pre-INIT(σ) ↔ **TRUE**
db. pre-OP(σ$_1$) ∧ post-INIT(σ$_1$,σ$_2$) ⇒ pre-LOOP(σ$_2$)
dc. pre-LOOP(σ$_1$) ∧ e-expr(e,σ$_1$) ∧ post-BODY(σ$_1$,σ$_2$) ⇒ pre-LOOP(σ$_2$)
dd. pre-LOOP(σ) ∧ e-expr(e,σ) ⇒ pre-BODY(σ)
ra. pre-BODY(σ$_1$) ∧ post-BODY(σ$_1$,σ$_2$) ∧ to-end(σ$_2$,σ$_3$) ⇒ to-end(σ$_1$,σ$_3$)
rb. pre-LOOP(σ) ∧ ~e-expr(e,σ) ⇒ to-end(σ,σ)
rc. pre-OP(σ$_1$) ∧ post-INIT(σ$_1$,σ$_2$) ∧ to-end(σ$_2$,σ$_3$) ⇒ post-OP(σ$_1$,σ$_3$)
ta. pre-LOOP(σ) ⇒ term(σ)≥0
tb. pre-LOOP(σ) ∧ term(σ)>0 ⇒ e-expr(e,σ)
tc. pre-LOOP(σ) ∧ term(σ)=0 ⇒ ~e-expr(e,σ)
td. pre-BODY(σ$_1$) ∧ post-BODY(σ$_1$,σ$_2$) ⇒ term(σ$_2$)<term(σ$_1$)

★   ★   ★

WHILEDN (cf. fig. 25)
For:

$OP \triangleq DO\ WHILE(e);\ BODY;\ END;$

to be correct, find:

$term:\ State \rightarrow Int$

and show:

da. $pre\text{-}OP(\sigma_1) \wedge e\text{-}expr(e,\sigma_1) \wedge post\text{-}BODY(\sigma_1,\sigma_2) \Rightarrow pre\text{-}OP(\sigma_2)$
db. $pre\text{-}OP(\sigma) \wedge e\text{-}expr(e,\sigma) \Rightarrow pre\text{-}BODY(\sigma)$
ra. $pre\text{-}BODY(\sigma_1) \wedge post\text{-}BODY(\sigma_1,\sigma_2) \wedge post\text{-}OP(\sigma_2,\sigma_3) \Rightarrow$
      $post\text{-}OP(\sigma_1,\sigma_3)$
rb. $pre\text{-}OP(\sigma) \wedge \sim e\text{-}expr(e,\sigma) \Rightarrow post\text{-}OP(\sigma,\sigma)$
ta. $pre\text{-}OP(\sigma) \Rightarrow term(\sigma) \geq 0$
tb. $pre\text{-}OP(\sigma) \wedge term(\sigma) > 0 \Rightarrow e\text{-}expr(e,\sigma)$
tc. $pre\text{-}OP(\sigma) \wedge term(\sigma) = 0 \Rightarrow \sim e\text{-}expr(e,\sigma)$
td. $pre\text{-}BODY(\sigma_1) \wedge post\text{-}BODY(\sigma_1,\sigma_2) \Rightarrow term(\sigma_2) < term(\sigma_1)$

★ ★ ★

DO/BY/TO (see fig. 30)
For:

$OP \triangleq DO\ i\ =\ l\ BY\ 1\ TO\ u;\ BODY(i);\ END;$

BODY
state: State
type: Int $\rightarrow$

to be correct, find:

pre-LOOP: State Int $\rightarrow$ *Bool*
so-far: State Int State $\rightarrow$ *Bool*

and show:

da. $pre\text{-}OP(\sigma) \Rightarrow pre\text{-}LOOP(\sigma,l)$
db. $pre\text{-}LOOP(\sigma_1,i) \wedge i \leq e\text{-}expr(u,\sigma_1) \wedge post\text{-}BODY(\sigma_1,i,\sigma_2)$
      $\Rightarrow pre\text{-}LOOP(\sigma_2,i+1)$
dc. $pre\text{-}LOOP(\sigma,i) \wedge i \leq e\text{-}expr(u,\sigma) \Rightarrow pre\text{-}BODY(\sigma,i)$

ra. $pre\text{-}OP(\sigma) \Rightarrow so\text{-}far(\sigma,l,\sigma)$
rb. $so\text{-}far(\sigma_1,i,\sigma_2) \wedge pre\text{-}LOOP(\sigma_2,i) \wedge i \leq e\text{-}expr(u,\sigma_1)$
      $\wedge post\text{-}BODY(\sigma_2,i,\sigma_3)$
            $\Rightarrow so\text{-}far(\sigma_1,i+1,\sigma_3)$
rc. $so\text{-}far(\sigma_1,i,\sigma_2) \wedge pre\text{-}LOOP(\sigma_2) \wedge i = e\text{-}expr(u,\sigma_1)+1 \Rightarrow post\text{-}OP(\sigma_1,\sigma_2)$

Data Refinement

Preservation of validity (see chapter 10)

va. $(\mathbf{A}\sigma)(inv(\sigma) \wedge pre\text{-}OP(\sigma,args) \wedge post\text{-}OP(\sigma,args,\sigma',res) \Rightarrow inv(\sigma'))$

$$\star \quad \star \quad \star$$

Data type adequacy (see chapter 11)

aa. $(\mathbf{A}\sigma1)(inv1(\sigma1) \Rightarrow (\mathbf{E}\sigma)(\sigma=retr(\sigma1)) \wedge inv(retr(\sigma1)))$
ab. $(\mathbf{A}\sigma)(inv(\sigma) \Rightarrow (\mathbf{E}\sigma1)(inv1(\sigma1) \wedge \sigma=retr(\sigma1)))$

$$\star \quad \star \quad \star$$

Operation modelling (see chapter 12)

da. $(\mathbf{A}\sigma1)(inv1(\sigma1) \wedge pre\text{-}OP(retr(\sigma1),args) \Rightarrow pre\text{-}OP1(\sigma1,args))$
ra. $(\mathbf{A}\sigma1)(inv1(\sigma1) \wedge pre\text{-}OP1(\sigma1,args) \wedge post\text{-}OP1(\sigma1,args,\sigma1',res) \Rightarrow post\text{-}OP(retr(\sigma1),args,retr(\sigma1'),res))$

Appendix C

PROPERTIES OF OPERATORS

This appendix contains a quick reference to the functions and properties which have been given either as examples or exercises in the body of the book. (See also the Table of Symbols.) The notation used here is a subset of that covered, and defined, in Bjorner(78)

Logic Notation

(See chapter 2.)

Properties of Logical Operators

Tautologies

$a \lor \sim a$
$a \Rightarrow (a \lor b)$
$b \Rightarrow (a \lor b)$
$(a \land b) \Rightarrow a$
$(a \land b) \Rightarrow b$
FALSE $\Rightarrow a$
$a \Rightarrow$ **TRUE**

Equivalent Pairs

$a \land b$, $b \land a$	*Commutative law for and*
$a \land$ **TRUE** , a	
$a \lor b$, $b \lor a$	*Commutative law for or*
$a \lor$ **FALSE** , a	
$(a \land b) \land c$, $a \land (b \land c)$	*Associative laws*
$(a \lor b) \lor c$, $a \lor (b \lor c)$	
$a \land (b \lor c)$, $(a \land b) \lor (a \land c)$	*Distributive laws*
$a \lor (b \land c)$, $(a \lor b) \land (a \lor c)$	

$\sim(a \lor b)$, $\sim a \land \sim b$ *De Morgan's laws*
$\sim(a \land b)$, $\sim a \lor \sim b$

$\sim(\sim a)$, a *double negation*

$a \Rightarrow b$, $\sim a \lor b$ *implication*
$\sim(a \Rightarrow b)$, $a \land \sim b$

$a \Leftrightarrow b$, $(a \Rightarrow b) \land (b \Rightarrow a)$ *equivalence*

$\sim(\mathbf{A}i\epsilon D)(p(i))$, $(\mathbf{E}i\epsilon D)(\sim p(i))$ *Quantifiers*
$\sim(\mathbf{E}i\epsilon D)(p(i))$, $(\mathbf{A}i\epsilon D)(p(i))$
$(\mathbf{E}!i\epsilon D)(p(i))$, $(\mathbf{E}i\epsilon D)(p(i)) \land (p(i) \land p(j) \Rightarrow i=j)$
$(\mathbf{E}!i\epsilon D)(p(i)) \Rightarrow p((\iota i)(p(i)))$

Auxiliary Definitions

is-divisor$(x,y) \triangleq (x \bmod y) = 0$

is-common-divisor$(x,y,d) \triangleq$ *is-divisor*$(x,d) \land$ *is-divisor*(y,d)

is-odd$(x) \triangleq (x \bmod 2) = 1$
is-even$(x) \triangleq (x \bmod 2) = 0$

is-multiple$(x,m) \triangleq (m \bmod x) = 0$
is-common-multiple$(x,y,m) \triangleq$ *is-multiple*(x,m) & *is-multiple*(y,m)

mod: Int Int $\rightarrow$ *Int*
pre-mod$(x,y) \triangleq y \neq 0$
post-mod$(x,y,r) \triangleq (0 \leq r < y \lor y < r \leq 0)$ & $(\mathbf{E}m\epsilon Nat)(m*y+r=x)$

is-prime$(x) \triangleq (\mathbf{A}d\epsilon Nat)($*is-divisor*$(x,d) \Rightarrow d=1 \lor d=x)$

Set Notation

(See chapter 8.)

$\{x \mid p(x)\}$

$x \epsilon X$
$S \cup T \triangleq \{e \mid e\epsilon S \lor e\epsilon T\}$
$S \cap T \triangleq \{e \mid e\epsilon S \land e\epsilon T\}$
$S - T \triangleq \{e \mid e\epsilon S \land \sim(e\epsilon T)\}$
$S \subseteq T \triangleq x\epsilon S \Rightarrow x\epsilon T$
$S \subset T \triangleq S \subseteq T \land (\mathbf{E}e\epsilon S)(\sim(e\epsilon T))$
union$SS \triangleq \{e \mid (\mathbf{E}S\epsilon SS)(e\epsilon S)\}$

Auxiliary Definitions

$is\text{-}disj(S,T) \triangleq S \cap T = \{\}$

$applys(S,f) \triangleq$
 if $S=\{\}$ **then** $\{\}$
 else
   (let $e \epsilon S$
    $\{f(e)\} \cup applys(S-\{e\},f))$

$maxs:\ Int\text{-}set \rightarrow Int$
$maxs(S) \triangleq$
 let $e \epsilon S$
 if card$S=1$ **then** e
 else $max(e,maxs(S-\{e\}))$
$pre\text{-}maxs(S) \triangleq S \ne \{\}$

List Notation

(See chapter 9)

hd$list$
$pre\text{-}hd(list) \triangleq list \ne \diamond$

tl$list$
$pre\text{-}tl(list) \triangleq list \ne \diamond$

len$list \triangleq$ **if** $list=\diamond$ **then** 0 **else** $1 + $ **len**$(tllist)$

$list(i) \triangleq$ **if** $i=1$ **then** **hd**$list$ **else** $(tllist)(i\text{-}1)$
$pre\text{-}index(list,i) \triangleq 1 \le i \le$ **len**$list$

$list1 \mid \mid list2 \triangleq$
 $(\iota list)$
  $($**len**$list = $ **len**$list1 + $ **len**$list2 \wedge$
  $(\mathbf{A}i \epsilon \{1:$**len**$list1\})(list(i)=list1(i)) \wedge$
  $(\mathbf{A}i \epsilon \{1:$**len**$list2\})(list($**len**$list1+i)=list2(i))))$

conc$listl \triangleq$ **if** $listl=\diamond$ **then** $\diamond$ **else** **hd**$listl \mid \mid$ **conctl**$listl$

elems$list \triangleq \{list(i) \mid 1 \le i \le$**len**$list\}$

Auxiliary Definitions

$is\text{-}disjl(setl) \triangleq (\mathbf{A}i,j \epsilon \{1:$**len**$setl\})(i=j \vee is\text{-}disj(setl(i),setl(j)))$

$rev(list) \triangleq$ **if** $list=\diamond$ **then** $\diamond$ **else** $rev(tllist) \mid \mid <$**hd**$list>$

is-permutation(list,list') ≜ *bagol(list')=bagol(list)*

is-uniquel(list) ≜ *(**A**i,jε{1:len*list*})(i=j* ∨ *list(i)≠list(j))*

front(list,k) ≜ **if** *k>0* **then** *<hdlist>| | front(tllist,k-1)* **else** *<>*
pre-front(list,k) ≜ *k≤len*list

subl(list,i,k) ≜
    if *i=1* **then** *front(list,k)* **else** *subl(tllist,i-1,k-1)*
pre-subl(list,i,k) ≜ *1≤i≤len*list*+1* & *0≤k≤len*list

rest(list,i) ≜ *subl(list,i,len*list*)*
pre-rest(list,i) ≜ *1≤i≤len*list*+1*

back(list,j) ≜ *subl(list,len*list*-j+1,len*list*)*
pre-back(list,j) ≜ *0≤j≤len*list

del(list,i) ≜ **if** *i=1* **then** tl*list* **else** *<hdlist>| | del(tllist,i-1)*
pre-del(list,i) ≜ *1≤i≤len*list

modl(list,i,e) ≜
    if *i=1* **then** *<e>| |* tl*list*
    else *<hdlist>| | modl(tllist,i-1,e)*
pre-modl(list,i,) ≜ *1≤i≤len*list

repeat(e,n) ≜ **if** *n=0* **then** *<>* **else** *<e>| | repeat(e,n-1)*

interval(i,j) ≜ **if** *j<i* **then** *<>* **else** *<i>| | interval(i+1,j)*

applyl(list,f)
    if *list=<>* **then** *<>*
    else *<f(hdlist)>| | applyl(tllist,f)*

limitl(list,p) ≜
    if *list=<>* **then** *<>*
    else
        if *p(hdlist)* **then** *<hdlist>| | limitl(tllist,p)*
        else *limitl(tllist,p)*

sel-subl(list,indl) ≜
    if *indl=<>* **then** *<>*
    else *<list(hdindl)>| | sel-subl(list,tlindl)*
pre-sel-subl(list,indl) ≜ **elems***indl* ⊆ *{1:len*list*}*

mask-l: Sym-list Bool-list → Sym-list
mask-l(sl,bl) ≜
    if *sl=<>* **then** *<>*
    else if hd*bl* **then** *<hdsl>| | mask-l(tlsl,tlbl)*
    else *mask-l(tlsl,tlbl)*

tally: Bool-list → Nat0
tally(bl) ≜ **card** $\{i \mid 1 \leq i \leq \textbf{len}bl \wedge bl(i)\}$

Proven Results

for $1 \leq i \leq \textbf{len}list$:
  del(list,i) = *front(list,i-1)* | | *rest(list,i+1)*

rev(rev(list)) = *list*

Mapping Notation

(See chapter 12)

$[x \rightarrow y \mid p(x,y)]$
rng M ≜ $\{M(d) \mid d \epsilon \textbf{dom}M\}$

$M \dagger N$ ≜ $[d \rightarrow r \mid$
    $d \epsilon \textbf{dom}N \wedge r=N(d) \vee$
    $d \epsilon (\textbf{dom}M \text{-} \textbf{dom}N) \wedge r=M(d)]$
$M \mid S$ ≜ $[d \rightarrow M(d) \mid d \epsilon (\textbf{dom}M \cap S)]$

build-set: D (D → D) D-set → D-set
build-set(d,m,ds) ≜
  if $d \epsilon ds$ **then** *ds*
  else *build-set(m(d),m,ds* $\cup$ $\{d\})$

reachable: D (D → D) → D-set
reachable(d,m) ≜ *build-set(d,m,*$\{\})$

exmpty-bag() ≜ $[]$

plus-bag: D (D → Nat0) → (D → Nat0)
plus-bag(v,m) ≜ **if** $v \epsilon \textbf{dom}m$ **then** $m \dagger [v \rightarrow m(v)+1]$ **else** $m \dagger [v \rightarrow 1]$

mpc-bag(v,m) ≜ $m(v)$

bagol(l) ≜ $[v \rightarrow$ **card** $\{i \mid l(i)=v\} \mid v \epsilon \textbf{elems}l]$

trans(m) ≜ $[d \rightarrow reachable(d,m) \mid d \epsilon \textbf{dom}m]$

Operations

(See chapter 4)

OP
states: S
type: D → R
pre-OP: S D → Bool
post-OP: S D S R → Bool

Abstract Syntax

(See chapter 14)

A = B	*equality (as sets)*
A = B │ C	*union of sets*
A = [B]	*optional*
A = B-set	*set*
A = B → C	*mapping*
A = B-list	*list*
A = B-list1	*non-empty list*
A:: B C	*introduces a constructor*
mk-A(b,c)	*constructor*
A:: s-1:B s-2:C	*introduces selectors as well*

Appendix D

*SELECTED DETAILED PROOFS

Two of the sets of properties, which are used to reason about programs, are here proved correct with respect to the language definition of appendix A.

Proof of SEQ

Theorem, given the results in fig. 17:

$pre\text{-}OP(\sigma_1) \Rightarrow$
$$((\mathbf{E}\sigma_2)(\sigma_2=i\text{-}stmt\text{-}list(C,\sigma_1)) \wedge post\text{-}OP(\sigma_1,i\text{-}stmt\text{-}list(C,\sigma_1)))$$

where:

$C = <OP1,OP2>$

Proof:
Assume:

1. $pre\text{-}OP(\sigma_1)$

From this and *da*:

2. $pre\text{-}OP1(\sigma_1)$

Therefore, with the correctness of *OP1*:

3. $(\mathbf{E}\sigma_3)(\sigma_3=i\text{-}stmt(OP1,\sigma_1))$

Let σ_3 be such. With *1*, *2*, *4*, and *db*:

4. $\sigma_3=i\text{-}stmt(OP1,\sigma_1) \wedge post\text{-}OP1(\sigma_1,\sigma_3)$
5. $pre\text{-}OP2(\sigma_3)$

Therefore:

6. $(\mathbf{E}\sigma_4)(\sigma_4=i\text{-}stmt(OP2,\sigma_2))$

Let σ_4 be such. With *5*:

7. $\sigma_4 = i\text{-}stmt(OP2,\sigma_3) \wedge post\text{-}OP2(\sigma_3,\sigma_4)$

But, from the language definition:

8. $i\text{-}stmt\text{-}list(C,\sigma_1) = i\text{-}stmt(OP2,i\text{-}stmt(OP1,\sigma_1))$

thus:

9. $(\mathbf{E}\sigma_2)(\sigma_2 = i\text{-}stmt(C,\sigma_1))$

Thus from ra, 1, 4, 7 and 8:

10. $post\text{-}OP(\sigma_1,i\text{-}stmt\text{-}list(C,\sigma_1))$

Proof of WHILEDN

Theorem, given the results in fig. 25:

$pre\text{-}OP(\sigma_1) \Rightarrow$
$\qquad ((\mathbf{E}\sigma_2)(\sigma_2 = i\text{-}do\text{-}while\text{-}stmt(OP,\sigma_1)) \land$
$\qquad\qquad post\text{-}OP(\sigma_1,i\text{-}do\text{-}while\text{-}stmt(OP,\sigma_1)))$

Proof:
Assume:

1. $pre\text{-}OP(\sigma_1)$

From ta:

2. $term(\sigma_1) \geq 0$

By induction on $term(\sigma_1)$, basis, assume:

3. $term(\sigma_1) = 0$

From 1, 3, and tc:

4. $\sim e\text{-}expr(e,\sigma_1)$

From the language definition:

5. $i\text{-}do\text{-}while\text{-}stmt(OP,\sigma_1) = \sigma_1$
6. $(\mathbf{E}\sigma_2)(\sigma_2 = i\text{-}do\text{-}while\text{-}stmt(OP,\sigma_1))$

Then from 1, 4, and rb:

7. $post\text{-}OP(\sigma_1,\sigma_1)$

Therefore, noting 5, 7:

8. $post\text{-}OP(\sigma_1,i\text{-}do\text{-}while\text{-}stmt(OP,\sigma_1))$

Induction step, assume:

9. $term(\sigma_1) > 0$

From 1, 9, and tb:

10. $e\text{-}expr(e,\sigma_1)$

From the language definition:

11. $i\text{-}do\text{-}while\text{-}stmt(OP,\sigma_1) =$
$\qquad i\text{-}do\text{-}while\text{-}stmt(OP,i\text{-}stmt\text{-}list(BODY,\sigma_1))$

And from 1, 10, and db:

12. pre-BODY(σ_1)

therefore:

13. ($\mathbf{E}\sigma_2$)(σ_2=i-stmt-list(BODY,σ_1))
$\land$ post-BODY(σ_1,i-stmt-list(BODY,σ_1))

Let σ_2 be such, it follows from *12, 13,* and *da*:

14. pre-OP(σ_2)

Then from *12, 13,* and *td*:

15. term(σ_2) < term(σ_1)

Thus, by induction hypothesis:

16. ($\mathbf{E}\sigma_3$)(σ_3=i-do-while-stmt(OP,σ_2)) $\land$
post-OP(σ_2,i-do-while-stmt(OP,σ_2))

Let σ_3 be such. Then, from *11, 13,* and *16*:

17. ($\mathbf{E}\sigma_3$)(σ_3 = i-do-while-stmt(OP,σ_1))

Finally, from *12, 13, 16,* and *ra*:

18. post-OP(σ_1,i-do-while-stmt(OP,σ_1))

GLOSSARY

This glossary defines technical terms used within the book. References to the relevant chapter are given where necessary. The Index can also be used to locate definitions and uses of terms.

Abstract data types: data types which, in general, are not available in programming languages. They are normally specified using the notations (e.g. sets, mappings) introduced in part B.

Abstract syntax: an abstract syntax is a set of rules defining a class of objects; such objects can be visualized as trees—the structure of the generating rules is preserved. (See chapter 14.) In contrast to *concrete syntax*, the details of different, but semantically equivalent, concrete strings are avoided.

Abstraction: the process of abstraction involves ignoring irrelevant details so that the main points are brought into focus. An abstraction is something which results from this process (e.g. road map, circuit diagram).

Abstraction, operational: (term due to E.W.Dijkstra) the use of specifications of operations by predicates which define the required input-output relation (see *implicit definition*).

Abstraction, representational: (term due to E.W.Dijkstra) the use, in specifications, of data types which possess only those properties necessary to specify the result required (see *abstract data types*).

Active decomposition: a principle to be followed in choosing the specifications of sub-operations during decomposition. The aim is to isolate the sub-operations from their context. (See chapter 5.)

Adequacy: property of a representation (of an abstract data type). A representation is said to be adequate if there is at least one value of the representation corresponding to each abstract value. More precisely, every valid value of the abstract type can be created by applying the retrieve function to a valid member of the representation type. (See chapter 11.)

Algebraic definition of a data type: see *implicit definition of a data type*.

Algorithm: an algorithm is a set of rules which defines a way of computing some result (e.g. Euclid's algorithm for finding the greatest common divisor of two numbers). An algorithm can be embodied in a program, but the two should not be confused. (See Documenting Algorithms in chapter 6).

Apply: a function is applied to arguments in order to determine its value. The process is described in chapter 2 in terms of substituting the argument values for the parameter names in the function definition. The application of mappings is discussed in chapter 12.

Arguments: values to which a function is applied. (See chapter 2.)

Axiom: a statement on which deductions are to be based and whose truth is accepted (e.g. the properties of factorial shown in chapter 2 or Euclid's axioms of geometry).

Axiomatic definition of a data type: see *implicit definition of a data type*.

Bag: an unordered collection of values which can contain duplicates. (See chapter 12.)

Bias: a constructive specification of a data type is said to be biased (towards certain realizations) if equality of the underlying objects cannot be tested using the operators of the data type. The effect of bias is to make the proofs of some realizations more difficult. (See chapter 15.)

Boolean values: the two truth values **TRUE** and **FALSE**. The set containing these two values is called *Bool*. (See chapter 2.)

Bound variables: those variables whose identifiers are given a local significance by either a quantifier (see chapter 2):

$(\mathbf{E}x)(x*x = y)$ *x is bound and y is free,*

or by their use in an implicit definition (see chapter 8), e.g. in:

$\{x \mid p(x)\}$ *x is bound,*

Cardinality: the number of elements in a set.

Coding: final stage of the development of a program.

Composite objects: those with structure (cf. *elementary objects*), for example, sets, lists. (See chapter 14.)

Concatenation: the operation which links two lists together. (See chapter 9.)

Concrete syntax: a set of rules for producing the strings of the language (cf. *abstract syntax*). (See chapter 14.)

Conditional expression: an expression of the form:

if *b* **then** *e1* **else** *e2*

Its value is either the value of expression *e1* or that of *e2* depending on the value of *b*. (See chapter 3.) See also *extended logical expressions*.

Conjunction: logical expression whose main operator is *and*. (See chapter 2.)

Constructive definition: an abstract data type can be defined constructively by stating what each of its operators does in terms of collections of previously understood objects. (See chapter 7.) Contrast with *implicit definition of data types*.

Correctness: of a program—no errors with respect to the specification.

Correctness argument: an indication of why a step of development is correct with respect to its specification. A correctness argument may take many forms: for straightforward expansion of a schema, a reference (e.g. see Jackson(75) chapter 4) may be adequate; for most loop decompositions, a record of the invariant may be acceptable; at the extreme, a formal proof may be necessary.

Data refinement: a step of development which provides a representation for abstract data types. (See chapter 11.)

Data type: a data type is characterized in this book by its operators (see chapter 7). New, or abstract, data types are defined by constructive specifications. See also *extension of a data type*.

Data type invariant: a predicate which defines a subset of a class of objects—it is *invariant* with respect to the operators. (See chapter 10.)

Decomposition: a step of development which provides a realization for implicitly defined operations in terms of control structures. (See chapter 5.)

Design: a stage development which shows the structure of the solution (HOW) to a problem given in a specification (WHAT).

Development: stepwise evolution of a system from specification to code. See *decomposition* and *refinement*.

Disjoint Sets: two sets are said to be disjoint if they have no common elements. (See chapter 8.)

Disjunction: logical expression whose main operator is *or*. (See chapter 2.)

Domain: of a map or function, is the set of values from which arguments may be selected. A function (see chapter 2) may have defined results over a more restricted set (cf. *pre-condition*). The set of values over which a mapping (see chapter 12) is defined can be determined by the **dom** operator.

Elementary objects: objects whose structure is of no interest (see chapter 14), denoted by sequences of capital letters, e.g. **NIL**.

Equivalence relation: a relation which is reflexive, symmetric and transitive. (See chapter 8.)

Extended logical expressions: logical expressions some of whose operands may be undefined. *More on Logic in chapter 3 explains how such expressions may themselves be given a defined meaning.

Extension of a data type: a data type is extended by defining new operators. Such operators may be characterized by predicates—using inverses, axioms or recursive functions. (See chapter 7.)

Formal language: one whose semantics are precise. (See chapter 2.) Thus, in a programming language, each string of statements has a precise meaning (cf. *natural language*).

Formal proof: one whose individual steps only require manipulations of symbols (e.g. application of a substitution rule). A formal proof could be mechanically checked (cf. *correctness argument*).

Free variables: those whose meaning is given by a larger environment (i.e. not locally bound), cf. *bound variables*.

Function: a function will yield, when applied to arguments (chosen from its domain), values (in its range), see chapter 2. It is important to keep separate the implicit view of a function, which is its specification, and its explicit definition, which is the rule to compute the result.

Hashing: a way of computing addresses from character strings such as names. The key is manipulated so as to form an address in a defined range—allowance must be made for two names coming to the same address.

Hypothesis: temporary assumption, in particular left-hand side of an implication.

Implementation bias: see *bias*.

Implication: logical expression whose main operator is *implies*. (See chapter 2.)

Implicit definition of a data type: a definition given by relating the operators of the data type, (cf. *constructive definition*). (See chapter 16.)

Implicit specification: specification of a function or operation in terms of predicates defining its required input/output relation (i.e. without giving any algorithm to achieve the task). (See chapter 2.)

Induction: is a way of proving results about properties of infinite (ordered) sets of values. Inductive proofs contain a basis and an inductive step. For application to correctness proofs for recursive functions see chapter 3. For appropriate rules for sets see chapter 8, for lists chapter 9, and for abstract syntax chapter 14.

Induction hypothesis: the assumption of the property one is trying to prove for some value n, to be used in proving the property for $n+1$. (See chapter 3.)

Integers: the infinite set of numbers:

... , -2, -1, 0, 1, 2, ...

Language definition: a documentation of the precise semantics of the constructs of a language. (See appendix A.)

Linked list: data structure used in list processing where elements contain data and a pointer to the next element.

List: ordered collection of values which can be accessed by position. Their use in defining abstract data types is described in chapter 9.

Logic (predicate): see *predicate calculus*.

Logic (propositional): see *propositional calculus*.

Many-one: a many-one function or mapping can map several different argument values onto the same result (cf. one-one).

Mapping: an object which can be used to look up values. (See chapter 12.) Mappings are a restricted form of functions.

Mathematical semantics: a language definition style in which each construct in the language to be defined is associated with a denotation which is a mathematical object (e.g. a function). See Stoy(77) or Bjorner(78).

Meta-language: a formal language used to describe systems, in particular languages.

Meta-IV: a meta-language devised in the IBM Laboratory Vienna as a successor to *VDL*. The notation used in this book is a subset of Meta-IV (see Bjorner(78)). The underlying approach is basically that of mathematical semantics.

Model: the operations of the representation of an abstract data type are said to model those of the abstraction. (See chapter 11.)

Modulus: x **mod** y is the remainder when x is divided by y; all values concerned being integers.

Multi-set: see *bag.*

Natural language: one used by human beings in natural communication, e.g. English, French, German. Such languages are inherently imprecise in that sentences can be constructed whose meaning is not unique. Contrast with *formal language.*

Natural number: member of the infinite set $\{1, 2, 3, ...\}$.

One-one: a one-one function or mapping yields different results for each of its argument values.

Operations: program-like constructs which change a state as well as, possibly, accepting arguments and yielding results. (See chapter 4.)

Operators: a data type is manipulated (created, changed or interrogated) via its operators: they may be functions or operations.

Parameter: the parameter names of a function are those identifiers which are replaced by values of arguments when the function is evaluated. (See chapter 2.)

Partial correctness: a result which shows that any generated results will be in a specified relation to the given initial values but which does not show that the function (or operation) terminates for all values in its domain, (cf. *total correctness*).

Partial function: is one which does not deliver results for all values of its domain—for some arguments its result is undefined.

Partition: of a set, a splitting of its elements into disjoint sets, each of which is a subset of the original set. (See chapter 8.)

Post-condition: a predicate which characterizes the input/output relation of a function (see chapter 2) or operation (see chapter 4).

Pre-condition: a predicate which characterizes the valid inputs of a function (see chapter 2) or operation (see chapter 4).

Predicate: a function whose range is the set of Boolean values, see chapter 2.

Predicate calculus: calculus of expressions which include predicates, quantifiers and propositional connectives. (See chapter 2.)

Proof: see formal proof.

Proof by contradiction: proof by reducing an assumption to a contradiction, thus proving the converse of the assumption. See for example *Predicates and Sets in chapter 8.

Proposition: expression whose value is **TRUE** or **FALSE**. (See chapter 2.)

Propositional calculus: calculus of expressions which include propositions and propositional connectives. (See chapter 2.)

Propositional operators: *and, or* etc. (See chapter 2.)

Quantifiers: Universal (**A**)—*for all,* and existential (**E**)—*there exists.* (See chapter 2.)

Range: set of values which can be generated as the result of a mapping (see chapter 12), or function (see chapter 2).

Rational numbers: those numbers which can be expressed as a division of two integers.

Real numbers: a larger class than the rational numbers—it includes values like the square root of two—excluded are the numbers which involve the square root of negative numbers.

Realization: an implementation in terms of less abstract primitives of an implicitly defined operation (see decomposition) or abstract data type (see refinement).

Recursive function: a function whose definition involves a reference to the name of the function itself. (See chapter 3.)

Refinement of objects: realization of abstract data types in terms of more concrete objects. (See chapter 11.)

Relation: see section Recording Equivalence Relations of chapter 8.

Representation: an implemention of an abstract data type in terms of a more concrete one. (See chapter 11.)

Requirements: business-oriented statement of the need for a system.

Retrieve functions: used to express the (one-many) relationship between elements of an abstract data type and those of its realization. (See chapter 11.)

Rigorous argument: organized and sound reasoning which is not necessarily formal.

Rigorous method: see chapter 17.

Satisfy: a value is said to satisfy a predicate if evaluation of the predicate yields **TRUE** for that value. (See chapter 2.)

Semantics: the semantics of, for example, a programming language gives the meaning of each of its constructs. (See appendix A.)

Set: unordered collection of values—use in describing abstract data types is explained in chapter 8.

Specification: precise statement of the properties of a system (WHAT it does, not HOW it is to be done). See chapters 2, 4 and 7-16.

States: collections of values for variables. For the description of classes of states, see chapter 4.

Structural induction: see chapter 14.

Substitution: the obvious way of using a general definition for particular values, remembering to substitute only for free variables. Thus if:

$$p(x) \triangleq x>2 \land (\mathbf{E}x)(x = 2)$$

then:

$$p(7) = 7>2 \land (\mathbf{E}x)(x = 2)$$

Symbolic execution: execution with symbols rather than actual values for variables to establish more general results than by test cases. See Hantler(76) and, for application to proofs, Burstall(74).

Syntax: see *concrete syntax* and *abstract syntax*.

Tautology: a logical expression which evaluates to **TRUE** whatever values are substituted for its variables. (See chapter 2.)

Theorem: a true statement which is often supported by an argument that it is indeed always true.

Theory: a theory of a data type is a collection of properties which can be used in establishing theorems about programs using the data type. (See chapter 13.) The development of a theory for a particular application area makes subsequent proofs both shorter and clearer.

Three-valued logic: see *extended logical expressions*.

Top-down: a hierarchical structure for documenting a development.

Total function: one which yields a defined result for all arguments in the domain defined by the type clause of the function.

Total correctness: a program is said to be totally correct, with respect to its specification, if (in addition to partial correctness) it terminates for all permissible inputs. (See chapter 5.)

Type clause: of a function specifies its domain and range (see chapter 2), e.g.:

$$f: D \rightarrow R$$

Vacuously true: an implication whose left-hand side is **FALSE** or whose right-hand side is **TRUE** is said to be vacuously true because its truth can be determined without checking the other part of the expression.

Validity: the valid objects of a data type are those which satisfy the data type invariant. It is necessary to prove that the operations of a data type preserve validity. (See chapter 10.)

Vienna Definition Language (VDL): a meta-language used by the IBM Laboratory Vienna in the 1960's for the definition of programming languages (e.g. PL/I, see Lucas(69)) and systems (cf. Meta-IV).

ANSWERS TO SELECTED EXERCISES

Answers are provided to those exercises which are essential for an understanding of the notation.

Exercises from Chapter 2

Exercise 2.1

a)

a	b	a ∨ b
TRUE	TRUE	TRUE
TRUE	FALSE	TRUE
FALSE	TRUE	TRUE
FALSE	FALSE	FALSE

b)

a	b	a ⇔ b
TRUE	TRUE	TRUE
TRUE	FALSE	FALSE
FALSE	TRUE	FALSE
FALSE	FALSE	TRUE

c)

a	~ a
TRUE	**FALSE**
FALSE	**TRUE**

Exercise 2.3

d)

a	b	b⟹a	a ⟹ (b⟹a)
TRUE	**TRUE**	**TRUE**	**TRUE**
TRUE	**FALSE**	**TRUE**	**TRUE**
FALSE	**TRUE**	**FALSE**	**TRUE**
FALSE	**FALSE**	**TRUE**	**TRUE**

Exercise 2.6

nth-root: Real Int → Real
pre-nth-root(x,n) $\triangleq$ *is-odd(n)* $\lor$ *x≥0*
post-nth-root(x,n,r) $\triangleq$ *r**n = x*

Exercise 2.7

rdiv: Real Real → Real
pre-rdiv(x,y) $\triangleq$ *y≠0*
post-rdiv(x,y,d) $\triangleq$ *d*y = x*

Exercise 2.8

post-idiv(a,b,q,r) $\triangleq$ *(b*q+r = a)* $\land$ *0≤r<b*

Exercise 2.9

a) true, b) false, c) false—the remainder can never exceed the divisor, d) true—any number can be divided by itself, e) true—more difficult, *1* is a divisor which will divide any number, f) true—where *x* and *y* are relatively prime, e.g. *5,6*, g) true, h) false—because *2* is considered to be prime.

Exercise 2.11

is-multiple(x,m) ≜ *m***mod***x = 0*
is-common-multiple(x,y,m) ≜ *is-multiple(x,m)* ∧ *is-multiple(y,m)*

scm: Nat Nat → *Nat*
post-scm(x,y,m) ≜
    is-common-multiple(x,y,m) ∧
    ~*(***E***n∈Nat)(n<m* ∧ *is-common-multiple(x,y,n))*

Exercise 2.12

mod: Nat0 Nat → *Nat0*
post-mod(x,y,r) ≜ *0≤r<y* ∧ *(***E***m∈Nat)(m*y+r=x)*

Exercises from Chapter 3

Exercise 3.1

Statement to be proved:

*(***A***x∈Int)(pre-double(x)* ⇒ *post-double(x,double(x)))*

Using the predicate definitions, gives:

TRUE ⇒ *double(x)=2*x*

Using definition of *double*, and omitting the left of the implication, gives:

x+x = 2*x

which is true from a property of arithmetic.

Exercise 3.10

a) **if** *a* **then** *b* **else FALSE**
b) **if** *a* **then** *b* **else TRUE**
c) **if** *a* **then** *b* **else** *(***if** *b* **then FALSE else TRUE***)*

Exercise 3.11

a)

if *(***if** *a* **then TRUE else** *b)* **then TRUE else** *c*

by identity (f):

if *a* **then** *(***if TRUE then TRUE else** *c)* **else** *(***if** *b* **then TRUE else** *c)*

by identity (b):

if *a* **then TRUE else** *(***if** *b* **then TRUE else** *c)*

Exercises from Chapter 4

Exercise 4.1

(This includes exercise 4.3).

Sexp:: X: Int   Y: Int   R: Int

EXP
states: Sexp
pre-EXP(<,y,>) ≜ y≥0
post-EXP(<x,y,>,<,,r'>) ≜ r'=exp(x,y)

Exercise 4.4

Sgcd:: X: Int   Y: Int

GCD
states: Sgcd
pre-GCD(<x,y>) ≜ x>0 ∧ y>0
post-GCD(<x,y>,<x',>) ≜
     is-common-divisor(x,y,x') ∧
     *~(**E**d'∊Nat)(d'>x' ∧ is-common-divisor(x,y,d'))*

Exercise 4.5

IDIV:: Sidiv: →

pre-IDIV(<a,b,,>) ≜ a≥0 ∧ b>0
*post-IDIV(<a,b,,>,<,,q',r'>) ≜ q'*b+r'=a ∧ 0≤r'<b*

Exercises from Chapter 5

Exercise 5.1

For *da*, *db*, observe both right-hand sides are true—the implications are therefore vacuously true.

ra.
pre-MKODD-BODY(s₁) ∧ post-DIVX(s₁,s₂) ∧ post-MULTY(s₂,s₃)
     ⇒ post-MKODD-BODY(s₁,s₃)

$MOD(x_1,2)=0 \land x_1>0 \land x_3=x_2=x_1/2 \land y_3=y_2*2 \land y_2=y_1 \land r_3=r_2=r_1$
     $\Rightarrow r_3+x_3*y_3=r_1+x_1*y_1 \land 1\le x_3<x_1$

Noting:

$r_3+x_3*y_3$
$$= r_1+(x_1/2)*y_1*2$$
$$= r_1+x_1*y_1$$

and that x_1 being positive and even guarantees that:

$1 \leq (x_1/2) < x_1$

concludes the proof.

Exercises from Chapter 8

Exercise 8.1

a) true, b) true, c) false, d) true, e) false, f) false.

Exercise 8.2

a) $\{1\}$
b) $\{1,4,9,16\}$
c) $\{1,4,9,16\}$
d) $Nat0$
e) 2
f) $\{1,2,3,4\}$

Exercise 8.3

a) $\{x \mid x \epsilon \{100:200\} \wedge x \textbf{mod} 9 = 0\}$
b) $\{x \mid x \epsilon \{200:300\} \wedge \textit{is-prime}(x)\}$
c) $Nat \subseteq Nat0 \subseteq Int$

Exercise 8.5

a) $S_1 \cup S_2 = S_2 \cup S_1$
   $S_1 \cap S_2 = S_2 \cap S_1$
b) $S_1 \cup (S_2 \cup S_3) = (S_1 \cup S_2) \cup S_3$
   $S_1 \cap (S_2 \cap S_3) = (S_1 \cap S_2) \cap S_3$
c) $S_1 \cap (S_2 \cup S_3) = (S_1 \cap S_2) \cup (S_1 \cap S_3)$
   $S_1 \cup (S_2 \cap S_3) = (S_1 \cup S_2) \cap (S_1 \cup S_3)$

Exercises from Chapter 9

Exercise 9.1

a) $<2>$
b) 2
c) $<1,2>$
d) $<1,2,3>$
e) $\{2,\{3,4,2\}\}$
f) $<1,<2>>$

Exercise 9.2

a) $l=<<1>,\{1\},a>$
b) $l=<1,2,2>$

Exercise 9.3

$<1,1>$

Exercises from Chapter 11

Exercise 11.1

Studx1:: N: Student-name-list   Y: Student-name-list

retr-Studx(<n,y>) $\triangleq$ *<***elems***n,***elems***y>*

Exercise 11.2

retr-Studx(<nml,ynl>) $\triangleq$
   *<***elems***(mask-l(nml,ynl)),*
    elems*nml -* **elems***(mask-l(nml,ynl))>*

Exercise 11.3

retr-Dict(wgl) $\triangleq$ **elems** *(***conc** *wgl)*

Exercises from Chapter 12

Exercise 12.1

a) 2
b) [11→22, 13→26, 17→34, 19→38]
c) 81
d) 24
e) {1,4,9}
f) b
g) c

Exercise 12.3

$M1 = [1→2]$ $M2 = [1→3]$

BIBLIOGRAPHY

Alagic(78): *The Design of Well-Structured and Correct Programs.*, S.Alagic and M.A.Arbib, Springer-Verlag, 1978.

Backus(78): *Can Programming be Liberated from the von Neumann style? A Functional Style and its Algebra of Programs.*, J.Backus, Communications of ACM, vol.21, no.8, pp 613-641, Aug. 1978.

Baker(72): *Chief Programmer Team Management of Programming.*, F.T.Baker, IBM Systems Journal, Vol. 11, pp 56-73, 1972.

Barron(68): *Recursive Techniques in Programming.*, D.W.Barron, MacDonald, 1968.

Bekic(71): *Formalization of Storage Properties.*, H.Bekic and K.Walk, (in) Engeler(71).

Bekic(74): *A Formal Definition of a PL/I Subset.*, (2 parts), H.Bekic, D.Bjorner, W.Henhapl, C.B.Jones and P.Lucas, IBM (Vienna) Technical Report TR25.139, Dec. 1974.

Berthaud(78): *Towards a Formal Language for Functional Specifications.*, M.Berthaud, in: *Constructing Quality Software.*, North-Holland, 1978.

Berztiss(75): *Data Structures Theory and Practice.*, A.T.Berztiss, Academic Press, 1975.

Bjorner(78): *The Vienna Development Method: The Meta-Language.*, (eds) D.Bjorner and C.B.Jones, Springer-Verlag Lecture Notes in Computer Science, No. 61, 1978.

Bjorner(79): *Formalization of Data Base Models.*, D.Bjorner, presented at the Copenhagen Winter School on *Abstract Software Specifications.*, proceedings to be published, 1979.

Bron(76): *A Proposal for Dealing with Abnormal Termination of Programs.*, C.Bron, M.M.Fokkinga and A.C.M.De Haas, T.H. Twente, Memo No. 150, Nov. 1976.

Burge(75): *Recursive Programming Techniques.*, W.H.Burge, Addison-Wesley, 1975.

Burstall(69): *Proving Properties of Programs by Structural Induction.*, R.M.Burstall, Computer Journal, Vol. 12, pp 41-47, 1969.

Burstall(74): *Program Proving as Hand Simulation with a Little Induction.*, R.M.Burstall, IFIP Congress, 1974.

Burstall(77): *Putting Theories Together to Make Specifications.*, R.M.Burstall and J.A.Goguen, International Joint Conference on Artificial Intelligence, Boston, Aug. 1977.

Coleman(79): *The Clean Termination of Pascal Programs.*, D.Coleman and J.W.Hughes, Acta Informatica, Vol.11, pp 195-210, 1979.

Comer(79): *The Ubiquitous B-Tree.*, D.Comer, ACM Computing Surveys, Vol.11, No.2, pp 121-137, 1979.

Cooper(66): *The Equivalence of Certain Computations.*, D.C.Cooper, Computer Journal, Vol.9, pp 45-52, 1966.

Correll(78): *Proving Programs Correct through Refinement.*, C.H.Correll, Acta Informatica, Vol. 9, pp 121-132, 1978.

Dahl(72a): *Structured Programming.*, O.-J.Dahl, E.W.Dijkstra and C.A.R.Hoare, Academic Press, 1972.

Dahl(72b): *Hierachical Program Structures.*, O.-J.Dahl and C.A.R.Hoare, in: Dahl(72a), pp 197-220.

Dahl(78): *Can Program Proving be Made Practical?.*, O.-J.Dahl, Oslo University, Institute of Informatics, Report No. 33, ISBN 82-90230-26-5, May 1978.

Dershowitz(79): *Proving Termination with Multisets Orderings.*, N.Dershowitz and Z.Manna, Communications of ACM, to appear.

Dijkstra(68): *Goto Statement Considered Harmful.*, E.W.Dijkstra, Letter to the Editor, Communications of ACM Vol.11, pp 147-148, March 1968.

Dijkstra(69): *Notes on Structured Programming.*, E.W.Dijkstra, Note EWD249, (later in Dahl(72a), pp 1-82), Aug. 1969.

Dijkstra(75): *Guarded Commands, Nondeterminacy and Formal Derivation of Programs.* E.W.Dijkstra, Communications of ACM, Vol.18, No.8, pp 453-457, Aug. 1975.

Dijkstra(76): *A Discipline of Programming.*, E.W.Dijkstra, Prentice-Hall, 1976.

Earley(68): *An Efficient Context-Free Parsing Algorithm.*, J.Earley, Ph.D. Thesis, Carnegie-Mellon University, 1968.

Earley(70): *An Efficient Context-Free Parsing Algorithm.*, J.Earley, Communications of ACM, Vol. 13, No. 2, pp 94-102, Feb. 1970.

ECMA(76): *American National Standard Programming Language PL/I.*, ECMA/TC10 and ANSI.X3.53-1976, July 1976.

Engeler(71): *Symposium on Semantics of Algorithmic Languages.*, E.Engeler (ed.), Springer-Verlag Lecture Notes in Mathematics, No. 188, 1971.

Fagan(76): *Design and Code Inspections to Reduce Errors in Program Development.*, M.E.Fagan, IBM Systems Journal, Vol.15, pp 182-211, 1976.

Fleck(65): *Formal Definition of the PL/I Compile Time Facilities.*, M.Fleck, IBM (Vienna) Technical Report TR25.095, June 1965.

Floyd(67): *Assigning Meaning to Programs.*, R.W.Floyd, Proceedings of Symposia in Applied Mathematics, Vol. 19, *Mathematical Aspects of Computer Science.*, (J.T.Schwartz—ed.), American Math. Soc., 19-32, 1967.

Fokkinga(77): *Axiomatization of Declarations and the Formal Treatment of an Escape Construct.*, M.Fokkinga, IFIP Working Conference on Formal Description of Programming Concepts, St.Andrews, Canada, Aug.1977.

Gerhart(76): *What Goes Down Should Also Come Up: Some Issues about Abstraction.*, S.L.Gerhart, 5th. Texas Conference on Computer Systems, Oct. 1976.

Gerhart(77): *A Unified View of Current Program Testing and Proving· Theory and Practice.*, Duke University, 1977.

Gerhart(78): *Program Verification in the 1980s: Problems, Perspectives, and Opportunities.*, S.L.Gerhart, University of Southern California, Report ISI/RR-78-71, Aug. 1978.

Goguen(75): *Abstract Data Types as Initial Algebras and Correctness of Data Representations.*, J.A.Goguen, J.W.Thatcher, E.G.Wagner and J.B.Wright, Conference on Computer Graphics, pp 89-93, May 1975.

Goguen(76): *An Initial Algebra Approach to the Specification, Correctness and Implementation of Abstract Data Types.*, J.A.Goguen, J.W.Thatcher and E.G.Wagner, IBM (Research) RC6487, Nov. 1976.

Gries(78): *A Linear Sieve Algorithm for Finding Prime Numbers.*, D.Gries and J.Misra, Communications of ACM, Vol.21, No.12, pp 999-1003, Dec. 1978.

Gull(79): *Recursive Data Structures in APL.*, W.E.Gull and M.A.Jenkins, Communications of ACM, Vol.22, No.2, pp 79-96, 1979.

Guttag(75): *The Specification and Application to Programming of Abstract Data Types.*, J.V.Guttag, Ph.D Thesis, University of Toronto, 1975.

Guttag(77): *Abstract Data Types and the Development of Data Structures.*, J.Guttag, Communications of ACM, Vol.20, No.6, June 1977.

Guttag(78): *Abstract Data Types and Software Validation.*, J.V.Guttag, E.Horowitz and D.R.Musser, Communications of ACM, Vol.21, No.12, pp 1048-1064, Dec. 1978.

Hall(75): *Computational Structures: An Introduction to Non-Numerical Computing.*, P.A.V.Hall, MacDonald and Jane's, 1975.

Hansal(74): *'Software Devices' for Processing Graphs Using PL/I Compile Time Facilities.*, A.Hansal, Information Processing Letters, No.2, pp 171-179, 1974.

Hansal(76): *A Formal Definition of a Relational Data Base System.*, A.Hansal, IBM (Peterlee) UKSC0080, June 1976.

Hantler(75): *EFFIGY Reference Manual.*, S.L.Hantler and A.C.Chibib, IBM Research RC5225, Jan. 1975.

Hantler(76): *An Introduction to Proving the Correctness of Programs.*, S.L.Hantler and J.C.King, IBM (Research) RC5893, March 1976.

Henderson(72): *An Experiment in Structured Programming.*, P.Henderson and R.A.Snowden, BIT 12, pp 38-53, 1972.

Henhapl(78): *A Formal Definition of ALGOL 60 as Described in the 1975 Modified Report.*, W.Henhapl and C.B.Jones, (in) Bjorner(78).

Hill(72): *Wouldn't it be nice if we could write computer programs in ordinary English—or would it?.*, I.D.Hill, BCS Computer Bulletin, Vol.16, No.6, pp 306-312, June 1972.

Hitchcock(72): *Induction Rules and Termination Proofs.*, P.Hitchcock and D.M.R.Park, (in) *Automata, Languages and Programming.*, pp 225-251, M.Nivat (ed.), North-Holland, 1972.

Hitchcock(74): *An Approach to Formal Reasoning about Programs.*, P.Hitchcock, Ph.D. Thesis, University of Warwick, June 1974.

Hitchcock(77): *An Approach to Conceptual Data Analysis.*, P.Hitchcock and F.Pace, IBM (UK) Report UKSC0090, Dec.1977.

Hoare(69): *The Axiomatic Basis of Computer Programming.*, C.A.R.Hoare, Communications of ACM, Vol.12, pp 576-583, Oct. 1969.

Hoare(71): *Proof of a Program: FIND.*, C.A.R.Hoare, Communications of ACM, Vol.14, pp 39-45, 1971.

Hoare(72a): *Notes on Data Structuring.*, C.A.R.Hoare, in Dahl(72a), pp 83-174, 1972.

Hoare(72b): *Proof of Correctness of Data Representations.*, C.A.R.Hoare, Acta Informatica, Vol. 1, pp 271-281, 1972.

Hoare(72c): *An Axiomatic Definition of the Programming Language Pascal.*, C.A.R.Hoare and N.Wirth, E.T.H. Zurich, Report No. 6, Nov.1972.

Hoare(72d): *Proof of a Program: 'The Sieve of Eratosthenes' .*, C.A.R.Hoare, BCS Computer Journal, Vol.15, No.4, pp 321-325, Nov. 1972.

Hoare(73): *A Structured Paging System.*, C.A.R.Hoare, BCS Computer Journal, Vol.16, No.3, pp 209-215, Aug. 1973.

Hoare(74): *Consistent and Complementary Formal Theories of the Semantics of Programming Languages.*, C.A.R.Hoare and P.E.Lauer, Acta Informatica, Vol.3, pp 135-153, 1974.

IBM(a): *OS PL/I Checkout and Optimizing Compilers: Language Reference Manual.*, IBM GC33-0009.

IBM(b): *Improved Programming Technologies: An Overview.*, IBM, GHC20-1850.

Izbicki(75): *On a Consistency Proof of a Chapter of a Formal Definition of a PL/I Subset.*, H.Izbicki, IBM (Vienna) Technical Report TR25.142, Feb. 1975.

Jackson(75): *Principles of Program Design.*, M.A.Jackson, Academic Press, 1975.

Jensen(76): *Pascal User Manual and Report.*, K.Jensen and N.Wirth, Lecture Notes in Computer Science, No.18, Springer-Verlag, 1976.

Jones(71): *Proving Correctness of Implementation Techniques.*, C.B.Jones and P.Lucas, (in) Engeler(71), pp 178-211, 1971.

Jones(72): *Formal Development of Correct Algorithms: An Example Based on Earley's Recognizer.*, C.B.Jones, ACM SIGPLAN Notices Vol.7 No.1. (also IBM (Hursley) Technical Report TR12.095), Jan. 1972.

Jones(73): *Formal Development of Programs.*, C.B.Jones, IBM (Hursley) Technical Report TR12.117, June 1973.

Jones(76a): *Formal Definition in Compiler Development.*, C.B.Jones, IBM (Vienna) Technical Report TR25.145, Feb. 1976.

Jones(76b): *Program Development Using Data Abstraction.*, C.B.Jones, Presented at IFIP WG2.3, Grenoble, manuscript, Dec. 1976.

Jones(77a): *Structured Design and Coding: Theory versus Practice.*, C.B.Jones, Informatie, Jaargang 19, nr.6, pp 311-319 June 1977.

Jones(77b): *Implementation Bias in Constructive Specifications.*, C.B.Jones, manuscript, Sep. 1977.

Jones(78): *The Meta-language: A Reference Manual.*, C.B.Jones, (in) Bjorner(78).

Jones(79a): *Constructing a Theory of a Data Structure as an aid to Program Development.*, C.B.Jones, Acta Informatica 11, pp 119-137, 1979.

Jones(79b): *The Vienna Development Method: Examples of Compiler Development.*, C.B.Jones, in: *Le Point sur la Compilation.*, M.Amirchahy and D.Neel (eds.), IRIA-SEFI, 1979.

T.C.Jones(77): *Program Quality and Programmer Productivity.*, Capers Jones, IBM (San Jose) Technical Report TR02.764, Jan. 1977.

Kahn(79): *Semantics of Concurrent Computation.*, (ed) G.Kahn, Springer-Verlag Lecture Notes in Computer Science, No.70, 1979.

Kapur(79): *Specifications of Majster's Traversable Stack and Veloso's Traversable Stack.*, D.Kapur, ACM SIGPLAN Notices, Vol.14, No.5, pp 46-53, 1979.

Katzenelson(79): *Clusters and Dialogues for Set Implementations.*, J.Katzenelson, to be published in IEEE Transactions, 1979.

Kernighan(74): *The Elements of Programming Style.*, B.W.Kernighan and P.J.Plauger, Mc Graw-Hill, 1974.

Kernighan(76): *Software Tools.*, B.W.Kernighan and P.J.Plauger, Addison-Wesley, 1976.

Knuth(68): *The Art of Computer Programming: Volume 1: Fundamental Algorithms.*, D.E.Knuth, Addison-Wesley, 1968 (second edition 1973).

Knuth(74): *Structured Programs with goto Statements.*, D.Knuth, ACM Computer Surveys, Vol.6, No.4, Dec.1974.

Knuth(75): *Sorting and Searching.*, D.E.Knuth, Addison-Wesley, 1975.

Langefors(73): *Theoretical Analysis of Information Systems.*, B.Langefors, Studentlitteratur, 1973.

Linden(72): *A Summary of Progress Toward Proving Program Correctness.*, T.A.Linden, ACM Fall Joint Computer Conference, 1972.

Lipschutz(64): *Theory and Problems of Set Theory and Related Topics.*, S.Lipschutz, Schaum Outline Series, McGraw-Hill, 1964.

Liskov(74): *Programming with Abstract Data Types.*, B.H.Liskov and S.Zilles, ACM SIGPLAN Notices, Vol. 9, No.4. April 1974.

Liskov(75): *Specification Techniques for Data Abstractions.*, B.H.Liskov and S.N.Zilles, IEEE Transactions, Vol. SE-1, No. 1, pp 7-19, March 1975.

Liskov(77): *Abstraction Mechanisms in CLU.*, B.H.Liskov, A.Snyder, R.Atkinson and C.Shaffert, Communications of ACM 20, 8, pp 564-576, Aug. 1977.

London(72): *A Correctness Proof of the Fischer-Galler Algorithm Using Inductive Assertions.*, R.L.London, in Rustin(72), 1972.

Lucas(68): *Two Constructive Realizations of the Block Concept and Their Equivalence.*, P.Lucas, IBM (Vienna) Technical Report TR25.085, June 1968.

Lucas(69): *On the Formal Description of PL/I.*, P.Lucas and K.Walk, Annual Review in Automatic Programming, Vol. 6, Part 3, 1969.

Lucas(71): *Formal Definition of Programming Languages and Systems.*, P.Lucas, IFIP Congress, Ljubljana, 1971.

Lucas(73): *On Program Correctness and the Stepwise Development of Implementations.*, P.Lucas, (in) Proceedings Convegno di Informatica Teorica, pp 219-251, University of Pisa, Mar. 1973.

Lucas(78): *On the Formalization of Programming Languages: Early History and Main Approaches.*, P.Lucas, (in) Bjorner(78).

Lucas(79): *On the Structure of Application Programs.*, presented at the Copenhagen Winter School on *Abstract Software Specifications.*, proceedings to be published, 1979.

McCarthy(63): *A Basis for a Mathematical Theory of Computation.*, J.McCarthy, (in) *Computer Programming and Formal Systems.*, North-Holland, 1963.

Manna(78): *Is SOMETIME sometimes better than ALWAYS?: Intermittent Assertions in Proving Program Correctness.*, Z.Manna and R.J.Waldinger, Communications of ACM, Vol.21, pp 159-172, Feb. 1978.

Milner(70): *A Formal Notion of Simulation Between Programs.*, R.Milner, Swansea University Memo No. 14, Oct. 1970.

Morris(72): *A Correctness Proof Using Recursively Defined Functions.*, J.H.Morris Jr., (in) Rustin(72), 1972.

Myers(75): *Reliable Software Through Composite Design.*, G.J.Myers, Petrocelli Charter, 1975.

Naur(66): *Proof of Algorithms by General Snapshots.*, P.Naur, BIT Vol. 6, pp 310-316, 1966.

Naur(69): *Programming by Action Clusters.*, P.Naur, BIT Vol. 9, pp 250-258, 1969.

Naur(72): *An Experiment on Program Development.*, P.Naur, BIT Vol. 12, pp 347-365, 1972.

Naur(74): *Concise Survey of Computer Methods.*, P.Naur, Studentlitteratur, 1974.

Nilsson(76): *Relational Data Base Systems—Formalization and Realization.*, J.F.Nilsson, (Ph.D. Thesis), Technical University of Denmark, ID641, Aug. 1976.

North(77): *ELIZA.*, S.North, Creative Computing, July/Aug 1977.

Park(70): *Fixpoint Induction and Proofs of Program Properties.*, D.Park, (in) Machine Intelligence, Vol.5, Meltzer and Mitchie (eds.), Edinburgh University Press, pp 59-78, 1970.

Parnas(72): *A Technique for Software Module Specification with Examples.*, D.L.Parnas, Communications of ACM, Vol.14, No.5, May 1972.

Randell(75): *System Structure for Software Fault Tolerance.*, B.Randell, IEEE Transactions, Vol.SE-1, No. 2, June 1975.

Randell(78): *Reliability Issues in Computing System Design.*, B.Randell, P.A.Lee and P.C.Treleaven, Comp. Surveys, Vol.10, No.2, pp 123-166, June 1978.

Reynolds(78): *Reasoning about Arrays.*, J.C.Reynolds, (submitted to Communications of ACM), 1978.

Robinet(74): *Programming Symposium: Proceedings, Colloque sur la Programmation, Paris, April 9-11,1974.*, B.Robinet (ed.), Lecture Notes in Computer Science, No. 19, Springer-Verlag, 1974.

Rosenberg(74): *On Storing Arbitrarily Many Extendible Arrays of Arbitrary Dimensions.*, A.L.Rosenberg, IBM Research Report RC4800, 1974.

Rustin(72): *Formal Semantics of Programming Languages.*, R.Rustin (ed.), Prentice-Hall, 1972.

Schwartz(73): *The SETL Language and Examples of its Use.*, J.T.Schwartz, Courant Institute, New York University, 1973.

Sites(74): *Proving that Computer Programs Terminate Cleanly.*, R.L.Sites, Thesis Stanford University, STAN-CS-74-418, May 1974.

Stay(76): *HIPO and Integrated Program Design.*, J.F.Stay, IBM Systems Journal, Vol. 15, pp 143-154, 1976.

Stoy(77): *Denotational Semantics—the Scott-Strachey Approach to Programming Language Theory.*, J.E.Stoy, MIT Press, 1977.

Tennent(73): *Mathematical Semantics of SNOBOL4.*, R.D.Tennent, ACM SIGPLAN Conference, Oct. 1973.

Urschler(69a): *Concrete Syntax of PL/I.*, G.Urschler, IBM (Vienna) Technical Report TR25.096, June 1969.
Urschler(69b): *Translation of PL/I into Abstract Syntax.*, G.Urschler, IBM (Vienna) Technical Report TR25.097, June 1969.

Walk(69): *Abstract Syntax and Interpretation of PL/I (ULD Version III).*, K.Walk, K.Alber, M.Fleck, H,Goldmann, P.Lauer, E.Moser, P.Oliva, H.Stigleitner and G.Zeisel, IBM (Vienna) Technical Report TR25.098. Apr. 1969.
Warnier(74): *Logical Construction of Programs.*, J.D.Warnier, H.E.Stenfert Kroese B.V.—Leiden, 1974.
Wegbreit(76): *Verifying Program Performance.*, B.Wegbreit, J.ACM, Vol.23, No.4, Oct. 1976.
Weinberg(71): *The Psychology of Computer Programming.*, G.M.Weinberg, Van Nostrand, 1971.
Weissenboeck(75): *A Formal Interface Specification.*, F.Weissenboeck, IBM (Vienna) Technical Report TR25.141, Feb. 1975.
Weizenbaum(67): *Contextual Understanding by Computers.*, J.Weizenbaum, Communications of ACM, Vol.10, No.8, Aug. 1967.
Whitehead(59): *An Introduction to Mathematics.*, A.N.Whitehead, Oxford University Press, 1959.
Wirth(71): *Program Development by Stepwise Refinement.*, N.Wirth, Communications of ACM, Vol. 14, No.4, pp 221-227, April 1971.
Wirth(76): *Algorithms + Data Structures = Programs.*, N.Wirth, Prentice-Hall, 1976.
Wulf(76): *An Introduction to the Construction and Verification of Alphard Programs.*, W.A.Wulf, R.L.London and M.Shaw, IEEE SE-2, 4, pp 253-265, Dec. 1976.

Zemanek(66): *Semiotics and Programming Languages.*, H.Zemanek, Communications of ACM, pp 139-143, 1966.

INDEX

This book has been produced with the aid of a computer text processing system—the IBM Document Composition Facility. Its Generalized Markup Language (GML) permitted working versions of the text to be printed on a standard computer line printer, even before final layout of the book was chosen. It was then possible for the system to generate input to a composition program which caused a photocomposer to produce camera-ready master pages to the publisher's specifications.